# Hiking Colorado

# Hiking Colorado

A Guide to the State's Greatest Hiking Adventures

Third Edition

**Maryann Gaug**

**FALCON**GUIDES

GUILFORD, CONNECTICUT
HELENA, MONTANA
AN IMPRINT OF GLOBE PEQUOT PRESS

# FALCONGUIDES®

Copyright © 2003, 2011 by Morris Book Publishing, LLC
Published by Globe Pequot Press in 2002 as *Hiking Colorado III*

FalconGuides is an imprint of Globe Pequot Press.
Falcon, FalconGuides, and Outfit Your Mind are registered trademarks of Morris Book Publishing, LLC.

Interior photos: Maryann Gaug
New maps created by Mapping Specialists; map revisions by Melissa Baker and Daniel Lloyd © Morris Book Publishing LLC
Project editor: Julie Marsh
Layout artist: Kevin Mak

ISSN 1542-8648
ISBN 978-0-7627-5982-8

Printed in the United States of America
10 9 8 7 6 5 4 3 2 1

# Contents

# Overview

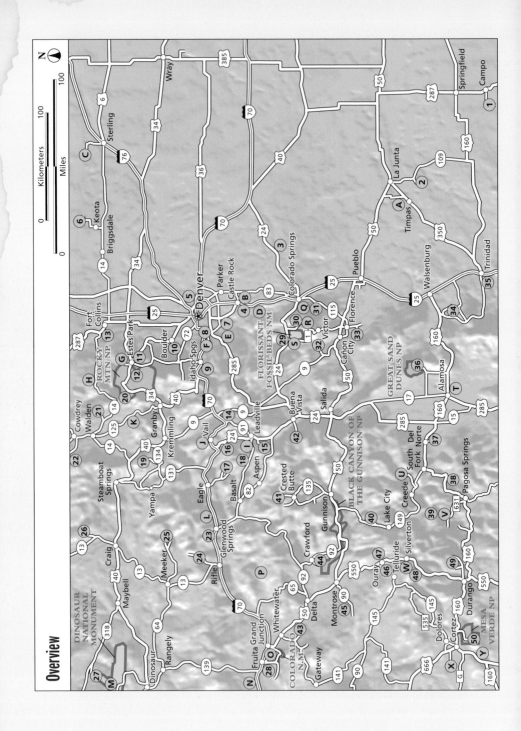

# Acknowledgments

Where to begin? First let me thank Anne Robinson and Jacque Kriegel for doing several hikes with me, especially the ones needing car shuttles. Because I hiked most of the trails by myself, my good friend, Keith Brown, anxiously awaited my phone calls that I was safe and not lost in the woods.

In researching hikes and asking questions afterwards, I talked with and/or met many wonderful and interesting people who care about our public lands and work hard to maintain trails and preserve wild country. Despite the "big brother" image federal and state employees often have, these people love the backcountry and were eager to answer questions and help me. They took time from busy schedules to review the chapters from their areas and provide feedback. If I name everyone, I'll bore you to tears and would accidentally forget someone for sure. My thanks go to all of these very helpful land agency people!

I enjoyed traveling around the state, meeting Forest Service and Bureau of Land Management employees with whom I've taken various classes over the years. Seeing old friends again, while they shared their insights and advice with me, was truly a great experience!

I would especially like to thank all those people who came before, who not only saw the need to preserve open space and wildlands, but who followed through on their visions. Over the years many people have continued working to create the wonderful collection of parks and open space lands, along with the national forests, parks, and wildlife refuges, that we enjoy today in Colorado. Thanks also go to the citizens of various cities and counties for consistently voting to tax themselves to purchase and preserve more lands, not only for recreation, but also to protect wildlife habitat. We all owe a great debt to these people, and to the people who continue the work of maintaining existing lands and procuring new ones.

Thanks to all the individuals in the many volunteer groups who help the land management agencies with everything from trail maintenance and construction to fund-raising to keep these special lands . . . well, special! Please consider joining one of these groups, and add your talents to help in whatever way you can.

Thanks also to all the friends and coworkers who put up with two years of "I have to work on the hiking guide" when they asked me to do things.

Hiking so many trails reminded me that fellow hikers are very friendly folk. I also had some interesting conversations with mountain bikers and horseback riders. Many people wondered why I hiked with ski poles. It was fun to demonstrate my hiking poles with shock absorbers!

A special thanks to my Mom and my Dad, both dead, for encouraging me to do what I want to do and strive for peace and happiness.

Last, but not least, thanks to you readers and fellow hikers for buying the third edition of *Hiking Colorado*. I hope you find it useful and interesting, and may you enjoy many hours hiking the trails described between these covers.

# Introduction

Colorado! The word conjures images of rugged peaks, cascading mountain streams, and crystal clear alpine lakes. Indeed, the state's middle section lives up to those expectations, but the state as a whole offers so much more. Colorado's western canyon country, carved by raging torrents, is rich in dinosaur graveyards and the artifacts and ruins of Ancestral Puebloan and Fremont Indians, all well worth exploring. The Eastern Plains, long thought too flat to be scenic, have plenty of natural delights tucked away for the hiker. Buttes rise above the plains, providing a haven for hawks and falcons, while southeastern canyons cache signs of ancient inhabitants including American Indian petroglyphs and North America's largest known dinosaur tracksite.

About 355 million years ago, Colorado sat near the equator. Little crustaceans in shallow seas died and were compressed into limestone. The Ancestral Rockies were uplifted from the seas and formed part of the supercontinent Pangaea. As time progressed the mountains eroded, and coastal dunes became today's magnificent sandstone cliffs. The present Rocky Mountains were uplifted starting 70 million years ago. Volcanic activity 25 million years ago created plateaus and several mountain ranges. Then, 25 million to 5 million years ago, the entire region began to rise 5,000 feet to its present elevation. Ice ages took hold of Colorado (by that time located north of the equator around the thirty-ninth parallel), and from 1.8 million to 12,000 years ago, glaciers carved the magnificent craggy peaks and U-shaped valleys we see today.

Human history in Colorado started with hunter-gatherers, followed by the Ancestral Puebloan culture that, from 500 BC to AD 1300, farmed then built pueblos and magnificent cliff dwellings in the southwest corner of the state. After AD 1300, other Native Americans moved into the Eastern Plains and mountain valleys. Spanish explorers arrived in the late 1500s, followed by trappers and traders. The gold rush of 1859 was perhaps the most significant event in the state's history, bringing settlers, fortune seekers, and improved transportation. The railroad companies performed engineering miracles to conquer impassable mountains, hastening both the transportation of ore and the state's development. Later, equally impressive roads were built for the automobile.

Today these roads provide us with relatively easy travel to hiking trails. Hiking is one of the best ways to explore Colorado. The fifty featured hikes in this guide offer a sample of Colorado's beautiful and varied terrain, its fascinating geology, flora and fauna, and human history. Honorable Mention hikes are included to give the hiker more options in a particular region. Hikes range from easy to strenuous, from a 1-mile loop around a waterfowl-filled lake to overnight backpacking trips. I included some classic trails and found several new ones. I especially tried to find trails in lesser-known and quieter areas. Because wilderness areas closest to Front Range metro areas

*Indian paintbrush*

are being "loved to death" and opportunities for solitude have greatly decreased, I avoided including trails in those areas.

Featured trails in this guide were originally hiked between 1999 and 2002. For those trails that were changed after 2002, and for several new trails, I hiked or rehiked them in 2009 and 2010. Please realize that trail locations and conditions, roads, and signage are subject to change over time. Trail mileage is as much an art as a science, even for land managers. Finding accurate historical information was sometimes interesting when different books contained conflicting information! I've included appropriate websites to assist in finding further information, but note that website addresses can change too. Times change and so do trail conditions. Remember to check with the appropriate land management agency for current fees, regulations, and trail information before heading out, then have a great hike!

Henry David Thoreau said, "In wildness is the preservation of the world." Aldo Leopold added years later: "When we see land as a community to which we belong, we may begin to use it with love and respect." My wish for you is to enjoy hiking, and learn about yourself and the world around you, to which we all belong. Remember, only we can preserve wildlands for current and future generations.

As you hike around our beautiful state, capture part of nature's spirit and hold it close to your own. Leave a piece of your spirit as well, so that no matter where you travel or live, the peace and beauty of Colorado's wild country—its mountains, plains, and canyons—will remain with you forever.

Thanks for purchasing *Hiking Colorado*. Happy hiking!

## Weather

Difficult to forecast and prone to change quickly, Colorado's weather is a wonder in itself. The mountains often create their own weather, with summer thunderstorms being a prime example. Rains may drench the Front Range and Eastern Plains while western mountains and canyons remain sunny and warm. Snow can fall in higher elevations at any time.

Spring is a great time to hike at lower elevations, renewing yourself after the chill of winter. The weather tends to be unpredictable and wet, especially in April and May. Spring runoff starts in May and typically peaks around mid-June.

Summer attempts to begin in June in the high country. June also begins thunderstorm season. As the sun heats the ground, warm air rises, cools, and releases moisture that condenses into clouds. Three problems result from thunderstorm development. One is lightning, a killer from above. The second is flash flood, which can roar out of nowhere into mountain and desert canyons. The third is more subtle: Rain in Colorado tends to be cold, and unprepared hikers can become hypothermic very quickly, even in summer. Monsoon season brings occasional gray, rainy days and increased thunderstorms from mid-July to early September.

◀ *Colorado columbine*

Colorado's fall season (September to mid-October) is perhaps the best time of year to hike. Thunderstorms are less frequent and the air is crisp and cool, with dazzling blue skies. Winds pick up on the mountain peaks, so be aware! Aspen trees turn gold and red about the last two weeks in September. By early October the Gambel oak and cottonwood trees are in prime color at lower elevations. Mid-October snows tend to bring an end to high altitude hiking, while lower elevations become the perfect place to hike.

Winter brings deep snow to the mountains, requiring foot travel by snowshoes or skis. If you venture out on backcountry trails, take an avalanche awareness course. Colorado typically leads the nation in avalanche deaths. At lower elevations in the eastern and western parts of the state, year-round hiking is the norm, interrupted only by snowfalls that normally melt quickly.

Whatever the season, always bring layers of clothes and rain (or snow) gear. Weather can change quickly and a temperature drop of 10°F to 20°F in one hour is not unheard of. Be prepared!

An interesting rule of thumb: For every 1,000 feet of elevation gained, the temperature drops about 4°F. So when Denver, at 5,280 feet, registers 80°F, it may only be 60°F in Leadville at 10,190 feet. Another tidbit: Research in Colorado has measured a 26 percent increase in ultraviolet radiation between 5,500 feet and 14,000 feet on a cloudless summer day. Remember your sunscreen!

## Flora and Fauna

Colorado ranges in elevation from 3,337 feet at its lowest point in the northeastern plains to 14,433 feet at the top of Mount Elbert near Leadville. In the rain shadow of the Rocky Mountains, the Eastern Plains are high and dry, with less than 15 inches of annual precipitation. Wolf Creek Pass on the Continental Divide often receives over 300 inches of snow annually. Just east of Wolf Creek Pass, the San Luis Valley is a true desert, receiving less than 8 inches of moisture per year. With such environmental extremes, Colorado has a wide diversity of flora and fauna.

At the lowest elevations, shortgrass prairie dominates the Eastern Plains, while semidesert scrub and sagebrush shrublands populate the west side of the Rockies. As elevation and precipitation increase, you pass from mountain shrublands into piñon-juniper forest, then ponderosa pine and Douglas fir forests. Continue to climb through lodgepole pine and aspen forests into forests of spruce-fir, and limber and bristlecone pine. Mountain grasslands and wetlands punctuate the forest blanket. Finally, alpine tundra at the highest elevations supports miniature vegetation.

Starting in the late 1990s and continuing through the time of publication, aging lodgepole pine forests have been killed by mountain pine (bark) beetles. Although these tiny insects are part of the natural forest cycle, they reproduced in epidemic proportions due to drought, which also weakened trees, making them more susceptible to the beetles. Very cold winters kill many beetles, but recent winters have been relatively mild. Treating over 1 million acres of infested trees with insecticides became

*Arctic gentians*

impossible, resulting in millions of dead trees. Please be aware that these dead trees can fall at any time, particularly in high winds. Please park your car and place your tent away from them. Be careful while hiking, too!

As you hike through these different ecosystems, notice which plants and animals live among which trees and the different soil types. For example, aspens grow in moist, protected areas. Bushes provide browse for mule deer. Grasses offer good eats for elk, which also scrape the bark off aspen in winter. Prairie dogs, mule deer, white-tailed deer, coyotes, and pronghorn antelope rule the plains. Little critters provide food for coyotes, foxes, eagles, hawks, and great horned owls. Elk, mule deer, and black bears live in forested areas, while mountain lions prowl rocky slopes. On cliffs and rocky steeps, mountain goats and Rocky Mountain bighorn sheep somehow survive. A good place to see bighorn sheep right from your car window is along I-70 near Georgetown. Long gone are the wild bison, grizzly bear, and wolf populations. Canada lynx were reintroduced in the San Juan Mountains in 1999 amid much controversy. You can still see bison on ranches around the state, as well as at Genesee and Daniels parks, and in the Rocky Mountain Arsenal National Wildlife Refuge near Denver.

As you gain elevation, animals and plants show their adaptations to shorter summers, less oxygen, and colder temperatures. Above treeline, you can't miss the cute little pikas scurrying around with mouthfuls of grasses and flowers, or lazy marmots sunning themselves on rocks. In some heavily visited areas chipmunks, ground squirrels, and marmots will practically attack you, expecting a handout. Please don't feed them, as they may not forage for themselves. Crows, magpies, blue Steller's jays with their black crowns, and pesky Clark's nutcrackers and gray jays (nicknamed camp robbers) are easily spotted birds.

Fishing in Colorado can be superb. Native cutthroat trout are making a recovery after introduced sport fish such as rainbow and brown trout increased competition for the food supply.

By July, wildflowers are blooming in the cool air of the high mountains. If summer has experienced normal or greater precipitation, mushrooms pop out in August and early September. Many mushrooms are poisonous, while others are edible and incredibly delicious. Do not pick mushrooms unless you know what you are doing!

The dry western side of the state is covered with sagebrush, greasewood, four-winged saltbush, skunkbrush, and shadscale. Rattlesnakes, eastern fence and other lizards, coyotes, jackrabbits, and deer mice are just a few of the reptiles and mammals living in this dry country that fluctuates between extremes of heat and cold. Desert bighorn sheep were reintroduced to several western canyons in the 1980s.

Bristlecone pines grow in Colorado generally south of I-70. These amazing trees live 1,500 to 2,000 years in the state. In the transition zone between alpine tundra and subalpine zone, you will notice islands of stunted trees with a few flag trees sticking up—a pattern called krummholz. The deadwood on the windward side protects the rest of the tree island, so please don't use it for firewood.

Above treeline, each incredible tiny flower has its own particular niche, whether on wind-blown slopes or next to sheltering rocks. Although the terrain above treeline can appear tough or barren, it's an ecosystem distinguished by its delicate flora. Be sure to tread lightly and stay on designated trails. Just a few steps off trail can cause plant damage requiring years to repair.

## Wilderness Restrictions/Regulations

Colorado's two national grasslands, eight national wildlife refuges, twelve national forests, forty-three wilderness areas (not counting wilderness study areas), and nine national parks and monuments provide numerous opportunities for hiking and backpacking in many different settings and ecosystems. Colorado also has forty-three state parks, plus various county and city open space areas and mountain parks.

If you plan to hike or backpack in a wilderness area, contact the responsible USDA Forest Service, National Park Service, or Bureau of Land Management (BLM) office by phone or check the appropriate website for up-to-date restrictions and regulations. By law, each national forest must have a forest management plan, and each plan must be reviewed every ten to fifteen years. Some plans are in the revision process as this guidebook is being published and some regulations may change. In general, each wilderness area has specific group size limitations, usually applying to both people and pack stock. A few wilderness areas have designated campsites in heavily used areas. Indian Peaks Wilderness has a backcountry permit requirement for overnight camping for all users and for day use year-round by organized groups. A free self-issued Wilderness Use Permit is required to use the Holy Cross, Maroon Bells–Snowmass, and Mount Evans Wilderness Areas. Wilderness areas closest to urban areas tend to have more regulations because of the large number of recreational users. See "In Addition: What Is Wilderness?" (in the North Central Mountains section) for more information on this topic.

Non-Wilderness parts of national forests and BLM lands tend to have fewer regulations. Some popular areas charge fees as specified by the Federal Lands Recreation Enhancement Act. Eighty percent of collected fees are retained locally for enhancement and services for those sites. National parks and monuments charge entrance fees and require backcountry permits for camping and sometimes for hiking. State parks charge entrance fees and separate camping fees. Each county and city open space or mountain park area has its own regulations.

Leave No Trace outdoor skills and ethics are increasingly important for the preservation of Colorado's wildlands and parks. For further information, visit the website at www.LNT.org. Also, see "In Addition: Leave No Trace" (in the South Central Mountains section). **Note:** Leave No Trace principles state that you should camp at least 200 feet from streams, lakes, and trails. Most state and local agencies ask that you camp at least 100 feet from water sources, trails, and roads. Please err on the side of caution, and camp as far from streams and lakes as you can—at least 100 feet and preferably 200 feet away.

## Winter Hiking

The hikes in this book were chosen for enjoyment and adventure during snow-free times. Trails open year-round are listed as such. Winter in Colorado's high country brings deep snows or wind-blown drifts that close many trailhead access roads from the time when winter gets serious (October to November) to when the snowpack melts and muddy roads dry (June to mid-July). Some snow-closed roads can be skied or snowshoed, with most such roads also being used by snowmobiles.

Don't attempt to drive a snow-closed road in a 4WD vehicle. One forest ranger commented that he has seen vehicles stuck a mile down a closed road after the drivers broke through the compacted snow. Use skis, snowshoes, or snowmobiles as allowed by local regulations.

The hikes were not evaluated for avalanche danger. As noted elsewhere in this book, Colorado typically leads the nation in avalanche deaths. Many avalanche awareness and field clinics are offered around the state. If you venture into the high country in winter, take clinics and be prepared for variable and extreme winter conditions. The winds can blow steadily at 60 miles per hour and gust to over 100 miles per hour in higher elevations.

*Elk browsing in Rocky Mountain National Park*

The Colorado Avalanche Information Center provides daily avalanche forecasts but always reminds people that conditions vary with each location and aspect. Check out the website at http://avalanche.state.co.us.

"Hiking" snow-covered trails in winter typically implies snowshoeing or cross-country skiing. Those methods of transportation are described in greater detail at the end of the Front Range hiking chapter. Another challenge in winter is locating high country trails. Snow-covered trails can be difficult if not impossible to find. Featured trails that are marked by blue diamonds on trees, which denote ski touring trails (orange diamonds typically denote snowmobile trails), are noted. Many trails, especially those in wilderness areas, are neither maintained nor marked for winter use. They may not be the best ski or snowshoe routes either. In winter, excellent route-finding skills and winter ski or snowshoe skills are mandatory. Some trails are not skier friendly because they are narrow and steep. Snowshoes are sometimes the best way to travel. And sometimes it's best to wait until summer to travel the trail.

Check with the local land management agency for winter trail recommendations, but be aware that they may not always have up-to-date information on winter trail conditions.

## Hiking with Dogs

Under Canine Compatibility in the hike specs, the words "Dogs must be under control" mean dogs can be off leash but must be under immediate voice control. If you cannot control your dog by voice command, regulations typically require the dog be leashed. This information was obtained from public land managers contacted while researching this hiking guide. According to the Colorado Division of Wildlife, harassment of wildlife (even chasing squirrels) by dogs and humans is illegal in Colorado.

## Levels of Difficulty

This rating system was developed from several sources and personal experience. These difficulty levels are meant as guidelines; the trails may prove easier or harder depending on ability and physical fitness. Hikes are rated by having one or more of the noted characteristics.

**Easy**—4 miles or less total trip distance in one day; elevation gain less than 600 feet; paved or smooth-surfaced dirt trail; less than a 6 percent grade average

**Moderate**—Up to 8 miles total trip distance in one day; elevation gain of 600 to 1,200 feet; a 6 to 8 percent grade average

**Difficult**—Up to 12 miles total trip distance in one day; elevation gain of 1,200 to 2,500 feet; an 8 to 10 percent grade average

**Most difficult**—Up to 16 miles total trip distance in one day; elevation gain of 2,500 to 3,500 feet; trail not well defined in places; a 10 to 15 percent grade average

**Strenuous**—Mainly reserved for peak climbs or canyon descents; greater than 15 percent grade average

## Getting around Colorado

### Area Codes

Colorado currently has four area codes: The Denver/Boulder metro area (extending out to Longmont, Idaho Springs, and Castle Rock) uses 303 and 720 (this area requires a ten-digit phone number even when calling from one house in Denver to the house next door). The 719 area code services the greater south-central and southeastern part of the state, including Colorado Springs, Pueblo, Buena Vista, Leadville, Alamosa, and Del Norte. The 970 area code covers the northern Front Range, Eastern Plains, and West Slope, extending east from Craig to Sterling and south from Craig to Durango and Cortez.

## Roads

For current information on statewide weather, road conditions, and road closures, contact the Colorado Department of Transportation (CDOT) at their toll-free hotline: (877) 315-7623 or 511 on your cell phone (Colorado only). Denver metro area and out-of-state callers can access the hotline by calling (303) 639-1111. The same information can also be found by visiting CDOT's website at www.cotrip.org.

## By Air

Denver International Airport (DIA) is 23 miles northeast of downtown Denver. Along with servicing the majority of flights into Colorado, DIA also links flights throughout the global village. For more information, contact its website at www.flydenver.com or call (303) 342-2000 or (800) AIR2DEN (247-2336).

Roughly 60 miles south of Denver lies the Colorado Springs Airport (COS). The Colorado Springs Airport services the southern half of the Front Range and Eastern Plains. For more information, contact its website at www.flycos.com or call (719) 550-1972.

Servicing the northwestern towns of Steamboat Springs and Hayden, the Yampa Valley Regional Airport (HDN) can be reached by calling (970) 276-5001 or visiting www.co.routt.co.us.

The Grand Junction Regional Airport (GJT) in Grand Junction services western Colorado and eastern Utah. This airport features commercial carrier service with more than 500 nonstop and one-stop connections to cities in the United States, Canada, Europe, and Central America. For more information, check out its website at www.gjairport.com or call (970) 244-9100.

Two airports serve the towns of the central Rockies: Aspen and Eagle. Aspen Airport is located just north of the town of Aspen, surrounded by mountains on three sides. For information, call (970) 920-5380 or check out the website at www.aspenairport.com. Eagle County Regional Airport (EGE) lies between Vail and Glenwood Springs. Contact them at (970) 328-2680 or www.eaglecounty.us/airport/.

To the southwest lies the Durango–La Plata County Airport (DRO). The Durango–La Plata County Airport is located about 14 miles southeast of Durango. For more information, contact its website at www.flydurango.com or call (970) 247-8143.

To book reservations online, check out your favorite airline's website or search one of the following travel sites for the best price: www.cheaptickets.com, www.expedia.com, www.priceline.com, www.orbitz.com, http://travel.yahoo.com, www.travelocity.com, www.trip.com, or www.kayak.com—just to name a few.

## By Rail

Amtrak has two routes that travel through Colorado daily. The California Zephyr travels between Chicago and San Francisco via Fort Morgan, Denver, Winter Park, Granby, Glenwood Springs, and Grand Junction. The stations in Grand Junction,

Glenwood Springs, and Denver have checked baggage service. The Southwest Chief travels between Chicago and Los Angeles via Lamar, La Junta, and Trinidad. For more details, call (800) 872-7245 or visit www.amtrak.com for more information.

## By Bus

Greyhound or partners serve most cities in Colorado and the major ski resorts along Interstates 25, 76, and 70 and US Highways 40, 50, and 550. Call Greyhound at (800) 231-2222 or visit www.greyhound.com for more information.

Roaring Fork Transit Authority (RFTA) runs frequent service from Glenwood Springs to Aspen, making it a convenient connection with Amtrak and Greyhound. For more information, check out the website at www.rfta.com or call (970) 925-8484.

Denver/Boulder Regional Transportation District (RTD) serves Boulder and metro Denver, including downtown and the airport. For more information call (303) 299-6000 or (800) 366-7433, or visit www.rtd-denver.com.

## Shuttles

From Denver International Airport, taxicabs, charters, vans, and luxury limousines can deliver you to most any Colorado location by prior arrangement. Check the Denver International Airport website at www.flydenver.com for a detailed listing of all available shuttle options.

## Visitor Information

For general information on Colorado, visit the official website of Colorado travel: www.colorado.com. The site contains a wealth of vacation information.

Visitors to Colorado can find vacation information, free state maps and brochures, and clean restrooms at Colorado's welcome centers, located near most of the major highways entering Colorado. For more information, visit www.colorado.com/WelcomeCenters.aspx.

## Wildland and Park Contact Information

For information about Colorado's parks and public wildlands, contact the following:

- USDA Forest Service: www.fs.usda.gov/r2/
- Bureau of Land Management: www.blm.gov/co/st/en.html
- Colorado State Parks: http://parks.state.co.us
- National Park Service: www.nps.gov
- US Fish & Wildlife Service: www.fws.gov/mountain-prairie/co.html

## How to Use This Guide

Each region begins with a section introduction, where you're given a sweeping look at the lay of the land. After this general overview, specific hikes within that region are described. You'll learn about the terrain and what surprises each route has to offer.

Next, you'll find the quick, nitty-gritty details of the hike: where the trailhead is located, the nearest town in which you'll find services, hike length, approximate hiking time, difficulty rating, elevation gain/loss, best hiking season, type of terrain, and what other trail users you may encounter. Elevation gain attempts to give you an approximate idea of the real gain or real loss of a trail as it roller coasters across the landscape.

The Finding the Trailhead section gives you dependable directions from a nearby city right down to where you'll want to park. (By the way, Trailhead GPS coordinates are in NAD 27 datum.) The Hike section is the meat of the chapter. Detailed and honest, it's the author's carefully researched impression of the trail. While it's impossible to cover everything, you can rest assured that we won't miss what's important.

In Miles and Directions, mileage cues are provided to identify all turns and trail name changes, as well as points of interest. And again, trailhead GPS coordinates are in NAD 27 datum. Between this and the route map, you simply can't get lost.

The Hike Information section is a hodgepodge. In it you'll find trail hotlines (for updates on trail conditions), as well as where to stay, what to eat, and what else to see while you're hiking in the area.

Lastly, the Honorable Mentions section details all of the hikes that didn't make the cut, for whatever reason—in many cases it's not because they aren't great hikes, but because they're overcrowded or environmentally sensitive to heavy traffic. Be sure to read through these. A jewel might be lurking among them.

## How to Use the Maps

### Regional Location Map
These maps (one presented in each section intro) help you find your way to the start of each hike from the nearest sizeable town or city. Coupled with the detailed directions provided in the Finding the Trailhead entries, these maps should visually lead you to where you need to be for each hike.

### Route Map
This is your primary guide to each hike. It shows all of the accessible roads and trails, points of interest, water, towns, landmarks, and geographical features. It also distinguishes trails from roads. The selected route is highlighted, and directional arrows point the way. Shaded topographic relief in the background gives you an accurate representation of the terrain and landscape in the hike area.

# Trail Finder

| | Back-packers | Waterfall | Geology Lovers | Dinosaur Lovers | Children | Dogs | Peak Baggers | Great Views | Lake Lovers | Canyons | Nature Lovers | History Lovers |
|---|---|---|---|---|---|---|---|---|---|---|---|---|
| **Eastern Plains** | | | | | | | | | | | | |
| 1. Homestead Trail | | | ● | | | | | | | ● | ● | ● |
| 2. Picket Wire Canyonlands | | | | ● | | | | | | ● | | ● |
| 3. Paint Mines Interpretive Park | | | ● | | ● | | | | | | | ● |
| 4. Dawson Butte Ranch Open Space | | | | | ● | | | | | | | |
| 5. Rocky Mountain Arsenal National Wildlife Refuge | | | | | ● | | | | | | ● | ● |
| 6. Pawnee Buttes | | | ● | | ● | ● | | | | | ● | |
| **Front Range** | | | | | | | | | | | | |
| 7. Fountain Valley and South Rim Trails | | | ● | | ● | | | | | | | ● |
| 8. Mount Falcon Park Upper Loop | | | | | | | | | | | | ● |
| 9. M. Walter Pesman Trail | | | | | ● | | | ● | | | ● | |
| 10. Bear Canyon Trail | | | ● | | | | ● | | | ● | | |
| 11. Kruger Rock Trail | | | | | | | | ● | ● | | | |
| 12. Fern Lake | ● | ● | | | | | | | | | | ● |
| 13. Lory State Park Loop | ● | | ● | | | | | | | | | |

| | Back-packers | Waterfall | Geology Lovers | Dinosaur Lovers | Children | Dogs | Peak Baggers | Great Views | Lake Lovers | Canyons | Nature Lovers | History Lovers |
|---|---|---|---|---|---|---|---|---|---|---|---|---|
| **North Central Mountains** | | | | | | | | | | | | |
| 14. Wheeler Trail | | | | | | • | | | | | | • |
| 15. North Mount Elbert Trail | | | | | | | • | • | | | | |
| 16. Notch Mountain | | | | | | | • | • | | | • | • |
| 17. Mount Thomas Trail | | | | | | | • | • | | | | |
| 18. Granite Lakes Trail | • | | | | | | | | • | | | |
| 19. Silver Creek Trail | • | | | | | | | | | | | • |
| 20. Lulu City (Site) | | | | | • | | | | | | | |
| 21. Kelly Lake | • | | | | | | | | • | | | |
| 22. Seven Lakes | • | • | | | | | | | • | | | |
| **Northwest** | | | | | | | | | | | | |
| 23. Storn King Fourteen Memorial Trail | | | | | | | | | | | | • |
| 24. Coyote and Squirrel Trails | | • | • | | • | | | | | | | |
| 25. Marvine Loop | • | | | | | | | | • | | | |
| 26. Black Mountain (West Summit) trail | | | | | | • | | | | | • | |
| 27. Gates of Lodore Nature trail | | | • | | • | | | | | • | | • |
| 28. Devils Canyon | | | • | | | | | | | • | | |

| | Back-packers | Waterfall | Geology Lovers | Dinosaur Lovers | Children | Dogs | Peak Baggers | Great Views | Lake Lovers | Canyons | Nature Lovers | History Lovers |
|---|---|---|---|---|---|---|---|---|---|---|---|---|
| **Southeast Mountains** | | | | | | | | | | | | |
| 29. Twin Rock Trail | | | | | ● | | | | | | | ● |
| 30. Rock Pond to Werley Ranch Loop | | | | | | | | | | | | ● |
| 31. Aiken Canyon | | | | | | | | | | | ● | |
| 32. Thompson Mountain | | | | | | ● | | | | | | |
| 33. Newlin Creek Trail | | | | | | ● | | | | ● | | ● |
| 34. Spanish Peaks Traverse | | | ● | | | | | | | | | ● |
| 35. Reilly and Levsa Canyons | | | | | | | | | | | | ● |
| **South Central Mountains** | | | | | | | | | | | | |
| 36. Dunes Hiking | | | ● | | | | | | | | ● | |
| 37. Middle Frisco Trail | | | | | | ● | | | ● | | | |
| 38. Alberta Peak: Continental Divide National Scenic Trial | | | | | | ● | ● | ● | | | | |
| 39. Williams Creek Trail | ● | | | | | | | | | | | |
| 40. Devils Creek and Lake | ● | | | | | | | | ● | | | |
| 41. Washington Gulch Trail | | | | | | | | | | | ● | |
| 42. Ptarmigan Lake | | | | | | ● | | ● | ● | | | |

## Southwest

| | Back-packers | Waterfall | Geology Lovers | Dinosaur Lovers | Children | Dogs | Peak Baggers | Great Views | Lake Lovers | Canyons | Nature Lovers | History Lovers |
|---|---|---|---|---|---|---|---|---|---|---|---|---|
| 43. Big Dominquez Canyon | | | ● | | | | | | | ● | ● | ● |
| 44. North Vista Trail | | | ● | | | | | ● | | ● | | |
| 45. Upper Roubideau Area Loop | | | | | | | | | | | | |
| 46. Jud Wiebe Memorial Trail | | | | | | | | ● | | | | |
| 47. Cascade and Portland Loop | | | | | | | | ● | | | | |
| 48. Pass and Coal Creek Loop | | | | | | ● | | ● | | | ● | |
| 49. First Fork and Red Creek Loop | | | | | | ● | | | | | ● | |
| 50. Petroglyph Point Trail | | | | | ● | | | | | ● | | ● |

# Map Legend

## Transportation

- ══5══ Interstate Highway
- ══8══ U.S. Highway
- ══3══ State Highway
- ═CR 23═ Local Road
- = = = Unpaved Road
- = = = Jeep Trail
- ├──┼──┤ Railroad Tracks

## Trails

- ------- Featured Trail
- ------ Trail
- ............ Paved Trail
- ——— Special Trail
- → Direction of Travel

## Water Features

- Body of Water
- Marsh/Swamp
- River/Creek
- Intermittent Streams
- ⫽ Rapids
- ⟔ Springs
- ⋙ Waterfall

## Land Management

- ─ ─ ─ State Line
- National Park/National Forest
- National Monument/ Wilderness Area
- Local/State Park/Wildlife Refuge

## Symbols

- ≍ Bridge
- ▲ Campground
- ✪ Capital
- Ⅲ Cattle Guard
- ⛰ Continental Divide National Scenic Trail
- ▯ Firetower
- ⚑ Gate
- 🐎 Horse Trail
- ▲ Mountain Peak/Summit
- 🅿 Parking
- ⟩⟨ Pass
- ⛱ Picnic Area
- ■ Point of Interest/Structure
- ((A)) Radio Tower
- 🏢 Ranger District Office
- 🚻 Restroom
- ○ Town
- ① Trailhead
- 💧 Water
- ◄ Viewpoint/Overlook
- ❓ Visitor/Information Center

# Eastern Plains Overview

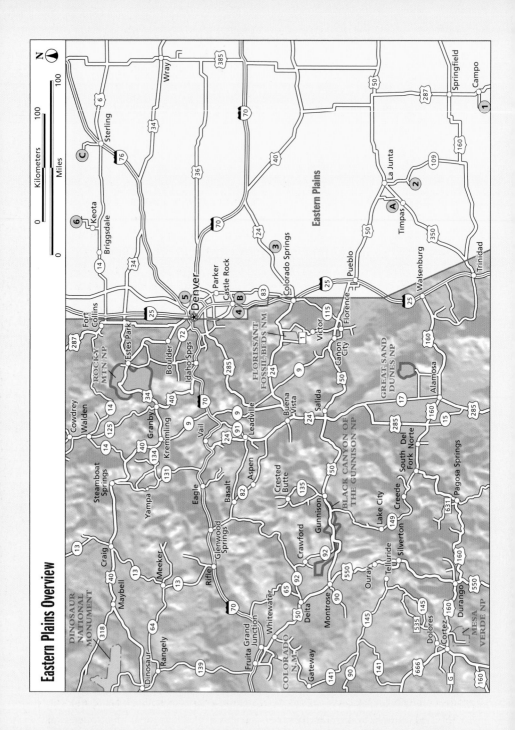

# Eastern Plains

Almost half of Colorado lies on the Great Plains where they bump into the Rocky Mountains. Even the lowest point in Colorado, at 3,337 feet near the Nebraska border east of Wray, is lofty compared to most of the nation. The Dust Bowl of the 1930s ended many dreams, yet it created the situation that ultimately resulted in the formation of the Pawnee National Grassland and Comanche National Grassland. The latter contains not only remains of pioneer settlements, but also those of Native American inhabitants who left rock carvings and an equinox marker tucked away in a cave.

Most hikers ignore the plains, thinking they are flat and boring, not to mention most of the land is private. But the plains have hidden spots every hiker should take time to explore. With most people dismissing the plains as a good hiking destination, what a great place to go for solitude!

Pawnee National Grassland lies north of Greeley and east of Fort Collins. The Pawnee Buttes section has a 1.8-mile hiking trail open year-round. Spring brings forth beautiful flowers, including prickly pear cactus, yucca, sunflowers, prairie cone-flower, prairie clover, locoweed, and prairie evening primrose, to name a few. This area is popular for bird watching. Seasonal closures of the overlook and cliffs protect birds during nesting season.

Comanche National Grassland lies south of La Junta, with another section southwest of Springfield in the southeastern corner of the state. A section of the Mountain Branch of the Santa Fe Trail can still be seen and hiked southwest of La Junta. Be sure to stop at Bent's Fort National Historic Site to step back in time to the days of trappers and early travelers in this area. Vogel Canyon offers some loop hikes with petroglyphs and remains of old stage stops. Beyond that, a must see is the largest known dinosaur tracksite in North America in Picket Wire Canyonlands. You can hike or bike into the area or take a guided 4WD tour offered by the Forest Service. Several trails in Picture Canyon take you almost into Oklahoma and feature petroglyphs, old homesteads, an arch, and a windmill.

Since Denver is the Queen City of the Plains, trails at the Rocky Mountain Arsenal National Wildlife Refuge are included in this chapter. Rocky Mountain Arsenal once produced chemical weapons, and later pesticides. Nevertheless, as urban development encroached on wildlands, a variety of wildlife took refuge in the buffer zone around the manufacturing facility. Manufacturing operations ceased in 1982. Today the wildlife refuge offers tours and a variety of trails for short and long hikes. New hikes on the Eastern Plains include one in the Paint Mines Interpretive Park, opened in 2005, and one in Dawson Butte Ranch Open Space, opened in 2008.

Several state parks, mainly located at reservoirs, offer hiking opportunities virtually year-round. In addition, North Sterling Reservoir State Park near Sterling offers short trails.

Take a trip to explore the eastern section of Colorado. You'll be pleasantly surprised by the subtle beauty. Interesting geological features, wildlife and birds, and historical places await your visit. Scenic and historic byways to explore include the Santa Fe Trail, Pawnee Pioneer Trails, and the South Platte River Trail.

# 1  Homestead Trail

The Homestead and Arch Rock Trails travel across a variety of landforms and through human history. Rock art from 2,000 years ago to the modern era is pecked and painted onto canyon walls. An equinox carving exists in a crack on a canyon wall. Remains of homesteads from the late 1800s and early 1900s dot the landscape. Hells Half Acre, a rock arch, numerous little canyons, springs, a forlorn windmill, wind-blown plains, prairie flowers, and juniper trees are some sights you can see as you hike this loop. Watch for great horned owls!

**Start:** From Picture Canyon picnic ground
**Distance:** 8.5-mile loop (9.5 miles if you include three spur trails)
**Approximate hiking time:** 3 to 5 hours
**Difficulty:** Moderate due to length
**Elevation gain:** 570 feet total; 280 feet plus another 290 feet in ups and downs
**Seasons:** Best in spring and fall. Summer can be very hot and winter can bring blizzards and snow.
**Trail surface:** Dirt trail, Forest roads, shortgrass prairie
**Land status:** National Grassland
**Nearest town:** Springfield
**Other trail users:** Equestrians, mountain bikers, motorists (in a few places), hunters (in season)

**Canine compatibility:** Dogs must be under control. Water is scarce along the trail.
**Schedule:** Year-round. Call for road and trail conditions after big snowstorms.
**Fees and permits:** None
**Maps:** USGS Campo SW and Tubs Springs
**Trail contact:** Comanche National Grassland, Carrizo Unit, Springfield; (719) 523-6591; www.fs.usda.gov/psicc
**Other:** You can camp in the parking lot. There are three covered picnic tables and one vault toilet. It's a very pleasant area next to canyon cliffs. There's no garbage service available here—pack it out!
**Special considerations:** No water, so bring your own.

**Finding the trailhead:** From the junction of US 287/385 and US 160 in Springfield, drive south on US 287/385 for 16.4 miles to just south of mile marker 13. Turn right onto Baca County Road (BCR) M. The road is wide and well graded dirt, but it can have washboards. The rest of the drive to the trailhead in the Picture Canyon Picnic Area is on maintained dirt roads. Drive 9 miles west to BCR 18 and turn left (south). Drive another 7.9 miles to the entrance to Picture Canyon Picnic Area and turn right on FR 2361. The road splits in 0.6 mile; take the left branch. The picnic area is another 1.4 miles south. Trailhead GPS: N37 00.73'/W102 44.66'

## The Hike

Most people think of eastern Colorado as a flat, uninspiring expanse, but the south-eastern corner bordering Oklahoma is full of interesting canyons, rock formations, wildlife, reptiles, birds, and human history.

*Arch Rock on spur trail*

There's evidence of people dwelling in Picture Canyon as far back as 2,000 years ago. The canyons provided their inhabitants with abundant wildlife and shelter from the elements, and supported wet bottomlands and running streams and springs, which made life in the canyons even more attractive. The first inhabitants were hunter-gatherers. By AD 1000, farming enabled a more settled lifestyle. In Crack Cave within Picture Canyon, ancient residents carved lines onto the wall. Experts surmise the markings may have been used to help with crop planting and harvesting, or to indicate ceremonies. During spring and fall equinox, the sun's rays illuminate these lines at sunrise. Because of vandalism, a locked gate now prevents the casual visitor from entering the cave, but festivals held in spring and fall allow a limited number of people to see the sunrise illumination.

About 0.4 mile from the trailhead on a side spur, numerous petroglyphs and pictographs are displayed on the canyon wall. A sea that covered much of Colorado back in Cretaceous times (about 100 million years ago) deposited these sandstone cliffs. Depictions of horses (which were introduced to North America by the Spanish) indicate that some of the artwork was done as recently as 500 years ago. Sadly, in more recent times, visitors have carved or painted initials and drawings over pre-existing artwork. It's sometimes hard to tell what is old and what is new. In one large opening, look for parallel lines carved in the rock. Some people believe these lines to be related to ohgam writing, an alphabet used in the British Isles from about AD 0 to 500. Some of the drawings have been interpreted as compasses and sundials, as well as equinox indicators.

The Jicarilla Apache are known to have inhabited this area since the early 1600s, and the Comanches arrived around 1700. In 1541, the conquistador Coronado claimed this land for Spain during his search for the legendary cities of gold. By 1846, the United States declared ownership of the region. Cattle barons grazed their herds on the endless grasslands in the 1870s and 1880s. Homesteaders arrived between 1890 and 1926 in search of a new life. But making a living was tough in the arid climate. A continuous water supply was of utmost importance, and visitors today can still see the remains of rock houses close to the springs at Crack Cave and Cave Springs.

▶ The Antiquities Act of 1906 and the Archaeological Resources Act of 1979 protect rock art and homestead ruins. Please respect the rock art by not touching it. Others arriving after you want to see original, not scarred, rock art. Touching rock art with hands, chalk, or even paper can hasten deterioration, plus it can interfere with new archaeological dating techniques.

Unfamiliar with the dry climate, settlers practiced ranching and farming methods they had brought from wetter homelands. Overgrazing and plowing methods combined to damage the fragile land. Several drought years, in conjunction with the normally windy weather, blew away the topsoil in the Dust Bowl of the 1930s. By 1938, farmers and ranchers were broke and begged the federal government for relief. A federal land purchase program was created, and between 1938 and 1942 the government bought thousands of farms, totaling 11.3 million acres of land. The USDA Forest Service was assigned to manage 5.5 million of these acres, and, in 1960, 4 million acres were designated a national grasslands, where restoration efforts continue today. Presently 200 grazing allotments are managed by the Forest Service in Comanche National Grassland.

The prairies also attract diverse wildlife, including approximately 275 species of birds, 40 reptiles, 9 amphibians, 11 fish, and 60 different mammals, including bear, mountain lion, bobcat, coyote, deer, and antelope. **Caution:** Watch for rattlesnakes in the grass, rock crevices, and ruins.

Although the trail is decently marked, this hike is often an exercise in *Where's the next trail marker?* Occasionally markers have fallen over or are farther apart. Trail markers consist of juniper logs with white paint on top, rock cairns, and carsonite posts (like highway reflector posts, but brown). Some trail sections follow forest roads. Three spurs are included in the hike description: one to rock art, one to homestead ruins and Crack Cave (closed), and the other to a rock arch and rock molar.

*Posts showing route at mile 7*

## Miles and Directions

**0.0**  Start at the trail register box by Picture Canyon Picnic Ground after checking out the big interpretive sign with the trail map and three smaller signs. The Homestead Trail quickly joins a non-motorized two-track road—turn left. Elevation: 4,300 feet.

**0.4**  A faint trail heads left near a sign about protecting Indian pictures and carvings. **(Side trip:** You can turn left here to see the rock art on the canyon walls. It's about 0.4 mile out-and-back. Return the way you came and turn left on the road to continue on Homestead Trail.)

**0.6**  Arrive at a trail and road junction. The road goes left and the Homestead Trail makes a very sharp right onto a singletrack trail. Follow the Homestead Trail, following the wooden posts with white tops. GPS: N37 00.40' / W102 45.01'. **(Side trip:** You can continue on the two-track road slightly to the right to the base of the cliff, where you'll see house ruins and Crack Cave [closed]. This spur is about 0.3 mile out-and-back.)

**0.8**  Arrive at a check dam and Homestead Trail and Arch Rock Trail sign with left arrow. Turn left and walk across the check dam, continuing to curve left to the next post. Turn right and walk up the trail. Some juniper trees almost cover the trail, and it crisscrosses a little dry creek several times. Keep following the wooden posts.

**1.1**   The trail forks. The right fork is a hiker bypass trail and offers an interesting glimpse of Hells Half Acre. The Homestead Trail goes left and is better marked. Turn left onto this trail, which soon makes a left turn to climb up out of the canyon. Continue following wooden posts. **(Note:** Watch out for yucca plants—members of the lily family—as their pointy leaves tend to hurt if you bump into them.)

**1.3**   Reach the ridgetop. The trail tread disappears, so follow the white-topped posts. GPS: N37 00.55'/W102 45.39'.

**1.7**   Cross a doubletrack trail just before the next wooden post. At the post, a sign indicates the horse trail goes right and the hiker bypass goes left. GPS: N37 00.85'/W102 45.61'. Turn left and follow the cairns down into a little slickrock canyon, following more cairns and rock-lined trail. **(FYI:** Toward the bottom, if there's water in a pond, look for little frogs. You'll also see Indian marbles on the nearby rocks.)

**1.9**   Arrive at the junction where the Homestead Trail and Arch Rock Trail split. Turn left onto Homestead Trail. **(Side trip:** It's worth the 0.25-mile out-and-back hike on Arch Rock Trail (the right fork) to see the arch and molar [as in tooth] rock.)

**2.8**   The trail intersects a road (FR 2361.E). Turn left and walk down the road.

**3.25**  An old rock house is on the right. GPS: N37 00.03'/W102 46.36'. OKLAHOMA STATE LINE sign is on the left.

**3.5**   Cave Spring is on your right. **(Note:** Although the water comes from a spring, the Forest Service suggests treating it as a safety precaution.) Continue walking down the road, which turns into a singletrack soon after Cave Spring. The trail heads through a wonderful cottonwood grove, then across a lush grassy area.

**3.9**   Arrive at the ruins of an old homestead. Look for the wooden post at the top of the slick-rock. The trail goes up the slickrock.

**4.75**  Arrive at a broken windmill. GPS: N37 00.94'/W102 47.23'. Elevation: 4,473 feet. The trail turns right. The trail tread disappears. Follow the white-topped trail posts.

**5.25**  The trail leads to a post at the canyon edge. GPS: N37 01.06'/W102 46.80'. Look for rock cairns as the trail drops down into the next canyon. Walk a little right, follow the water line down the slickrock, and then turn a little left. You'll see some big cairns. Follow them down to the canyon bottom.

**5.4**   Arrive at a dirt road (FR 2361.L) and turn right, walking on the road, which is the Homestead Trail.

**5.7**   The road forks. Take the left fork (FR 2361.E).

**5.8**   The road forks. Take the right fork (FR 2361.E).

**6.25**  The Homestead Trail turns right off of FR 2361.E at a sign. Follow the trail right, up a little canyon of sorts and past some interesting rock formations. Continue following wooden posts. As you reach the high area, head to the post on the right. The trail curves right here as the tread disappears.

**6.8**   Reach the junction of Arch Rock and Homestead Trails. GPS: N37 01.28'/W102 45.67'. Go straight (southeast); do not turn right. Continue on Arch Rock (also Homestead) Trail ignoring any doubletrack trails.

**7.3**   Turn left up an open area, following the posts. GPS: N37 01.17'/W102 45.21'. Once up on the ridge, turn right, and walk along the high area for a while, heading generally southeast.

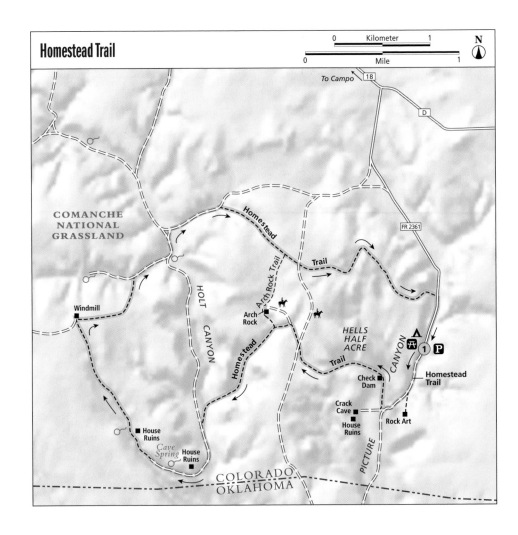

# Homestead Trail

0    Kilometer    1

0    Mile    1

N

To Campo    18

D

COMANCHE
NATIONAL
GRASSLAND

FR 2361

Homestead

Trail

HOLT
CANYON

Arch Rock Trail

Arch
Rock

HELLS
HALF
ACRE

Homestead

Trail

PICTURE CANYON

Check
Dam

Crack
Cave

House
Ruins

Rock Art

Windmill

House
Ruins

Cave
Spring

House
Ruins

COLORADO
OKLAHOMA

1    P

Homestead
Trail

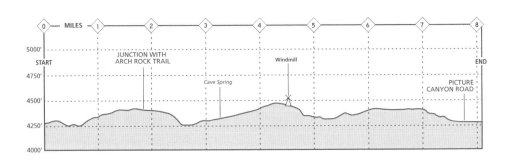

MILES    0    1    2    3    4    5    6    7    8

5000'

START

JUNCTION WITH
ARCH ROCK TRAIL

Windmill

END

4750'

Cave Spring

PICTURE
CANYON ROAD

4500'

4250'

4000'

**8.0** At the post, the trail starts heading downhill to FR 2361 (the road to the picnic area). Follow the cairns down a little slickrock area.

**8.2** Reach FR 2361. Turn right, and walk down the dirt road.

**8.5** Arrive back at the trailhead.

## Hike Information

### General Information
**Springfield Chamber of Commerce:** Springfield; (719) 523-4061; www.springfieldcolorado.com /chamber.html

### Local Events/Attractions
**Kirkwell Cattle Company:** custom ranch adventures—wagon and horseback trips; Springfield; (719) 523-3294, (719) 324-5225; www.kirkwellcattle.com
**Spring Equinox Festival (the first day of spring) and Fall Equinox Festival (the first day of fall):** Springfield; (719) 523-6591; www.fs.usda.gov/psicc (search for Crack Cave)

### Restaurants
**Longhorn Steakhouse:** 400 Main St., Springfield; (719) 523-6554
**La Mission at Main Cafe:** Main St., Springfield; (719) 523-4888
**Trails End Dining:** 964 Main St., Springfield; (719) 523-4460

### Hike Tours
See the Spring and Fall Equinox Festivals above under Local Events

# 2 Picket Wire Canyonlands

Picket Wire Canyonlands is a trip back in time, visiting early homesteads, a mission, and traveling even farther back to dinosaurs. It is a beautiful rimrock canyon with junipers, cactus, grasses, cottonwoods, and the Purgatoire River. Once down in the wide canyon, the hike is mostly gentle with a few hills. Intricately carved headstones in an old cemetery, and dinosaur tracks from 150 million years ago, are the highlights of this hike. The dinosaur tracksite is the largest documented in North America.

**Start:** From Withers Canyon trailhead
**Distance:** 10.8 miles out and back
**Approximate hiking time:** 5.5 to 7 hours
**Difficulty:** Difficult due to distance
**Elevation gain/loss:** 150-foot gain / 415-foot loss, including undulations
**Seasons:** Spring and fall are best
**Trail surface:** Dirt road, mainly doubletrack, sometimes rocky, with one steep section
**Land status:** National grassland
**Nearest town:** La Junta
**Other trail users:** Equestrians, mountain bikers, and hunters (in season), 4WDs during tours
**Canine compatibility:** Dogs must be under control
**Schedule:** Year-round, dawn to dusk
**Fees and permits:** None

**Maps:** USGS Riley Canyon and Beaty Canyon; USDA Forest Service Comanche National Grassland
**Trail contact:** Comanche National Grassland, La Junta; (719) 384-2181; www.fs.usda.gov /psicc
**Other:** No camping allowed in the canyon. Primitive camping is allowed on top of the canyon near Withers Canyon trailhead. A vault toilet, pullouts, and fire grates are available year-round. Camping is also available at Picket Wire Corrals, along with a vault toilet. Visiting equestrians may use the corrals for their horses. Only day use is allowed in the canyon itself, and a dusk-to-dawn closure order is in effect. Bring water. If you want to cross the river to explore more of the tracksite, bring old shoes with you. Be careful crossing, because dinosaur tracks create drops in the streambed.

**Finding the trailhead:** From La Junta Drive, drive south on CO 109 for 13.6 miles (past mile marker 43) to Forest Road (FR) 2200, with a sign to Vogel and Picket Wire Canyons. Turn right onto FR 2200 and drive about 8 miles to Otero County Road 25, also with a sign for Picket Wire Canyonlands. Turn left and continue for 6 miles to FR 2185. Turn left at Picket Wire Corrals. FR 2185 is to the left of the vault toilet. Drive 3.3 miles to Withers Canyon Trailhead and park. Trailhead GPS: N37 39.59' / W103 34.22'

## The Hike

Although people often visualize eastern Colorado as endless and uninteresting plains, the southeastern part of the state is punctuated by canyons and juniper forests. Established in 1960, Comanche National Grassland is one of the exclamation points within the text of this land. The Forest Service manages some 435,000 acres

*Remains of the Dolores Mission and its cemetery*

here in Comanche National Grassland, and has since the U.S. government gave it the charge of rehabilitating the area in 1954. The government bailed out Dust Bowl victims whose property had been rendered virtually worthless due to poor farming techniques and overgrazing. Thanks to revegetation efforts and the protection of natural grasses—still ongoing—the grassland today serves as both a wildlife habitat and a playground for human recreation. Conservation and control methods have also allowed for the reintroduction of livestock grazing.

Humans have lived in the Purgatoire Valley for perhaps as long as 10,000 years. Experts place rock art in the canyonlands between 375 and 4,500 years old. Spanish explorers first came to the area in the 1500s, when the Purgatoire Valley was verdant and full of wildlife. Legend has it that a group of early Spanish military explorers met their deaths in the Purgatoire Valley, either due to exposure or conflict with the Native Americans. Either way, the men were said to have died before having their last rites administered, thus the river that courses through the canyon was named El Rio de las Animas Perdidas en Purgatorio (the River of Lost Souls in Purgatory). French trappers who wandered into the canyon during the eighteenth century shortened the name to Purgatoire. Settlers struggled with the French pronunciation, and the river became known as Picket Wire. (By the way, Purgatoire is pronounced "purgatory" in these parts.)

Jicarilla Apaches hunted and farmed the area for about a century, between 1620 and 1720, after which the Comanches took control. French traders and trappers arrived prior to 1800 and hunted the plentiful beaver down to very low levels. Without a healthy beaver population to build and maintain dams, the pools and marshes of the Purgatoire River disappeared. Today you see a small river meandering along a broad valley between rimrock walls.

Leave the parking area by the bulletin board, pass through a wide opening in a fence, sign the trail register, and descend to a pipe gate. Please close any gates behind you. From the gate, the trail drops steeply through the rimrock layer of Withers Canyon, losing 250 feet in the next 0.25 mile. Right after the trail joins another double-track road in Purgatoire Canyon, ruins of an old homestead appear on the right. The trail goes up and over a few side ridges, bringing you close to the cliffs. Farther upstream, remains of adobe walls rise from the ground just past the river water sign. (Remember to treat any river water before drinking it.)

Just a little farther down the trail are the remains of the Dolores Mission, with its small cemetery. In 1871 Damacio Lopez led twelve families here, where they remained for two generations. The little headstones are intricately carved with a variety of symbols (like hearts) and inscribed with dates between 1896 and 1900. They are fragile and several are broken, so avoid touching them. A vehicle turnaround for guided tours is located here. A smoother dirt road takes you to the dinosaur tracksite another 1.6 miles upstream.

Envision yourself here 150 million years ago. Imagine a large lake of about 6 miles in diameter, set in a semiarid region. Algae, snails, minute crustaceans, fish, and horsetail plants live in and along the lake. Watch as a group of brontosaurs walk along the shore, side by side. Come another time, as brontosaurs and two-legged dinosaurs use the area heavily, trampling anything underfoot. Visit yet another time to see three-toed carnivorous dinosaurs, perhaps allosaurus, walk near the lake. Today, interpretive signs explain the fossil footprints.

By the river, the three-toed footprints jump out at you. Compare your foot size with theirs. Depending on the river flows, tracks can sometimes be filled with mud. The brontosaur tracks lie on the south side of the river. They extend for 0.25 mile and contain about one hundred different trackways with 1,300 visible footprints. Dinosaur science has not progressed enough to verify which dinosaurs created the tracks; however current speculation includes members of the brontosaur order (large terrestrial plant eaters) such as brachiosaurid, camarasaurid, and diplodocid families, and the theropod order (terrestrial carnivores) such as allosaurus. Take care while here—help preserve the tracks for future generations. If you wander off trail, remember the U.S. Army's Pinyon Canyon Maneuver Site is just north of Picket Wire Canyonlands and is off-limits, besides being dangerous.

◀  *Dinosaur Trackway in Picket Wire Canyon*

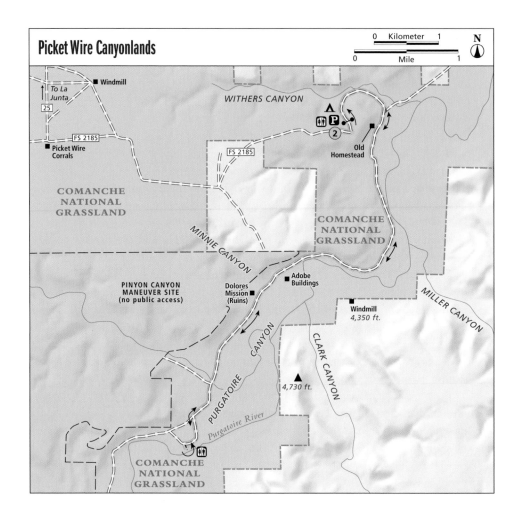

# Picket Wire Canyonlands

0    Kilometer    1

0    Mile    1

N

■ Windmill

To La Junta

25

FS 2185

■ Picket Wire Corrals

WITHERS CANYON

FS 2185

Old Homestead

COMANCHE NATIONAL GRASSLAND

COMANCHE NATIONAL GRASSLAND

MINNIE CANYON

PINYON CANYON MANEUVER SITE (no public access)

Dolores Mission ■ (Ruins)

Adobe Buildings

Windmill 4,350 ft.

MILLER CANYON

CLARK CANYON

PURGATOIRE CANYON

▲ 4,730 ft.

Purgatoire River

COMANCHE NATIONAL GRASSLAND

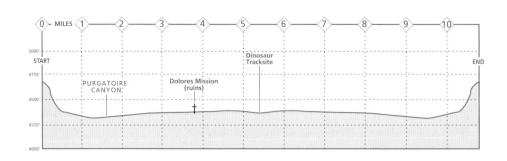

0 — MILES — 1 — 2 — 3 — 4 — 5 — 6 — 7 — 8 — 9 — 10

5000'

START

END

4750'

Dinosaur Tracksite

PURGATOIRE CANYON

Dolores Mission (ruins)

4500'

4250'

4000'

## Miles and Directions

**0.0** Start at the Withers Canyon Trailhead. Elevation: 4,630 feet.

**0.05** Arrive at the trail register. Turn left on Picket Wire Trail.

**0.2** Reach a pipe gate and walk around it.

**0.9** Reach the intersection with a nonmotorized dirt road (doubletrack) in Purgatoire Canyon, and turn right. GPS: N37 39.73'/W103 33.70'

**1.1** Reach the remains of an old homestead.

**3.5** Reach the remains of old adobe buildings.

**3.8** Reach the Dolores Mission ruins and cemetery.

**5.1** The road forks. Take left road branch to reach the vault toilet and the trail to the dinosaur tracksite. Turn left.

**5.4** Stop and read the interpretive signs before looking for tracks along the riverbank (both sides). Elevation: 4,360 feet. GPS: N37 37.05'/W103 35.78'. Return the way you came.

**10.8** Arrive back at the trailhead.

## IF YOU MEET A RATTLESNAKE

Rattlesnakes tend to avoid humans. They will strike if surprised, threatened, or hassled. Watch where you step or before you put your hands on rocks or ledges. If it's really hot, snakes rest in shaded areas. In spring and fall, they try to warm up in sunny areas. If you see or hear a rattlesnake, *freeze!* That may be hard to do, but rattlesnakes strike at motion and heat. Stand still and look for the snake. Be quiet until the snake calms down, uncoils, and slithers away. If you see the snake 4 to 5 feet or more from you, back away slowly.

## Hike Information

### General Information
**La Junta Chamber of Commerce:** La Junta; (719) 384-7411; www.lajuntachamber.com
**Unofficial Comanche National Grasslands website:** www.vipgrafx.com/misc/cng.htm

### Local Events/Attractions
**Bent's Old Fort National Historic Site:** La Junta; (719) 383-5010; www.nps.gov/beol
**Koshare Indian Museum:** La Junta; (719) 384-4411; www.kosharehistory.org
**Otero County Museum:** La Junta; (719) 384-7500

### Accommodations
**KOA:** La Junta; (719) 384-9580 or (800) 562-9501; www.koa.com
**Vogel Canyon Picnic Ground:** camp in parking lot; Comanche National Grassland, La Junta; (719) 384-2181; www.fs.usda.gov/psicc

**Withers Canyon trailhead area:** Comanche National Grassland, La Junta; (719) 384-2181; www.fs.usda.gov/psicc

## Restaurants
**The Junction Grill:** 27866 Highway 50, La Junta; (719) 384-8488
**Mexico City Cafe:** 1617 Raton Ave., La Junta; (719) 384-9818

## Clubs and Organizations
**Rocky Mountain Nature Association:** Comanche National Grassland, La Junta; (719) 384-2181; www.rmna.org

## Hike Tours
**Comanche National Grassland:** La Junta; (719) 384-2181; www.fs.usda.gov/psicc. Offers 4WD tour to the dinosaur tracksite from the opposite direction on Saturdays in May, June, Sept, and Oct.

*Purgatoire River and trail about 2.8 miles*

# 3  Paint Mines Interpretive Park

The figure-eight trail through Paint Mines Interpretive Park is a real treat! The trail winds through shortgrass and midgrass prairie, where you can see blue grama, Colorado's state grass. Chokecherry, mountain mahogany, wild rose, and a variety of other plants find moisture in the natural drainages. The trail follows a creekbed for part of the journey, while a graveled path finishes the tour, including a great view of brilliantly colored hoodoos and other eroded features. The designated trail takes you close to the formations, but not in them, to prevent damage to these fragile outcrops.

**Start:** From the Paint Mines Interpretive Park trailhead

**Distance:** 4.0-mile figure eight with spur

**Approximate hiking time:** 1.5 to 3 hours

**Difficulty:** Easy due to distance and elevation gain

**Elevation gain:** 450 feet, including various ups and downs

**Seasons:** Year-round except after a big snow

**Trail surface:** Dirt trail

**Land status:** El Paso County Parks

**Nearest town:** Calhan

**Other trail users:** Hikers only

**Canine compatibility:** Dogs and pets are prohibited

**Schedule:** Year-round from dawn to dusk

**Fees and permits:** None

**Map:** USGS Calhan

**Trail contact:** El Paso County Parks, 2002 Creek Crossing, Colorado Springs; (970) 520-6375; www.elpasoco.com/parks

**Special considerations:** Be aware of flash floods in drainages if the weather is stormy. Rain can cause flash floods in a flash!

**Finding the trailhead:** From I-25 north of downtown Colorado Springs, take exit 149, and head east on East Woodmen Road about 13 miles to US 24. Turn left onto US 24 and head northeast about 19.3 miles to Yoder Street at the east end of Calhan. Turn right and drive 0.7 mile to Paint Mine Road and turn left. Follow Paint Mine Road 1.4 miles to the parking lot on the left. Turn in and park. A vault toilet is available but no water, so bring your own. Trailhead GPS: N39 01.23'/W104 16.40'

## The Hike

While you're driving from Colorado Springs toward Calhan, past farms, ranches, and subdivisions housing an expanding population, fly back in time about 70 million years. That was when the Rocky Mountains, including Pikes Peak, started rising from the inland Cretaceous Seaway. Familiar features like the flatirons and hogbacks that stretch from Colorado Springs to Fort Collins tilted toward the sky. The Denver Basin formed to the east, and erosion from the new mountains filled the basin with many types of sediment.

Fast forward 6 million years. The dinosaurs, along with many plants, trees, and other animals, had disappeared about 1 million years ago. Colorado was situated at a lower elevation, and wet monsoons dropped close to 120 inches of rain a year,

creating a tropical rain forest, the remains of which have been uncovered near Castle Rock and while building Denver International Airport. As time marched on, soil built up in the rain forest, to 20 feet deep in some places. This fossil clay soil is called paleosol. Erosion from the granitic Pikes Peak eventually covered the paleosol, burying trees and animals, and hardening into a white sandstone over time. In more recent times, forces uplifted Colorado about 5,000 feet and glaciers covered the high peaks. As the glaciers melted, rushing rivers eroded the sediments in the foothills and plains.

In today's Paint Mines Interpretive Park, water and wind have worn through the layers of clay of the paleosol, creating gullies and hoodoos, interesting shapes topped with the white sandstone from Pikes Peak. Minerals in the clay create colorful layers of beige, gray, yellow, orange, pink, maroon, and purple, while quartzite produces a blinding white—a real rainbow. Artifacts found on the property indicate that Paleo-Indians used the area 9,000 years ago, while they roamed the plains hunting mammoths and giant bison. Petrified wood unearthed in the clay layers became tools for these and later peoples. Bison bones exposed in the gullies suggest that native peoples may have chased bison over the cliffs and harvested the dead animals for food, clothing, and lodging. When the art of making pottery developed, people gathered the colorful clay to make their earthenware and ceremonial paints, hence the name: Paint Mines.

By the 1880s white people arrived to settle homesteads on the high plains. One legend says Dad McRae looked around the area where the Rock Island railroad was planned and found the site where Calhan now sits. Mike Calahan had the contract to build the section of railroad through this area. Someone probably dropped an "a" when naming the town. The first train arrived in 1888, as well as the post office.

Dr. Abraham Scott and his wife, Harriet, arrived in Calhan in the 1890s, and he became the town's first doctor. His daughter Caroline married Henry Freeman. One of their sons, Harry, owned land southeast of Calhan, including the Paint Mines. Caroline's brother, Lewis, developed the mines, hauling the colorful clay to Denver and Pueblo by wagon, mainly for creating fire brick, pottery, and tile. Several buildings in Pueblo and Colorado Springs were built with bricks made from Paint Mines clay.

Eventually clay shipments stopped and Calhan's residents used the area for picnics and sometimes Easter sunrise services. People partied in the gullies, leaving graffiti as well as beer cans. In 1997, El Paso County started to buy land to preserve this unique area. The county closed the area, conducted archaeological and geologic surveys, and with the help of volunteers, cleaned up the land and built trails. Great Outdoors Colorado (GOCO) and The Conservation Fund helped with funding. The 750-acre Paint Mines Interpretive Park opened to the public in June 2005.

The hike as featured is a figure eight. Start by heading down the trail to the northeast, winding along a creekbed. This part of the trail can be very slippery when the

*Ponderosa pine and yucca from overlook*

*View of the Paint Mines from overlook*

clay is wet. Follow the green carsonite posts along the way. This section gives you an idea of the eroding force of water, as well as of plains flora. You'll eventually approach the colorful hoodoos and arrive at an interpretive sign about geology. Please stay on marked trails (as of 2010 hiking off the main gully into the colorful formations is prohibited). Stay on the trails posted on the map on the interpretive sign at the trailhead, and in the area brochure.

This unique area, a special combination of interesting geology, archaeology, and high plains ecosystems, is listed on the National Register of Historic Places. Interpretive signs along the trail explain diverse features and history. Keep an eye open for the various animals and birds that live and visit here.

## Miles and Directions

**0.0** Start at the interpretive signs by the Paint Mines Interpretive Park parking lot. Elevation: 6,655 feet. At the first junction, continue straight ahead. (You'll return on the trail to the right.)

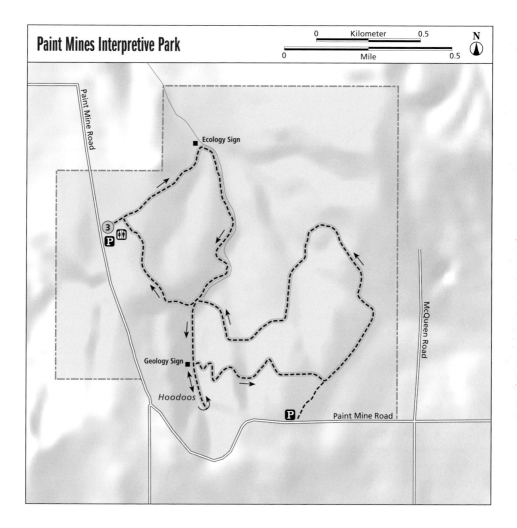

Paint Mines Interpretive Park

0  Kilometer  0.5

0  Mile  0.5

N

Paint Mine Road

Ecology Sign

3

P

McQueen Road

Geology Sign

Hoodoos

P

Paint Mine Road

**0.4** Pass the ecology interpretive sign. The low point of the hike is just beyond here. The trail enters a typically dry creekbed that can be very slippery when wet. Avoid this section of trail during wet weather. Follow the green carsonite posts if you're unsure of the trail's line.

**0.7** Pass by eroded cliffs along the creek. Notice the soil breaks off easily, to be worn down when water flows in the creek.

**1.1** Arrive at an X junction, the middle of the figure eight. Continue straight ahead in the creekbed. Ignore the social trail to the right a little farther along the trail. Some colorful hoodoos are ahead.

**1.3** Arrive at the junction with a gravel trail coming in from the left. GPS: N39 00.89'/W104 16.12'. Continue straight ahead to the geology interpretive sign. The designated trail continues straight ahead for another 0.2 mile along the main gully. Please do not hike on the social trails into the hoodoo formations or climb on the formations. Turn around at the end of the trail and retrace your steps.

**1.7** Arrive back at the junction with the gravel trail; turn right and head uphill.

**1.8** A bench and scenic overlook of the hoodoos is on the right. A lone ponderosa pine grows below.

**2.3** Arrive at the junction with the trail that goes right to another parking area. Continue to the left on the main trail. Elevation 6,745 feet. GPS: N39 00.84'/W104 15.68'.

**3.0** A little eroded area is off to the left.

**3.6** Arrive back at the X junction, the middle of the figure eight. Continue straight ahead and uphill back toward the parking lot.

**3.7** Stop at the bench for a great overview of the Paint Mines area and the plains to the east.

**3.9** Turn left to return to the trailhead.

**4.0** Arrive back at the trailhead by the parking lot.

## Hike Information

### General Information
**Town of Calhan:** 556 Colorado Ave., Calhan; (719) 347-2586; www.calhan.net

### Local Events/Attractions
**El Paso County Fair:** 366 10th St., Calhan; (719) 520-7880; www.elpasocountyfair.com
**Serenity Springs Wildlife Center:** big cats and exotics; 24615 Scott Rd., Calhan; (719) 347-9200; www.serenityspringswildlife.org

### Restaurants
**Hearthstone Kitchen Restaurant:** 520 Colorado Ave., Calhan; (719) 349-2490
**Rooster's Grille & Pizzaria:** 100 5th St., Calhan; (719) 347-3280

### Clubs and Organizations
**El Paso County Parks Volunteers:** 2002 Creek Crossing, Colorado Springs; (719) 520-6384; www.elpasoco.com/parks

### Hike Tours
**El Paso County Parks:** fee required; 2002 Creek Crossing, Colorado Springs; (719) 520-6387; www.elpasoco.com/parks

# 4 Dawson Butte Ranch Open Space

The loop trail in Dawson Butte Ranch Open Space winds gently through ponderosa pine and Gambel oak (oakbrush) forest and across several meadows on the south side of Dawson Butte. Occasionally you get glimpses of the tops of Pikes Peak and Devils Head, along with the ridge of the Rampart Range to the west. This open space features separate bridle trails complete with over sixty horse jumps. The area is excellent wildlife habitat with a good diversity of birds. With a picnic table almost halfway around the loop, this trail provides for a leisurely hike.

**Start:** From the Dawson Butte Ranch trailhead on the north side of the parking lot
**Distance:** 5.0-mile loop
**Approximate hiking time:** 1.5 to 2.5 hours
**Difficulty:** Moderate due to distance
**Elevation gain:** 320 feet including undulations
**Seasons:** Best Apr through Nov—you can cross-country ski or snowshoe when there's enough snow
**Trail surface:** Natural surface trail
**Land status:** Douglas County Open Space
**Nearest town:** Castle Rock

**Other trail users:** Equestrians and mountain bikers
**Canine compatibility:** Dogs must be on leash
**Schedule:** Year-round, from one hour before sunrise to one hour after sunset
**Fees and permits:** None
**Maps:** USGS Dawson Butte; Douglas County Open Space Dawson Butte Ranch Trail map at www.douglas.co.us/openspace/Dawson_Butte _Ranch.html
**Trail contact:** Douglas County Open Space, 100 Third St., Castle Rock; (303) 663-7495; www.dcoutdoors.org

**Finding the trailhead:** From Castle Rock, head south on I-25 to exit 181, Plum Creek. At the traffic light, go straight ahead on the Frontage Road. Drive south 5.3 miles to Tomah Road. Turn right (west) on Tomah Road, cross the railroad tracks (coal trains may take a long time to clear the crossing), and drive 1.6 miles to the Dawson Butte Ranch entrance on the right. A portable toilet and picnic tables are located by the parking lot. Bring your own water as none is available along the trail. There is no access or trail to the top of Dawson Butte, both to protect wildlife and because part of the top is private property. Please stay on established trails. Trailhead GPS: N39 17.70'/W104 55.23'

## The Hike

In June 1820 Major Stephen H. Long set out from the area around Council Bluffs, Iowa, with a group of nineteen men under orders from the Secretary of War to explore the Platte River and its tributaries. His expedition included a naturalist, a landscape painter, a zoologist, and a physician with a background in geology and botany. Doctor James, the physician, kept a detailed diary of the trip, describing vegetation, climate, fauna, geology, and geography. On July 10, the group arrived at and described Dawson Butte. On July 13, Doctor James and two others started to ascend Pikes Peak. They arrived on the summit at 4 p.m. on July 14.

Some forty years later, Thomas Dawson established squatters' rights on the area below the butte that now bears his name. He became the first postmaster at nearby Bear Canyon.

Dawson's name also became attached to the sandstone formation that makes up a good portion of the buttes and cliffs east of the foothills in Douglas County. About 70 million years ago, the Rocky Mountains started slowly rising, and Pikes Peak, a huge block of granite, emerged. While the mountains rose, erosion wore them down, creating large alluvial fans at their bases. No buttes existed back in those early times. Instead, dinosaurs like triceratops, as well as crocodiles and turtles, roamed what is now the plains. In a temperate climate fig trees, palms, magnolias, willows, and maples grew instead of today's ponderosa pines. The coarse eroded granite from Pikes Peak became the 55-million-year-old white-and-buff rock (mostly quartz and feldspar) called "Dawson Arkose." Petrified wood is the most common fossil found in this formation. Some layers erode very easily, leaving behind the many buttes along I-25, such as Castle Rock and Dawson Butte, as well as hoodoos (rock columns weathered into interesting shapes). The caps on the buttes are held together by a harder, iron-containing rock layer that covered the looser rocks, pebbles, and sand. Imagine this area 50 million years ago when no buttes existed—only a high plain at the base of the mountains.

Today Gambel oak (oakbrush) and ponderosa pines have replaced palms and magnolias. Oakbrush produces small acorns, about 1 inch long. Native Americans shelled the nuts and soaked them in water to release the bitter tannic acid. Then they ground the nuts into acorn meal that became bread, mush, and pancakes. Deer enjoy browsing oakbrush, while birds and bears eat the acorns. Oakbrush only grows roughly south of Morrison (CO 74) on the eastern slope of the Colorado Rockies, but on the western slope it grows in most locations between 5,500 to 10,000 feet.

Ponderosa pines live in dry, warm places between 5,500 and 9,000 feet elevation. Trees can grow 150 feet tall and 3 to 4 feet in diameter. Bigger trees may live 300 to 500 years. Their needles are long and grow in packets of two or three. Some people say the bark smells like butterscotch. The bark of a mature ponderosa is fairly thick and fire-resistant. However, if the fire reaches the tree crown, then the tree will burn. Douglas County thinned the ponderosa forest in 2009 to provide more space between the trees to suppress potential wildfires.

The Chapman Young family owned the Dawson Butte Ranch between 1950 and 2004. Douglas County purchased 828 acres of land from the family between 2004 and 2007, with help from Great Outdoors Colorado, the Douglas County Open Space fund, and some private donations. The land is protected by a conservation easement, meaning it cannot be developed or subdivided. Douglas Land Conservancy holds the conservation easement, while Douglas County owns the land. A little piece of private property exists in the middle of this open space area, so please respect the property owners' rights. The Youngs had designed and created many horse paths and

*Trail and Dawson Butte* ▶

# Dawson Butte Ranch Open Space

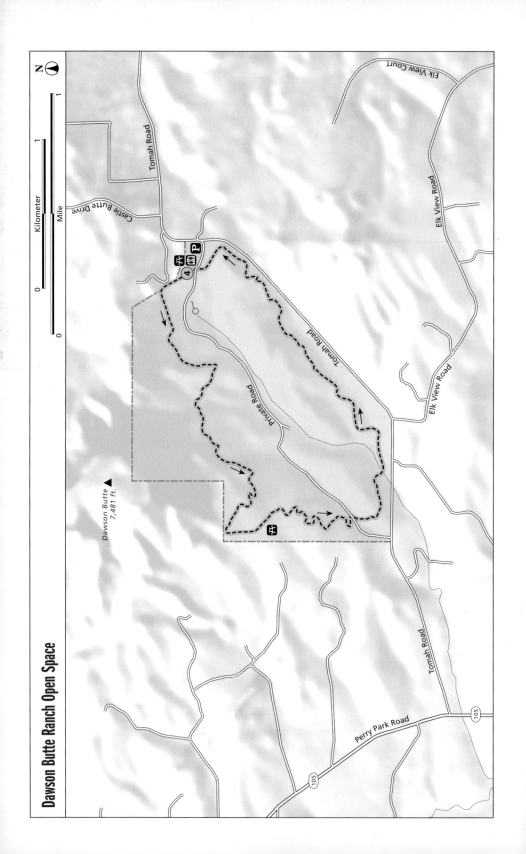

*Dawson Butte framed by ponderosa pine*

jumps on their property. The county selected sixty of the jumps and kept them for local equestrians to enjoy with their horses.

Douglas County was especially interested in the Dawson Butte Ranch because of the good wildlife habitat. The land also supports a diversity of birds. Some that come to nest at Dawson Butte Ranch include prairie falcons, ovenbirds, western tanagers, and black-headed grosbeaks. The Audubon Society sponsors a Christmas Bird Count over about a three-week period starting in mid-December each year, and Dawson Butte Ranch Open Space is one of their locations. Results are used to study the status of wintering bird populations across North America, and to create strategies for habitat protection and resolution of any environmental threats.

Dawson Butte Ranch Open Space is a wonderful little area to escape from the crowded city and enjoy a day in the rolling woodlands with your family. Come often to see what changes the different seasons bring to this special place.

## Miles and Directions

**0.0**   Start at the trailhead on the north side of the parking lot. Elevation: 6,815 feet. The loop is described in a counterclockwise direction. You can also start at the trailhead on the south side.

**0.9**   Reach the junction with Manger Meadow Trail, one of the many bridle paths with horse jumps. Continue straight ahead.

**1.4** Over the next 0.5 mile, you'll come to junctions with several bridle paths. All are well marked. Stay on the main trail for hikers and mountain bikers.

**2.0** Look to the right—you'll see a picnic table down Picnic Tree Trail. This is a good place for lunch if you'd like to take this spur trail. GPS: N39 17.41'/W104 56.40'

**2.8** Reach the junction with the private road. Continue straight ahead on the trail.

**3.3** Cross a little creek, which is the low point of the hike.

**3.5** At the junction with Tomah Meadow Path, continue straight ahead.

**4.4** Reach the four-way junction of the Dawson Butte, Tomah Meadow, and Play Pen Path trails. Continue straight ahead.

**5.0** Pass three picnic tables to the right. Play Pen Path comes in from the left. Arrive back at the parking lot.

## Hike Information

### General Information
**Castle Rock Chamber of Commerce:** (303) 688-4597; www.castlerock.org

### Local Events/Attractions
**Castle Rock Wine Fest:** (303) 688-4597; www.castlerockwinefest.com
**Colorado Renaissance Festival and Artisan Marketplace:** Larkspur; (877) 259-3328; www.coloradorenaissance.com

### Accommodations
**Colorado State Parks–Chatfield State Park:** 11500 North Roxborough Park Rd., Littleton; (303) 791-7275; http://parks.state.co.us/Parks/Chatfield
**Jellystone Castle Rock Campgrouund:** 6527 South I-25, Castle Rock; (303) 681-3169; www.gocampingamerica.com/parkInfo.aspx?campID=14349

### Restaurants
**Dream Pastries:** 370 Perry St., Castle Rock; (303) 814-1991; www.dreampastries.com
**Siena:** 333 Perry St., Castle Rock; (303) 688-2622; www.sienacr.com
**Union Bistro:** 3 Wilcox St., Castle Rock; (303) 668-8159

### Clubs and Organizations
**Douglas Land Conservancy:** Castle Rock; (303) 688-8025; www.douglaslandconservancy.org
**Volunteer opportunities:** Douglas County Open Space, Castle Rock; (303) 660-7495; www.douglas.co.us/openspace

### Hike Tours
**Douglas County Open Space:** Castle Rock; (303) 660-7495; www.douglas.co.us/openspace

# 5 Rocky Mountain Arsenal National Wildlife Refuge

Created in 1992, Rocky Mountain Arsenal National Wildlife Refuge (RMANWR) is a serene wildlife oasis near a bustling urban area. Over the years, the mile-wide buffer around the former chemical weapons plant provided a refuge for prairie animals and birds as the Denver metro area expanded. White-tailed and mule deer, eagles, prairie dogs, hawks, waterfowl, burrowing owls, and more thrive here, so close to millions of people. Enjoy watching wildlife on your hike through shortgrass prairie, woodlands, and wetlands rich in farming and military history.

**Start:** From the trailhead by interpretive signs southwest of the contact station.
**Distance:** 5.3-mile loop with spur
**Approximate hiking time:** 1.75 to 2.75 hours
**Difficulty:** Moderate due to distance; easy loop is available
**Elevation gain:** 40 feet
**Seasons:** Year-round except after big snowstorms; summer can be very hot
**Trail surface:** Natural surface trail, crusher fines, dirt road, and some paved roads
**Land status:** National Wildlife Refuge
**Nearest towns:** Commerce City and Denver
**Other trail users:** Hikers only; anglers around Lakes Mary and Ladora
**Canine compatibility:** Assistance dogs allowed
**Schedule:** Year-round 6 a.m. to 6 p.m. (closed Monday and all federal holidays). Check the website or call the visitor center (9 a.m. to 4 p.m.) before heading out to hike. RMANWR may close quickly and unexpectedly for wildlife needs or inclement weather.
**Fees and permits:** None, except for catch-and-release fishing
**Map:** USGS Montbello
**Trail contact:** U.S. Fish & Wildlife Service, Rocky Mountain Arsenal National Wildlife Refuge, 5650 Havana St., Building 121, Commerce City; (303) 289-0930; www.fws.gov/rockymountainarsenal
**Other:** RMANWR offers many different wildlife-viewing tours and nature programs. Visit the website for more information. RMANWR does not have an auto tour route.
**Special considerations:** Please remain on the trails and obey all posted signs. Alcohol and firearms are prohibited.

**Finding the trailhead:** From I-70 in Commerce City, take exit 278, Northfield/Quebec Street, and head north on Quebec 2.5 miles to Prairie Parkway. Turn right onto Prairie Parkway and drive 0.5 mile to Gateway Road. Turn left onto Gateway Road and continue 1.1 miles to the Visitor Center. Please check in at the Visitor Center (opened May 21, 2011), where water, restrooms, exhibits, and a bookstore are available. You can then drive to the Contact Station and park by the trailhead; or you can walk about 1 mile on a trail from the Visitor Center to the trailhead by the Contact Station. Ask for directions at the Visitor Center. Trailhead GPS: N39 49.27' / W104 51.84'

## The Hike

Originally shortgrass prairie, RMANWR was home to antelope, deer, gray wolf, black-footed ferret, and bison. The Arapaho and Cheyenne made their living here

*Lake Mary*

before homesteaders arrived in the late 1800s. The new residents built houses, grew crops, dug irrigation ditches, and planted nonnative trees. The bombing of Pearl Harbor in 1941 changed the fate of these 27 square miles (17,000 acres). The U.S. Army purchased the land from the farmers and built a chemical weapons manufacturing complex, the Rocky Mountain Arsenal.

After World War II, the army leased some facilities to private companies to offset operational costs and maintain the complex for national security. One company manufactured agricultural pesticides. Although waste generated during production years was disposed of according to accepted practices in those days, part of the arsenal became contaminated. It was declared a Superfund site in 1987. The cleanup program was completed in 2010.

As a result of the buffer zone established around the manufacturing facilities, over the years a large animal population began to thrive in the arsenal. With the discovery of a communal roost of bald eagles, the U.S. Fish & Wildlife Service (the Service) became involved in the area. In 1992 Congress designated the Rocky Mountain Arsenal National Wildlife Refuge, which at 15,000 acres, is one of the largest urban wildlife refuges in the country. Exhibits in the visitor center and interpretive signs at several trail junctions relate more historic and natural history details.

The Service offers numerous environmental education programs to school children. During one class, teachers and students gathered near a prairie dog town to observe these little critters. While they watched, a young badger grabbed a prairie dog for its lunch. Nothing like seeing nature in action!

During your first visit, take a wildlife viewing bus tour that gives a great overview of the refuge. Then take a hike! The featured loop takes you on a tour of the various facets of RMANWR.

Swallow boxes line the shore of Lake Mary, while ducks and geese enjoy the water. Partway around the lake, watch for the Prairie Trail to the right. This trail switchbacks out of a little gully then heads across the plains. Listen for the prairie dogs' warning yips as you approach. They scurry about and are vigilant for hawks. Sometimes when a hawk catches a prairie dog, an eagle will come along and steal the hawk's catch. On a clear day you can see forever, from the downtown Denver skyline to the majestic Front Range beyond.

Woodland Trail makes a rectangle through an old homestead area. Cottonwoods line abandoned lanes, and elm, fruit trees, white poplar, New Mexico locust, and even a ponderosa pine reveal a human touch. White-tailed deer, a woodland species, roam freely here. They bound away as you approach, white tails held high. Refuge staff revegetated the old lanes and fields to restore the native shortgrass prairie. Native grass seed is purchased, but the native wildflower seeds must be collected from similar sites in eastern Colorado or other states.

## HOME WHERE THE BISON ROAM

March 17, 2007, was a very special day at Rocky Mountain Arsenal National Wildlife Refuge. Sixteen bison from the National Bison Range (NBR) in Montana arrived at their new home here. The U.S. Fish & Wildlife Service will allow the herd to expand to approximately 250 animals. Bison once roamed the shortgrass prairie where the Denver metro area now lies. This small herd will help the Service evaluate the bison's impact on RMANWR's native shortgrass ecosystem. The Service operates a bison conservation program that includes the NBR, established in 1908 to conserve the American bison.

Some bison have been crossbred with domestic cattle. The DNA of the bison chosen for RMANWR was tested, and the results showed no cattle genes in their ancestry. By moving pure bison to different appropriate wildlife refuges in at least five states, the Service hopes to ensure the long-term conservation of the species.

You can take a tour by reservation only to see these original natives of Colorado's Eastern Plains.

*Deer near Lake Ladora*

A viewing blind down a spur trail off Rod and Gun Club Trail overlooks a wetland area, where the vegetation is very different from that along Prairie Trail. Redwinged blackbirds sing a symphony, with other birds joining the chorus. Ladora Trail presents opportunities to watch ducks, great blue herons, various shorebirds, and other waterfowl enjoying Lake Ladora—watch for cormorants with their outspread wings. Deer wander around, browsing the grasses, casting a glance toward hikers.

RMANWR is an oasis in a bustling urban area. Check the website frequently for new interpretive programs and tours as well as any sudden closures. Visit often when you have a little time. Watch the seasons change and take advantage of the many nature programs, kids' programs, and tours that are offered throughout the year.

## Miles and Directions

**Note:** These directions assume you drive from the visitor center to the contact station (old visitor center) to start your hike. You can start hiking from the interpretive signs east of the visitor center to reach the trailhead by the contact station. That will add 2 miles out and back to your hike.

**0.0** Start at the trailhead by the interpretive signs southwest of the contact station. Elevation: 5,210 feet. After 500 feet reach a T intersection with the Prairie Switchback Trail. Turn left and head to Lake Mary.

**0.15** Reach a Y intersection by interpretive signs. Turn right (west) onto the Lake Mary Trail.

**0.2** Reach the junction with Prairie Switchback Trail. Continue straight ahead. The little bird-houses on poles along the trail are for tree swallows.

**0.4** Arrive at the junction with the Prairie Trail. Turn right. At the top of the switchbacks, enjoy the antics of the prairie dogs.

**0.9** Reach a junction with a road from the visitor center. Turn right and walk down the road. No restrooms are available here.

**1.0** At the junction with the 6th Avenue Trail, go across the road to the continuation of Prairie Trail. GPS: N39 48.78'/W104 51.64'

**1.6** Reach the four-way junction with the Havana Ponds Trail and Woodland Trail. Go a tad left to continue the hike, heading east on the Woodland Trail.

**2.1** Reach the junction with the D Street Trail and the Rod and Gun Club Trail. Go straight ahead on the Rod and Gun Club Trail.

**2.4** Start the little loop on the Rod and Gun Club Trail by turning right. There's a bench here.

**2.5** At the spur trail to the Rod and Gun Club viewing blind, turn right on the spur.

**2.6** Arrive at the viewing blind, with interpretive signs and views of the wetland. GPS: N39 48.60'/W104 50.35'

**2.7** Return the way you came to the Rod and Gun Club Trail and turn right to complete the loop.

**2.9** Reach the end of the loop. Turn right to continue on the Rod and Gun Trail.

**3.1** At the junction of the Rod and Gun Club Trail with the Woodland and D Street Trails, turn right (north) onto the D Street Trail.

**3.5** Reach the junction of the D Street Trail and the 6th Avenue Trail. Continue straight ahead on the semipaved trail.

**3.7** Arrive at the junction of the D Street Trail and the Ladora Trail. GPS: N39' 48.94'/W104 50.75'. Turn left onto the dirt Ladora Trail.

**4.7** The trail jogs right, then left.

**4.8** The trail curves over the Lake Ladora dam.

**5.1** Turn right to return to the contact station. GPS: N39 49.18'/W104 51.63'

**5.2** Head to the left and walk through the picnic area to the contact station.

**5.3** Arrive back at the contact station.

## Options

1. For a very short and easy hike, walk the 0.9-mile lollipop from the contact station around Lake Mary and back.

2. For a 1.9-mile loop, start as in the featured hike, but at mile 0.9 turn left and walk across the old parking area to a trail. Walk 0.25 mile to Ladora Trail; turn left. At the paved road turn right, then in about 200 feet turn left on the trail that switchbacks down to Lake Mary. Turn left at the next junction, then right to walk on the floating bridge on the east side of Lake Mary. Follow the instructions from the 0.15-mile mark in the Miles and Directions in reverse back to the contact station.

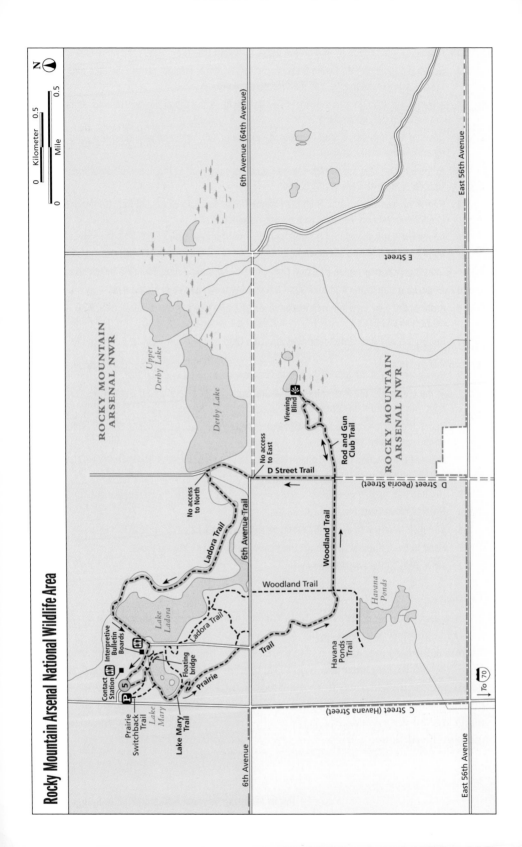

# Rocky Mountain Arsenal National Wildlife Area

# Hike Information

## General Information

**Aurora Chamber of Commerce:** (303) 344-1500; www.aurorachamber.org
**Denver Metro Convention & Visitors Bureau:** (800) 233-6837, (303) 892-1505; www.denver.org
**Metro North Chamber of Commerce:** Westminster; (303) 288-1000; www.metronorthchamber.com

## Local Events/Attractions

**Denver Botanic Gardens:** Denver; (720) 865-3500; www.botanicgardens.org
**Denver Museum of Nature & Science:** Denver; (800) 925-2250, (303) 322-7009; www.dmns.org
**Denver Zoo:** Denver; (303) 376-4800; www.denverzoo.org
**RMANWR Visitor Center:** various nature programs; Refuge Roundup celebrating National Wildlife
Refuge Week; Commerce City; (303) 289-0930; www.fws.gov/rockymountainarsenal

## Clubs and Organizations

**Fish and Wildlife Volunteers at RMANWR:** (303) 289-0930; www.fws.gov/rockymountainarsenal
**Friends of the Front Range Wildlife Refuges:** RMANWR, Commerce City; (303) 287-8734 or
(303) 287-0210; www.ffrwr.org

## Hike Tours

**RMANWR Visitor Center:** Commerce City; (303) 289-0930; www.fws.gov/rockymountainarsenal

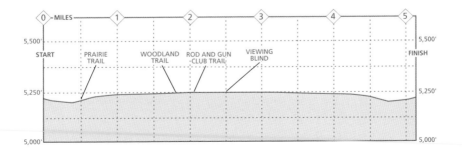

# 6 Pawnee Buttes

The Pawnee Buttes protrude 200 to 250 feet above this trail like upside-down vases. The surrounding shortgrass prairie is home to many birds, including great horned owls, American kestrels, eagles, hawks, swallows, and mountain plover, to mention a few of the 296 species that have been spotted in Pawnee National Grassland. Coyotes, foxes, deer, mountain lions, pronghorns, rattlesnakes, and an assortment of mice, voles, jackrabbits, and prairie dogs call this special place home. Spring fills the prairie with colorful wildflowers and is a great time for bird watching.

**Start:** From Pawnee Buttes Trail (Trail 840) trailhead
**Distance:** 3.6 miles out and back
**Approximate hiking time:** 1.5 to 2.5 hours
**Difficulty:** Easy
**Elevation gain/loss:** 30-foot gain / 290-foot loss
**Seasons:** Year-round except after big snowstorms; summer can be very hot. Spring and fall are best for hiking.
**Trail surface:** Dirt trail
**Land status:** National Grassland
**Nearest town:** Ault
**Other trail users:** Equestrians

**Canine compatibility:** Dogs must be on leash
**Schedule:** Year-round
**Fees and permits:** None for hiking, except for groups larger than 75 people
**Maps:** USGS Grover SE and Pawnee Buttes
**Trail contact:** Pawnee National Grassland, Greeley; (970) 346-5000; www.fs.usda .gov/arp
**Special considerations:** Please obey any seasonal closures and avoid disturbing nesting birds. Hawks and falcons nest in the cliffs while others nest in the grasses. Rattlesnakes live in this area too, so keep an eye and ear open for them.

**Finding the trailhead:** From I-25 east of Fort Collins, take exit 269A (Ault). Drive 50.4 miles east on CO 14, through Briggsdale, to the sign for Keota at Weld County Road (WCR) 103, just east of mile marker 189. Turn left and drive 4 miles to where the road curves right onto WCR 98. In another 0.8 mile, you're at Keota. Head northeast on WCR 98½. In another 0.3 mile, turn left onto WCR 105. The road turns a few times, but follow the signs for Pawnee Buttes. In 2.9 miles, turn right onto WCR 104 and drive another 3 miles to WCR 111. Turn left. When you reach WCR 110 in 3 miles, continue straight ahead. Drive another 1.2 miles to Forest Road (FR) 685, which heads north from a left curve. Turn right and you'll reach the trailhead in 1.2 miles. Turn left into the parking lot. There are no facilities or water at the trailhead or the Overlook, another 0.5 mile past the parking lot. Bring water with you. Trailhead GPS: N40 48.83' / W104 00.00'

## The Hike

Driving from Ault to the Keota turnoff on CO 14, the world around you is a far cry from the nonstop traffic of I-25 and the congestion of the Denver/Boulder/Fort Collins metro areas. Rolling hills of grass stretch to the horizon on each side of the road, punctuated with a lone tree here and there. A ranch house may appear in the distance.

*Pawnee Buttes and surrounding area*

A few rows of little trees have been planted on the north side of the highway, probably for a windbreak, if the trees can survive the dry, windy climate of Colorado's high plains.

Before you turn into the trailhead parking lot, you'll pass an old-time windmill still used to pump water for cattle. Listen to it creak and groan; watch the tail and vane keep the wheel into the wind. To the north, you'll see the Cedar Creek wind farm, its 274 turbines generating 300 megawatts of electricity. Located on private land, the wind farm began operation in October 2007. The old and the new are quite a contrast, but each serves its purpose. Unfortunately, large birds, raptors in particular, can't see the rotating turbine blades and a collision results in the bird's death.

Colorado was covered by the Cretaceous Seaway from 114 million to 65 million years ago. After the dinosaurs disappeared 65 million years ago, the Rockies were uplifted and volcanoes ejected ash high into the sky. The inland sea receded, but sediments eroded from the mountains to the west covered the old seabed. For more than 10 million years sandstone, siltstone, and ashy claystone were deposited on the plains, eventually becoming the White River Formation.

The opening acts of the Age of Mammals starred camels, rhinoceros, three-toed

*Trail and juniper trees*

horses, and hippopotamus-like animals grazing on the grasslands and woodlands that had developed. Erosion continued to wear down the Rockies, and the deposits on the plains became the Arikaree Formation and the Ogallala Formation, the latter comprising sandstone and conglomerate (rocks and stones cemented together).

Around 5 million years ago the whole area was uplifted about 5,000 feet. Rivers increased in speed and volume, sometimes fed by melting mountain glaciers. Water eroded through the sediment layers on the plains, especially the softer White River Formation. Some of the harder Ogallala Formation remained, protecting the underlying materials. The Pawnee Buttes are remnants of those early plains, as are the Chalk Bluffs to the north. The White River Formation in the Pawnee Buttes area contains one of the prime deposits of vertebrate fossils in the world. Please remember fossils are protected by law and must not be removed from the area.

Erosion continues today, creating the badlands features found along the trail as it drops down a little gully between the trailhead area and Lips Bluff. Just enough moisture allows junipers to grow, with an occasional piñon pine or limber pine for good measure. Prickly pear cactus blooms brightly in mid-June, along with purple locoweed, white yucca, and white prairie phlox. While hiking, you might notice tufted sandwort, a pincushion-like plant that grows on the siltstone barrens in the area. One general aspect of shortgrass prairie is that vegetation covers less than 50 percent of it.

Bison once roamed this area in herds as large as 60 million. Blue grama and buffalo grass satiated these large animals, which moved constantly in search of new food. The grasslands and bison adapted to each other. As settlers moved west to homestead, they turned the sod, exposing the prairie soil to wind erosion. Unlike the bison, cattle continually grazed the same area, giving the grasses no time to recover. With low annual precipitation rates, farming was marginal at best. High winds accompanied the drought of the 1930s, blowing loose soil everywhere. Many people left their farms during this Dust Bowl.

In 1934 the U.S. government created a program to purchase marginal lands. By 1946, the government had purchased 11.3 million acres, of which 5.5 million acres came under the jurisdiction of the Department of Agriculture, and eventually the Forest Service. In 1960 about 3.8 million acres were designated as national grasslands. The Pawnee National Grassland consists of 193,060 acres. One of the Forest Service's duties is to manage national grasslands for forage and recreation resources, while another is to manage the resources to "maintain and improve soil and vegetative cover and to demonstrate sound and practical principles of land use for the areas in which they are located."

Because the buttes are crumbling sandstone, please refrain from climbing them. While you hike, keep an eye out for prairie residents: antelope, deer, rabbits, and of course the birds. Enjoy some peaceful time in this unique section of Colorado's Eastern Plains.

## Miles and Directions

**0.0**  Start at the interpretive signs in the parking lot. The trail is to the right. Elevation: 5,420 feet. Hike down the little gully.

**0.4**  Reach a fence and bulletin board. Just beyond the trail branches. Go left on the main Pawnee Buttes Trail. The right branch goes to Lips Bluff, which is closed Mar 1 to June 30 to protect nesting birds.

**0.6**  The trail winds through a little juniper forest.

**1.0**  An overgrown doubletrack comes in from the right (also closed Mar 1 to June 30.) Continue on the main trail to the left.

**1.1**  A trail comes in from the right. Continue on the main trail to the left.

**1.4**  A faint trail crosses the main trail. Continue straight ahead on the main trail.

**1.5**  Arrive at the west butte.

**1.8**  Arrive at the grassland/private property boundary. Elevation: 5,160 feet. GPS: 40 49.32'/W103 58.48'. You're in between the west and east buttes. Turn around and return the way you came.

**3.6**  Arrive back at the trailhead.

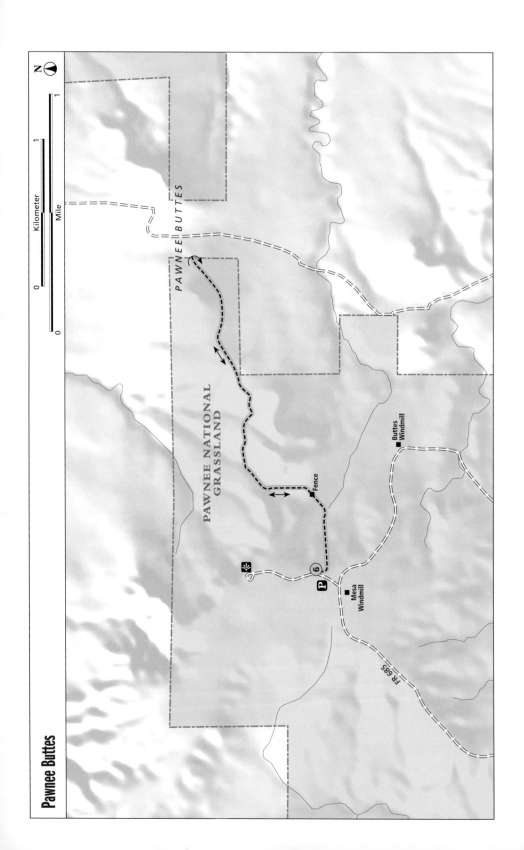

Pawnee Buttes

# Hike Information

## General Information

**Pawnee National Grassland:** Greeley; (970) 346-5000; www.fs.usda.gov/arp

## Local Events/Attractions

**Pawnee Pioneer Trails Scenic Byway:** Pawnee National Grassland, Greeley; (970) 346-5000; www.coloradobyways.org

## Accommodations

**Crow Valley Recreation Area:** Pawnee National Grassland, Briggsdale; (970) 346-5000; www.fs.usda.gov/arp

# Honorable Mentions

## Eastern Plains

Compiled here are some great hikes in the Eastern Plains region that didn't make the A-list this time around, but deserve recognition. Check them out and let us know what you think. You may decide that one or more of these hikes deserves higher status in future editions or, perhaps, you may have a hike of your own that merits some attention.

### A  Santa Fe National Historic Trail

You can walk a 3-mile section of the Mountain Branch of the Santa Fe Trail southwest of La Junta. Trade between the United States and Santa Fe in what was then Mexico prospered via this route in the mid-1800s. Settlers followed, spreading across Colorado and northern New Mexico. Spanish Peaks, a landmark for those long-ago travelers, is visible from this section of trail. From La Junta, drive south on US 350 for about 13 miles. Turn right onto CO 71 and drive for about 0.5 mile, then turn left into the Sierra Vista Overlook parking lot. There are no facilities here. Hike up to the overlook for an overview of the surrounding territory. The trail is marked by stone posts and ends 3 miles southwest at the Timpas Picnic Area. If you have two cars, leave one at the picnic area, which is an additional 3 miles down US 350. Turn right at Otero CR 16.5, cross the railroad tracks, then turn right into the parking lot. A 0.5-mile nature loop leads from the picnic area (vault toilet but no water) to Timpas Creek and back. The creek was a welcome relief for travelers on the trail, for it was the first water source in this very dry country after leaving the Arkansas River. You can also reach the trailheads from Trinidad, with Sierra Vista Overlook at 56 miles and the town of Timpas at 53 miles on US 350. Spring and fall are the best times to hike; summer can be really hot. Make sure to bring water with you. For more information, contact Comanche National Grassland at (719) 384-2181 or visit the website at www .fs.usda.gov/psicc.

### B  Castlewood Canyon State Park Loops

Castlewood Canyon lies in the Black Forest on the high plains. Views of Pikes Peak and the Front Range are spectacular. This canyon once held a dam, which was built in 1890 to store irrigation water from Cherry Creek. Its collapse in 1933 caused two deaths and about $1 million damage. This state park is day use only, open from sunrise to sunset. Dogs must be on leash. Elevations range from 6,100 to 6,600 feet. About 13 miles of trails allow you to explore this interesting canyon. The Inner Canyon–Lake Gulch Loop is a moderate 1.8-mile hike. For a slightly longer hike that has some steep sections, try the Creek Bottom–Rim Rock Loop hike at 4 miles. From I-25 at

Castle Rock, drive east on CO 86 for 6 miles to Franktown. Turn right (south) onto CO 83 (South Parker Road) for 5 miles to the park entrance. For more information contact Castlewood Canyon at (303) 688-5242, or visit the website at parks.state.co .us/parks/castlewoodcanyon.

## ◯ North Sterling Reservoir

Shortgrass prairie and cottonwoods surround North Sterling Reservoir, originally called Point of Rocks Reservoir. Chimney Canyons' chalk cliffs lie to the north. Monuments commemorate the Battle of Summit Springs, between the Cheyenne and the U.S. Cavalry, while a large boulder saved from construction contains the fossilized jawbone of an archaic plains mammal. The South Shoreline Trail is a 7-mile out-and-back trek along the south shore. Balanced Rock, Sunset Point Overlook, and Quarry Loop Trails are each 0.25-mile long, leading from Chimney View and Inlet Grove Campgrounds. These trails providing a sampling of northeastern Colorado. From Main Street and North 7th Avenue (which becomes Logan County Road [LCR] 39 and wiggles through a few more county road designations) in Sterling, drive north on North 7th Avenue to LCR 46 and turn left to the park's south entrance. Total distance is about 12 miles. For further information contact North Sterling State Park at (970) 522-3657, or visit the website at http://parks.state.co.us /parks/northsterling.

# Front Range Overview

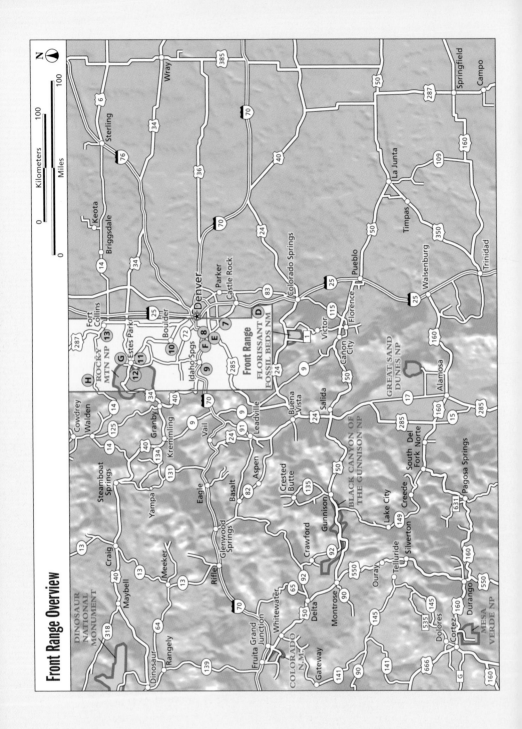

# Front Range

The easternmost spine of mountains in Colorado, running from the Wyoming border to Colorado Springs, is known as the Front Range. Rising first in foothills, then into high mountains, they provided a formidable barrier and foreboding of what was yet to come for any explorer or pioneer trying to cross the North American continent. Five of Colorado's fifty-four peaks over 14,000 feet, including Longs Peak and Mount Evans, are located in this region. Another famous Front Range peak, Pikes Peak, can be seen from three hikes featured in the Southeast Mountains section of this guide.

The Front Range foothills contain fun hiking trails and interesting geology. A rock feature known as the Flatirons protrudes like standing irons from the foothills in the Boulder area. Another great example of these tilted rocks, created from the Fountain Formation, can be seen in Red Rocks Park and Roxborough State Park. A real gem, Roxborough has received numerous state and national designations for its tilted geology and rich natural and human history. Dinosaur Ridge, a National Natural Landmark west of Denver, preserves dinosaur tracks from eons ago in the Dakota Hogback. Foothills canyon topography creates a perfect funnel for flash floods.

About 80 percent of Colorado's population lives in the metropolitan areas just east of the Front Range. Within a short driving distance, recreational opportunities abound. With altitudes between 5,000 and 14,264 feet, hikers can enjoy their sport nearly year-round. As summer temperatures rise beyond 90°F in the foothills, backcountry trails to mountain peaks and lakes offer a great respite.

Rocky Mountain National Park is one of the crown jewels of the national park system, with its glacially sculpted peaks and high alpine lakes. Trail Ridge Road, the highest continuous automobile road in the United States, takes you to the "land above the trees," the alpine tundra. An interesting land of small microclimates, the ecosystem is very fragile. The Rocky Mountain Nature Association offers great classes in all aspects of the region's natural history, including this remarkable ecosystem. Rocky, as locals call the park, contains an incredible number of hiking trails to lakes, historic sites, mountaintops, and even across the Continental Divide. Backpacking permits are required in the park and guarantee you a spot, often secluded from others. Most of the park's backcountry is located within the Rocky Mountain National Park Wilderness Area, designated by Congress in 2009.

Although several other wilderness areas have been designated in the Front Range, the trails are not included in this guide because of their popularity and high volume of hikers. Should you hike in these wilderness areas, be careful to keep impact at an absolute minimum. See "In Addition: Leave No Trace" in the South Central Mountains section of this guide for more information.

Many Front Range cities and counties have open space programs, and those parks, along with state parks, offer a great variety of hiking venues. Boulder started its open space program in 1967 when citizens passed a 0.4 percent sales tax to acquire and manage open space. The City of Boulder and Boulder County have preserved many acres between them. In spring, while the mountain trails are still buried in the white stuff, trails in Boulder's Open Space and Mountain Parks provide an excellent way to get in shape for summer hiking.

Jefferson County citizens approved a sales tax in 1972 to acquire, maintain, and preserve open spaces. As of January 2010, Jefferson County operated twenty parks, a nature center, one museum, and several other open space properties.

Douglas County started its Open Space program in 1994, when voters approved a 0.6 percent sales and use tax to acquire land. The open space program preserves wildlife habitat and creates buffers between communities, while conserving the rural landscape, historic properties, archaeological sites, and agricultural heritage of the county.

Scenic and historic byways winding through this area include the Cache La Poudre–North Park, Guanella Pass, Trail Ridge Road, Peak to Peak, Lariat Loop, and Mount Evans.

# 7 Fountain Valley and South Rim Trails

Roxborough State Park is a land of red rock slabs sticking up like upside-down spear points. The Fountain Valley Trail provides a close-up view of the rocks and the historic Persse Place. The South Rim Trail circles Roxborough's south end, winding through Gambel oak past some of the huge rocks. Crossing over grassland and past ponderosa pines, it ascends a ridge for an almost aerial view of the interesting rock formations. The geology is easy to see and examine from the ridge. Skyscrapers to the north form a contrasting backdrop to the natural "buildings" of the tilted rocks.

**Start:** From Willow Creek and Fountain Valley trailhead interpretive signs just southwest of the Roxborough State Park visitor center
**Distance:** 5.5-mile figure-eight loop with one spur
**Approximate hiking time:** 2.25 to 3 hours
**Difficulty:** Moderate due to length; easy if the loops are done separately
**Elevation gain:** 440 feet
**Seasons:** Year-round, except after a big snowstorm (open for snowshoeing or cross-country skiing)
**Trail surface:** Natural surface trail, closed dirt roads, paved walkway, and parking lot
**Land status:** State park
**Nearest town:** Littleton

**Other trail users:** Hikers only
**Canine compatibility:** Dogs not permitted
**Schedule:** Year-round. Roxborough is a day-use only park. The park is open from 8 a.m. to 5 p.m. daily; until 8 p.m. in the summer. Call or check the website for exact hours as they can change monthly. The visitor center hours also change with the season. Park gates are locked at closing!
**Fees and permits:** Daily entrance fee or annual parks pass required
**Maps:** USGS Kassler; Nat Geo Trails Illustrated 135 Deckers/Rampart Range
**Trail contact:** Roxborough State Park, 4751 North Roxborough Dr., Littleton; (303) 973-3959; parks.state.co.us/parks/roxborough

**Finding the trailhead:** From the C-470 and Wadsworth Boulevard (CO 121) interchange west of Littleton, drive south on Wadsworth for 4.5 miles to Waterton Road (Douglas CR 217). Turn left onto Waterton Road, drive 1.7 miles to North Rampart Range Road, and turn right. Drive another 2.1 miles on North Rampart Range Road, then turn left onto North Roxborough Park Drive. Turn immediately right by the fire station and follow the road into the park. Stop at the entrance station to pay the fee, or if it is unattended, use the self-serve station. The visitor center parking lot is 2.2 miles from the fire station. Water and restrooms are available at the visitor center, a 0.1-mile walk from the main parking lot. Trailhead GPS: N39 25.77'/W105 04.13'

## The Hike

Roxborough State Park has received several designations over and above "state park": Colorado Natural Area, National Natural Landmark, and National Archaeological District. Once you arrive, you will understand why so many "labels" have been bestowed upon the area. The tilted red slabs of sandstone immediately catch your eye,

*View from Fountain Valley Trail*

but look around and you will discover other geologic formations that have developed over 500 million years. The area also exemplifies the transition zone between prairie and mountains. Around and between the towering rocks, many natural microcosms provide homes for very diverse vegetation, including yucca and Gambel oak (oak-brush), stately ponderosa pine, aspen and wild rose, and marsh plants. With a variety of food available, mule deer, foxes, rock squirrels, coyotes, and black bears populate the area, with an occasional visit from a mountain lion. Raptors love the ridges. Opportunities to learn about geology, natural history, prehistoric peoples, and early Colorado history give you an excuse to return time and again.

Because Roxborough Park is so special, its different designations require conservation for present and future generations. Emphasis is placed on protecting the total park resource. For example, assuring grasses grow undisturbed by humans means the local rodents, rabbits, and other little critters have enough to eat. These small mammals are an important food source for the many raptors in the area, including golden eagles. Therefore restrictions and regulations, such as the day-use only rule, have been instituted.

Everyone can help preserve the uniqueness of Roxborough by staying on the trails, not feeding or disturbing wildlife, and leaving what you find. With so many visitors, hiking off-trail can lead to vegetation damage and destruction. Collecting samples of vegetation and rocks only robs others of the chance to see nature at its best, and picking flowers or fruits deprives wildlife of needed nutrients. One autumn day, a woman visiting the park loudly challenged the various rules. People later observed her leaving with some bright red branches, presumably for home decoration. Imagine her surprise upon discovering she had an armful of poison ivy!

To truly experience this unique area, visit Roxborough at various times of year. In winter, the towering rocks wet from melting snow contrast sharply against a brilliant blue Colorado sky and snow-draped hills and trees. Spring brings fragrant blossoms and colorful flowers with changing variety throughout summer. Oakbrush turns blazing red in fall, while aspens don regal gold. Although you may not always see wildlife when you visit, you might catch a glimpse of a new fawn or a fledgling (young bird) spreading its wings. No matter the season, something is always new for the observant hiker!

Start your hike on the easy Fountain Valley Trail, which wanders among the tilted rocks. A borrowed trail guide from the visitor center will give you additional insight into the features focused on at various numbered posts. Take a few minutes to hike up to Lyons Overlook, which provides almost a bird's-eye view of the rock formations. Persse Place is about halfway around the loop. Henry Persse, owner of much of the land that is now the park, suggested renaming the area Roxborough, after his family's estate in Ireland. Originally called Washington Park (see if you can find the rock that looks like George Washington), confusion with Denver's Washington Park necessitated the name change. Denver's elite enjoyed the Persse Resort in the early 1900s.

Back at the trailhead, head south on Willow Creek Trail—a separate trail guide is available. While walking you can learn about geology and plants and animals living in the grasslands and oakbrush along the trail. Pass a couple of large Fountain Formation rock slabs that create a "feel small" perception. Poison ivy and rattlesnakes live here, so be careful not to tangle with either. Watch for deer along the way.

At the junction, head south on South Rim Trail. It gently climbs past ponderosa pines, eventually gaining a ridge (rim) with a unique perspective of the park's standing rock formations. On a clear day you can see tall buildings in the south metro area and out onto the plains. Dropping down from the ridge, switchback to a junction with the Willow Creek Trail and stay to the right. The trail crosses a bridge over Willow Creek. Return to the visitor center via a trail north of the entrance road.

Enjoy the special features of Roxborough State Park and return often to watch the seasons change!

## Miles and Directions

**0.0** Start on the visitor center's west patio and walk northwest to the trailhead for the Willow Creek Loop, South Rim Loop, and Carpenter Peak Trails. Elevation: 6,200 feet.

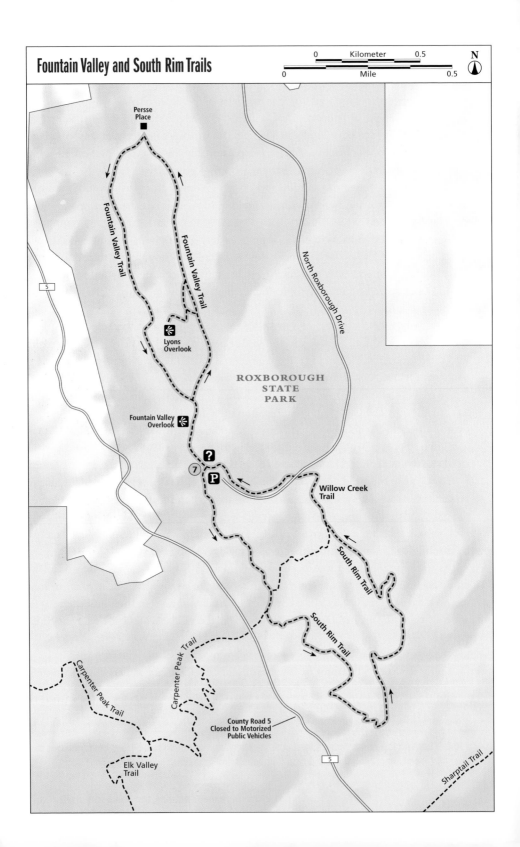

# Fountain Valley and South Rim Trails

0 Kilometer 0.5

0 Mile 0.5

N

Persse Place

Fountain Valley Trail

Fountain Valley Trail

5

Lyons Overlook

Fountain Valley Overlook

ROXBOROUGH
STATE
PARK

North Roxborough Drive

7

P

Willow Creek Trail

South Rim Trail

Carpenter Peak Trail

South Rim Trail

Carpenter Peak Trail

County Road 5
Closed to Motorized
Public Vehicles

5

Elk Valley Trail

Sharptail Trail

*View of Roxborough State Park from South Rim Trail*

**0.1** Pass the junction with Fountain Valley Overlook Trail on the left. **(Side trip:** A less-than-0.1-mile out-and-back spur leads to an overlook.) Continue straight ahead on Fountain Valley Trail.

**0.2** Reach a Y; the start and end of Fountain Valley loop. Follow the loop counterclockwise, heading to the right first. GPS: N39 25.95' / W105 04.18'

**0.6** Reach the south end of the Lyons Overlook spur. Turn left onto the spur. In about 200 feet, turn left and continue uphill to the overlook.

**0.8** Arrive at an observation deck with nice views of the tilted rocks, ridges, and trail. Elevation: 6,240 feet. GPS: N39 26.13' / W105 04.25'. Return to the last turn, then turn left and walk downhill 0.2 mile to rejoin Fountain Valley Trail.

**1.0** Turn left onto Fountain Valley Trail.

**1.4** Persse Place is on the right. GPS: N39 26.60' / W105 04.33'

**2.4** Arrive back at the start/end of the Fountain Valley loop. Turn right to return to the trailhead.

**2.6** Arrive back at the trailhead. To reach the South Rim Trail, hike down the Willow Creek Trail, to the left of the bulletin board.

**3.05** At the junction, turn right on the South Rim Trail / Carpenter Peak Trail.

**3.1**  Reach the junction with Carpenter Peak Trail. Turn left on South Rim Trail. There's a nice bench under a huge cottonwood just down the trail.

**3.6**  A little trail to the right goes to a bench with a great view of the tilted rocks to the north.

**4.1**  A little trail to the right leads to a bench shaded by oakbrush. There are nice views to the south and east. The trail reaches its high point near here, at 6,480 feet. GPS: N39 25.23'/W105 03.55'

**5.0**  Reach the junction of the South Rim and Willow Creek Trails. Continue straight ahead and downhill. There's a bench here.

**5.2**  The trail arrives at a Y. Turn left and cross the entrance road, then continue to the left on the other side of the road.

**5.4**  The trail enters a parking lot. There's a restroom here. Continue straight through the lot, which will lead you to a trail to the parking lot closest to the visitor center.

**5.5**  Arrive back at the parking lot closest to the visitor center.

## Hike Information

### General Information
**South Metro Denver Chamber of Commerce:** Littleton; (303) 795-0142; www.bestchamber.com

### Local Events/Attractions
**Chatfield State Park:** Littleton; (303) 791-7275; parks.state.co.us/parks/chatfield

### Accommodations
**Chatfield State Park Campgrounds:** Littleton; (303) 791-7275; parks.state.co.us/parks /chatfield
There are many other accommodations in the south metro area as well.

### Restaurants
There are many restaurants in the south metro area.

### Clubs and Organizations
**Friends of Roxborough:** volunteer naturalists and trail stewards; Roxborough State Park, Littleton; (303) 973-3959; http://parks.state.co.us/parks/roxborough

### Hike Tours
**Roxborough State Park:** Littleton; (303) 973-3959; http://parks.state.co.us/parks/roxborough

# 8 Mount Falcon Park Upper Loop

Mount Falcon Park provides not only pleasant hiking country, with rolling meadows and shady forests on small hills, but also a walk back into history. Once owned by visionary John Brisben Walker, the remains of his mansion and the start of a futile dream lie ready for exploration. A former summer cabin has been remodeled into a viewpoint and picnic pavilion. This lollipop hike visits these sites on a tour of the western part of the park. Excellent interpretive signs explain the human and natural history. The park protects wildlife habitat and offers recreational trails near the cultural features.

**Start:** At the edge of the west parking lot on the dirt road (Castle Trail)

**Distance:** 4.3-mile lollipop, with the loop in the middle

**Approximate hiking time:** 2 to 3 hours

**Difficulty:** Moderate due to length and one steep section

**Elevation gain:** 210-foot loss/355-foot gain

**Seasons:** Best from May through Nov

**Trail surface:** Natural surface and rocky trail, and old roads (closed to the motorized public)

**Land status:** Jefferson County Open Space

**Nearest town:** Lakewood

**Other trail users:** Mountain bikers and equestrians

**Canine compatibility:** Dogs must be on leash

**Schedule:** Year-round, from one hour before sunrise to one hour after sunset

**Fees and permits:** None for day hikes. Large groups and unique activities require special permits.

**Maps:** USGS Morrison; Nat Geo Trails Illustrated 100 Boulder/Golden; Latitude 40° Colorado Front Range

**Trail contact:** Jefferson County Open Space, 700 Jefferson County Parkway, Golden; (303) 271-5925; www.co.jefferson.co.us/openspace

**Other:** During spring snowmelt, trails in the eastern section of the park, including Castle Trail, may be closed to protect them from deterioration. Call the trails hotline at (303) 271-5975 for up-to-date information.

**Special considerations:** Bring water, as none is available along the trail. Leave valuables at home.

**Finding the trailhead:** From C-470, take the US 285 exit and head southwest. In 4.5 miles turn right (north) onto Parmalee Gulch Road. Follow Parmalee Gulch for 2.7 miles, then turn right at the Mount Falcon sign onto Picutis Road. The route to Mount Falcon Park is very circuitous, but it is well marked, so just follow the signs. The Mount Falcon Park information sign is 1.8 miles from Parmalee Gulch Road. Turn right into the upper parking lot 0.1 mile past the information sign. There are picnic tables near the parking lot, but no water is available. Vault toilets are located about 0.1 mile down the trail past the interpretive signs. Trailhead GPS: N39 38.17' / W105 14.31'

## The Hike

John Brisben Walker and his wife named Mount Falcon while watching one of the beautiful birds circling overhead as they were visiting the site of their new home.

*Brick wall remains of Walker Castle*

Walker, a visionary and entrepreneur, lobbied for a system of mountain parks for Denver and envisioned concerts at the Red Rocks Amphitheater, which he once owned. He built an incline railroad up Mount Morrison, manufactured Stanley Steamers, owned *Cosmopolitan* magazine, and dreamt of creating a Summer White House for U.S. presidents. Interpretive signs at Mount Falcon Park give a detailed history of the man and his pursuits.

Walker's second wife, Ethel, died in 1916; his Mount Falcon home burned in 1918; and World War I took a toll on his finances. He died penniless in 1931. However, a number of his dreams came true. Denver created a system of mountain parks and built an amphitheater in Red Rocks Park, a popular modern venue for summer concerts. Walker donated Inspiration Point near I-70 and Sheridan Boulevard to Denver for a park, and Regis University sits on land he gave to the Jesuits. In 1914, when Frederick Law Olmstead Jr. recommended lands for Denver to obtain for its mountain parks system, Mount Falcon made his list. Although Denver did not buy Mount Falcon, in 1974 the Mount Falcon Association approached Jefferson County (Jeffco) to see if it wanted to purchase 1,490 acres. With the help of the Colorado Open Lands Foundation, Jeffco procured Walker's old property—very appropriate because of his vision to acquire mountain lands for preservation of forests and for people to enjoy.

Numerous overlooks on this hike offer views of the Eastern Plains and the Continental Divide, one of the reasons Walker enjoyed Mount Falcon. From the scenic view spur trail near the Summer White House, you'll find a good view of Red Rocks Park and its amphitheater, the hogback running north, Green Mountain, and Mount Morrison. Castle Trail drops steeply below you—it's hard to believe people raced cars up this old road during Walker's time.

A lookout tower stands on Mount Falcon's summit along the Tower Trail. Besides views to the plains and the Continental Divide, the tower puts you at eye level with the cones on nearby Douglas fir trees. Look closely at the cones, and you'll see three-pronged bracts sticking out. The story goes that a fox was chasing a little mouse one day. A kindly Douglas fir looked down and invited the mouse to jump into its branches for safety. As a result, you can see the mouse's hind feet and tail as they disappear into the cone. Douglas firs are not true firs, because their cones hang down. Cones point up on true firs, such as the subalpine firs found at higher elevations. When the bracts fall off the cones, they look like small candles in the tree tops. Douglas firs typically grow on shady, cooler northern exposures in the foothills.

> ▶ John Brisben Walker believed that reason could bring about world peace. In 1914 he invited President Woodrow Wilson to a meeting of 500 of the most capable men in the United States at the Camp of the Red Rocks to promote better understanding, broader ideas, and more tolerance for the nation.

After you descend from the tower, look for the fancy old steps with white, black, and red stones. Perhaps people once walked this decorative path to Mount Falcon's summit. The trail leads to the Eagle Eye Shelter, a 1930s-style former summer home. Jeffco Open Space's crew built a nice picnic pavilion and observation deck here. Views include Turkey Creek Canyon, Indian Hills, and the Continental Divide. Near the walk leading to the shelter, look for an old well. An arch over the well reads AM BRUNNEN VOR DEM THORE (TORE), the first line of Franz Schubert's song "At the Well Before the Town Gate"—a touch of culture in the foothills.

## Miles and Directions

**0.0** Start from the southeast edge of the parking lot where the dirt road (Castle Trail) starts. Elevation: 7,720 feet. Walk down Castle Trail.

**0.1** The Parmalee Trail crosses the road. Continue straight ahead on Castle Trail. Vault toilets are to the left.

**0.25** Pass an interpretive sign about fire. The Castle Trail starts to climb slightly.

**0.4** At the junction of the Castle Trail and Meadow Trail, turn left onto Castle Trail (still a dirt road). There's a bench here and, to the right, a little trail to an overlook.

**0.8** Reach the junction of the Castle Trail, Meadow Trail, and the spur trail to Walker Home ruins. Turn left here to check out the remains of the Walker mansion. GPS: N39 38.12' / W105 13.59'. Out-and-back distance from the trail junction to the interpretive sign in the ruins' courtyard is about 500 feet. When you return to the junction, turn left onto Castle Trail. You'll soon come to a gate that is closed when the trails beyond are muddy.

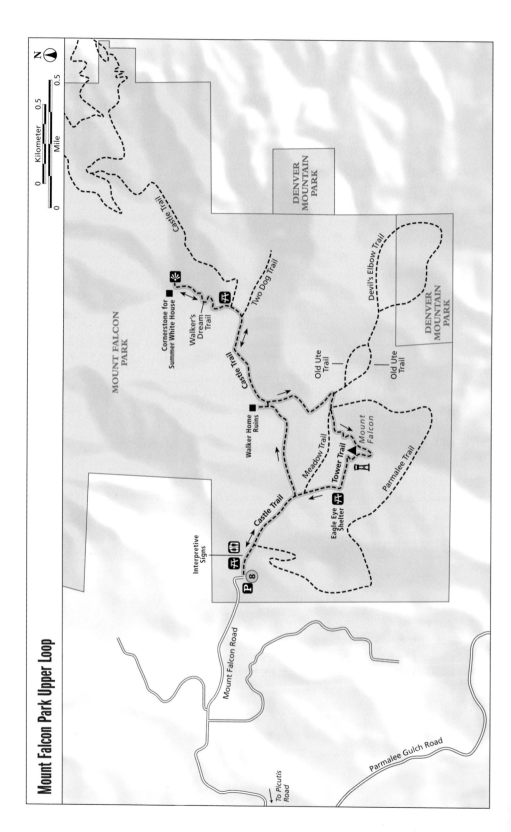

# Mount Falcon Park Upper Loop

N

0    0.5
Kilometer

0    0.5
Mile

MOUNT FALCON PARK

Castle Trail

Cornerstone for
Summer White House

Walker's Dream Trail

Castle Trail

Two Dog Trail

Walker Home Ruins

Devil's Elbow Trail

Castle Trail

Old Ute Trail

Old Ute Trail

DENVER MOUNTAIN PARK

DENVER MOUNTAIN PARK

Meadow Trail

Mount Falcon

Tower Trail

Parmalee Trail

Eagle Eye Shelter

Interpretive Signs

P  8

Mount Falcon Road

To Picutis Road

Parmalee Gulch Road

**1.3**  At the junction with the Two Dog Trail, continue straight ahead on the road.

**1.4**  Arrive at the junction with Walker's Dream Trail. Turn left and head uphill toward Walker's proposed location for the Summer White House. **(Option:** At mile 1.7, turn right to walk to an overlook with a good view to the east and south [about 350 feet out and back]. Return the way you came, then turn right and continue uphill on Walker's Dream Trail.)

**1.8**  Reach the interpretive sign and cornerstone for the Summer White House. Elevation: 7,613 feet. GPS: N39 38.43'/W105 13.07' Retrace your steps down Walker's Dream Trail.

**2.2**  At the junction with the Castle Trail, turn right.

**2.7**  Return to the junction of the Castle Trail, Meadow Trail, and the trail to Walker Home ruins. Turn left onto Meadow Trail.

**3.0**  Reach the junction of the Meadow Trail and Old Ute Trail. Turn right to continue on the Meadow Trail.

**3.1**  Arrive at the junction of the Meadow Trail, Tower Trail, and Parmalee Trail. Go about 45 degrees to the left onto the Tower Trail.

**3.5**  The trail splits, with equestrians going to the left. Just beyond the split is the tower. Walk up the stairs for nice views. GPS: N39 37.78'/W105 13.79'

**3.7**  Descend the white stone path to the Eagle Eye Shelter. Turn left onto the stone path to check out the observation deck, with nice views, and have a bite to eat (about 0.1 mile out and back). Picnic tables are in the shelter. GPS: N39 37.83'/W105 13.96'. When you return, turn left on Tower Trail.

**3.9**  At the junction of the Tower Trail and Meadow Trail, turn left.

**4.0**  Reach the junction of the Meadow Trail and Castle Trail. Turn left and return the way you came.

**4.3**  Arrive back at the trailhead.

## Option

For a shorter, easy 3.5-mile out-and-back, hike to the Summer White House then return the way you came, instead of hiking the middle loop to the lookouts.

## Hike Information

### General Information
**Town of Morrison:** (303) 697-8749; www.town.morrison.co.us

### Local Events/Attractions
**Morrison Natural History Museum:** (303) 697-1873; www.mnhm.org
**Red Rocks Park and Amphitheater:** Morrison; (303) 697-6047; www.redrocksonline.com. Tours available May through Oct or by appointment.

### Organizations
**Jefferson County Open Space Volunteers:** Golden; (303) 271-5922; www.co.jefferson.co.us /openspace

# 9 M. Walter Pesman Trail

Mount Goliath Natural Area contains subalpine and alpine ecosystems along Mount Evans Road. The M. Walter Pesman Trail (Trail 50) winds and climbs through an ancient bristlecone pine forest (some trees are over 1,500 years old) in the natural area. It crosses alpine tundra with fantastic tiny wildflowers (peak bloom is in mid-July) to the upper trailhead. To return, hike a little higher on Alpine Garden Loop (Trail 49) for great 360-degree views, then rejoin the Pesman Trail. End your hike by exploring the Bristlecone Loop Trail and Interpretive Gardens by the Dos Chappell Nature Center.

**Start:** From the lower Mount Goliath trailhead interpretive sign behind the Dos Chappell Nature Center

**Distance:** 2.5 miles out and back, with two little half-loops

**Approximate hiking time:** 1.5 to 3 hours

**Difficulty:** Moderate due to altitude and rocky trail in spots

**Elevation gain:** 680 feet

**Season:** Best from late June through Sept. Mount Evans Road must be open at least to Summit Lake for hikers to reach the trailhead.

**Trail surface:** Dirt trail with some rocks

**Land status:** National forest

**Nearest town:** Idaho Springs

**Other trail users:** Hikers only

**Canine compatibility:** Dogs must be on leash

**Schedule:** Mount Evans Road is closed for the winter starting the first Mon in Oct or after the first major snowfall until Memorial Day, depending on weather.

Nature center is open 10 a.m. to 5 p.m. every day when Mount Evans Road is open.

**Fees and permits:** Entrance fee, annual pass, or an America the Beautiful pass required

**Maps:** USGS Idaho Springs; Nat Geo Trails Illustrated 104 Idaho Springs/Loveland Pass; Latitude 40° Colorado Front Range

**Trail contact:** Arapaho National Forest, Clear Creek Ranger District, Idaho Springs; (303) 567-3000; or www.fs.usda.gov/arp

**Finding the trailhead:** From Idaho Springs, take exit 240 off I-70 onto CO 103. Drive up CO 103 about 13 miles to CO 5 (Mount Evans Scenic Byway), by Echo Lake Lodge. Turn right onto CO 5, drive to the fee station, and pay the fee. Continue up the twisty road about 3 miles to the lower trailhead and the Dos Chappell Nature Center. Vault toilets, but no water, are available at the nature center. Trailhead GPS: N39 38.56' / W105 35.53'
**(Option:** If you have two cars, leave one at the lower trailhead and drive to the upper trailhead, another 1.8 miles up Mount Evans Road. There is a very small parking lot at the upper trailhead.)

## The Hike

The Mount Evans area harbors a very large stand of bristlecone pine trees. Some of these twisted and contorted trees are more than 1,600 years old! The USDA Forest Service set aside 160 acres of this ancient forest as a Research Natural Area (RNA) many years ago. The RNA is protected from development and most human activity,

*Pesman Trail through krummholz*

enabling scientists to study a relatively untouched area. In the 1950s the Denver Botanic Gardens developed a program of "planned altitude units" and surveyed potential areas. The area near Mount Goliath RNA appeared to be a perfect match. The botanic gardens approached the Forest Service, and they formed a partnership for the Alpine Unit. A trail was built along the flank of Goliath Peak (12,216 feet), allowing people to see the bristlecone pines and the abundant alpine tundra flowers along the route. In August 1962 the botanic gardens and the Forest Service dedicated the M. Walter Pesman Trail. About 0.5 mile of the trail is in the RNA. Mount Goliath RNA was also designated a Colorado Natural Area in 1980.

M. Walter Pesman arrived in Fort Collins, Colorado, in 1908. A native of the Netherlands, he earned his Bachelor of Science degree in horticulture from Colorado State College (now University) in 1910. Although his career revolved around landscape architecture, he loved the native flora of Colorado. He wrote the first Colorado wildflower identification book geared toward laypeople instead of botanists. In *Meet the Natives* he separated flowers by colors and also by the life zones in which they were usually found. The Denver Botanic Gardens' Board of Trustees decided to name the trail at Mount Goliath in Pesman's honor in appreciation of his many years of teaching the general public about natural landscapes and native plants.

Over time the Pesman Trail deteriorated as a result of the elements and general use. In 1996, the Garden Club of Denver made a three-year commitment to repair the trail and to develop guided tours. Volunteers for Outdoor Colorado (VOC), under the direction of Dos Chappell, pitched in with manual labor to fix the trail. A Forest Service trail crew worked on the more difficult sections. The groups created a plan for a nature center for Mount Goliath, to be located in the lower parking lot. A new trail was built through the first part of the bristlecone forest—a fairly level and easy dirt trail, usable by wheelchair users and others unable to hike the Pesman Trail.

The Denver Botanic Gardens also planted an alpine garden at the lower trailhead. This garden contains alpine tundra plants found along the Pesman Trail, allowing those who cannot hike to see these amazing plants. Receipts from the initial Mount Evans fee demonstration project were combined with funds raised by the botanic gardens and the Garden Club to pay for these projects. The Dos Chappell Nature Center was completed in 2004 and contains many interesting exhibits.

Begin the hike by the Lower Mount Goliath interpretive sign behind the nature center. The Pesman Trail begins in the interpretive gardens, then leads into the bristlecone forest. Engelmann spruce trees also live here, along with colorful yellow cinquefoil, bright red Indian paintbrush, fuzzy purple fringe, white chickweed, and blue Jacob's ladder. As you climb toward treeline, small bristlecone pines next to the trail provide a closer glimpse of needles and cones. Tiny flowers bloom at this elevation. Please stay on the trail because the tundra is very fragile. Plants may grow only 0.25 inches in one year and can be easily damaged. The yellow sunflowers, large by alpine standards, are called old-man-of-the-mountain. Purple sky pilot, yellow cinquefoil, white American bistort, alpine phlox, and lots of little sages line the trail. Occasionally look behind you for a view of the Eastern Plains south of Denver.

Once above treeline you are exposed to the ever-present wind. Make sure to bring extra layers, as it is mighty chilly at 12,000 feet. The trail also becomes rougher and rockier above treeline. After reaching the upper trailhead, return via the Alpine Garden Loop 49, to the left of the interpretive signs. The trail gently ascends between rock outcroppings, where you get a great 360-degree view that includes Mount Evans (14,264 feet). Dropping down, rejoin the Pesman Trail. Remember to take a walk around the interpretive gardens at the lower trailhead. Come often to this trail as various weather conditions change the feel of the area.

## Miles and Directions

**0.0** Start at the Lower Mount Goliath trailhead interpretive sign behind the Dos Chappell Nature Center. Start hiking on the M. Walter Pesman Trail, which goes straight ahead through the interpretive gardens. Elevation: 11,540 feet.

**0.1** Reach the intersection with the Bristlecone Loop Trail. Continue straight ahead, uphill on the Pesman Trail.

**0.3** What looks like a trail comes in from the right (it goes to a little overlook). Continue to the left around the switchback.

**0.75** The trail makes a short right switchback and seems to disappear. It then makes an immediate left switchback.

**0.9** You're basically above treeline at this point.

**1.0** Reach the trail junction with Alpine Garden Loop (Trail 49). Continue to the left to the upper trailhead.

**1.2** Arrive at the Upper Mount Goliath trailhead. On your return, hike up Alpine Garden Loop to the left of the interpretive sign. Elevation: 12,152 feet. GPS: N39 37.98' / W105 36.21'.

**1.4** Reach the top of the ridge and look at the great 360-degree view. Elevation: 12,220 feet.

**1.5** Arrive at the trail junction with Pesman Trail. Turn left and head downhill the way you came.

**2.4** Return to the trail junction with Bristlecone Loop Trail. Turn right onto Bristlecone Loop Trail.

**2.5** Arrive back at the trailhead.

# THE ANCIENT ONES

Bristlecone pines, *Pinus aristata,* can witness many happenings in their 1,500- to 2,000-year lifespans. Contorted by wind and often polished on one side by ice crystals and blowing dirt, it is hard to imagine how the trees survive.

Bristlecone pines grow in windy areas in coarse, rocky soils. They thrive where the slope is sunny and dry, well drained, and prone to cold temperatures and frost. Bristlecones are reasonably easy to spot, sporting fairly dense needles that grow in packets of five. The needles are no longer than 2 inches and are usually coated with sticky resin drops. The thick clusters produce a brush-like effect, thus the name *bristle.* Purplish-brown female cones with prickles grow near the tips of branches. Male cones are small, oval, and dark orange, growing in clusters near the branch tips.

During tough years, bristlecones may shut off nutrients to a branch or two, killing the branch to save the rest of the tree. They also survive with much of their bark blasted off, although enough has to be left to carry nutrients. Another survival secret is slow growth, which produces very dense wood that protects the tree from fire, insects, and disease. A living tree may consist of both live and dead parts. Even after death, the twisted, contorted ghost tree attracts photographers and artists with its interesting shapes and gray to brown to black hues.

Take a moment to be quiet with these trees, which have seen so many changes in their lives. Think about the survival mechanisms that allow them such longevity. Be kind and do not damage them—let them continue to live, much longer than any one human ever will.

# M. Walter Pesman Trail

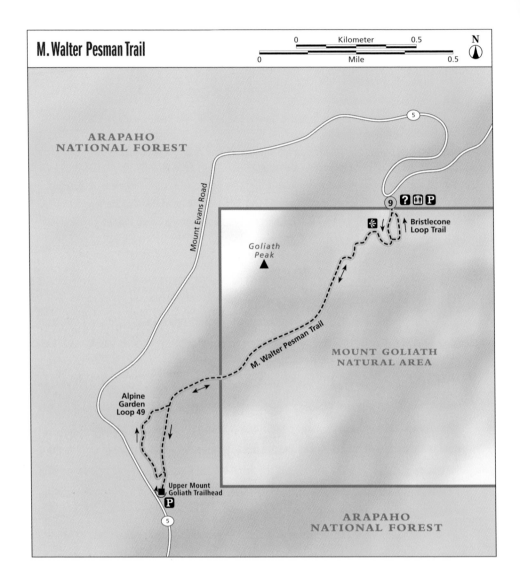

ARAPAHO
NATIONAL FOREST

Mount Evans Road

Goliath
Peak

9

Bristlecone
Loop Trail

M. Walter Pesman Trail

MOUNT GOLIATH
NATURAL AREA

Alpine
Garden
Loop 49

Upper Mount
Goliath Trailhead

5

ARAPAHO
NATIONAL FOREST

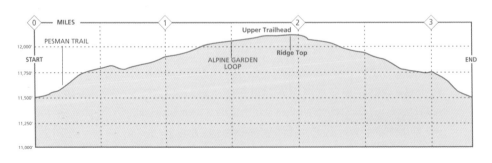

MILES

PESMAN TRAIL

Upper Trailhead

START

ALPINE GARDEN
LOOP

Ridge Top

END

12,000'

11,750'

11,500'

11,250'

11,000'

# Hike Information

## General Information
**Clear Creek County Chamber & Tourism Bureau:** Idaho Springs; (303) 567-4660; (866) 674-9237; www.clearcreekcounty.org

## Local Events/Attractions
**Argo Gold Mine & Mill:** Idaho Springs; (303) 567- 2421; www.historicargotours.com
**Indian Hot Springs:** Idaho Springs; (303) 989-6666; www.indianspringsresort.com
**Mount Evans Scenic Byway:** Clear Creek County Chamber & Tourism Bureau, Idaho Springs; (303) 567-4660; (866) 674-9237; www.clearcreekcounty.org
**Phoenix Gold Mine:** Idaho Springs; (303) 567-0422

## Accommodations
**National Forest campgrounds:** Arapaho National Forest, Clear Creek Ranger District, Idaho Springs; (303) 567-3000; www.fs.usda.gov/arp

## Restaurants
**Beau Jo's Pizza Restaurant:** 1517 Miner St., Idaho Springs; (303) 567-4376; www.beaujos.com
**Echo Lake Lodge:** 13264 State Highway 103, Idaho Springs; (303) 567-2138
**Tommyknocker Brewery & Pub:** 1401 Miner St., Idaho Springs; (303) 567-2688; tommy knocker.com
**Two Brothers Delicatessen:** 1424 Miner St., Idaho Springs; (303) 567-2439; www.twobrothers deli.com

## Clubs and Organizations
**Denver Botanic Gardens:** Denver; (720) 865-3500; www.botanicgardens.org

## Hike Tours
**Denver Botanic Gardens:** Denver; (720) 865-3500; www.botanicgardens.org

# 10 Bear Canyon Trail

The hike up lush Bear Canyon takes you past tilted flatirons and interesting rock formations. Occasionally a view of the high plains to the east opens up. An old wagon road (not obvious) carried ore from the mines near Central City down to Boulder and was also used to transport goods to the miners in the late 1800s. Wander up to the junction of Green Bear and Bear Peak West Ridge Trails for a picnic along the way. For a tougher option, summit Green Mountain after a stairmaster-like climb up log and stone steps for the last 0.2 mile.

**Start:** From the National Center for Atmospheric Research (NCAR) trailhead

**Distance:** 6.8 miles out and back

**Approximate hiking time:** 3 to 4.5 hours

**Difficulty:** Difficult for Bear Canyon due to elevation gain

**Elevation gain/loss:** 1,430-foot gain / 350-foot loss

**Seasons:** Best from May (after the snow has melted) through Oct

**Trail surface:** Dirt trail, rocky in a few areas

**Land status:** City of Boulder Open Space & Mountain Parks

**Nearest town:** Boulder

**Other trail users:** Hikers only on NCAR property; equestrians on the other trails

**Canine compatibility:** Dogs must be leashed on NCAR property. Dog regulations vary from trail to trail and even seasonally; check www.osmp.org for dog regulations or call (303) 441-3440.

**Schedule:** Year-round, but Bear Canyon Trail may be snow covered in winter due to being mostly in shadow. NCAR Road is open 6 a.m. to 10 p.m. Check www.osmp.org for conditions and any seasonal closures.

**Fees and permits:** None required for groups of fewer than 25 people, unless you plan to travel off-trail. Free off-trail permits are available online.

**Maps:** USGS Eldorado Springs; Nat Geo Trails Illustrated 100 Boulder/Golden; Latitude 40° Boulder County Trails

**Trail contact:** City of Boulder Open Space & Mountain Parks, Boulder; (303) 441-3440; www.osmp.org

**Special considerations:** Bring water with you as little is available along the trail; what is there needs to be treated.

**Finding the trailhead:** From the intersection of Broadway and Table Mesa Drive in Boulder, head west on Table Mesa Drive for 2.5 miles to the parking lot at NCAR. The NCAR access road (starts at the end of Table Mesa Drive) opens at 6 a.m. While you're driving along the curving NCAR road, keep an eye out for deer, as well as joggers, walkers, and bicyclists. Park in the large parking lot. You passed the trailhead next to the driveway to the NCAR building. Walk back to where NCAR Drive heads downhill; the trailhead starts to the left by a big rock with a sign for the WALTER ORR ROBERTS NATURE TRAIL, aka Walter Orr Roberts Weather Trail. A bulletin board is on the right. Restrooms and water are available when NCAR is open. Trailhead GPS: N39 58.72' / W105 16.50'

*Lead climber just off Bear Canyon Trail* ▶

## The Hike

The first thing you notice from your car is the interesting design of the Mesa Laboratory of the National Center for Atmospheric Research (NCAR), a scientific research laboratory that focuses on the atmosphere. Designed by architect I. M. Pei, the research facility opened in 1966. The cliff dwellings at Mesa Verde inspired his design, and sand obtained from a nearby quarry was mixed with concrete to match and blend in with the backdrop of the Flatirons. The internal design provides researchers with personal space yet enables them to partake in informal meetings in the maze of halls and the common areas. NCAR is a program of the National Science Foundation. The University Corporation for Atmospheric Research (UCAR), founded in 1960 by fourteen member universities, provides administrative services and manages funding for NCAR. Walter Orr Roberts became UCAR's president and NCAR's first director.

The first part of the hike is along the Walter Orr Roberts Weather Trail (also called the Walter Orr Roberts Nature Trail). Take a few minutes either at the start or end of your hike to read the interesting interpretive signs about weather.

As you climb the little ridge to the water tank, you're walking on Dakota sandstone, the shore of a salty sea about 100 million years ago. When the present Rocky Mountains started to rise, they tilted the sandstone into this ridge, called the Dakota Hogback. The hogback runs intermittently along the Front Range from Douglas County to the Wyoming border.

As you drop from the hogback to the Mesa Trail, the famous Boulder Flatirons appear. These slanted rocks are the Fountain Formation, a combination of sandstone and conglomerate, the latter being a mixture of pebbles and sand cemented together. About 300 million years ago the Ancestral Rockies, also known as Frontrangia, slowly rose above the surrounding land parallel to today's Front Range, but about 30 to 50 miles west. Frontrangia eroded into red-colored gravel and sand that reached depths of 7,000 to 12,000 feet. Over time, the sand became sandstone, and the gravel turned into conglomerate. When the present Rockies started to rise about 64 million years ago, the land tilted sharply. Softer materials eroded away, leaving the interesting sandstone formations that look like the bottom of a standing iron. After you hike up the service road past the mouth of Bear Canyon, look to the southwest for Seal Rock, which just needs a beach ball–shaped rock on top to complete the image.

Near the beginning of the Bear Canyon Trail, you'll pass a small electric substation. A power line follows Bear Canyon all the way to Flagstaff Road, then north to the Boulder Canyon hydroelectric plant (built in 1910) at the east end of Boulder Canyon. The trail slowly climbs along the shady left side of Bear Canyon Creek. To the north, some flatirons emerge just across the tiny creek. You may see rock climbers practicing their skills on the slanty rocks.

A toll (wagon) road once took miners up Bear Canyon and on to the mines in Central City and Black Hawk. Residents of Boulder and Marshall wanted to bring ore from the mines to smelters near their towns, instead of the smelters in Denver. They could transport and sell equipment, produce, and other goods to the mines. Built in 1862 by Henry Clay Norton and George Williamson, floods washed out the road in 1864. Four years later the Bear Canyon and Black Hawk Wagon Road Company formed and made improvements to the road the following summer. Floods continued to take their toll, with the road being reconstructed in 1885, 1907, and 1935.

> You can download the Illustrated Geology Tour for NCAR area from www .bouldercolorado.gov /files/openspace/pdf _education/NCARGeology Tour.pdf. This tour goes from the NCAR parking lot to the Mesa Trail (part of this hike) and then up toward Mallory Cave (not part of this hike).

The toll road brought another commodity to the Boulder area—timber. Lumbering operations began in the thick forests up Bear Canyon, on the Kossler Ranch, and near South Boulder Creek. Mary Collins lived on a ranch up Bear Canyon, and in 1909 wrote of her childhood memories driving with her father in an ox-drawn wagon full of lumber or potatoes headed for Boulder. " . . . there was a sheer descent of hundreds of feet on the lower side and above us and across, the many colored rocks towered like the mighty battlements of giant castles." She mentioned that the road could be treacherous, as witnessed by bleaching horse bones and a wrecked buggy down in the canyon.

Today the trail up Bear Canyon is a delight to hike. In addition to majestic flatirons and castle-like rock formations, Douglas fir, aspen, ponderosa pine, Rocky Mountain juniper, and various riparian area bushes and trees surround the trail. Boulder Mountain Parks crews have upgraded the trail to make it more user and environmentally friendly and sustainable. Most of the trail is in the Western Mountain Parks Habitat Conservation Area, created to protect a large block of naturally functioning ecosystem including the habitat of some rare and threatened species.

## Miles and Directions

**0.0** Start at the Walter Orr Roberts Nature Trail trailhead. Elevation: 6,120 feet.

**0.1** Turn right onto the north loop of the nature trail. Follow the signs To Mesa Trail.

**0.2** Turn left. Come to a bulletin board sign where you turn left and hike on the trail that drops into a saddle then climbs the Dakota Hogback. You are now leaving the weather trail and heading toward the Mesa Trail.

**0.5** Turn left at the junction with a service road and walk past the green water tank.

**0.6** Turn left at the Y junction and head downhill to the Mesa Trail. (The right branch goes to the Mesa Trail as well, but intersects it farther north.)

**0.7** Arrive at the four-way junction with the Mesa, Mallory Cave, and NCAR Mesa Trails. Turn left (south) onto the Mesa Trail. GPS: N39 58.68' / W105 17.02'.

# Bear Canyon Trail

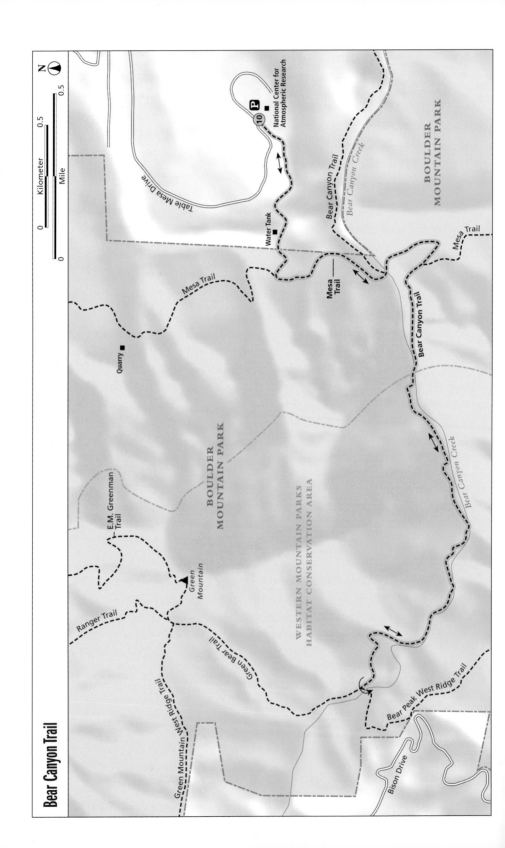

**1.0** Reach the junction of the Mesa Trail and Bear Mountain Drive. Turn right onto the Mesa Trail, which is a service road in this area.

**1.1** Cross Bear Canyon Creek on the road. Elevation: 6,080 feet (low point on the hike). Continue around the left curve and up the road (Mesa Trail) toward the Bear Canyon Trail.

**1.4** Arrive at the junction of the Mesa Trail and Bear Canyon Trail. Turn right onto Bear Canyon Trail. GPS: N39 58.27' / W105 16.98'.

**1.8** Enter the Western Mountain Parks Habitat Conservation Area.

**3.4** Reach the three-way intersection of the Bear Canyon, Bear Peak West Ridge, and Green Bear Trails. Elevation: 7,200 feet. GPS: N39 58.45' / W105 18.44'. Turn around here and retrace your steps.

**6.8** Arrive back at the trailhead.

## Option

For an 8.8-mile, most difficult hike to the top of Green Mountain, turn right at mile 3.4 onto the Green Bear Trail and head north. Reaching the summit and returning to the trailhead will take a total of 4 to 6 hours; elevation gain will be 2,374 feet, with a 350-foot loss. At mile 4.2 arrive at the four-way intersection of Green Mountain West Ridge, Green Bear, and Ranger Trails. Turn right onto the Green Mountain West Ridge Trail, which rises steeply to the summit. A 0.2-mile climb brings you to the top of Green Mountain. Elevation: 8,144 feet. GPS: N39 58.93' / W105 18.05'. On the summit, to both the right and left, are boulders you can scramble up for views to the east and of Boulder. To the left is a big boulder with a cairn on top. The summit register tube is cemented into the cairn. On the north side of this big rock lump are great views of Longs Peak, Twin Sisters, and Mount Audubon to the south. The E. M. Greenman Trail heads downhill from this point. Return the way you came.

# Hike Information

## General Information
**Boulder Chamber of Commerce:** (303) 442-1044; www.boulderchamber.com
**Boulder Colorado Convention and Visitors Bureau:** (303) 442- 2911, (800) 444-0447; www
.bouldercoloradousa.com

## Local Events/Attractions
**Colorado Music Festival:** Chautauqua Auditorium, Boulder; (303) 449-1397; www.coloradomu
sicfest.org
**Colorado Shakespeare Festival:** University of Colorado, Boulder; (303) 492-0554

## Restaurants
**Boulder Cork:** 3295 30th St., Boulder; (303) 443-9505; www.bouldercork.com
**Boulder Dushanbe Teahouse:** 1770 13th St., Boulder: (303) 442-4993; www.bouldertea
house.com
**Ras Kassa's Ethiopian Restaurant:** 2111 30th St., Suite E, Boulder; (303) 447-2919; www
.raskassas.com/home.html

## Clubs and Organizations

**Colorado Mountain Club–Boulder Group:** Boulder; (303) 554-7688; www.cmcboulder.org

**OSMP Volunteers:** City of Boulder Open Space & Mountain Parks; (303) 441-3440; www.osmp.org

## Hike Tours

**City of Boulder Open Space & Mountain Parks:** (303) 441-3440; www.osmp.org

# GEOLOGY BABBLE

metamorphic rock—A rock formed when high heat or intense pressure causes one type of rock to be transformed into another type of rock

gneiss—A metamorphic rock with light and dark bands (think "nice" lines)

schist—A metamorphic rock, usually dark-colored, with lots of mica (a shiny mineral)

igneous rock—A rock formed when magma (molten rock) cools

granite—A light-colored igneous rock formed when magma cooled under the earth's surface, usually in rock cracks; often with pink minerals and quartz embedded

erosion—The process of losing material, usually due to water, wind, or glacial ice

freeze-thaw cycle—When water freezes in a rock crack it expands; when the ice thaws, the water takes less space, and the crack contracts. The repeated process can eventually break a rock apart.

joint—A fracture or crack in rock

glacier—A flowing compacted mass of ice that moves because of its own weight on a sloping surface

# 11 Kruger Rock Trail

Kruger Rock is a rocky knob on a ridge overlooking a large meadow in Hermit Park Open Space (HPOS), opened in 2008 for public use. Wildlife viewing includes elk, mule deer, bobcat, black bear, and moose. A rare cinquefoil (potentilla) species is found in HPOS, which also contains two high-quality wetlands. Ranching history lives on in legends, sensitive areas are restricted for preservation, and amenities provide for human recreation. The trail to Kruger Rock winds through a mixed conifer forest. Enjoy the wonderful 360-degree views from the high point near this special open space park.

**Start:** From the Kruger Rock Trail parking lot near the group pavilion
**Distance:** 4.0 miles out and back
**Approximate hiking time:** 1.5 to 2.5 hours
**Difficulty:** Moderate due to elevation gain
**Elevation gain:** 975-foot gain/50-foot loss
**Seasons:** Best from May through Oct
**Trail surface:** Dirt trail, rocky in a few areas
**Land status:** Larimer County Department of Natural Resources; national forest
**Nearest town:** Estes Park
**Other trail users:** None
**Canine compatibility:** Dogs must be on leash

**Schedule:** Year-round, sunrise to sunset
**Fees and permits:** Day use fee required
**Maps:** USGS Panorama Peak; Nat Geo Trails Illustrated 101 Cache La Poudre/Big Thompson; Latitude 40° Colorado Front Range
**Trail contact:** Hermit Park Open Space, Larimer County Department of Natural Resources, 1800 South County Rd. 31, Loveland; (970) 679-4570 or (970) 577-2090; www.co .larimer.co.us/naturalresources
**Other:** Vault toilets located near pavilion
**Special considerations:** No water on trail; bring your own.

**Finding the trailhead:** From Estes Park, head southeast on US 36 and drive just past the top of the hill to Hermit Park Open Space. The turnoff is right before mile marker 4. Turn right onto the access road. The entrance station is in 0.2 mile. Continue on the park road for 2.9 miles, passing various turns to different camping and picnic areas, until you reach the first turnoff to the group-use area and the Kruger Rock Trail parking area. Turn left to the parking lot. A short trail starts from the north edge of the parking lot. GPS: N40 20.46'/W105 28.36'

## The Hike

The road into Hermit Park Open Space (HPOS) winds up several switchbacks to a ridge. As you cross the crest, Longs Peak appears, almost startling you with its huge presence. The road winds down through mixed conifer forest, past a cabin area along Big Gulch, then into Hermit Park, with its group picnic area, pavilion, and trails. The little rocky knob atop a nearby hill is Kruger Rock, the destination of this hike.

Kruger Rock is named after either Christina (or Christianne) Krueger or her husband, Alfred. They purchased some of the land in this area in 1909 and received a patent for the rest through the Homestead Act of 1862. One account indicates they purchased land around and north of the pavilion in 1910. Someone, somewhere,

probably dropped the "e" from Krueger when naming the rock knob.

> **A valley surrounded by hills or mountains in Colorado is often called a "park."**

Local kids named the high meadow Hermit's Park after a loner called Dutch Louie, who squatted on the Crocker Ranch near the head of Big Gulch and built a two-story cabin around 1910. He ran cattle, hunted, and grew potatoes on the land. Legend says he was hung for cattle rustling. However, records are sketchy about whether F. W. Crocker actually owned Hermit's Park. Crocker owned the Crocker Biscuit Company (later National Biscuit Company) in Denver. In 1905 he purchased land at the base of Mount Olympus to the northwest of Hermit Park, shown as Crocker Ranch on the USGS topo map, but no records indicate he actually owned the land on which Dutch Louie squatted. He did run a large cattle operation. Perhaps others owned the land and Crocker leased it from them. The "Line Shack" near the pavilion supposedly was used by Crocker's ranch hands.

Records do show that John L. Jacobi purchased 160 acres of land in 1898 (near the Hermit's Cabin). His obituary called him "Dutch Louie" and reported he owned thousands of acres of land. In February 1901 Christ Wilhelm Deushcle purchased 143 acres near the head of Big Gulch, northeast of the pavilion. Is "Dutch" a mispronunciation of his name? Who "Dutch Louie" was remains a mystery, but his two-story cabin still stands, with signs identifying it as "Hermit's Cabin" of "Dutch Louie."

Hewlett-Packard Company (HP) purchased Hermit Park in 1967 as a retreat for its personnel and built cabins, campgrounds, trails, and a picnic pavilion. HP deeded the land to Agilent Technologies, Inc., in 1999. The company's employees approached Larimer County Department of Natural Resources to see if the county would purchase the well-loved property so others could enjoy it and to preserve it. A huge capital campaign ensued, with many partners participating. With help from the Estes Valley Land Trust, the Estes Valley Recreation and Park District, the Town of Estes Park, City of Loveland, City of Fort Collins, Town of Berthoud, Great Outdoors Colorado (GOCO), and many private donors, Larimer County purchased the 1,362-acre Hermit Park in February 2007. According to the Hermit Park Open Space Education Plan, "Hermit Park Open Space was acquired with the intent of protecting the native vegetation and wildlife populations, preserving scenic views, and providing outdoor recreation opportunities."

Most of HPOS is under a conservation easement held by the Estes Valley Land Trust, which determines the type of development allowed and where. To meet the above intentions, 25 percent of HPOS is used for developed recreation and relaxation, while the other 75 percent protects natural and cultural resources as well as habitat. Sandwiched between the Roosevelt National Forest and the Meadowdale Conservation Easement to the east, HPOS provides a corridor of more than 41,000

*Longs Peak and Continental Divide*

acres for elk and other wildlife. Visitors are requested to stay on established trails and in developed areas to protect the unique resources, including a rare cinquefoil species, wetlands, and wildlife habitat.

HPOS is a great place to visit, with both campgrounds and cabins available for overnight stays. If there's enough snow, you can cross-country ski or snowshoe during winter, but check first with the park for conditions.

The well-designed and well-built trail up to Kruger Rock opened in 2008. It winds up a grassy hillside, through ponderosa pine and Douglas fir forest, over some granitic rocks, and past a vista point that provides excellent views of the Estes Park area. The trail continues to climb, and its switchbacks make the elevation gain relatively easy. Stone steps take you up a few steep sections. The final scramble is up a wide crack with good handholds and footholds. From the top of the rock, you get a fantastic view of peaks in Rocky Mountain National Park, the Eastern Plains, and points south along the Front Range. The summit is rocky but broad—a pleasant place for lunch if the wind's not blowing.

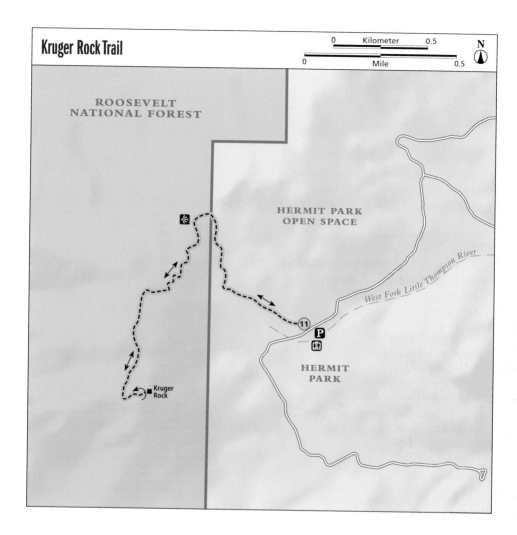

# Kruger Rock Trail

ROOSEVELT
NATIONAL FOREST

HERMIT PARK
OPEN SPACE

West Fork Little Thompson River

HERMIT
PARK

Kruger
Rock

0        Kilometer        0.5

0              Mile              0.5

N

## Miles and Directions

**0.0**  Start at the Kruger Rock Trail parking area. The access trail starts in northwest corner of parking lot. Walk past the vault toilets and picnic pavilion. Turn right on the road beyond the pavilion, and head to the trailhead near the winter closure gate on the main park road. Elevation: 8,430 feet.

**0.1**  Find the Kruger Rock Trail at the edge of the main park road near the gate. GPS: N40 20.49'/W105 28.47'.

**0.8**  A little trail to the right leads to a viewpoint.

*Final scramble to the top*

**2.0** Reach the base of Kruger Rock. Scramble up the gully to the top, using good handholds and footholds. Elevation 9,355 feet. GPS: N40 20.30'/W105 29.11'. Retrace your steps from here.

**4.0** Arrive back at the trailhead.

## Hike Information

### General Information
**Estes Park Convention & Visitors Bureau:** Estes Park; (970) 577-9900 or (800) 44-ESTES; www.estesparkcvb.com
**Hermit Park Open Space:** Larimer County Dept. of Natural Resources; (970) 577-2090; www.co.larimer.co.us/naturalresources

### Local Events/Attractions
**Estes Park Area Historical Museum:** Estes Park; (970) 586-6256; www.estesnet.com/Museum/
**Longs Peak Scottish/Irish Highland Festival:** Estes Park; (970) 586-6308 or (800) 90ESTES (800-903-7837); www.scotfest.com
**MacGregor Ranch Museum:** Estes Park; (970) 586-3749; www.macgregorranch.org

### Accommodations
**Hermit Park Open Space:** campgrounds and cabins; (800) 397-7795; www.larimercamping.com

### Restaurants
**Big Horn Restaurant:** 401 West Elkhorn Ave., Estes Park; (970) 586-2792; www.estesparkbighorn.com
**Ed's Cantina & Grill:** 390 East Elkhorn Ave., Estes Park; (970) 586-2919; www.edscantina.com
**Nepals Cafe:** 184 East Elkhorn Ave., Estes Park; (970) 577-7035
**Smokin' Dave's BBQ & Taphouse:** 820 Moraine Ave., Estes Park; (866) 674-2793; www.smokindavesbbqandtaphouse.com

### Clubs and Organizations
**Friends of Larimer County Parks and Open Lands:** 1800 South County Rd. 31, Loveland; (970) 679-4570; www.co.larimer.co.us/naturalresources/volunteer/

### Hike Tours
**Hermit Park Open Space:** Larimer County Department of Natural Resources, 1800 South County Rd. 31, Loveland; (970) 679-4570, (970) 577-2090; www.co.larimer.co.us/naturalresources

# 12 Fern Lake

The Fern Lake Trail wanders through lush vegetation near the Big Thompson River to The Pool, a quiet section in an otherwise fast-flowing river. The trail then climbs along a ridge of lodgepole pine to pretty Fern Falls. The hike continues up into spruce/fir forest to Fern Lake, where winter carnivals once took place near a cozy lodge. Visitors in the early 1900s enjoyed vacations and overnights near The Pool and at Fern Lake Lodge (removed 1979). For an optional extension, follow the trail farther uphill to Odessa Lake, nestled between pointy peaks including the Little Matterhorn—a touch of Switzerland in Colorado.

**Start:** From the Fern Lake trailhead
**Distance:** 7.6 miles out and back
**Approximate hiking time:** 3 to 5 hours
**Difficulty:** Difficult due to elevation gain
**Elevation gain:** 1,375 feet
**Seasons:** Best from June through early Oct
**Trail surface:** Dirt trail, rocky in a few areas
**Land status:** National park wilderness
**Nearest town:** Estes Park
**Other trail users:** Equestrians
**Canine compatibility:** Dogs are not permitted
**Schedule:** Year-round. The access road is closed by snow in winter just past the Cub Lake trailhead, about 0.7 mile from the Fern Lake trailhead. The trail is neither marked nor maintained for winter use.
**Fees and permits:** Entrance fee, annual pass, or America the Beautiful pass required.

Backcountry permits are required for overnight camping (970-586-1242; a fee is charged). Download the Backcountry Camping Guide from the park website.
**Maps:** USGS McHenrys Peak and Longs Peak; Nat Geo Trails Illustrated 200 Rocky Mountain National Park; Latitude 40° Colorado Front Range
**Trail contact:** Rocky Mountain National Park, Estes Park; (970) 586-1206; www.nps.gov /romo
**Other:** Bear-proof food canisters are required below treeline between May 1 and Oct 31.
**Special considerations:** No facilities at trailhead. No potable water along the trail—bring your own water. Water and restrooms at the main visitor center and at the Moraine Park Visitor Center.

**Finding the trailhead:** From Estes Park drive west on US 36 to the Beaver Meadows entrance station to Rocky Mountain National Park, just past the visitor center. Pay your fee or show your pass. Drive 0.25 mile west and turn left onto Bear Lake Road. Drive 1.2 miles and turn right towards Moraine Park Campground. In 0.5 mile, turn left toward the Fern Lake trailhead. After 1.25 miles you'll come to a small parking area with a vault toilet. The shuttle bus stops here. Continue driving down the dirt road another 0.7 mile to Fern Lake trailhead parking lot. **Note:** You'll pass three little parking areas on the way. Please observe the parking regulations and park only in specified places off the road. Alternately, you can drive to the main shuttle parking area and take a shuttle to the shuttle stop, then walk 0.7 mile to the trailhead. GPS: N40 21.29'/W105 37.84'

## The Hike

Before Rocky Mountain National Park (RMNP) was created in 1915, much of Moraine Park was private land and the surrounding forests were part of the Colorado National Forest. Then, as now, visitors flocked to the beautiful mountain valleys for rest, relaxation, and adventure.

The Brinwood Ranch and Hotel, located just east of the present Moraine Park Stables, opened in 1911 and attracted visitors from all over. The nearby Fern Lake Trail tempted people to explore the forest and high lakes either by foot or by horseback.

The first part of the hike, along the Big Thompson River, is quite mellow. Ferns, riparian bushes of various types, aspen, Rocky Mountain juniper, ponderosa pine, Douglas fir, Rocky Mountain maple, and a beautiful mixture of wildflowers line the trail. Occasionally granitic boulders of different shapes and sizes rise above the vegetation, creating a forested rock garden. In one place the rock-lined trail wanders beneath a canopy of tree branches.

At 1.7 miles, the trail crosses the Big Thompson on a substantial bridge with large handrails. To the right is The Pool, a calm spot in the otherwise rushing river. On the other side of the bridge, the trail to Fern and Odessa Lakes turns right among some boulders.

A little farther up the trail is the turnoff to the Old Forest Inn campsite. The Higby Brothers owned a small lodge where the Old Forest Inn campsite is located. The original lodge consisted of two wooden walled tents. The Teckers purchased the three-acre area in 1917. Although partially burned by a lightning-caused fire in 1919, the Teckers continued their operations, building a small dining room and serving 500 people annually for the next three years. By 1929 the Forest Inn consisted of fourteen tents with concrete floors, a main lodge, and two log cabins. In the 1930s a few more cabins replaced the tents. A night at the lodge in 1949 cost $5.25 per person, including meals. Then in his 80s, Mr. Tecker operated the lodge for the last summer in 1952. The National Park Service purchased his lodge for $14,000 and removed the buildings by 1959.

Dr. William Jacob Workman practiced medicine in Denver and traveled often to the Estes Park area. He loved to fish and found that Fern Lake, which he named, was an ideal place to practice his hobby. He obtained permission from the Forest Service to build a cabin on the east shore, 5 miles from the Brinwood. After completion in 1911, Workman built tent-cabins and tents around the main lodge. Inside, people ate meals at a large wooden table, which seated twenty-one. The table surrounded a large log stump on which another table revolved, creating a lazy susan. Hungry diners helped themselves to various delicious courses as they rotated by.

After the creation of RMNP, Dr. Workman sold the permit to operate the lodge, and the Higby Brothers took over operations. Lodging cost $1 per night per person. In 1916 the Estes Park Outdoor Club invited directors of the Colorado Mountain Club to Fern Lake Lodge to check out winter sports possibilities. They obviously

## Accommodations

**Rocky Mountain National Park:** Estes Park. Camping reservations accepted for Glacier Basin, Moraine Park, and Aspenglen campgrounds (877-444-6777 or online at www.recreation.gov). First-come, first-served at Longs Peak campground (tents only).

**YMCA of the Rockies:** 2515 Tunnel Rd., Estes Park; (970) 586-3341 or (800) 777-9622; www.ymcarockies.org

## Restaurants

**Big Horn Restaurant:** 401 West Elkhorn Ave., Estes Park: (970) 586-2792; www.estesparkbighorn.com

**Ed's Cantina & Grill:** 390 East Elkhorn Ave., Estes Park; (970) 586-2919; www.edscantina.com

**Nepals Cafe:** 184 East Elkhorn Ave., Estes Park; (970) 577-7035

**Smokin' Dave's BBQ & Taphouse:** 820 Moraine Ave., Estes Park; (866) 674-2793; www.smokindavesbbqandtaphouse.com

## Clubs and Organizations

**Colorado Mountain Club:** Contact CMC's state office at (303) 279-3080 or at www.cmc.org. There are CMC groups in Longmont, Fort Collins, Greeley, and Boulder.

**Rocky Mountain Nature Association:** Estes Park; (970) 586-0108; www.rmna.org

## Hike Tours

**Rocky Mountain National Park:** Estes Park; (970) 586-1206; www.nps.gov/romo

**Rocky Mountain Nature Association:** Estes Park; (970) 586-0108; www.rmna.org

◀ *Fern Falls*

# 13　Lory State Park Loop

Lory State Park is a hiker's dream, with many trails designated for "foot only." Situated next to Horsetooth Reservoir, trails climb into the nearby montane foothills with ponderosa pine and Douglas fir forests. Wild turkeys hide, mule deer browse, and Abert's squirrels and cottontail rabbits frolic. Lory even has six backcountry campsites available by permit. At a lower elevation, this is a perfect place to satisfy early-season hiking and camping urges. Arthur's Rock protrudes above the park, providing views of the Fort Collins area. This hike makes a loop using sections of six different trails.

**Start:** From the Well Gulch Nature Trail trailhead by the South Eltuck Picnic Area

**Distance:** 6.6-mile loop

**Approximate hiking time:** 2.5 to 4 hours

**Difficulty:** Difficult due to elevation gain and some steep spots

**Elevation gain:** 1,670-foot gain, including three elevation gains/losses

**Seasons:** Year-round, except after a big snowstorm

**Trail surface:** Dirt trail, sometimes steep and rocky, sometimes gentle

**Land status:** State park

**Nearest towns:** Laporte and Fort Collins

**Other trail users:** Some trail sections open to mountain bikers and equestrians, while others are hiker only; hunters in season

**Canine compatibility:** Dogs must be on leash; little to no water along the trail

**Schedule:** Year-round. Summer: 6 a.m. to 10 p.m. Winter: 5 a.m. to 6 p.m. Call for trail conditions in winter.

**Fees and permits:** Daily fee or annual parks pass required. Permit required (with fee) for backpacking (overnight camping at designated campsites only). Campfires are not allowed in the backcountry.

**Maps:** USGS Horsetooth Reservoir; Latitude 40° Colorado Front Range

**Trail contact:** Lory State Park, 708 Lodgepole Drive, Bellvue; (970) 493-1623; http://parks .state.co.us/parks/lory

**Special considerations:** Vault toilets but no water. Bring water with you.

**Finding the trailhead:** From Fort Collins take US 287 north. Just past mile marker 350, US 287 turns right. Continue straight ahead onto Larimer County Road (LCR) 54G. Drive 2.7 miles through Laporte, then turn left to Rist Canyon (LCR 52E). Turn left after 1 mile onto LCR 23N in Bellvue, drive 1.4 miles south, and then turn right onto LCR 25G. Drive another 1.7 miles to the park entrance and turn left. Pay the entrance fee and stop in the visitor center to check out the interpretive displays. Restrooms and water are available at the visitor center. Drive 0.9 mile south to the South Eltuck Picnic Area, across from the Well Gulch Nature Trail trailhead kiosk. GPS: N40 34.70'/W105 10.70'

## The Hike

Human activity around present-day Fort Collins can be traced back about 11,000 years. The largest Folsom culture campsite is located north of town. The term "Folsom culture" comes from archaeological evidence first found in 1926 near Folsom, New Mexico, that distinguished this group's tools and culture from those of other

*Hikers on Arthur's Rock Trail and view*

ancient Native Americans. More modern tribes of the area included the Arapaho, Cheyenne, and Ute.

In the early 1800s, fur traders came to the area in search of pelts. In 1836, a party of trappers climbed into the foothills west of the Fort Collins area. Their supplies became too heavy and they decided to hide them. The supposed location of this cache was near today's Bellvue. Because the cache included gunpowder, the river near their cache became known as the Cache la Poudre.

One of the party members, Antoine Janise, returned a few years later to settle down. Janise saw his opportunity for success after gold was discovered near Denver. Near present-day Laporte, he established a settlement called Colona in 1859, after receiving permission from the local Arapaho tribe. Prospectors began combing all the tributaries of the South Platte River, including the Cache la Poudre. Settlers continued to arrive, establishing farms to feed themselves and the miners.

One settler was John Kimmons, who homesteaded 160 acres in the area of today's Lory State Park. In 1897, he exchanged his land for John Howard's family ranch in North Park. The Howards appreciated the milder winters near Fort Collins, plus the

nearby schools for their children. They grew hay, raised cattle, and harvested timber in the foothills. Purchasing adjacent lands over the years, their ranch expanded to 3,600 acres. Stop by Homestead Picnic Area to see the three cedar trees and sandstone slabs where the Howards' house used to stand.

The plains and foothills of Colorado are known to be dry, and early farmers looked to the Cache la Poudre River for relief. G. R. Sanderson built the first irrigation ditch in northern Colorado, diverting water from the Poudre above Bellvue. By 1933, irrigation took much water from the Poudre and the Big Thompson River to the south. The U.S. Bureau of Reclamation started the Colorado–Big Thompson Project, to divert west slope water to the thirsty farms and growing population of the east. A 9.75-foot diameter tunnel, up to 3,600 feet underground, was drilled under the Continental Divide. The Alva B. Adams Tunnel transports water from Grand Lake on the west side of the Continental Divide to Marys Lake near Estes Park on the east. Water from Marys Lake flows through various reservoirs and ultimately to Horsetooth Reservoir, which was completed in 1949.

By 1967, after three generations, ranching became unprofitable for the Howard family. Part of the land was sold and developed into Soldier Canyon Estates, which you drive past to reach the park. The state of Colorado procured the remaining land for the park, which opened in May 1975. A later land purchase added about 100 acres, and presently Lory State Park consists of 2,591 acres. The park is named in honor of Dr. Charles A. Lory, a former president of Colorado Agricultural College (today's Colorado State University), and an early settler. As Fort Collins and the surrounding area quickly expanded, Lory State Park's role in wildlife preservation became very important. Recreational opportunities within Lory State Park, Horsetooth Mountain Open Space, and Horsetooth Reservoir also provide welcome relief from the fast pace of the modern world.

This hike starts at the Well Gulch Nature Trail trailhead near the South Eltuck Picnic Area. Following Well Gulch through yucca, wooly mullein, and shortgrass prairie, the trail enters ponderosa pine and Douglas fir forests. Watch out for poison ivy along this trail. It then joins the Timber Trail and climbs steadily and sometimes steeply to a ridge. As the trail turns from south- to north-facing slopes, notice how the vegetation changes in response to a slightly cooler and wetter climate on the north faces. At various points check out the excellent views of the Eastern Plains and Fort Collins.

At the ridgeline, numbered poles mark campsites. Near campsites 1 and 2, look straight ahead to see Arthur's Rock. A short trail scrambles to its top for even better views. Return to the main trail and head downhill on the Arthur's Rock Trail, which drops and twists below granitic cliffs to the Overlook Trail. This trail travels the edge

*Little waterfall on Well Gulch Nature Trail*

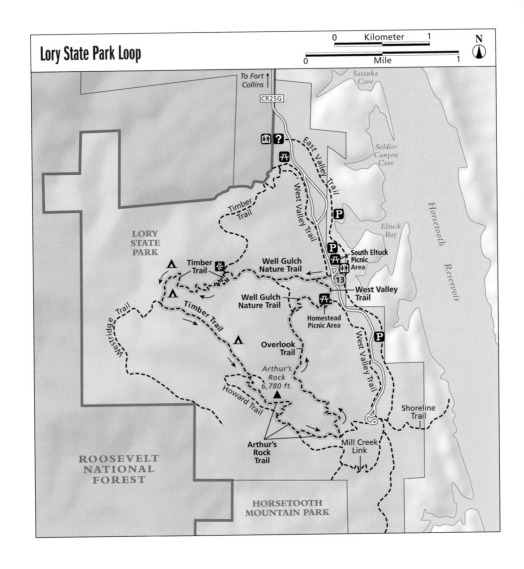

# Lory State Park Loop

0 Kilometer 1

0 Mile 1

N

To Fort Collins

CR25G

East Valley Trail

West Valley Trail

Timber Trail

LORY STATE PARK

Timber Trail

Well Gulch Nature Trail

South Eltuck Picnic Area

13

West Valley Trail

Well Gulch Nature Trail

Homestead Picnic Area

Westridge Trail

Timber Trail

Overlook Trail

Arthur's Rock 6,780 ft.

West Valley Trail

Howard Trail

Shoreline Trail

Arthur's Rock Trail

Mill Creek Link

ROOSEVELT NATIONAL FOREST

HORSETOOTH MOUNTAIN PARK

Satanka Cove

Soldier Canyon Cove

Eltuck Bay

Horsetooth Reservoir

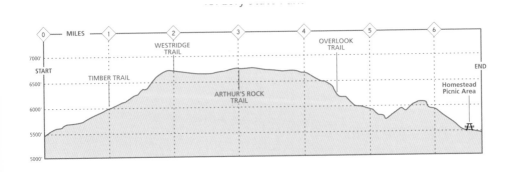

MILES

WESTRIDGE TRAIL

OVERLOOK TRAIL

7000'

START

END

TIMBER TRAIL

6500'

ARTHUR'S ROCK TRAIL

Homestead Picnic Area

6000'

5500'

5000'

of forest and plains, climbing and dropping across drainages below Arthur's Rock before finally emerging onto the prairie for the last leg of the loop.

## Miles and Directions

**0.0** Start at Well Gulch Nature Trail trailhead by South Eltuck Picnic Area. Elevation: 5,480 feet. Stop at the kiosk for information and a *Well Gulch Self-Guided Nature Trail* brochure.

**0.1** Reach the intersection with West Valley Trail. Cross the bridge and turn right on Well Gulch Nature Trail.

**0.5** Come to the intersection of Well Gulch Nature Trail and the access trail to Timber Trail. Continue straight ahead on the access trail to reach Timber Trail.

**1.0** Reach a T intersection with Timber Trail. GPS: N40 34.71'/W105 11.51'. Turn left onto the Timber Trail and head uphill. The trail switchbacks up an open, south-facing slope.

**1.3** The trail swings left, from a south-facing to a north-facing slope. **(Note:** Check out the change in vegetation with the change in slope aspect.)

**2.3** Westridge Trail comes in from the right. Curve left on Timber Trail. **(FYI:** The flat ponderosa-filled area is a nice place for a little break. You'll be passing by the designated campsites on this section.)

**3.0** Reach the Campsite 1 sign on the left and Campsite 2 sign on the right. As you continue along the trail, Arthur's Rock is ahead.

**3.1** Arrive at the three-way junction with Howard, Arthur's Rock, and Timber Trails. Turn left onto Arthur's Rock Trail.

**3.2** Come to the intersection with the spur trail to Arthur's Rock summit. GPS: N40 34.09' /W105 11.30'. **(Side trip:** Turn left to scramble to the top of Arthur's Rock [6,780 feet] for great views. It's 0.1 mile out and back to the saddle between rock lumps.) Curve right and head downhill on Arthur's Rock Trail. The trail switchbacks and drops down along the side of Arthur's Rock. **(FYI:** You'll get a good view of what 1.7-billion-year-old rock looks like.)

**3.8** The trail curves right as it drops below the ridge at the end of Arthur's Rock.

**4.0** An access trail to a bouldering area is on your right. Continue downhill to the left on Arthur's Rock Trail.

**4.3** Reach the intersection with the Mill Creek Link. Turn left at this fork, staying on Arthur's Rock Trail.

**4.6** Reach the intersection with Overlook Trail. GPS: N40 33.81'/W105 10.66'. Turn left and follow Overlook toward Well Gulch Nature Trail. Overlook Trail meanders up and down at the edge of the forest but eventually levels out.

**5.8** Arrive at the intersection of Overlook Trail and Well Gulch Nature Trail. Turn right and follow the nature trail downhill toward Homestead Picnic Area.

**6.3** Reach the intersection of Well Gulch Nature and West Valley Trails. Turn left and walk on West Valley Trail, past Homestead Picnic Area, heading mostly north.

**6.5** Reach the intersection of West Valley Trail and Well Gulch Nature Trail. Turn right, cross the bridge, turn right, and return to South Eltuck Picnic Area.

**6.6** Arrive back at the Well Gulch Nature Trail trailhead kiosk.

# THE WOOD TICK

Colorado has relatively few poisonous or irritating plants, insects, and reptiles. Be aware, however, of the wood tick, *Dermacentor andersoni*. The small insect is about ⅛ inch long, with a flat body. Ticks are active from late March into early July and live in grassy, woody, or brushy areas, waiting for a warm-blooded body. Humans and dogs can easily pick up ticks by brushing against vegetation. The tick embeds itself head first into your flesh, with its body sticking out. Unlike mosquitoes, ticks feed on the host's blood for hours. An anchor below their mouths keeps them attached.

The wood tick may carry one of two infections that are threatening to human hosts. If the tick bite goes undetected, a person may develop the virus Colorado tick fever. Symptoms appear within three to six days after the bite and include head and body aches, lethargy, nausea, vomiting, and abdominal pain. The illness lasts for five to ten days. These wood ticks also carry the bacterium causing Rocky Mountain spotted fever. Symptoms appear in two to four days, including fever, spotted rash, headache, nausea, vomiting, and abdominal and muscle pain. If Rocky Mountain spotted fever is suspected, seek medical attention immediately as this illness can be life threatening.

When hiking during tick season, check yourself (skin, hair, clothes) often to remove any ticks before they can transmit disease. Applying deet- and permethrin-based repellents on skin and clothes can help. Wear light-colored clothing so you can see ticks more easily. Tuck loose clothing into your socks and pants. If you find a tick embedded in your skin, grasp the skin as close as possible to the tick with a pair of tweezers and gently pull it straight out. Remove the tick intact. Do *not* leave the head and neck in your skin. Other removal methods, such as covering the insect with alcohol, fingernail polish, or oil, may cause the tick to regurgitate and pass infection on to its host. If you cannot effectively remove the tick, seek medical attention.

## Hike Information

### General Information
**Fort Collins Chamber of Commerce:** 225 South Meldrum, Fort Collins; (970) 482-3746; www.fcchamber.org
**Fort Collins Convention & Visitor Bureau:** 19 Old Town Sq., Suite 137; (800) 274-3678 or (970) 232.3840; www.ftcollins.com

## Local Events/Attractions

**New Belgium Brewery:** 500 Linden St., Fort Collins; (888) NBB-4044 or (970) 221-0524; www.newbelgium.com

**Rocky Mountain Raptor Center:** 720B East Vine Dr., Fort Collins; (970) 484-7756; www.rmrp.org

## Restaurants

**Coopersmith's Pub & Brewing:** 5 Old Town Sq., Fort Collins; (970) 498-0483; www.coopersmithspub.com

**Panhandler's Pizza:** 1220 West Elizabeth St., Fort Collins; (970) 221-4567; www.panhandlerspizza.com

**Pickle Barrel:** 122 West Laurel, Fort Collins; (970) 484-0235

## Clubs and Organizations

**Colorado Mountain Club–Fort Collins group:** (303) 279-3080; http://fortcmc.org

**Volunteer at Lory State Park:** (970) 493-1623; http://parks.state.co.us/parks/lory

# In Addition

## Winter Hiking

When winter brings a blanket of snow to Colorado's mountains, don't hibernate! Cross-country skis and snowshoes open a new world to summer hikers. Many trails are still used in the winter, and ski trails are often marked with blue diamonds. Orange diamonds typically denote snowmobile routes. Be aware that unmarked trails may be extremely hard to find as a snow-blanketed forest looks very different in winter than in summer. Also be aware of and avoid avalanche danger.

The type of equipment you buy depends on how you are going to use it. Lightweight, small snowshoes are great on packed trails, but sink in deep, off-trail snow where larger snowshoes work better. Snowshoeing is like walking with wide and long feet. Hiking or ski poles can help with balance.

Colorado hosts numerous Nordic centers and guest ranches with groomed trails where skinny track skis, skating skis, or snowshoes are the mode of travel. For where to go, check the website www.coloradocrosscountry.com. If you've never cross-country skied before, take a couple of lessons at one of these centers. You'll learn correct technique, which will make backcountry skiing more enjoyable. It's also easier to learn on groomed trails.

Backcountry skiing comes in three varieties: touring, telemarking, or downhill. Wider skis are used in the backcountry, but several styles are available. For novices or spring skiing, waxless skis are the way to go. As you gain skill, Colorado's snow is great for waxed skis. Waxes grip the snow so you don't slide backward while going uphill, but let you slide downhill. Waxless skis work the same but are usually less efficient. Skins placed on the bottom of your skis can help you climb steep or hard-packed hills (remember avalanche danger though).

Then you need to decide if you are just touring or entering the downhill world of telemarking or randonée. Touring and telemarking require free-heel bindings, while randonée incorporates a binding that allows the heel to lift on the uphill but clamps down for parallel (alpine) turns on the downhill.

Colorado has fantastic backcountry hut systems. Traveling to these huts requires good winter backcountry and route-finding skills and equipment. Trails may not be obvious and many a skier has camped overnight outdoors without finding the hut.

Summer hiking trails may or may not be the best ski trails in winter. Check with the local offices of the Forest Service, Bureau of Land Management, and/or national, state, or local parks for recommended winter trails.

Then have a great winter "hike" on your snowshoes or skis!

# Honorable Mentions

## Front Range

Compiled here are some great hikes in the Front Range region that didn't make the A-list this time around but deserve recognition. Check them out and let us know what you think. You may decide that one or more of these hikes deserves higher status in future editions or, perhaps, you may have a hike of your own that merits some attention.

### D  Spruce Mountain

Spruce Mountain is a forested island in the sky rimmed with rock ledges. Views from the trail include Pikes Peak, Cheyenne Mountain, the old Greenland Ranch, thousands of acres of protected Douglas County Open Space, and points north to Longs Peak. Numerous view opportunities lie along the south rim, culminating at Windy Point on the southwest end. You can circle the top of Spruce Mountain or drop down and finish the hike around the north end of the pleasant mesa between the prairie and the foothills. The loop that drops down to the prairie is a moderate 5.6-mile lollipop. To reach Spruce Mountain from I-25 south of Castle Rock, take exit 173 (Larkspur), which becomes Spruce Mountain Road (Douglas CR 53). Drive 5.8 miles and turn right into the little parking lot for the Spruce Mountain Trail. GPS: N39 10.07'/W104 52.44'. You'll pass through the town of Larkspur on the way. A portable toilet is available at the trailhead. Hike or snowshoe the trail year-round, from one hour before sunrise to one hour after sunset. Bring water with you. Dogs must be on leash. For questions, contact Douglas County Open Space at (303) 660-7495 or www.douglas.co.us/dcoutdoors/.

### E  Meyer Ranch Park Loops

Meyer Ranch Park offers numerous loop trails appropriate for hikers of all abilities. Mountain bikers, joggers, and equestrians also enjoy the park. Typical of the Front Range foothills, various grasses, lodgepole and ponderosa pines, aspens, Douglas firs, and a few spruces cover the hills. Picnic tables are available along Owl's Perch Trail and under a shelter where Old Ski Run Trail heads uphill. This hike follows westside trails to the top of the park and returns on eastside trails. Near the top you can get a nice view of Mount Evans to the west. Hike up the service road to the vault toilet, follow the sign to the picnic tables (not the service road), and turn right onto Owl's Perch Trail. Continue taking right turns onto Lodgepole Loop and Sunny Aspen Trail to reach Old Ski Run Trail. Turn right near the picnic shelter onto Old Ski Run Trail, which is a lollipop. When you return to this junction at the picnic shelter, turn right onto Sunny Aspen Trail, then right again onto Lodgepole Loop to Owl's Perch

Trail. Turn right on Owl's Perch to return to the trailhead for a moderate 4.5-mile loop with a 900-foot elevation gain. To reach the trailhead from the intersection of C-470 and US 285 south of Morrison, drive about 11.2 miles west up Turkey Creek Canyon on US 285. Just past mile marker 239, take the South Turkey Creek exit. The exit loops around and under the overpass. In 0.1 mile turn right onto South Turkey Creek Road, then take an immediate left into the trailhead entrance. Elevation: 7,840 feet. GPS: N39 32.77'/W105 16.32'. There are no facilities at the trailhead but there is a composting toilet 0.2 mile up the trail, and a water pump a little farther. Dogs must be on leash. You can make shorter loops by just doing the Lodgepole Loop (2.5 miles) or combining the Lodgepole Loop and Sunny Aspen Trail (2.9 miles). For more information, contact Jefferson County Open Space at (303) 271-5925 or www .co.jefferson.co.us/openspace.

## F  Sisters/Bearberry Loop–Alderfer/Three Sisters Park

Located up Buffalo Park Road out of downtown Evergreen, Alderfer/Three Sisters Park offers over 15 miles of hiking trails. Roughly two-thirds of the miles are located in the northern half, which features the Precambrian rock formations called "The Three Sisters" and "The Brother." A nice 3.7-mile moderate loop starts at the east parking lot and includes Sisters, Bearberry, Homestead, Silver Fox, and Ponderosa Trails. Then hike up the Brother's Lookout Trail to the top of "The Brother" for a great view of the surrounding area. Ponderosa Trail takes you back to your car. Various families owned the present parklands, raising cattle, horses, silver fox, and hay. A sawmill even operated on the property. A number of other loop hikes of various lengths and levels of difficulty can be created from the different trails. From downtown Evergreen, travel south on Jefferson CR 73. Turn west (right) on Buffalo Park Road, then drive approximately 1.4 miles to the east parking lot. A second parking lot is located another 0.5 mile along Buffalo Park Road. Dogs must be on leash. For more information, contact Jefferson County Open Space at (303) 271-5925 or www .co.jefferson.co.us/openspace.

## G  Gem Lake

At 8,830 feet, Gem Lake lives up to its name. Granitic boulders, ledges, and cliffs surround this small rain-fed jewel. The trail travels along south- and east-facing slopes, wandering in and out of a couple of narrow canyons between granitic outcroppings. Interesting rock formations inspire the imagination. Several sections of trail offer great views of Estes Park, Twin Sisters, Longs Peak, and the Continental Divide in Rocky Mountain National Park. Colorful wildflowers grace the trail from mid-June to early July. This 3.5-mile out-and-back moderate trail is a good early and late season hike in the Rocky Mountain National Park Wilderness Area. From the intersection of US 34 and US 36 in Estes Park, follow US 34 west (bypasses downtown), and drive 0.4 mile to MacGregor Avenue (Larimer County Road 43/Devil's Gulch Road).

Turn right onto LCR 43 and drive 1.3 miles, just past mile marker 1, to the Lumpy Ridge trailhead sign. Turn left on Lumpy Ridge Road and drive another 0.4 mile to the trailhead parking lot. GPS: N40 23.80'/W105 30.75'. Vault toilets, but no water, are available at the trailhead. Dogs are not permitted. Bring water. A backcountry permit and bear-proof food container are required for overnight camping. An outhouse is located just below Gem Lake. For more information, contact Rocky Mountain National Park at (970) 586-1206 or www.nps.gov/romo.

## H Roaring Creek Trail (Trail 952)

Roaring Creek Trail climbs steeply up a south-facing slope through sagebrush, juniper, Douglas fir, and huge ponderosa pine. Roaring Creek roars even when the water is low, and becomes quite thunderous when full with spring runoff. Views of Poudre Canyon are great as you hike up this steep slope. After the first mile, the trail levels and continues along the creek, which is lined with willows, through a lodgepole pine forest. Occasionally an interesting rock outcropping punctuates the scenery. Native greenback cutthroat trout live in the creek, and moose or elk are sometimes seen at the upper end. A beautiful little meadow with huge ponderosa pines makes a perfect lunch spot at the turnaround point. Enjoy this 9.4-mile out-and-back trail (rated difficult). To reach the trailhead from Fort Collins, drive north on US 287 to Ted's Place. Turn left onto CO 14 and drive west up Poudre Canyon about 40.5 miles. The trailhead is on the right, just before mile marker 82 and about 1.2 miles west of Big Bend Campground. There are no facilities at the trailhead. Dogs must be under voice control. For more information, contact the Canyon Lakes Ranger District at (970) 295-6700 or www.fs.usda.gov/arp.

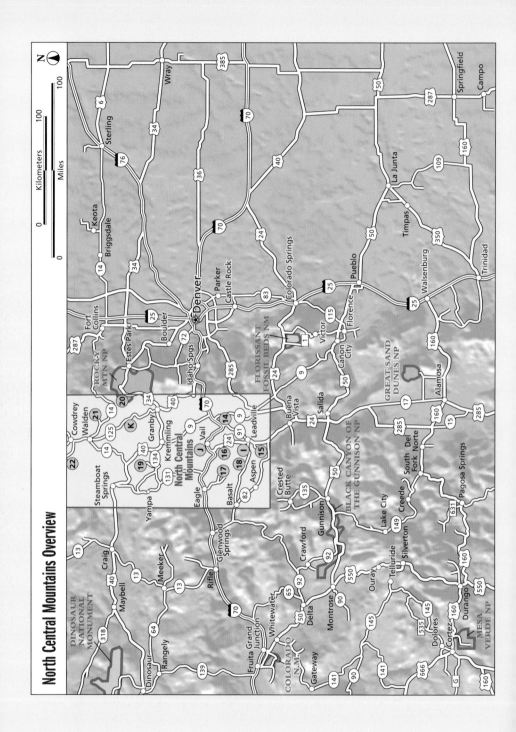

# North Central Mountains Overview

# North Central Mountains

N orth central Colorado is a land of sharp social and landscape contrasts. The northern half is still steeped in ranching, with one great ski area in the region, while the southern half contains numerous world-class ski (now year-round) resorts. All or parts of fourteen wilderness areas, plus trails throughout national forest lands, can keep you in new hiking terrain for many years. Fifteen of Colorado's fifty-four peaks over 14,000 feet are located in the area.

Ranching still provides the livelihood in most of the northern half of this region. From North Park—a huge valley between the Medicine Bow, Rabbit Ears, and Park mountain ranges—the North Platte River begins its journey to the Missouri River, then on to the Gulf of Mexico via the Mississippi. Bison once grazed here; now cattle and wildlife munch the tall grasses. Walden is the main town and the gateway to less-used areas of the Mount Zirkel Wilderness and Colorado State Forest State Park. North Park hides interesting treasures including sand dunes, Colorado's largest herd of moose, great hiking, and a yurt system. The Arapaho National Wildlife Refuge provides nesting habitat for waterfowl and other migratory birds. Moose were reintroduced to the area in the late 1970s. Elk, pronghorn, mule deer, and sage grouse also take advantage of the refuge's shrubland.

The Yampa River and its tributaries also support the ranching community, keeping the Old West spirit alive and well. Steamboat Springs keeps one foot on each side of the cultural divide—one with ranching, the other with tourists, a ski resort, and hot springs.

The western part of Rocky Mountain National Park, in the eastern part of this section, holds the headwaters of the Colorado River and offers wonderful wildlife viewing.

The southern half of the region contains the highest peaks in the state, along with much of the high-priced mountain real estate. The state's two highest peaks, Mount Elbert and Mount Massive, raise their lofty heads above Leadville, once home to rich mine owners such as Horace Tabor. It's hard to believe Mount Elbert (14,433 feet) is the tallest point of the state when its peak only rises 4,243 feet above the plains near

Leadville (10,190 feet). Mount Elbert's false summits drive hikers crazy, as does the rarefied air. Still, the view from the top is worth the effort! Colorado's high point lies in mining country that stretches from Aspen to the goldfields of Breckenridge. The incredible Hagerman Tunnel on the old Colorado Midland Railroad (an Honorable Mention hike) is only one of many engineering feats accomplished by men desperate for gold, silver, and promised fortunes.

Five hikes in this section are within the White River National Forest, 2.25 million acres of rugged mountains, beautiful streams, and lakes—a true hiker's paradise. It is consistently rated among the top five national forests in the United States for total recreation use. World-renowned ski resorts such as Aspen, Vail, Beaver Creek, Copper Mountain, Breckenridge, and Keystone are located in the White River National Forest, along with several smaller ski areas.

Scenic and historic byways for exploring the north central area include the Colorado River Headwaters, Flat Tops Trail, Cache La Poudre–North Park, Collegiate Peaks, West Elk Loop, and Top of the Rockies.

# 14 Wheeler Trail

This trail to the top of Wheeler Pass (unofficial name) is part of both the Wheeler National Recreational Trail and the Colorado Trail. It climbs steadily through spruce-fir and lodgepole forest on the western slope of the Tenmile Range. Views of the Gore Range, Copper Mountain, Breckenridge, French Gulch, and the Front Range are fabulous! Because this trail goes to a ridge above treeline, be sure to get an early start to avoid afternoon thunder and lightning storms.

**Start:** From the Wheeler Flats trailhead
**Distance:** 8.6 miles out and back (6.6 miles after trailhead moves)
**Approximate hiking time:** 5 to 6 hours
**Difficulty:** Most difficult due to elevation gain
**Elevation gain:** 2,730 feet
**Seasons:** Best from late June to mid-Oct
**Trail surface:** Dirt trail with some small creek crossings, rocks, and roots
**Land status:** National forest
**Nearest town:** Frisco
**Other trail users:** Equestrians, mountain bikers, and hunters (in season)

**Canine compatibility:** Dogs must be under control
**Schedule:** This trail crosses several avalanche chutes in the winter. It is neither maintained nor marked for winter use.
**Fees and permits:** None
**Maps:** USGS Breckenridge, Copper Mountain, and Vail Pass; Nat Geo Trails Illustrated 109 Breckenridge/Tennessee Pass and 108 Vail, Frisco, Dillon; Latitude 40° Summit County
**Trail contact:** White River National Forest, Dillon Ranger District, Silverthorne; (970) 468-5400; www.fs.usda.gov/whiteriver

**Finding the trailhead:** From Frisco head west on I-70 to exit 195 (for Copper Mountain and Leadville/CO 91). Exit and take CO 91 over I-70. The entrance to Copper Mountain Resort is on the right; turn left here onto an unnamed road, and drive past the gas station. It's 0.4 mile to the parking lot at Wheeler Flats trailhead. GPS: N39 30.55'/W106 08.50'. (The gas station has restrooms, food, and water.) **Note:** in 2011 or 2012, the trailhead will move 0.6 mile south of the entrance to Copper Mountain. It will be located in the parking lot on the left side of CO 91. Contact the Dillon Ranger District for status. Approximate GPS: N39 29.84'/W106 08.14'

## The Hike

Many summer moons ago, Ute Indians camped in this area and hunted bison, deer, elk, antelope, and mountain sheep in the surrounding high open areas. In 1879, Judge John Wheeler purchased 320 acres, now part of Copper Mountain Resort, and started a hay ranch. The next year silver miners arrived, and the ranch became a town known by various names: Wheeler's Ranch, Wheeler Station, Wheeler's, Wheeler, and Wheeler Junction. Wheeler prospered with a hotel, saloons, and a post office. Several sawmills provided lumber for the numerous mines along Tenmile Creek from Frisco to the top of Fremont Pass.

Despite its status as a mining town, tourists also came to Wheeler for the beautiful scenery and excellent fishing. In 1884, the Colorado & Southern Railroad finished laying tracks to Wheeler on the east side of Tenmile Creek. The railroad station at Wheeler was named Solitude Station. On the other side of the creek, the Denver & Rio Grande Railroad built a line with a station called Wheeler's. The Denver & Rio Grande serviced this area from 1880 to 1911. The Colorado & Southern ended its rail service around 1937.

▶ **In the first 1.5 miles of the Wheeler Trail, several little creeks fall steeply down gullies devoid of tall trees. These gullies are winter avalanche chutes. When seen from eastbound I-70 between Vail Pass and Copper Mountain, several chutes in this area (with the help of a little imagination) spell the word "SKY."**

The trail is mostly flat for the first mile, as it follows part of the old Colorado & Southern Railroad route, now covering a gas pipeline. In one place the trail seems lower than the creek! After 1 mile, you reach a junction with a post. Turn left, up the trail, to access Wheeler Pass. After the trailhead moves, you will cross a bridge to reach this post, eliminating 2 miles round-trip from your hike. Judge Wheeler used this trail to take his stock from Wheeler to his ranch in South Park. The trail now ends near Hoosier Pass, south of Breckenridge. It was designated a National Recreational Trail in 1979.

In about 3.4 miles, the trail exits the forest for a view of Climax Molybdenum Mine's settling ponds. Several prosperous mining towns, including Robinson and Kokomo of Wheeler's era, are buried under the ponds. Watch and listen for marmots. As the trail contours left into another drainage, you can see the ridge of the Tenmile Range and cairns marking the trail. From here the trail winds in and out of forest, meadow, and willows. Colorful wildflowers line the route. Trees become twisted krummholz near treeline, and finally give up. The trail is sometimes smothered by willows, but is passable. Three cairns built of good-size logs mark the way; the second one, however, is not on the trail, so stay alert. Finally, when your breath is short from elevation and the steep trail, the summit cairn comes into view.

That is, until you reach it and realize the trail continues farther up. Notice the vegetation along the trail. Willows and little red elephants grow in shallow depressions containing snow and water. The drier areas contain sedges and grasses, old-man-of-the-mountain, paintbrush, American bistort, chickweed, and alpine avens. The tundra is fragile. If you must go off trail, step on rocks as much as possible. When in a group, spread out.

The sign at the top of Wheeler Pass reports an elevation of 12,460 feet, but the topo map clearly indicates it's just under 12,400 feet. Be sure to hike to the little rocky knob on the left (12,408 feet) for the best easterly views. Breckenridge, French

◀ *Trail with pass in view*

*View from pass to east down Sawmill Gulch*

Gulch, and part of the Breckenridge ski area are on the east side; Copper Mountain and the Gore Range are to the northwest.

Founded in 1859 by General George E. Spencer, Breckenridge was named after U.S. vice president John Cabell Breckinridge to ensure the new town would receive a post office. During the Civil War, John Breckinridge joined the Confederate Army. Upset Breckinridge residents changed the "i" to "e," spelling the name "Breckenridge." Other stories indicate the town was named after Thomas E. Breckenridge, a member of the original mining party. At one time, men panning gold in the Blue River and French Gulch could earn as much as $12 to $20 a day each! Dredge boats came later to scoop up more gold, and mines were burrowed into the hills. The largest gold nugget ever found in Colorado came from this area. At thirteen pounds, it was called "Tom's Baby" (after Tom Groves, its finder; see "The Mystery of Tom's Baby" sidebar for more information).

Today both Breckenridge and Copper Mountain are known for their popular ski areas. Ski lifts at each area can be seen from various points along the trail. Skiing, other forms of outdoor recreation, and vacation homes have replaced mining in a new "gold rush" to the Rockies.

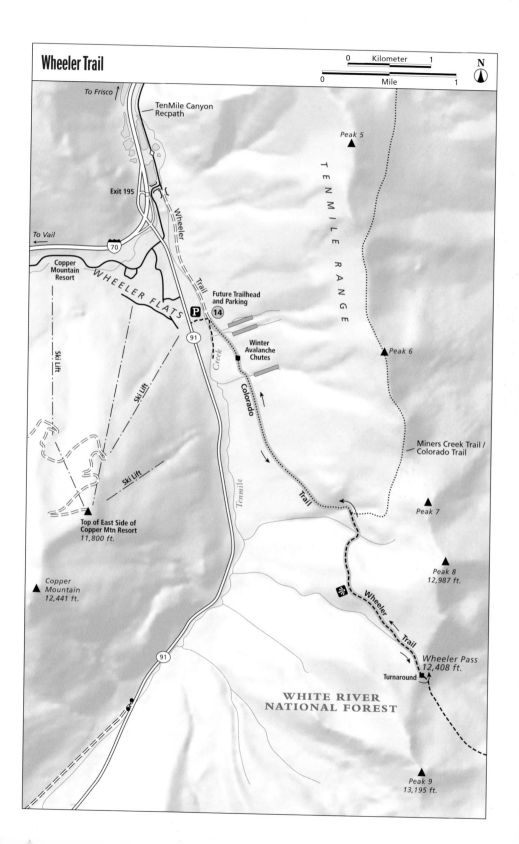

# Wheeler Trail

0       Kilometer      1

0          Mile        1

**N**

To Frisco

TenMile Canyon
Recpath

Peak 5

Exit 195

Wheeler

**70**

To Vail

Copper
Mountain
Resort

WHEELER FLATS

Trail

Future Trailhead
and Parking

**14**

**91**

Creek

Winter
Avalanche
Chutes

Peak 6

T E N M I L E   R A N G E

Colorado

Ski Lift

Ski Lift

Tenmile

Ski Lift

Trail

Miners Creek Trail /
Colorado Trail

Peak 7

Top of East Side of
Copper Mtn Resort
11,800 ft.

Copper
Mountain
12,441 ft.

Peak 8
12,987 ft.

Wheeler

**91**

Trail

Wheeler Pass
12,408 ft.

Turnaround

WHITE RIVER
NATIONAL FOREST

Peak 9
13,195 ft.

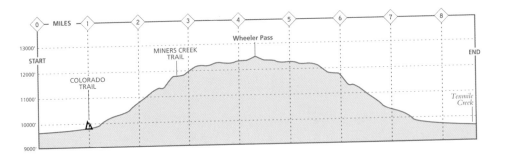

## Miles and Directions

**0.0** Start in the parking lot. Elevation: 9,680 feet. Cross the wooden bridge over West Tenmile Creek, turn right down the paved bike path, and in less than 0.1 mile come to a second bridge over Tenmile Creek. Veer right and walk across the gravel-topped bridge.

**1.0** Reach a junction with the Colorado Trail and turn left, heading uphill on the Colorado Trail, marked with a post. GPS: N39 29.83'/W106 08.08' **(FYI:** One trail [along the gas pipeline] goes straight along the creek and the other, the Colorado Trail, goes right to CO 91.) After the trailhead moves, you'll start the hike just west of here so subtract 1 mile from the one-way total; 2 miles from round-trip.

**2.8** Reach the trail junction with Miners Creek Trail. GPS: N39 28.63'/W106 06.93'. Go right on Wheeler Trail.

**4.3** Arrive at the top of Wheeler Pass. Elevation: 12,408 feet. GPS: N39 27.67'/W106 06.32'. Return the way you came.

**8.6** Arrive back at the trailhead.

## Hike Information

### General Information

**Breckenridge Resort Chamber:** Breckenridge; (970) 453-2918 or (888) 251-2417; www .gobreck.com

**Copper Chamber:** Copper Mountain; (970) 968-2318 ext. 40900; www.copperchamber.com

**Frisco Chamber of Commerce:** 416 Main St., Frisco; (800) 424-1554 or (970) 668-3050; www.friscocolochamber.com

### Local Events/Attractions

**Colorado Barbecue Challenge:** Frisco; (970) 668-5276; www.townoffrisco.com

**Country Boy Mine:** 0542 French Gulch Rd., Breckenridge; (970) 453-4405; www.countryboy mine.com

### Accommodations

**National Forest campgrounds:** Dillon Ranger District, Silverthorne; (970) 468-5400; www.fs .usda.gov/whiteriver or www.dillonrangerdistrict.com

## Restaurants

**Alpinista Mountain Bistro:** 172 Copper Circle, Copper Mountain; (970) 968-1144; www.alpinistabistro.com

**The Boatyard Pizzeria & Grill:** 304 Main St., Frisco; (970) 668-4728; www.boatyardgrillandpizza.com

**Downstairs at Eric's:** 111 South Main St., Breckenridge; (970) 453-1401; www.downstairsaterics.com

## Clubs and Organizations

**Friends of the Dillon Ranger District:** (970) 262-3449; www.fdrd.org

# THE MYSTERY OF TOM'S BABY

Tom Groves and Harry Lytton mined the area near Breckenridge known as Farncomb Hill. On July 23, 1887, Tom knocked down a clump of dirt and went to toss it in a dirt pile. The clump seemed heavier than usual, so he opened it with his shovel. Inside was a huge hunk of gold, or more precisely, crystallized gold. The two men ran down to Breckenridge, with Tom cradling the nugget as if it were a baby. Thus the name "Tom's Baby." The little darling weighed in at 160 ounces, which at twelve troy ounces per pound, put it at 13.3 pounds. After washing it off, it still weighed a respectable 136 ounces. From here a mystery developed—the nugget disappeared. What happened to Tom's Baby?

In 1973 Reverend Mark Fiester finished writing a book, *Blasted Beloved Breckenridge*. He had spent many hours researching the whereabouts of Tom's Baby. Since the nugget was supposedly Colorado's largest, it would have brought more money from being displayed than being melted. On July 5, 1965, the *Denver Post* revealed that a phony "Tom's Baby" had been created. Without clues to the whereabouts of the real one, Rev. Fiester suspected it had become part of John Campion's gold collection. Campion was associated with Tom Groves and the mine's owners. Finally, after the book's publication, the Denver Museum of Nature and Science, which had no record of Tom's Baby, found a box from Campion's gold collection in their vault. The box contained a large collection of crystallized gold, including a big hunk. Tom's Baby had been found!

And you'll find it on display in the Coors Mineral Hall of the Denver Museum of Nature and Science.

# 15 North Mount Elbert Trail

Mount Elbert is the highest point in Colorado and second highest in the Lower 48. The North Mount Elbert Trail climbs steeply through lodgepole, then spruce-fir forest and across alpine tundra. The worst parts of hiking Mount Elbert are its false summits and wind. The best parts include tremendous views and a feeling of great accomplishment. It's imperative to leave no later than 6:30 a.m. to avoid thunderstorms and lightning. Allow at least four to six hours for the hike to the top. Bring plenty of water and energy food.

**Start:** From the Mount Elbert trailhead near Elbert Creek Campground

**Distance:** 9.8 miles out and back

**Approximate hiking time:** 7 to 11 hours

**Difficulty:** Strenuous because of steepness and elevation

**Elevation gain:** 4,473 feet (including undulations)

**Season:** Best from July through Sept

**Trail surface:** Dirt trail; mostly steep, rocky in a few areas

**Land status:** National forest

**Nearest town:** Leadville

**Other trail users:** Equestrians, mountain bikers, and hunters (in season) on the Colorado Trail section only

**Canine compatibility:** Dogs must be under control: preferably on leash to avoid conflicts with other hikers and/or their dogs (very high volume of people/dogs on the trail)

**Schedule:** Year-round. The access road is closed by snow in winter about 4.8 miles from the trailhead. The road is still open to snowmobiles, skiing, and snowshoeing. The trail is neither marked nor maintained for winter use. Winds can blow over 100 mph above treeline.

**Fees and permits:** Groups of 10 or more people must get a permit from the Forest Service in Leadville

**Maps:** USGS Mount Elbert and Mount Massive; USFS San Isabel National Forest map; Nat Geo Trails Illustrated 127 Aspen/Independence Pass; Latitude 40° Summit County

**Trail contact:** San Isabel National Forest, Leadville Ranger District, Leadville; (719) 486-0749; www.fs.usda.gov/psicc

**Other:** Some dispersed camping is available along FR 110, the road to the trailhead. Please camp at least 100 feet away from roads and streams to help with restoration efforts. Halfmoon and Elbert Creek Campgrounds are also nearby.

**Special considerations:** FR 110/CR 11, the dirt road to the trailhead, is less than two cars wide, so be watchful for oncoming cars, especially around curves. It's passable by most vehicles, the worst problems being a few potholes and washboard sections.

**Finding the trailhead:** From Leadville, drive south on US 24 (Harrison Avenue in Leadville) for about 4 miles. Turn right onto CO 300 West, a well-marked road at mile marker 180. In 0.7 mile, turn left onto Lake County Road (LCR) 11 (Halfmoon Road), again well-signed. In another 1.3 miles, stay on LCR 11, which turns right and becomes dirt. In 2.2 miles this road becomes FR 110. Continue on for about 3 miles to the Mount Elbert trailhead parking lot on the left. The trailhead is 0.1 mile off of FR 110. There is a vault toilet but no water at the trailhead. Make sure to bring a lot of water with you as none is available along the trail. GPS: N39 09.10'/W106 24.72'

*Mt. Elbert from just below treeline*

## The Hike

When first seeing Mount Elbert from afar, you might wonder about its "highest in Colorado" status. Looming above the Arkansas Valley, which already lies at 10,000 feet, the elevation gain does not seem dramatic. North of Mount Elbert across Halfmoon Creek, the aptly named Mount Massive (14,421 feet) stands a mere 12 feet lower. Mount Elbert's long, smooth ridges make it a good first fourteener (peak over 14,000 feet in elevation) to climb. The magnificent views are reason enough to return.

French Mountain, Casco Peak, and Frasco form the foreground for summits to the west. Five of Colorado's fourteeners pierce the western sky: Capitol Peak (14,130 feet) with its distinctive knife-edge ridge, white-faced Snowmass Mountain (14,092 feet), the Maroon Bells with Maroon Peak (14,156 feet) and North Maroon Peak (14,014 feet), and Pyramid Peak (14,018 feet). To the south lies La Plata Peak (14,336 feet) in the Sawatch Range. To the north, Mount Massive, Mount of the Holy Cross (14,005 feet), and Notch Mountain (13,237 feet) dominate, with the Gore Range in the distance. The mighty Mosquito Range, which made Leadville a mining center, rises to the east. You can see all the way to Pikes Peak (14,110 feet) and the Sangre de Cristo Range. Down below lie the South Halfmoon and Arkansas Valleys and Twin Lakes.

When the current Rockies arose from the earth about 65 million years ago, mineral-rich liquid oozed into faults and cracks in the stressed rock. As the liquid

*View of Elk Mountains from summit*

cooled, rich ores formed. The Leadville area, located at the north end of the Arkansas Valley, has produced more than $500 million in silver, lead, zinc, gold, and other minerals. The Arkansas Valley is actually part of the Rio Grande Rift, a slice of land that stayed in place when the rest of Colorado rose about 5,000 feet, between 28 million and 5 million years ago. Glaciers later formed the cirque on Elbert's east side, while glacial moraines dammed Lake Creek, creating Twin Lakes. Mount Elbert itself is formed of 1.7-billion-year-old gneiss and schist.

Mount Elbert stood guardian as Leadville boomed first with gold, then with silver. In 1860, Abe Lee hit the first major gold strike. In 1874, as the gold dwindled, miners extracted silver-rich lead carbonate. The silver rush started, turning Leadville and surroundings into a large city, second to Denver. Enjoying prosperity, Leadville built a magnificent ice palace during the winter of 1896. It covered over three acres, with two 90-foot Norman towers. Inside, lighted dining rooms and an ice rink provided hours of entertainment. Ice sculptures of miners and prospectors decorated the palace.

The Hayden Survey of 1874 recorded the first ascent of Mount Elbert. The peak was named after Samuel Hitt Elbert, who first held the position of territorial secretary until the governor seized the state seal from him. Elbert resigned and left Colorado in 1866, only to return in 1873 as territorial governor. He held this post for one year before being appointed to the Colorado Supreme Court. Elbert was instrumental in formulating visionary conservation and irrigation concepts.

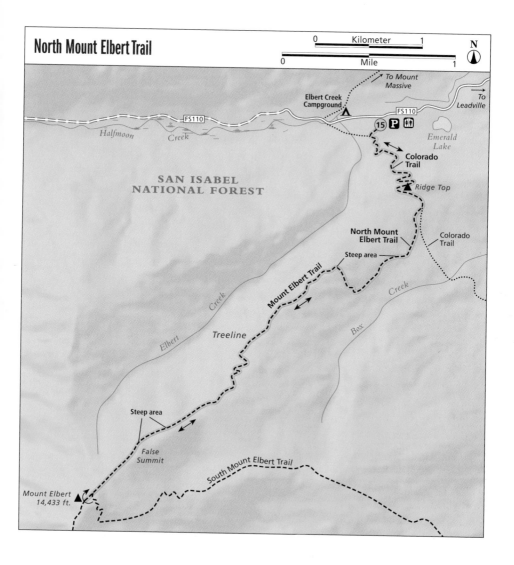

**North Mount Elbert Trail**

0     Kilometer     1

0     Mile     1

N

To Mount
Massive

Elbert Creek
Campground

FS110

To
Leadville

15 P

Emerald
Lake

Halfmoon    Creek

FS110

Colorado
Trail

SAN ISABEL
NATIONAL FOREST

Ridge Top

North Mount
Elbert Trail

Colorado
Trail

Steep area

Mount Elbert Trail

Creek

Box

Creek

Treeline

Elbert

Steep area

False
Summit

South Mount Elbert Trail

Mount Elbert
14,433 ft.

Hiking Mount Elbert is invariably an adventure. Snow falls at any time of year and the temperature seldom exceeds 50°F. The wind always seems to blow. Plan ahead and be prepared for adverse conditions. Weekends find the trail filled with people. Yet there is nothing like standing at the top of Colorado, beholding an endless horizon of mountains.

The first section follows part of the Colorado Trail, which traverses almost 500 miles of the state. About 1.2 miles into the hike you come to a juncture. Turn right onto the North Mount Elbert Trail. In the next trail section small groups of skinny lodgepole pines stand right in the middle of the trail, reminiscent of pictures with ski tracks each going on opposite sides of a tree. From here, the trail climbs steeply to a ridge. The Forest Service rerouted this section in 1992, a great improvement over the old trail. Along the ridge, a glimpse of the top comes to view. But it's really a false summit at about 13,880 feet—the real summit rises 550 feet higher.

Once above treeline, around 11,900 feet, the trail climbs through beautiful alpine tundra. The tiny plants are extremely fragile, so please stay on the trail. Yellow alpine avens, old-man-of-the-mountain with its large sunflower head, various paintbrushes, and blue–purple sky pilot brighten the surroundings. If stopping for a break on the tundra, watch out for marmots that might try to swipe your snack.

The trail is steepest along the right side of the false summit. Loose rocks and some big rock steps make this section challenging. After this part, the trail becomes gentler. The summit lies beyond the next rock hump. The last 0.1 mile crosses a somewhat skinny ridge where the wind can blast with fury. Finally the summit appears, complete with short rock walls to shelter hikers from the winds. Remember to sign the peak register. Enjoy the view and the top of Colorado!

▶ **The Colorado Fourteeners Initiative (CFI) started in 1994 when people realized the damage being caused by the alarming popularity of climbing Colorado's fourteeners. An estimated 200,000 people climbed fourteeners annually by 2002, a 300 percent increase in ten years. By 2010 that number had risen to 500,000 hikers annually. CFI forms partnerships with land agencies, hiking groups, and companies to protect and preserve both natural and recreational resources.**

## Miles and Directions

**0.0** Start at Mount Elbert trailhead near Elbert Creek Campground. Elevation: 10,040 feet.

**0.1** Reach the junction with the Colorado Trail. Turn left onto the Colorado Trail.

**0.9** Reach the top of a little ridge and descend slightly.

**1.2** Reach the junction of the Colorado Trail and the North Mount Elbert Trail. GPS: N39 08.65' / W106 24.45'. Turn right to climb Mount Elbert.

**2.2** Reach the northeast ridge.

**2.9** Reach the treeline.

**4.4** Arrive at a false summit. GPS: N39 07.34' / W106 26.34'. Now there are two smaller false summits to go.

**4.8** Reach the junction with the South Mount Elbert Trail, which comes in from the left. Continue straight ahead along the ridge.

**4.9** You're on top! Elevation: 14,433 feet. GPS: N39 07.06' / W106 26.69'. Return the way you came.

**9.8** Arrive back at the trailhead.

## Hike Information

### General Information
**Leadville/Lake County Chamber of Commerce:** Leadville; (888) 532-3845 or (719) 486-3900; www.leadvilleusa.com

### Local Events/Attractions
**Leadville, Colorado and Southern Railroad Company:** Leadville; (719) 486-3936; www.leadville-train.com

**Matchless Mine (Baby Doe Tabor Museum):** Leadville; (719) 486-3900

**National Mining Hall of Fame & Museum:** Leadville; (719) 486-1229

# TIPS FOR CLIMBING 14,000-FOOT PEAKS IN COLORADO

The first and foremost rule is to leave early enough to reach the summit and return to treeline before thunderstorms and lightning start. Thunderstorms can build quickly as the day warms. A good rule of thumb is to summit by 11 a.m. and head back by noon. If the weather looks iffy at any time, turn back. The peak will be there another day. Know your party's abilities and plan accordingly. One mile per hour or less is not an unreasonable estimate, given altitude and steep terrain.

Hiking fourteeners takes energy. In the cool, dry air, your body loses moisture from breathing and sweating. Drink a few mouthfuls of water every fifteen minutes or so to keep your body hydrated. Eating small amounts of food while drinking will keep your body fueled. A hydrated body also helps ward off altitude sickness, indicated by headache, nausea, and/or dizziness. Moving to a lower altitude cures the problem.

Bring layers of synthetic or wool clothing (no cotton) for wind, cold, and wet. Bring a winter hat—as much as 50 percent of your body heat can be lost through the top of your head. Pack a pair of gloves, too. Wear appropriate boots for the terrain. Snow and hail are common, and the winds usually blow above treeline. Cherish any summit with sun and no wind!

Carry topo maps and a compass or GPS unit, and know how to use them. Every year hikers need to be rescued because they lose their way coming down the mountain.

Tread lightly in high elevations. Fragile plants are critical to the land. Do not litter—a piece of trash covering a plant can kill it in a few weeks! Check the Colorado Fourteeners Initiative website for additional guidelines when traveling in the "land above the trees." Your actions, compounded by those of thousands of other visitors, determine the health of our natural environment.

## Accommodations

**The Delaware Hotel:** Leadville; (719) 486-1418 or (800) 748-2004; www.delawarehotel.com
**Leadville Hostel & Inn:** Leadville; (719) 486-9334; www.leadvillehostel.com
**National Forest campgrounds:** San Isabel National Forest, Leadville Ranger District, Leadville; (719) 486-0749; www.fs.usda.gov/psicc

## Restaurants

**The Grill Bar & Cafe:** 715 Elm St., Leadville; (719) 486-9930; www.grillbarcafe.com
**Quincy's Steaks & Spirits:** 416 Harrison Ave., Leadville; (719) 486-9765
**The Tennessee Pass Cafe:** 222 Harrison Ave., Leadville; (719) 486-8101; www.thetennessee passcafe.com

## Clubs and Organizations

**Colorado Fourteeners Initiative:** Golden; (303) 278-7650; www.coloradofourteeners.org
**Colorado Trail Foundation:** Golden; (303) 384-3729; www.coloradotrail.org

*Twin Lakes from Mount Elbert*

# 16 Notch Mountain

This hike takes you to the historic stone shelter on Notch Mountain for a fantastic view of Mount of the Holy Cross. The trail starts gently, passing through spruce-fir forest with occasional glimpses of the notch in Notch Mountain. Eventually the trail climbs to treeline, then through tundra and boulder fields via switchbacks. Watch for pikas, white-tailed ptarmigans, marmots, and beautiful alpine wildflowers. The switchbacks make the hike easier than most trails up 13,000-foot peaks. Remember to leave early to reach the summit by 11 a.m. so you can head back by noon and avoid thunderstorms.

**Start:** From the Fall Creek Trail trailhead

**Distance:** 10.8 miles out and back

**Approximate hiking time:** 5 to 7 hours

**Difficulty:** Most difficult due to length and elevation gain

**Elevation gain:** 2,763 feet, plus about 120 feet in undulations

**Seasons:** Best from late June to mid-Oct

**Trail surface:** Dirt trail, very rocky in spots

**Land status:** National forest and wilderness area

**Nearest towns:** Minturn and Vail

**Other trail users:** Equestrians (Fall Creek Trail section) and hunters (in season)

**Canine compatibility:** Dogs must be on leash

**Schedule:** The access road is closed by snow about 7.5 miles from the trailhead. Check the website or call for closure dates, which can run to June 20. The road is used by snowmobilers and cross-country skiers. The trail is neither maintained nor marked for winter use.

**Fees and permits:** No fees required. A free self-issued Wilderness Use Permit is required year-round for all users. One person in each group must carry a permit. Call the Holy Cross Ranger District for details. Group size limit: No more than 15 people per group with a maximum combination of 25 people and pack or saddle animals in any one group.

**Maps:** USGS Mount of the Holy Cross and Minturn; Nat Geo Trails Illustrated 126 Holy Cross/Ruedi Reservoir; Latitude 40° Vail & Eagle

**Trail contact:** White River National Forest, Holy Cross Ranger District, Minturn; (970) 827-5715; www.fs.usda.gov/whiteriver

**Other:** The dirt access road may be bumpy with rocks and potholes. Most passenger cars can make the trip with care. The road is narrow, so be careful when rounding curves. The parking lot gets crowded early as the trailhead for Mount of the Holy Cross is also here. Half Moon Campground near the trailhead has seven campsites.

**Special considerations:** Vault toilet at trailhead, but no water. Bring plenty of water with you.

**Finding the trailhead:** From Minturn, drive south on US 24 toward Leadville for about 3 miles (5 miles from the junction of I-70 and US 24). Just past mile marker 148, turn right onto Tigiwon Road (FR 707), which provides national forest access. Drive 8.1 miles up this dirt road to the trailhead. GPS: N39 30.02'/W106 25.94'

*Historic shelter and Mt. of the Holy Cross*

## The Hike

In the 1800s various stories about a mountain with a "snowy cross" circulated around Colorado. In 1869, William H. Brewer reported seeing Mount of the Holy Cross (14,005 feet) from the summit of Grays Peak (14,269 feet). As part of the Hayden Survey in the 1870s, William Henry Jackson photographed various areas of Colorado. The Hayden Survey was one of four great surveys of the West sponsored by the U.S. government between 1867 and 1878. From 1873 to 1875, leader Ferdinand V. Hayden concentrated on Colorado.

The 1873 survey set a goal to find this mysterious peak. Jackson climbed Grays Peak and also spotted the cross from the summit. By August the survey group arrived near present day Minturn. For three days they attempted in vain to find a route on Notch Mountain (13,237 feet) from which to view and photograph the "cross." Fallen trees and thick willows made the going too rough for pack animals, and the group ended up carrying Jackson's one-hundred pounds of photographic gear on

## BENEFITS OF LEASHING YOUR DOG

Keeping dogs leashed on the trail benefits you, your pet, other visitors, and wildlife. Dogs will surely come out the losers in a bout with the porcupines and mountain lions that live in these areas. Bears have also been known to chase dogs back to their owners. Freely roaming dogs can cause serious damage to delicate ecosystems. A leashed dog can also help you become more aware of wildlife, as dogs can easily detect smells and movement that would go unnoticed by humans.

foot. Jackson used a wet glass plate camera. Not only was the "film" made of glass, which had to be handled carefully, but also it needed to be developed soon after exposure. Jackson carried a portable darkroom tent and all necessary chemicals and supplies with him. Finally finding an approach, the still-difficult hike took two days, with little food and no shelter. (The surveyors thought they could do it in one day.) Finally atop Notch Mountain, fog decreased visibility to a few feet. Luckily, the fog broke briefly, giving Jackson a glimpse of the infamous cross across the valley. The next morning dawned clear and still, giving him a beautiful shot of the cross. He took several pictures, which caused a sensation across the country as people believed the snow-filled cross to be a sign from God.

The devout began to make annual pilgrimages to Mount of the Holy Cross in 1927. The USDA Forest Service issued a special use permit in 1928 to the Mount of the Holy Cross Pilgrimage Association, allowing the construction and maintenance of community houses and a semipublic campground. President Herbert Hoover proclaimed 1,392 acres around Mount of the Holy Cross as a national monument in 1929. Survey crews laid out an automobile route from US 24 to Tigiwon, and with help from citizens, the Eagle County government, and F. G. Bonfils, a road was completed to Tigiwon in 1932.

The Civilian Conservation Corps (CCC) improved the road in 1933, extending it to the present trailhead. The CCC also constructed the Notch Mountain Trail, the large community house at Tigiwon, and the stone shelter on Notch Mountain. The present Notch Mountain Trail, with its many switchbacks, stands as testimony to the excellent work done by the CCC. This trail was originally used by packhorses as well as hikers. Pilgrimages ceased in the early 1940s, presumably because of World War II. The U.S. Army actually controlled much of this area between 1938 and 1950. Nearby Camp Hale was a training ground for the famous 10th Mountain Division troops.

The cross is created by a 1,500-foot vertical gully and a 750-foot horizontal rock bench on the mountain's eastern face. Collected snow causes the formation to stand out against the mountainside. The right arm deteriorated due to rockslides, and access remained difficult even after the CCC's work. In 1950 President Harry Truman retracted national monument status and returned the land to the Forest Service.

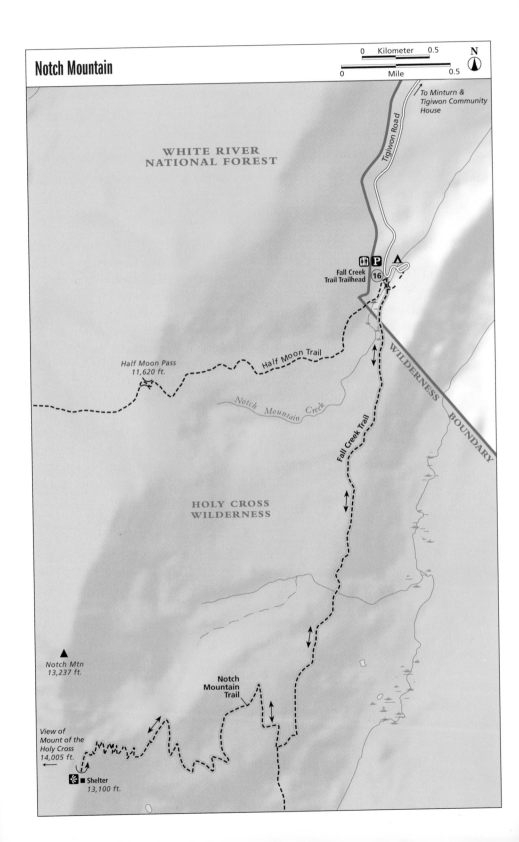

# Notch Mountain

0 Kilometer 0.5
0 Mile 0.5

N

WHITE RIVER
NATIONAL FOREST

*Tigiwon Road*

To Minturn &
Tigiwon Community
House

Fall Creek
Trail Trailhead

16

WILDERNESS BOUNDARY

*Half Moon Pass*
*11,620 ft.*

Half Moon Trail

*Notch Mountain Creek*

Fall Creek Trail

HOLY CROSS
WILDERNESS

▲
*Notch Mtn*
*13,237 ft.*

**Notch
Mountain
Trail**

View of
Mount of the
Holy Cross
14,005 ft.

■ Shelter
*13,100 ft.*

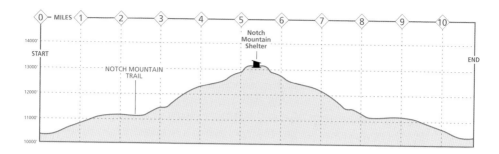

Even slightly damaged, a cross of snow still forms today. The Tigiwon Community House, after years of disrepair, has been mostly restored and is occasionally used for weddings. The Forest Service maintains the historic Notch Mountain stone shelter and its lightning rods to provide protection for hikers in case a thunderstorm moves in. Overnight camping is not allowed in the shelter.

Make sure to start on the Fall Creek Trail, not the Half Moon Trail. Just beyond the trailhead and creek crossing, take the right trail and head south, entering the Holy Cross Wilderness. The first mile is fairly gentle, but rocky. The trail then climbs, with occasional small elevation drops. The terrain drops steeply to the left, to Fall Creek below. After 2.4 miles the trail widens, with a scattering of boulders providing a perfect spot for a break before turning right up the Notch Mountain Trail.

From the rest spot, it's another 3 miles to the shelter and viewpoint. After a few switchbacks, the trail begins to pass through treeline and zigzags across the slope to the summit. More than twenty-seven switchbacks help you ascend the last 780 feet. Avoid the temptation to shortcut the switchbacks, as they keep the trail at a reasonable grade (which makes for easier hiking in the thinning air) and protect the terrain. Marmots and pikas zip around this area with amusing antics. Watch for white-tailed ptarmigan moms followed by a line of little chicks.

Once you reach the ridge and stone shelter, Mount of the Holy Cross looms large directly ahead. The alpine wildflowers grow thick and beautiful in July and early August. White arctic gentians signal summer's end. Please walk carefully on the fragile tundra, using rocks for steps as much as possible. And if you must, camp below treeline.

## Miles and Directions

**0.0**   Start at the Fall Creek Trail trailhead (versus the Half Moon Trail trailhead). Elevation: 10,314 feet. Cross a creek on a bridge and take the right fork in the trail (head south).

**1.4**   The trail traverses a landslide area.

**1.6**   Cross a wide creek on boulders. **(Note:** The crossing may be easier or harder depending on water volume. Be careful.)

**2.4**   Reach the trail intersection with Notch Mountain and Fall Creek Trails. GPS: N39 28.26' / W106 26.52'. This is a good place for a break. Turn right onto Notch Mountain Trail.

**3.5** Start to enter the land above the trees. **(Note:** Turn back if thunderstorms are imminent.)

**4.2** Switchbacks increase in number up to the ridge. Depending on where you start counting, you'll zigzag up more than twenty switchbacks in 780 feet. **(FYI:** Please do not shortcut the switchbacks. Shortcutting causes environmental damage and erosion that does not heal quickly at this elevation. Also, don't attempt this trail during whiteouts or low visibility. If you miss any of four particular switchbacks, you'll be freefalling over a cliff.)

**5.4** Reach the stone shelter on Notch Mountain, with a breathtaking view of Mount of the Holy Cross. Elevation: 13,077 feet. GPS: N39 28.17' / W106 27.52'. **(Note:** The shelter is meant for protection from lightning. Overnight camping is prohibited.) Return the way you came.

**10.8** Arrive back at the trailhead.

# WILDLIFE WATCHING ON NOTCH MOUNTAIN

Notch Mountain is a good area to see alpine animals and birds, particularly marmots, pikas, and white-tailed ptarmigan.

In summer, ptarmigan blend in perfectly with the mottled rocks, making them hard to see. Members of the grouse family, the males live in the alpine tundra all year. Ptarmigan blend in to the landscape so well, it's possible to almost step on one before noticing it's there.

Ptarmigan mate for life, although after breeding the couple goes their separate ways until the next spring. In summer tiny chicks line up to follow around after mom. When threatened, the mother will fake a broken wing to draw predators away from her offspring.

In winter ptarmigan plumage turns white, with feet and legs heavily feathered for warmth and flotation on the snow. Willows, which produce next year's buds in the fall, provide food for ptarmigan during long, cold winters. The birds might dive into a snowdrift, especially around willows, to stay warm on cold nights—a ptarmigan version of an igloo. Look for piles of ptarmigan droppings near willows while hiking.

The pika lives in rock piles in the alpine and subalpine zones year-round. The pika alert reverberates through the rocks. Active during winter as well as summer, the pika eats hay piles it busily collects during the summer. The small, mouselike creature with the short tail belongs to the rabbit order. Look closely or you might miss the busy critter as it scurries among the rocks. A mouthful of grass and flowers whizzes by as the pika stores its hay. Researchers have discovered that pikas will steal each other's piles. Watch for big white splotches on boulders along the trail. The splotches indicate pika restrooms. Bright orange lichen often grows near the splotches, energized by the nitrogen-rich fertilizer.

# Hike Information

## General Information
**Vail Valley Partnership (The Chamber and Tourism Bureau):** Avon; (970) 476-1000; www.visit vailvalley.com

## Local Events/Attractions
**Bravo! Vail Valley Music Festival:** Vail; (970) 827-5700; www.vailmusicfestival.org
**Camp Hale:** WWII training ground of the 10th Mountain Division); between Leadville and Minturn; (970) 527-8715; www.camphale.org
**Top of the Rockies Scenic and Historic Byway:** Leadville; (719) 486-3900 or (800) 933-3901; www.topoftherockiesbyway.org

## Accommodations
**National Forest campgrounds:** Holy Cross Ranger District, Minturn; (970) 827-5715; www.fs .usda.gov/whiteriver

## Restaurants
**Kirby Cosmo's BBQ Bar:** 474 Main St., Minturn; (970) 827-9027
**The Minturn Saloon:** 146 North Main St., Minturn; (970) 827-5954; www.minturnsaloon.com
**Paddy's Sports Bar and Grill:** 40801 Highway 6, Eagle-Vail; (970) 949-6093; www.paddysvail.com

## Clubs and Organizations
**Colorado Mountain Club–Gore Range Group:** www.cmc.org

## Hike Tours
**Paragon Guides:** Vail; (970) 926-5229 or (877) 926-5299; www.paragonguides.com
**Trailwise Guides:** Vail; (970) 827-5363 or (800) 261-5364; www.trailwiseguides.com

# 17 Mount Thomas Trail

The Mount Thomas summit, a bump on Red Table Mountain, offers spectacular 360-degree views of the central Colorado Rockies! Overwhelming views stretch from the Maroon Bells and Elk Mountains in the southwest, circling northwest to the Flat Tops, then I-70 north of Eagle. The Gore Range rises in the northeast, with the Sawatch Mountains towering in the east and southeast. Cattle still graze on some of the grassy southern slopes. Beautiful alpine wildflowers decorate the upper ridges. The trail traverses an open ridge for about 1.6 miles, so be sure to make the summit and be heading down before thunderstorms hit.

**Start:** 0.5 mile from the top of Crooked Creek Pass at the junction with FR 431

**Distance:** 9.2 miles out and back

**Approximate hiking time:** 4 to 7 hours

**Difficulty:** Difficult due to elevation gain and distance

**Elevation gain/loss:** 1,197-foot gain/370-foot loss

**Seasons:** Best from late June to mid-Oct

**Trail surface:** Dirt road and dirt trail with some steep sections and a boulder field

**Land status:** National forest, proposed wilderness area

**Nearest town:** Eagle

**Other trail users:** Equestrians, hunters (in season)

**Canine compatibility:** Dogs must be under control

**Schedule:** The access road is closed by snow just past Sylvan Lake State Park, 5.5 miles from the trailhead. The road is used by snowmobilers and cross-country skiers. The trail is neither maintained nor marked for winter use.

**Fees and permits:** None

**Maps:** USGS Crooked Creek Pass; Nat Geo Trails Illustrated 126 Holy Cross/Ruedi Reservoir; Latitude 40° Vail & Eagle

**Trail contact:** White River National Forest, Eagle Ranger District, Eagle; (970) 328-6388. White River National Forest, Sopris Ranger District, Aspen; (970) 963-2266; www.fs.usda .gov/whiteriver

**Special considerations:** No facilities or water available.

**Finding the trailhead:** From I-70 (exit 147) in Eagle, head south about 0.3 mile to US 6 and turn right in the traffic circle. Drive 1 mile, following the Sylvan Lake signs to a second traffic circle just past mile marker 149. You basically turn left via the traffic circle onto Sylvan Lakes Road. Continue 1.7 miles and turn right onto Brush Creek Road (Eagle CR 307). Drive about 8.8 miles to the fork in the road. Take the right branch, West Brush Creek (smooth dirt road), again to Sylvan Lake. Drive another 10 miles to the top of Crooked Creek Pass. The dirt road narrows and becomes FR 400 past Sylvan Lake State Park. You can park in the dirt area to the right at the top of the pass (add 1 mile round-trip to the hike mileage). Or, at the top of the pass, turn right onto an unmarked dirt road and drive 0.5 mile to the junction with FR 431. GPS: N39 26.34'/W106 41.10'. Park on the flat grassy area at the junction. With a 4WD, you can drive 0.2 mile from the junction with FR 431 to the actual trailhead, and park under the power lines.

*Summit cairn on Mt. Thomas*

## The Hike

Mount Thomas (11,977 feet) was named after the head of the St. Louis & Colorado Smelting Company. Thomas (the rest of his name apparently lost to history) started a smelter along the Colorado Midland Railroad in the Fryingpan Valley around 1890. The town that grew nearby, Thomasville, also bears his name. He became involved in some mining ventures north of town in the Lime Creek drainage. He did not have much luck—the mines produced little ore and his unprofitable smelter closed in 1892. A little peak on the ridge between Lime and Brush Creeks commemorates his involvement in the area. The ridge itself is known as Red Table Mountain.

Grassy meadows provide good grazing for cattle in the Lime Creek drainage. When settlers arrived in Colorado in the late 1800s, cattle and sheep grazed freely on public lands. Ranchers and sheepherders ran as much stock as possible, damaging many acres across the West from overgrazing. The Taylor Grazing Act of 1934 created grazing districts to minimize the degradation of public lands. Today the USDA Forest

Service grants grazing permits on the lands under its management. A rancher may hold several grazing allotments in an area. With guidance from the Forest Service, the rancher moves his herd at designated times, rotating cattle to different areas. Rotation has several benefits. The cattle continue to have fresh grass to eat. The grass in any given area is not totally consumed and has time to recover and stay healthy. Fences help keep cattle in designated areas. The rancher holding the grazing allotments is responsible for maintaining the fences. In the Lime Creek area, "lay down" fences are common. After the cattle leave the high country in the fall, the rancher lets the fences down. This practice prevents snow damage. In spring trees downed by winter snows and winds are removed from the fence line, the fences are set up again, and cattle are brought back to the grassy slopes. The rancher also helps maintain the hiking and other trails, which his cattle use.

During the hike, you may come across herds of cattle. They will not bother you and will just move up or off the trail as you approach. Please restrain dogs and do not harass the herd. Part of this area is currently (late 2010) being managed as a recommended wilderness area.

From the junction with FR 431, the hike follows a rough 4WD road, climbing steadily up to the trailhead located under some power lines. The turnoff to the trailhead is not marked, so follow the cues in the Miles and Directions carefully. A deep, thick, spruce-fir forest surrounds the trail, creating a dark primeval atmosphere where the appearance of elves and gnomes would hardly be surprising. Slip past the forest spirits into an open meadow with an airy view of the Lime Creek drainage. The trail winds between small stands of conifers and open, flower-covered meadows.

The trail continues up to a ridge and follows the north side. Below, the town of Eagle sits in the distance, with Sylvan Lake in the foreground. Catch a breather on a level area through the trees before negotiating an interesting skinny ridge. Red boulder fields drape the ridge to the north and south. The trail is tricky here, with a slippery climb up the next ridge. As the trail enters open meadow at treeline, the views are incredible. The Maroon Bells (Maroon Peak and North Maroon Peak), Pyramid, Snowmass, and Capitol peaks rear their 14,000-foot heads to the southwest.

The trail traverses below the ridge to the south side. After attaining the ridge again, turn right and hike to the red rock Mount Thomas summit. The rocks are the Maroon Formation, the same rocks that comprise the famous Maroon Bells near Aspen. This formation eroded from the Ancestral Rockies in western Colorado. As sediments were buried by streams, a rustlike stain formed, creating the red color. There is no official trail to the top, but it's easy to find the way. Views in every direction include the Gore Range, the Flat Tops, Mount Sopris near Carbondale, the Holy Cross Wilderness, and the peaks mentioned above. Keep an eye out for thunderstorms. The ridge is no place to be if lightning is flashing or approaching. Enjoy a picnic lunch and return the way you came!

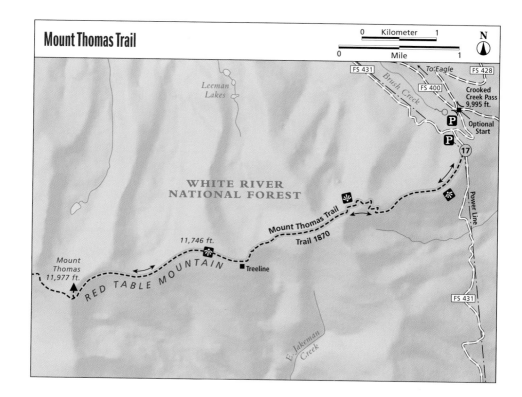

# Mount Thomas Trail

## Miles and Directions

**0.0**    Start at the junction with FR 431. Walk uphill on the rough 4WD road to the left. Elevation: 10,150 feet.

**0.2**    A side road heads to the right by some power lines. Turn right here and walk uphill. Follow the road as it curves left. The Mount Thomas Trail (Trail 1870) trailhead is on the right. GPS: N39 26.18′/W106 41.00′.

**0.6**    The trail enters a meadow. **(FYI:** Beautiful views of Lime Creek drainage.)

**1.3**    The trail starts to switchback up the ridge.

**2.0**    The trail crosses some meadows. Cairns mark the route.

**2.6**    Pass a sign at the boundary of the recommended Wilderness area. GPS: N39 25.51′/W106 42.85′. The trail climbs steeply up the ridge. Red boulder fields lie on both sides of the trail.

**3.0**    The trail is now above treeline. It is fairly easy to find, and is marked by cairns.

**3.2**    The trail crosses a hump on Red Table Mountain and descends a little from here. **(FYI:** Awesome views of the Maroon Bells are to the southwest.)

**4.0**    The trail leaves the ridge to traverse along the south side through a boulder field.

**4.5**   At a big cairn, turn right up the ridge to the summit of Mount Thomas. GPS: N39 25.12'/W106 44.59'. There's no trail, but there are some open areas between the krummholz (stunted trees) to walk on. Continue up a boulder field to the top.

**4.6**   Reach Mount Thomas summit. Elevation: 11,977 feet. GPS: N39 25.19'/W106 44.58' Return the way you came.

**9.2**   Arrive back at the trailhead.

## Hike Information

### General Information
**Eagle Valley Chamber of Commerce:** Eagle; (970) 328-5220; www.eaglevalley.org

### Local Events/Attractions
**Eagle County Historical Society's Visitor Center:** museum; Eagle; (970) 328-6464
**Sylvan Lake State Park:** Eagle; (970) 328-2021; http://parks.state.co.us/parks/sylvanlake

### Accommodations
**Sylvan Lake State Park Campground:** Eagle; (970) 328-2024; parks.state.co.us/parks /sylvanlake

### Restaurants
**The Eagle Diner:** 112 West Chambers Ave., Eagle; (970) 328-1919
**Grand Avenue Grill:** 678 Grand Ave., Eagle; (970) 328-4043
**Mi Pueblo:** 65 Market St., Eagle; (970) 328-5156

# 18 Granite Lakes Trail

The Granite Lakes Trail first wanders along the Fryingpan River, meandering up and down through thick forest and around some interesting granitic formations. The first 3.3 miles are fairly gentle. Turning up the Granite Creek drainage, the trail climbs steadily, and often steeply, to Lower Granite Lake, tucked in a bench above Granite Creek. Upper Granite Lake is about 0.75 mile farther along a fairly gentle path. Once in the subalpine zone, the wildflowers and views are beautiful. Backpack in and take an extra day or two to explore this beautiful and quiet area.

**Start:** From the Granite Lakes Trail (Trail 1922) trailhead
**Distance:** 13.6-mile out and back
**Approximate hiking time:** 8 to 12 hours (recommended 2- to 3-day backpack)
**Difficulty:** Most difficult due to elevation gain, length, and altitude
**Elevation gain:** 2,930 feet, plus some small undulations
**Seasons:** Best from late June to mid-Oct
**Trail surface:** Dirt trail, sometimes steep
**Land status:** National forest and wilderness area
**Nearest towns:** Basalt and Meredith
**Other trail users:** Equestrians, anglers, and hunters (in season)

**Canine compatibility:** Dogs must be on leash
**Schedule:** The trail is neither maintained nor marked for winter use.
**Fees and permits:** None. Group size limit: No more than 15 people per group with a maximum combination of 25 people and pack or saddle animals in any one group.
**Maps:** USGS Nast and Mount Champion; Nat Geo Trails Illustrated 126 Holy Cross/Ruedi Reservoir and 127 Aspen/Independence Pass; Latitude 40˚ Crested Butte, Aspen, Gunnison
**Trail contact:** White River National Forest, Sopris Ranger District, Carbondale; (970) 963-2266; www.fs.usda.gov/whiteriver

**Finding the trailhead:** From Basalt, drive east on the Fryingpan River Road (FR 105) about 31 miles (paved all the way) to a sign on the right side that says Nast Lake, Granite Lakes Trail Trailhead. Turn right and drive down a dirt road about 0.9 mile and cross the Fryingpan River bridge. On the other side of the bridge to the right is a parking area and the trailhead. Be sure to park here and do not drive any farther. There are no facilities here. Water from streams and lakes must be treated. Walk down the road to the Fryingpan River Ranch—the trail continues on the left past the mailboxes. Please stay on the trail and respect private property. GPS: N39 17.88'/W106 36.31'

## The Hike

Several stories recount the naming of the Fryingpan River. In one version, several miners ran across the mountains from a river drainage to escape angry Utes, only to find more Utes camped on the other side. One miner commented that it was like "jumping from the frying pan into the fire." The river from which they ran became known as the Fryingpan. Another account reports trappers being attacked by Utes,

*Upper Granite Lake*

with only two trappers surviving. One left his wounded companion in a nearby cave and hung a frying pan in a tree so he could find his buddy when he returned with help. Henry Gannet, one of the leaders of the Hayden Survey, officially named the river.

For many years, the Ute Indians hunted game in the Fryingpan and Roaring Fork River valleys. As miners swarmed over the area and homesteaders established ranches and farms, the Utes were forced from their cherished homelands. Mines were located near Meredith and Thomasville around 1882, but the ore soon played out. Other mines near Aspen were booming, but transportation proved to be an expensive nightmare. A race developed between railroad companies to provide rail service to Aspen and Glenwood Springs. The Colorado Midland Railway Company decided to build a railroad from Colorado Springs through Leadville and on to Aspen. The route tunneled through the Sawatch Range and down the Fryingpan River to its intersection with the Roaring Fork River. By November 1887, the railroad arrived at Aspen Junction, presently the town of Basalt.

As settlers moved into the area, they harvested its many resources. Some people provided elk and deer meat to the railroad workers and miners. By 1890 eight sawmills reportedly operated along the Fryingpan River, supplying lumber for building railroads, homes, buildings, and mine tunnels.

Even back in the 1890s the Fryingpan valley had earned a reputation as a sportsman's paradise, with large herds of elk and deer and abundant trout in lakes and streams. In the early 1900s, Arthur Hanthorn and James Morris built a tourist resort with a large lodge and several other buildings near the Nast railroad siding.

The mountains in the Fryingpan valley area became part of the Holy Cross Forest Reserve in 1905. Len Shoemaker served as a forest ranger in the area for about twenty years and in 1958 wrote a book, *Roaring Fork Valley,* in which he relates interesting historical tidbits. In 1918, the last Colorado Midland Railway train ran the Fryingpan route. The sawmills closed soon thereafter, and the Fryingpan River valley returned to a quieter existence.

In 1978, Congress designated the Hunter-Fryingpan Wilderness, named after two of its drainages. When the area around Mount Massive (14,421 feet) was considered for wilderness designation, Congress intended to include it in the Hunter-Fryingpan. An oversight, however, created a separate Mount Massive Wilderness in 1980. The Spruce Creek drainage was added to the Hunter-Fryingpan in 1993, for a total of 82,729 acres.

The first part of the hike crosses Mountain Nast Community, home to the private Fryingpan River Ranch and several summer cabins. Please respect the rights of property owners by staying on the trail. You'll pass through a few meadows, sometimes close to the creek, then enter thick forest. The trail crosses many small creeks while weaving up and down around various granitic formations. The Forest Service has worked on the trail with the help of Colorado Rocky Mountain School and others. Take time to appreciate their work in boggy areas. Part of the task of keeping an area pristine involves maintaining trails to avoid environmental damage. Volunteer and youth groups play an important role by helping the Forest Service with trail projects.

In about 3.3 miles the trail intersects the Fryingpan Lakes Trail. Taking a right turn, the Granite Lakes Trail climbs steeply out of the valley. The trail occasionally levels out, giving you a chance for a breather. Granite Creek cascades nearby, forming small waterfalls and interesting water slides. At 5 miles, the trail enters a beautiful meadow with sweeping views up the valley. After crossing Granite Creek twice, you begin climbing again.

Granite Lakes are nestled on a bench above Granite Creek. Trout jump and swim in the clear waters of Lower Granite Lake. The trail to the upper lake crosses flower-filled meadows. If you're backpacking, remember to camp at least 100 feet away from the lakes, streams, and trail. By making yourself less obvious, you and others can fully enjoy the peace and solitude.

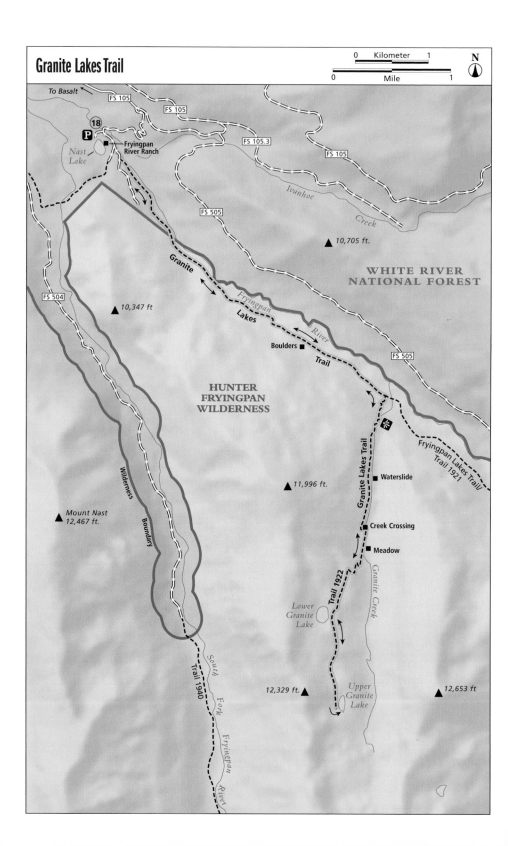

# Granite Lakes Trail

0 Kilometer 1
0 Mile 1

N

**To Basalt**
FS 105
FS 105
18
P
Nast Lake
Fryingpan River Ranch
FS 105.3
FS 105
FS 505
Ivanhoe
Creek
▲ 10,705 ft.

**WHITE RIVER NATIONAL FOREST**

Granite
Fryingpan
FS 504
▲ 10,347 ft
Lakes
River
Boulders ■
Trail
FS 505

**HUNTER FRYINGPAN WILDERNESS**

Granite Lakes Trail
Fryingpan Lakes Trail/
Trail 1921

▲ 11,996 ft.
■ Waterslide

Wilderness
Boundary

▲ Mount Nast
12,467 ft.

■ Creek Crossing
■ Meadow

Granite Creek

Lower Granite Lake

Trail 1922

South Fork Fryingpan River
Trail 1940

12,329 ft. ▲

Upper Granite Lake

▲ 12,653 ft

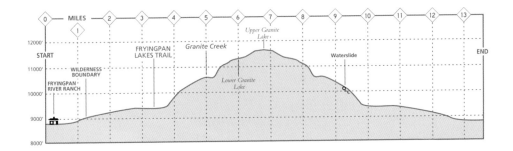

## Miles and Directions

**0.0** Start at the Granite Lakes Trail (Trail 1922) trailhead by Nast Lake. Please sign the trailhead register and read up-to-date regulations on the bulletin board. Elevation: 8,700 feet.

**0.2** Arrive at Fryingpan River Ranch. Walk on the road to the left past the mailboxes for Mountain Nast Community.

**0.3** Granite Lakes Trail turns left off the road. Follow the trail to the left along the river. GPS: N39 17.70'/W106 36.15'.

**1.2** Reach the wilderness area boundary sign.

**1.5** The trail comes very close to a U-curve on the Fryingpan River.

**2.3** The trail wanders through various granitic boulders and rock formations. Watch out for cairns marking the trail in rocky areas.

**3.3** Reach the junction with the Fryingpan Lakes Trail. Elevation: 9,480 feet. GPS: N39 16.05'/W106 33.73'. This is a good place for a break. Turn right onto the Granite Lakes Trail and head uphill. The trail starts to switchback steeply not too far from here.

**4.3** To the left is a waterslide down smooth granite.

**5.0** The trail comes to a beautiful meadow and goes downstream a little to a Granite Creek crossing over big boulders. **(Note:** Creek crossing can be tricky.) GPS: N39 15.10'/W106 33.88'. In a few feet you'll cross another little creek. Continue across the meadow, staying right of a big boulder in the meadow. There's a cairn near the trees.

**5.1** Cross Granite Creek again. You now leave Granite Creek and climb uphill to a bench above the drainage. The trail switchbacks steeply in spots (again).

**5.7** The trail climbs more gently through some wetter areas and more open areas.

**6.0** The trail crosses a little creek. Turn right at the cairn. **(Note:** Remember this spot on the way back as it's easy to miss.) Reach Lower Granite Lake. Elevation: about 11,400 feet. GPS: N39 14.50'/W106 34.22'.

**6.2** Come to a meadow with view. Cross a little flat area.

**6.4** Come to a creek crossing with lots of tree stumps. The trail is a little hard to find, but there are some cairns. Keep heading across the open area, slightly uphill. **(FYI:** Look behind for a good view of the Sawatch Range.) Come to a little flat area. The trail will drop down to the upper lake.

*Waterslide in Granite Creek*

**6.8** Reach Upper Granite Lake. Elevation: 11,600 feet. GPS: N39 13.87'/W106 34.15'. Return the way you came.

**13.6** Arrive back at the trailhead.

## Hike Information

### General Information

**Basalt Chamber of Commerce:** Basalt; (970) 927-4031; www.basaltchamber.org

### Local Events/Attractions

**Aspen Music Festival:** Aspen; (970) 925-9042; www.aspenmusicfestival.com
**Basalt River Days:** Basalt; (970) 927-4031; www.basaltchamber.org
**Strawberry Days:** Glenwood Springs; (970) 945-6589; www.strawberrydaysfestival.com

### Accommodations

**National Forest campgrounds:** Sopris Ranger District, Carbondale; (970) 963-2266; www.fs
.usda.gov/whiteriver

## Restaurants

**Riverside Grill:** 181 Basalt Center Circle, Basalt: (970) 927-9301; http://riversidegrillbasalt.com

**Smoke Modern BBQ:** 241 Harris St., Willits Town Center, Basalt: (970) 927-5158; www.smoke modernbbq.com

**Two Rivers Cafe:** 156 Midland Ave., Basalt; (970) 927-3348

## Clubs and Organizations

**Colorado Mountain Club–Aspen Group:** Aspen; www.cmc.org

**Roaring Fork Outdoor Volunteers:** Basalt; (970) 927-8241 or (877) 662-5220; www.rfov.org

**Wilderness Workshop:** Aspen; (970) 963-3977; www.wildernessworkshop.org

## Hike Tours

**Aspen Alpine Guides:** Aspen; (970) 925-6618; www.aspenalpine.com

# In Addition

## What Is Wilderness?

While you're hiking in Colorado, you'll inevitably find yourself in a "wilderness area." What is a designated wilderness area? What's different about wilderness than any other part of national forest, national park, or Bureau of Land Management (BLM) land?

Wilderness areas are very special places. The American people, through acts of Congress, designate certain pristine and primitive sections of undeveloped federal land as "wilderness." The Wilderness Act of 1964, which created a National Wilderness Preservation System (NWPS), gives Congress the authority to designate lands as wilderness.

First a little history. Back in the 1870s, people became alarmed at the rapid rate of development in America and the overuse of natural resources on public lands. Efforts were made to conserve and preserve certain areas. Yellowstone became our first national park in 1872. The first Primitive Area, a forerunner of wilderness, was designated in 1930. Concerns about development and abuse of public lands didn't stop then. Some believed that certain areas should be saved in their pristine condition. In 1955 the first draft legislation outlining the NWPS was written. After nine years of negotiations and rewrites, the Wilderness Act became law.

The purpose of the NWPS is to ensure that Americans now and in the future have the benefits of a wilderness resource. Those benefits include "outstanding opportunities for solitude or a primitive and unconfined type of recreation" and "the public purposes of recreational, scenic, scientific, educational, conservation, and historical use." The Wilderness Act specifically states that "A wilderness, in contrast with those areas where man and his works dominate the landscape, is hereby recognized as an area where the earth and its community of life are untrammeled by man, where man himself is a visitor who does not remain . . . an area of undeveloped Federal land retaining its primeval character and influence, without permanent improvements or human habitation, which is protected and managed so as to preserve its natural conditions and which . . . generally appears to have been affected primarily by the forces of nature . . ."

The Wilderness Act prohibits certain uses in designated wilderness areas, such as motorized equipment, landing of aircraft, nonmotorized mechanical transport (like mountain bikes), roads, and structures except in emergencies or administrative necessity. However, Congress allowed other uses to continue, such as grazing, hunting, and fishing. Since the end of 1983, new mining claims are prohibited, but patented claims existing prior to 1984 may be worked under certain restrictions.

Water in wilderness areas is a very touchy issue, especially in Colorado, where most of the major rivers originate within the state and flow outward. The state has historically held authority over water rights. As a result, "baby" wildernesses that do not contain the headwaters of their rivers, such as the Roubideau Area, are protected to maintain their wilderness characteristics except from a water standpoint. Occasionally a wilderness area surrounds private or state lands. The Act assures these landowners "reasonable access" that is consistent with wilderness preservation. As a result you might see a building (on private land) in the middle of a wilderness area!

Wilderness can be designated in national forests, on BLM lands, in national parks and monuments, and in national wildlife refuges. The agency responsible for the land administers the wilderness. Designation of new wilderness areas on national public lands is still ongoing. By late 2010, Colorado contained forty-three wilderness areas: thirty-nine areas managed by the USDA Forest Service and/or the BLM, and four managed by the National Park Service (one is jointly managed by the Forest Service and NPS). The U.S. Fish & Wildlife Service helps manage Mount Massive Wilderness. Colorado also has three "baby" wilderness areas.

Public lands managers face an interesting challenge in trying to provide solitude and a primitive and unconfined type of recreation while preserving the wilderness character of the lands "unimpaired for future use," lands that are primarily affected by natural forces. Human visitation is bound to leave scars on the land and impact other visitors unless each of us is very careful. Wilderness managers therefore strive to manage human behavior, mainly through education, access limitations, and regulations. Several wilderness areas require dogs to be on leash to minimize harassment of wildlife and other visitors. A camping permit system was created for the Indian Peaks Wilderness in the 1980s because the area was being "loved to death." A few wilderness areas have designated campsites in heavily used areas. In the Holy Cross and Maroon Bells–Snowmass Wilderness areas, one person in each group must carry a free self-registration wilderness use permit. The land agencies alone can't preserve and protect wilderness areas. Each of us plays an important role.

As you hike or backpack in a designated wilderness area, remember you are in a very special place. Keeping groups small, understanding the ecosystems well enough to make good decisions about where to hike and camp, keeping water clean, minimizing traces of your presence (for example fire rings and scars), and respecting wildlife and other visitors is extremely important. One hiker may not make a huge impact, but we are now hundreds of thousands of hikers each year. By understanding what designated wilderness is and taking the responsibility to act appropriately, we can preserve these special areas for ourselves and future generations.

For further information, check out www.wilderness.net, or find out more about The Wilderness Society at www.wilderness.org or by calling (800) 843-9453 or (303) 650-5818.

# 19 Silver Creek Trail

Silver Creek Trail starts out on closed logging roads, rising slightly to the Sarvis Creek Wilderness boundary. From here the trail mostly heads downhill, with a few uphills for variety. Silver Creek is a sparkling, crystal-clear stream, very worthy of its name. Interesting granitic formations appear occasionally on the north side of the trail. Lodgepole pine, Engelmann spruce, subalpine fir, aspen, and eventually ponderosa pine trees line the trail. This area is great for a quiet getaway, except during hunting season, which starts at the end of August.

**Start:** From east Silver Creek Trail (Trail 1106) trailhead on Red Dirt Road

**Distance:** 12.4 miles point to point (with opportunities for camping and an out-and-back return)

**Approximate hiking time:** 5 to 8 hours

**Difficulty:** Difficult due to length

**Elevation gain/loss:** About 300-foot gain/2,060-foot loss (plus little undulations)

**Seasons:** Best from mid-June through Oct

**Trail surface:** Dirt trail

**Land status:** National forest and wilderness area

**Nearest towns:** Kremmling, Yampa, and Steamboat Springs

**Other trail users:** Equestrians and hunters (in season)

**Canine compatibility:** Dogs must be under control

**Schedule:** FR 100 is closed by winter snow about 14 miles from the trailhead. The trail is neither maintained nor marked for winter use.

**Fees and permits:** None. Group size limit: No more than 15 people per group with a maximum combination of 25 people and pack or saddle animals in any one group. Camping and campfires are prohibited within 100 feet of all streams and trails.

**Maps:** USGS Gore Mountain, Tyler Mountain, and Green Ridge; Nat Geo Trails Illustrated 119 Yampa/Gore Pass

**Trail contact:** Medicine Bow-Routt National Forest, Yampa Ranger District, Yampa; (970) 638-4516; www.fs.usda.gov/mbr/

**Finding the trailhead:** *With shuttle:* These directions assume you would like to hike mostly downhill. From Yampa drive 8 miles north on CO 131 to Routt County Road (RCR) 14. Turn right onto RCR 14 and drive about 3.5 miles to RCR 16. Turn right onto RCR 16, following the Lynx Pass signs. Drive 1.6 miles, then turn left by some condo buildings to stay on RCR 16. In 1.3 miles, turn right, and continue on RCR 16 for another 5.4 miles. The trailhead is past mile marker 8.0, on the left side. There is parking on the left by the trailhead. Leave one car here. Continue south about 13.5 miles on RCR 16, which becomes FR 270, to Gore Pass Road (CO 134). Turn left on CO 134 and drive 3.1 miles east to FR 250. Turn left onto FR 250. At the first fork, stay left. At all junctions, stay on FR 250, driving for 11.1 miles to Red Dirt Road (FR 100). The last mile of FR 250 is a little rough, and low-clearance vehicles should go very slowly. Turn left onto Red Dirt Road (FR 100). Drive 5 miles north. The trailhead is on the left side of the road, past mile marker 11. You can camp near the east trailhead—remember to stay at least 100 feet from streams, trails, and the road. There are no facilities at either trailhead. GPS: N40 11.87'/W106 36.36'

*Without shuttle:* These directions assume you would like to hike mostly downhill. From Kremmling, drive west and north on US 40 about 6 miles to CO 134/Gore Pass Road. Turn left onto Gore

Pass Road and drive about 4.2 miles west to Red Dirt Road (FR 100). At the first two forks, stay right. At the third fork at FR 101 (also Grand CR 191), around mile 4.8, stay left. In another 1.7 miles, reach FR 250 and stay right. Follow the signs for Buffalo Park. The trailhead is on the left side of the road, about 11.6 miles from Gore Pass Road.

## The Hike

Silver Creek Trail traverses the southern part of the Sarvis Creek Wilderness, designated by Congress in 1993. This wilderness is unique because it is not composed of "rocks and ice" like so many other national forest wilderness areas in Colorado. Although heavily forested, its pristine and primitive nature qualified it for wilderness status.

The Sarvis Timber Company harvested trees in the Service Creek area in the mid-1910s using portable mills. Old-timers insist the area's original name was Sarvis. Some mapmaker, however, decided that "sarvis" was a common mispronunciation of the word "service" and placed the name "Service Creek" on the map. The wilderness area designation tried to right the incorrect spelling by using Sarvis.

The Civilian Conservation Corps (CCC) built much of the Silver Creek Trail. After the 1929 stock market crash and subsequent depression, 13.6 million Americans were unemployed by 1933. That year Congress passed the Emergency Conservation Work Act, creating what became known as the CCC. Young, unemployed, unmarried men between the ages of eighteen and twenty-five were eligible to join. Conservation of natural resources—reforestation, forest fire fighting, erosion control, trail building and maintenance, development of state parks, and other public works— became the CCC's mission. The U.S. Army built camps, the government furnished food and clothing, and the Departments of the Interior and Agriculture provided work projects and leadership. Each man earned $30 per month, of which $25 was sent home to his family.

The CCC is credited with building 46,854 bridges, 3,116 fire lookout towers, and 318,076 dams to help with erosion control, plus numerous buildings and trails. By 1937, the CCC employed more than 500,000 young men, working on projects all over the United States. The army operated more than 2,500 camps to house all the workers.

The men of the CCC performed excellent work. According to Forest Service personnel, the CCC workers who built the Silver Creek Trail created one that is easy to maintain. It has great drainage, rolling dips, and cribbed walls. Moss now covers the rock walls, making them difficult to see.

From the east trailhead, the hike follows several old logging roads, now closed to motorized travel. The trail gradually gains elevation to the wilderness boundary, which is nearly the highest point of the trail. From here you drop into the Silver Creek drainage, with marshy meadows hidden behind trees to the south. The granitic rocks along the trail take on some interesting shapes. After crossing a marshy section,

*Bend in Silver Creek*

the remains of a log cabin rest on the left. The former occupants are unknown, but the notched logs still show careful work by the cabin's builder. "Shiprock" sticks up its prow to the right a little farther down the trail. Colorful aspens frame the boulders in the fall.

As you round a ridge, check out the view down the drainage. The various lumps and cliffs of rock are composed of Precambrian granite (quartz monzonite). Precambrian rocks formed over 600 million years ago when molten magma oozed up into other rocks, cooled slowly, and became the granite you see today. Granite tends to erode like an onion peels, hence some of the rounded shapes. The red trees, or ghost trees, were killed by mountain pine beetles in the 1990s and early 2000s. Although these tiny insects are part of the natural forest cycle, they reproduced in epidemic proportions due to drought, which weakened trees, making them more susceptible to the beetles. Very cold winters kill many beetles, but winters have been relatively mild. Treating the acres of trees involved became impossible. Be aware that these dead trees can fall at any time, and particularly in high winds. Park your car and place your tent away from them. Be careful while hiking, too!

Sometimes Silver Creek runs swiftly down a tiny canyon, leaping over little cascades. Other times it broadens and sparkles in the sun. Deep pools attract fish—sit and watch for a while. Some good campsites can be found up on low ridges to the north of the trail—an appropriate 200-plus feet from the trail and creek, but close

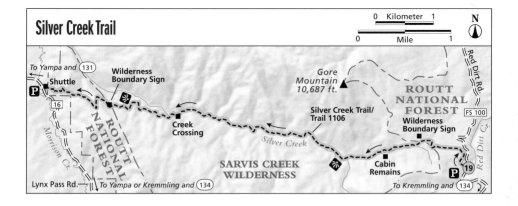

Silver Creek Trail

enough to fetch water easily. While you hike and camp, remember to use your Leave No Trace skills!

About two-thirds of the way into the hike, the trail crosses Silver Creek at a wide spot. The trail then swings away from the creek and eventually traverses a steep slope leaving the creek far below. After topping the ridge, you drop down on south- and west-facing slopes. The vegetation changes here, adapting to the dryness and heat. Ponderosa pines, Gambel oaks, sagebrush, and grasses replace the lodgepole and spruce-fir forest.

This area is very popular during hunting season. Bow and black powder hunters are plentiful during September. Be considerate and wear some blaze orange clothing.

## Miles and Directions

**0.0**    Start at the east Silver Creek Trail (Trail 1106) trailhead, by the bulletin board. Elevation: 9,730 feet. Walk back to road, turn left, and walk up the road, over the creek to the trail.

**0.1**    Silver Creek Trail starts to the left of the road at the big mounds of dirt that are used to close the old logging road to motorized vehicles. Hike up the dirt mound onto the double-track Silver Creek Trail.

**1.5**    The trail forks; turn left and walk up the old logging road.

**1.6**    Reach the Wilderness boundary sign. Elevation: 9,840 feet. GPS: N40 12.37'/W106 37.47'.

**2.5**    The cabin remains are on the left. GPS: N40 12.19'/W106 38.37'.

**3.6**    Round a ridge with a good view down Silver Creek drainage.

**8.0**    Cross Silver Creek. Elevation: 8,900 feet. GPS: N40 12.86'/W106 43.48'. **(Note:** Be careful in early summer when the creek runs high. The current may be swift.)

**10.2**   Reach the Wilderness boundary sign. GPS: N40 13.02'/W106 45.08'.

**11.5**   Top a ridge and begin the final descent to the west trailhead.

**11.6**   The trail forks; stay to the left (actually go straight downhill as there's a viewpoint off to the right).

**12.3** Reach the Silver Creek west trailhead bulletin board. If you're coming up from this direction, please stop to read up-to-date area information. (**Note:** From here to the trailhead parking, you'll be on private property. The Forest Service has permission for the trail to cross here. Please respect the private property!)

**12.4** Arrive at the west Silver Creek Trail trailhead. Elevation: 7,960 feet. GPS: N40 13.33'/W106 46.73'.

## Hike Information

### General Information

**Kremmling Visitor Center:** Kremmling; (970) 724-3472 or (877) 573-6654; www.kremmling chamber.com

### Local Events/Attractions

**Kremmling Days:** a celebration of the town's history; Kremmling; (970) 724-3472; www.kremm lingchamber.com

**Middle Park Fair & Rodeo:** Kremmling; (970) 724-3472

### Accommodations

**National Forest Service Campgrounds:** Medicine Bow–Routt National Forest, Yampa; (970) 638-4516; www.fs.usda.gov/mbr

### Restaurants

**Los Amigos Mexican Restaurant:** 109 South 6th Ave., Kremmling; (970) 724-9243

**Penny's Diner:** 98 Moffat Ave., Yampa; (970) 638-1000

### Clubs and Organizations

**Yampatika:** Steamboat Springs; (970) 871-9151; www.yampatika.org

*Rocks that look like Legos*

# 20 Lulu City (Site)

Follow traces of an old wagon road to the Shipler Mine, Shipler cabins, and the Lulu City site. Lodgepole pine and spruce-fir trees line this family-friendly trail. Hiking early in the morning or in the evening, you are likely to see elk, deer, moose, chipmunks, and birds (especially camp robbers). The infant Colorado River winds through the Kawuneeche Valley on its long journey to Mexico. Lulu City was a lively mining town from 1880 to 1884. The Grand Ditch, which still transports water from the Colorado River watershed to the Cache la Poudre River drainage on the east slope, is visible for much of the hike.

**Start:** From the Colorado River Trailhead
**Distance:** 7.4 miles out and back
**Approximate hiking time:** 3 to 5 hours
**Difficulty:** Moderate due to length
**Elevation gain:** 470 feet, plus about 150 feet in undulations
**Seasons:** Best from mid-June to mid-Oct
**Trail surface:** Dirt trail
**Land status:** National park wilderness
**Nearest town:** Grand Lake
**Other trail users:** Equestrians and anglers
**Canine compatibility:** Dogs not permitted
**Schedule:** Year-round. Park at the Timber Lake trailhead in winter.
**Fees and permits:** Entrance fee, annual pass, or America the Beautiful pass required for entry to Rocky Mountain National Park. Backcountry permits are required for overnight camping (970-586-1242; a fee is charged). Download the Backcountry Camping Guide from the park website.
**Maps:** USGS Fall River Pass; Nat Geo Trails Illustrated 200 Rocky Mountain National Park; Latitude 40° Colorado Front Range
**Trail contact:** Rocky Mountain National Park, Estes Park; (970) 586-1206. Kawuneeche Visitor Center, Grand Lake; (970) 627-3471; www.nps.gov/romo
**Other:** Bear-proof food canisters are required below treeline between May 1 and Oct 31.

**Finding the trailhead:** From Grand Lake, drive 1.8 miles north on US 34 to the Rocky Mountain National Park entrance station and pay the entrance fee. (The Kawuneeche Visitor Center, at mile 1.4, is an excellent place to start your visit.) From the entrance station, drive another 9.5 miles to the Colorado River trailhead entrance, on the left. The parking lot is another 0.1 mile. There are vault toilets and picnic tables. Drinking water is available at Timber Creek Campground, located 1.7 miles to the south, or at the visitor center. Trailhead GPS: N40 24.11' / W105 50.89'

## The Hike

On the way to the Colorado River trailhead, notice the broad valley through which you're driving. This U-shaped valley was carved by the 20-mile-long Colorado River Glacier, which melted about 12,000 years ago. We now call this the Kawuneeche (*kah-wu-NEE-chee*) Valley, an Arapaho term for "valley of the coyote." Coyotes still flourish here, as do deer and elk. In 1978 moose were reintroduced into North Park, northwest across the Continental Divide, and have since traveled to these wet valley meadows. Mountain lions also live here—so keep children close. Sometimes you can

*Lulu City site along the Colorado River*

see elk sitting in the grass among the trees, chewing their cud. When hiking here in the fall, watch for elk scat along the trail and imprints of elk beds in the grass, while listening for their eerie bugle.

The hike continues up the Kawuneeche Valley, along the North Fork of the Colorado River. Several high peaks to the west show the steep, sharp crags and cliffs formed by glacial carving. At about mile 0.5, cross a large meadow where the Colorado River Trail intersects the Red Mountain Trail. In 1907 Tober Wheeler (aka Squeaky Bob, due to his high-pitched voice) built a tent resort in this meadow to showcase the area's beautiful scenery and trophy hunting and fishing. In the mid-1920s Lester Scott bought the place and renamed it Phantom Valley Ranch—after the ghosts of American Indians, miners, and others whose presence he felt. In the 1960s NPS purchased and tore down the old ranch to let the land revert to a wild state.

After passing the mine tailings from the Shipler Mine, you arrive at the remains of two cabins at the edge of a meadow. These cabins were built in the 1870s by Joel Shipler, a prospector who just a few years later would discover a silver lode on the mountain that bears his name. Word of Shipler's strike spread, and miners quickly arrived in the upper part of the North Fork of the Grand River (later renamed Colorado River) valley in summer 1879. By June 1880 Lulu City started rising in the valley—exactly who Lulu was remains a question . . . perhaps the daughter of one of the town's founders?

Lulu City boasted a clothing store, a barbershop, an assay shop, a hardware store, and several grocery and liquor stores. Stagecoaches connected the town with Fort Collins and Grand Lake. A fine hotel and bank gave the little community a civilized air, while the red-light district, which operated a little north of town, satisfied the rowdier element. Two sawmills provided lumber for buildings and mines. Unfortunately, the extracted ore proved to be low-grade and not worth much money. By 1884 the death knell sounded for Lulu City.

Joel Shipler, however, continued to live in his cabins until about 1914. The Shipler Mine penetrated only about 100 yards into the mountain and probably didn't support his family very well. Still, Shipler reported abundant game in the area, knee-high grass, and catching "as many as 583 trout in one day." The leader of a Colorado Mountain Club outing in 1914 claimed to have caught 127 brook trout near Squeaky Bob's place.

After the Shipler cabins, the trail gradually climbs through thick forest, then turns east and heads uphill for about 0.2 mile. It then undulates along the side of Specimen Mountain. At the intersection with La Poudre Pass Trail, you drop somewhat steeply along a few switchbacks about 100 feet down into the valley and ultimately to the Lulu City site. A few log cabin ruins hide beneath trees. Wildflowers brighten the meadow, and ground squirrels might beg for lunch, but please don't feed them. Hike down to the river on a spur trail or farther north on the trail toward Thunder Pass. North across a little creek is the spur trail to a privy on the right. Just beyond the spur lies another ruin hidden by the branches of a tree growing where people once lived.

## Miles and Directions

**0.0** Start at the Colorado River trailhead interpretive bulletin boards. Elevation 9,010 feet.

**0.2** Top a little knoll after two switchbacks.

**0.5** The trail forks. Red Mountain Trail goes to the left. This is the site of Phantom Valley Ranch. Stay on the Colorado River Trail moving ahead and toward the right. GPS: N40 24.49'/W105 50.92'.

**1.7** The trail passes through a boulder field. (**FYI:** Watch for raspberries among the rocks. The tiny fruits are edible, but please take no more than one quart per person per day for personal consumption [park policy] because animals, like bears, depend on the berries for winter fat.)

**1.9** Arrive at the Shipler Mine tailings. GPS: N40 25.65'/W105 50.95'. (**FYI:** Look down to the left to see an old ore cart.)

**2.1** Reach Crater Creek bridge.

**2.2** Arrive at the remains of the Shipler cabins. Elevation: 9,240 feet. GPS: N40 25.86'/W105 51.02'. (**Option:** For a shorter 4.4-mile out-and-back hike, you can turn around here and return the way you came.) A little past the cabins on the left, a trail leads to a privy.

**2.8** The trail curves to the right and heads uphill more steeply.

**3.0** The trail curves to left and wiggles and undulates along the side of Specimen Mountain.

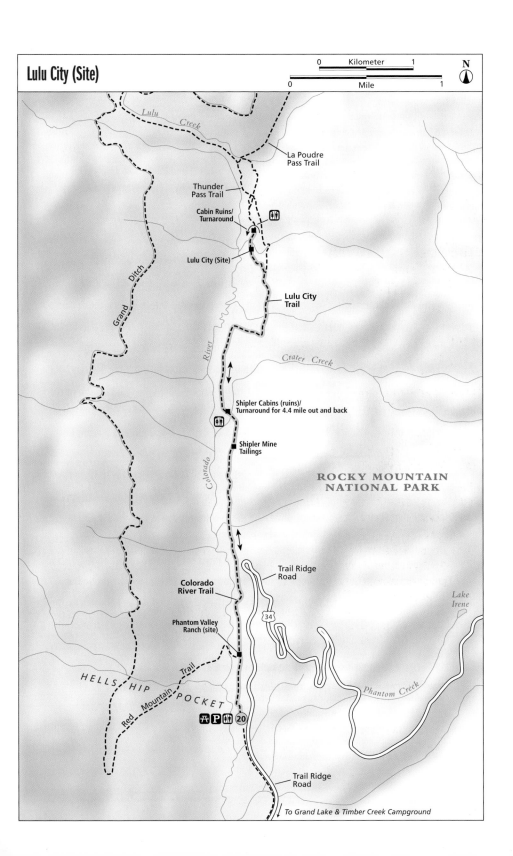

# Lulu City (Site)

0    Kilometer    1

0    Mile    1

N

La Poudre
Pass Trail

Thunder
Pass Trail

Cabin Ruins/
Turnaround

Lulu City (Site)

**Lulu City
Trail**

Grand Ditch

Lulu Creek

River

Crater Creek

Shipler Cabins (ruins)/
Turnaround for 4.4 mile out and back

Shipler Mine
Tailings

Colorado

**ROCKY MOUNTAIN
NATIONAL PARK**

Trail Ridge
Road

Lake
Irene

**Colorado
River Trail**

34

**Phantom Valley
Ranch (site)**

HELLS HIP POCKET

Red Mountain Trail

Phantom Creek

20

Trail Ridge
Road

*To Grand Lake & Timber Creek Campground*

**3.4** Arrive at a trail junction. The left fork takes you to the Lulu City site, while continuing straight will take you to La Poudre Pass. GPS: N40 26.63' / W105 50.72'. Take the left fork and head downhill to Lulu City.

**3.6** Arrive at the Lulu City site. (Old cabin ruins are on the right near the sign.) Elevation: 9,360 feet. GPS: N40 26.77' / W105 50.81'. **(FYI:** The left trail goes to the Colorado River, where you'll find good lunch spots.)

**3.7** Continue right through the Lulu City site toward the privy (spur trail to privy goes to the right). Just beyond the spur trail are cabin remains under a tree on the left. This the turn-around point, though the trail continues to Thunder Pass. Return the way you came.

**7.4** Arrive back at the trailhead.

# THE GRAND DITCH PROJECT

To the west of Lulu City, along the Never Summer Range, is a long, man-made scar in the earth known as the Grand Ditch. As people settled Colorado's dry Eastern Plains, the region's natural water supply proved insufficient to satisfy the developing cities, ranches, and farms. Colorado's West Slope receives more moisture, but it drains west into the Colorado River. People soon devised schemes to divert water from the west side to the east. The Larimer City Ditch Company was formed in 1881 to divert water toward Fort Collins and the Eastern Plains. By October 1890, the first section of the Grand Ditch brought water from the Never Summer Range over La Poudre Pass to Long Draw Creek, then to the Cache La Poudre River, which flows near Fort Collins. By 1936, the Grand Ditch extended to Baker Creek, a total of 14.3 miles. Built by Swedish, Japanese, Mexican, Chinese, and other laborers with little more than picks, shovels, and wheelbarrows, the ditch captures water from high alpine basins of the Never Summer Range. At its widest point, the ditch is 20 feet wide by 6 feet deep.

Water diversion is advantageous to humans, no question, but often it adversely impacts wildlife, forests, and ecosystems. Arguments have raged over the years, and continue today, over the issue of moving water from one side of the Continental Divide to the other.

Grand Ditch was named after the river whose waters it diverted. Grand River was the original name of the Colorado River within Colorado. Not until the Grand joined with the Green River in Utah did it become the Colorado River. In 1921, after some sneaky politics by Colorado Congressman Edward Taylor, President Harding signed a bill into law that renamed Grand River the Colorado River from its source high in Rocky Mountain National Park.

# Hike Information

## General Information

**Grand Lake Chamber of Commerce:** Grand Lake; (800) 531-1019 or (970) 627-3402; www.grandlakechamber.com

## Local Events/Attractions

**Annual Buffalo BBQ Weekend:** Grand Lake; (970) 627-3402; www.grandlakechamber.com

**Rocky Mountain Blues Festival:** Grand Lake; (970) 627-3402

**Rocky Mountain Repertory Theatre:** Grand Lake; (970) 627-3421; www.rockymountainrep.com

## Accommodations

**Arapaho-Roosevelt National Forest:** Sulphur Ranger District, Granby; (970) 887-4100; www.fs.usda.gov/arp

**Timber Creek Campground:** Rocky Mountain National Park (first-come, first-served); (970) 586-1206; www.nps.gov/romo

## Restaurants

**Grand Lake Brewing Company:** 915 Grand Ave., Grand Lake; (970) 627-1711; www.grandlakebrewing.com

**Sagebrush BBQ & Grill:** 11101 Grand Ave., Grand Lake; (970) 627-1404; www.sagebrushbbq.com

**Trail Ridge Grill:** US 34 and Golf Course Rd., Grand Lake; (970) 627-8182

## Clubs and Organizations

**Rocky Mountain Nature Association:** Estes Park; (970) 586-0108 or www.rmna.org

## Hike Tours

**Rocky Mountain National Park:** Kawuneeche Visitor Center (offers hikes to various locations on the west side, not necessarily to Lulu City); Grand Lake; (970) 627-3471; www.nps.gov/romo

**Rocky Mountain Nature Association:** Estes Park; (970) 586-0108; www.rmna.org

# 21 Kelly Lake

Beautiful Kelly Lake sits snuggled in a glacial basin between a high ridge to the west and the craggy Medicine Bow Mountains to the east. Overnight backpacking is the best way to explore this pleasant area, but don't rule out a long day hike to visit this little jewel. The trail starts out on logging roads through meadows, crosses two forks of the Canadian River, and passes through old timber cuts. The middle section of the hike travels on logging roads and singletrack trail. The final section is singletrack, gaining elevation to a scenic high alpine valley full of wildflowers.

**Start:** From the trailhead at the end of Jackson County Road (JCR) 41
**Distance:** 13.6 miles out and back
**Approximate hiking time:** 7 to 9 hours
**Difficulty:** Most difficult due to length
**Elevation gain/loss:** 2,545-foot gain / 400-foot loss
**Season:** Best from July through Sept
**Trail surface:** Dirt trail, rocky in a few areas
**Land status:** State park
**Nearest town:** Walden
**Other trail users:** Equestrians and mountain bikers; snowmobiles in winter
**Canine compatibility:** Dogs must be on leash
**Schedule:** Year-round

**Fees and permits:** Daily entrance fee or annual parks pass required
**Maps:** USGS Gould, Johnny Moore Mountain, and Rawah Lakes; Nat Geo Trails Illustrated 114 Walden/Gould and 112 Poudre River/Cameron Pass
**Trail contact:** State Forest State Park, 56750 Highway 14, Walden; (970) 723-8366; http://parks.state.co.us/Parks/StateForest
**Other:** Campfires are prohibited in the backcountry, so bring a stove. If you're backpacking, please sign the trailhead register.
**Special considerations:** Remember to treat any water from streams and lakes before drinking.

**Finding the trailhead:** From Walden, drive 19.2 miles east on CO 14 to the KOA Campground and entrance to State Forest State Park. Turn left onto JCR 41, and drive 0.2 mile to the entrance station and pay the fee. Continue driving on JCR 41 for 8.4 miles, past several turnoffs (4WD roads, campgrounds, and picnic areas). Watch for cattle and moose along the road. Arrive at the loop at the end of JCR 41. Parking is on the west side, along with a vault toilet. The trail starts at the northeast end of the loop. Bring your own water as none is available at the trailhead. GPS: N40 36.87' / W106 01.30'

## The Hike

Kelly Creek and Kelly Lake are named after an Irishman who lived in the area in the late 1800s. Not much is known about Crazy Kelly, but the story goes that he was very religious and would tell people he lived in heaven. He made his home in a cabin along Kelly Creek, and reportedly the local pack rats were his friends. Human friends found his body in the cabin on April 17, 1898, mostly consumed by pack rats. They burned his cabin, so the cabin remains you see along the trail did not belong to this interesting character.

State Forest State Park has an unusual history. When Colorado became a state on August 1, 1876, the federal government granted about 3 million acres of land and 4 million acres of mineral rights to the state to help fund public education. Sections 16 and 36 in every township became state school lands. The Colorado State Board of Land Commissioners (SLB) manages these areas. In 1938, a land exchange between the SLB and the USDA Forest Service occurred. Sections 16 and 36 in various national forests in Colorado were exchanged for national forest land near Gould, creating 70,980 contiguous acres. In 1953, the Colorado legislature passed legislation establishing the Colorado State Forest (CSF). Grazing, forestry, and recreation continued as it had before the designation.

Between about 1940 and 1970, lumber camps harvested timber in CSF, earning money for state schools. Today's Bockman Campground was the site of Bockman Lumber Camp, the largest in Colorado, supporting over one hundred men and their families. By 1955 several camps harvested close to 10 million board feet of lumber. Citizens complained about the timber operations, and by 1975 the lumber camps had closed.

CSF became a state park in 1970, and two years later the SLB leased the land to what has become Colorado State Parks for recreation management. The forest resource management contract was awarded to the Colorado State Forest Service. The state forest service was created by the Colorado legislature in 1955 as a division of what is now Colorado State University in Fort Collins. The state forest service provides protection and management of the state's forests (versus the national forests), and educates private landowners in forested areas about fire prevention and protection.

Today the state forest service uses adaptive management strategies to maintain a healthy forest. Some techniques include timber harvesting; researching and monitoring harvest results; wildlife monitoring (signs of healthy habitat) in conjunction with the Colorado Division of Wildlife; water quality monitoring (in particular for sediment loads); and livestock grazing from July through September to stimulate healthy range and forest.

State Forest State Park offers a wealth of recreation opportunities year-round. Four campgrounds with 158 developed campsites, over sixty dispersed campsites, and six cabins are available for your getaway. Never Summer Nordic, Inc. operates eight yurts (round Mongolian tents on wooden platforms) and two huts, available year-round.

Boating is allowed on North Michigan Reservoir, and fishing is popular on lakes and streams. Motorized trails provide hours of exploring. Hikers, mountain bikers, equestrians, cross-country skiers, and snowshoers enjoy many trails leading to high alpine lakes. Several geocache sites have been created throughout the park, and geocachers can rent GPS units at the Moose Visitor Center.

Moose were reintroduced to North Park in 1978 and 1979. These huge ungulates can grow to 6 feet tall at the shoulder, weigh up to 1,000 pounds, and reach 9.5 feet

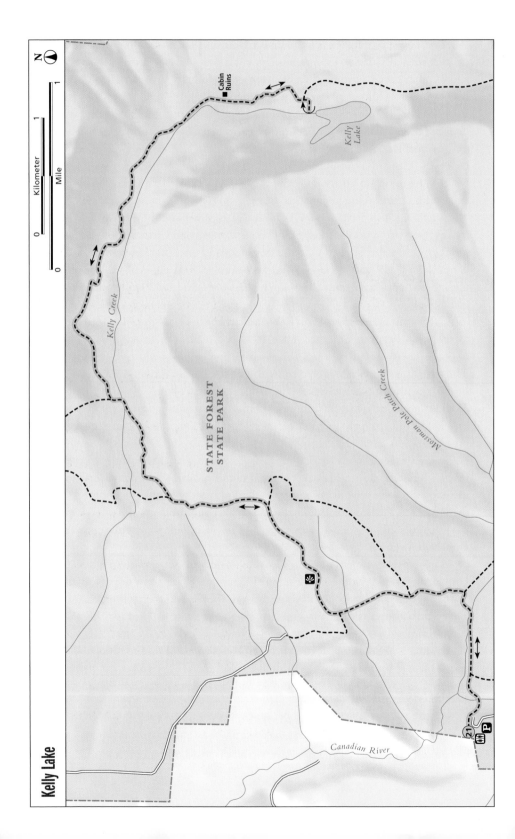

# Kelly Lake

N

0 1 Kilometer
0 1 Mile

Cabin Ruins

Kelly Creek

Kelly Lake

Mosman Pole Patch Creek

STATE FOREST STATE PARK

Canadian River

21

long. Their long spindly legs give them a top-heavy appearance. They typically live in forested areas near lakes and marshes. They graze on grasses, bushes, and underwater vegetation in summer, and on willows in winter. Being huge creatures, they have few predators and seldom show fear of humans. Extremely protective of their young and their private space, they will chase humans and dogs—and they are fast. Keep an eye out for these magnificent creatures while you're hiking, and give them plenty of space.

The hike starts by descending a ridge to the South Fork of the Canadian River through a lodgepole pine forest. The red dead trees have been killed by the mountain pine beetle. After crossing several meadows, the trail meanders through an aspen forest with colorful flowers. At about mile 4.3, the trail winds along the base of a boulder field, then climbs steeply uphill. Purple monkshood and larkspur line the path. By mile 6, you're in a beautiful alpine valley with Englemann spruce, subalpine fir, marshy areas, and gorgeous wildflowers. Kelly Creek sparkles in the sun. The trail climbs steeply up a ridge, passing a little waterfall. Suddenly Kelly Lake appears down in its bowl, craggy peaks bordering its east side. If you're camping, please remember to camp at least 100 feet (and hopefully 200 feet) away from streams and lakes and 0.25 mile from trails. Enjoy this special nook in State Forest State Park!

## Miles and Directions

**0.0** Start at the trailhead at the end of JCR 41. Elevation: 8,660 feet. The low point of this hike, near the South Fork of the Canadian River, is at 8,540 feet.

**0.75** An unmarked trail goes left. Continue hiking up the road.

**0.8** Reach the junction with a trail to the North Fork Canadian yurt. Continue to the left up the road.

**1.2** Reach the junction with the doubletrack trail to Kelly Lake and Clear Lake. Turn left. GPS: N40 37.15'/W106 00.49'. **(Option:** You can continue walking up the road. Skip ahead to mile 3.0.)

**1.6** Reach the junction with the trail to Clear Lake. Continue straight ahead and uphill.

**1.8** Reach a point with a nice view to the northwest of the Mount Zirkel Wilderness and North Park. GPS: N40 37.60'/W 106 00.49'.

**2.4** Arrive at the junction with a closed road. Walk a few more feet uphill to another road and turn left onto the road, heading north.

**3.0** Reach the junction with the Kelly Lake Trail. Turn right onto the singletrack trail. GPS: N40 38.29'/W105 59.90'.

**4.7** Reach the top of a steep section. You're entering a narrow valley. The trail crosses Kelly Creek several times in the next 1.3 miles. The trail can be wet and muddy in this section.

**6.1** Look for cabin ruins to your left. GPS: N40 38.03'/W105 57.45'. After a few more creek crossings, the trail climbs steeply for the last 0.6 mile. You'll drop about 70 feet from a ridge (10,875 feet) to the lake.

**6.8** Arrive at Kelly Lake. Elevation: 10,805 feet. GPS: N40 37.64'/W105 57.54'. Enjoy lunch and the beautiful scenery or set up your campsite. Return the way you came.

**13.6** Arrive back at the trailhead.

# Hike Information

## General Information
**North Park Chamber of Commerce:** Walden; (970) 723-4600; www.northparkchamber.com
**North Park Visitor's Bureau:** www.northparkvisitorsbureau.com

## Local Events/Attractions
**Arapaho National Wildlife Refuge:** Walden; (970) 723-8202; www.fws.gov/arapaho/
**McCallum Field (Oil & Gas) Auto Tour:** BLM Kremmling Field Office, Kremmling; (970) 724-3400
**North Park Museum:** 365 Logan St., Walden; (970) 723-8371

## Accommodations
**Colorado State Forest State Park campgrounds:** Colorado State Forest State Park, 56750 Highway 14, Walden; (970) 723-8366; reservations (800) 678-2267; http://parks.state.co.us/Parks/StateForest
**National Forest campgrounds:** Parks Ranger District, Walden; (970) 723-2700; www.fs.usda.gov/mbr
**Never Summer Nordic, Inc.:** yurts and huts in State Forest State Park, 247 County Road 41, Walden; (970) 723-4070; www.neversummernordic.com

## Restaurants
**Moose Creek Cafe:** 508 Main St., Walden; (866) 850-6971; www.moosecreekcafe.net
**Paradise Lanes:** 688 Main St., Walden; (970) 723-8616
**River Rock Cafe:** 460 Main St., Walden; (970) 723-4670; www.waldenriverrock.com

◀ *Kelly Lake*

# 22 Seven Lakes

The Seven Lakes Trail (Trail 1125) to Seven Lakes starts on the gentle Red Elephant Nature Trail, passing through lodgepole, spruce, and fir forest. Turning west, it climbs gently to the Mount Zirkel Wilderness boundary near Big Creek Falls. The trail wanders along Big Creek, then climbs a very steep section with many switchbacks. Excellent views of Big Creek Lakes can be seen from several viewpoints. The next section goes through old-growth forest and into flower-filled meadows just below Seven Lakes. The lakes are in a high, open area with views of Red Elephant Mountain and the Continental Divide. The lakes are a peaceful backpacking destination.

**Start:** From Seven Lakes trailhead near Big Creek Lakes Campground

**Distance:** 12.2 miles out and back

**Approximate hiking time:** 5 to 9 hours (recommended 2- to 3-day backpack)

**Difficulty:** Difficult due to length and one steep section

**Elevation gain:** 1,773-foot gain (with a 60-foot loss)

**Seasons:** Best from mid-June to mid-Oct

**Trail surface:** Dirt trail with some flat sections, occasional rocks and mud, and one section of many steep switchbacks

**Land status:** National forest and wilderness area

**Nearest town:** Walden

**Other trail users:** Equestrians, anglers, mountain bikers (not within the wilderness), and hunters (in season)

**Canine compatibility:** Dogs must be on leash on the Red Elephant Nature Trail (about the first mile), then under control on the rest of the trail

**Schedule:** The access road is closed about 13 miles from the trailhead in winter. Snowmobile or cross-country ski on the road; the trail is neither maintained nor marked for winter use.

**Fees and permits:** Day-use fee payable at the trailhead parking lot; America the Beautiful pass accepted (display in vehicle window). Group size limit: No more than 15 people per group with a maximum combination of 25 people and pack or saddle animals in any group

**Maps:** USGS Pearl and Davis Peak; Nat Geo Trails Illustrated 116 Hahns Peak/Steamboat Lake

**Trail contact:** Medicine Bow–Routt National Forest, Parks Ranger District, Walden; (970) 723-2700; www.fs.usda.gov/mbr

**Finding the trailhead:** From Walden, drive north a little more than 9 miles on CO 125 to Cowdrey. Turn left onto Jackson CR 6W. The road becomes gravel in about 5 miles. Drive a total of 18.8 miles from Cowdrey to FR 600/JCR 6A. Turn left. The road narrows as it enters the national forest. Be careful of oncoming vehicles as the road is not wide enough for two cars. Drive 5 miles to the junction with FR 689. Turn left, staying on FR 600. In 0.7 mile, enter the Big Creek Lakes Campground—go straight ahead at the campground entrance. Follow the hiker signs. There's a bulletin board with the campground fee station and rules 0.5 mile from the entrance. Continue another 0.2 mile and turn left into the Seven Lakes trailhead. Water is available at the campground. A vault toilet is located in the center of the parking circle. A day-use self-service pay station is located by the trailhead bulletin boards. Please sign the trail register. GPS: N40 55.88'/W106 37.15'

*Seven Lakes Trail*

## The Hike

The Mount Zirkel Wilderness was one of the original five Colorado wilderness areas designated by Congress in the Wilderness Act of 1964. This area around Big Creek Falls and Seven Lakes was added in 1993.

In 1867 Congress authorized a geological and natural resource survey along the fortieth parallel. Clarence King, just five years out of the Sheffield Scientific School at Yale, was appointed Geologist in Charge of the Geological Exploration of the Fortieth Parallel. King hired two assistant geologists, three topographic aides, two collectors, a photographer, and support men. He chose well-educated scientists who had studied at Yale or Harvard, and the geologists had even completed advanced studies in German universities. One geologist was Ferdinand Zirkel, who developed a common classification system for American and European rocks. For his contribution to science, a peak in the Park Range was named after him in 1874.

The Park Range forms the backbone of the Mount Zirkel Wilderness area. As the range stretches north toward Wyoming, it becomes known as the Sierra Madre. Part of the Sierra Madre near Seven Lakes produces the Encampment River, which flows north into the North Platte River. On the other side of the Continental Divide, the Elk River drains many of the high valleys, feeding its water into the Yampa River, and eventually into the Colorado. The Park Range is composed mainly of Precambrian metamorphic rocks like gneiss and schist, with some granite interspersed. These rocks are around 1.7 billion years old. Glaciers covered the area at various times, and Seven Lakes are probably one result.

This area escaped the miners' shovels and road-building. The land has not been altered or changed by humans as much as in other parts of Colorado. The Continental Divide by Seven Lakes appears to be a gentle ridge. The area hosts a spectacular display of July wildflowers, including paintbrushes, red elephants, pussytoes, penstemons, blue gentians, and varieties of yellow composites. Red Elephant Mountain (11,569 feet) raises its head and watches over the entire trail to Seven Lakes. This peak apparently reminded someone a long time ago of an elephant head and trunk. Can you see it?

The first part of the trail follows the Red Elephant Nature Trail. Pick up a nature guide at the trailhead. A forest fire swept through this area in the 1920s and the resulting lodgepole forest had little deadfall compared to the older, moister spruce-fir forest. Fire is important to the natural health of the forest, creating different vegetation pockets that support various plants and animals. However, by 2005, the mountain pine beetle invaded the lodgepole forest, killing many of the trees. The USDA Forest Service has removed many dead lodgepole, which pose a danger to hikers and could generate a hot fire. In several places, nice plank bridges cross wet areas. A lily pad-covered pond lies nestled in a cradle of trees.

After the trail turns west to follow Big Creek, an open area provides good views of Upper Big Creek Lake. A prominent cliff face towers above the wilderness boundary. Just beyond, down a little trail to the left, is Big Creek Falls. Not overly huge, they are still impressive. Take a break and enjoy the cool creek and falls before heading on. Beetle-kill trees are not removed in wilderness, so be aware of possible falling trees, especially on high-wind days.

The trail stays close to Big Creek for a while, then gradually climbs up a flower-filled section of trail with numerous seeps. Cow parsnip, pearly everlasting, and alder line the trail. After crossing an unnamed creek, take a quick break since the trail climbs steeply from here. More than fifteen switchbacks take you up 750 feet in a 0.5 mile. The trail then levels out and rolls gently through a nice old-growth forest past some beautiful meadows. A final climb threads through flower-filled meadows and on to Seven Lakes.

Follow the faint trail to the left of the first lake to reach the biggest lake, which is stocked yearly with native trout. There is a nice campsite above the largest lake, at

*Big Creek Falls*  ▶

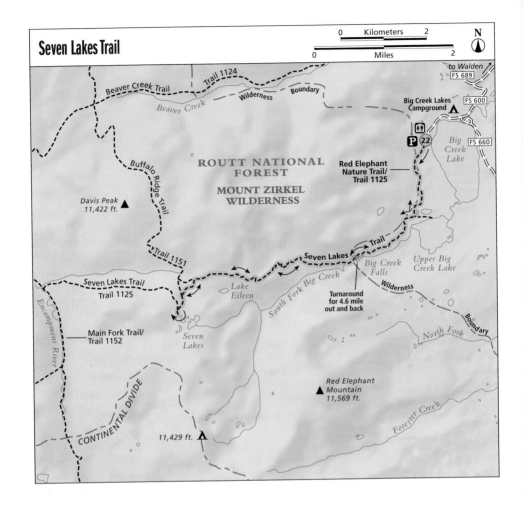

# Seven Lakes Trail

**ROUTT NATIONAL FOREST**

**MOUNT ZIRKEL WILDERNESS**

Trail 1124

Beaver Creek Trail

Beaver Creek

Wilderness Boundary

to Walden

FS 689

Big Creek Lakes Campground

FS 600

FS 660

Big Creek Lake

Red Elephant Nature Trail/ Trail 1125

Buffalo Ridge Trail

Davis Peak 11,422 ft.

Trail 1151

Seven Lakes Trail

Seven Lakes Trail Trail 1125

Lake Eileen

South Fork Big Creek

Big Creek Falls

Upper Big Creek Lake

Wilderness Boundary

Turnaround for 4.6 mile out and back

North Fork

Encampment River

Main Fork Trail/ Trail 1152

Seven Lakes

Red Elephant Mountain 11,569 ft.

CONTINENTAL DIVIDE

11,429 ft.

Forester Creek

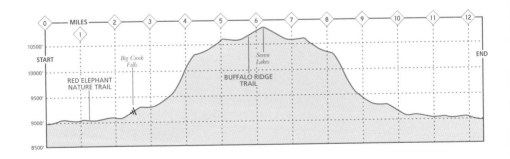

| MILES | 0 | 1 | 2 | 3 | 4 | 5 | 6 | 7 | 8 | 9 | 10 | 11 | 12 |

10500'

START

END

10000'

Big Creek Falls

Seven Lakes

RED ELEPHANT NATURE TRAIL

BUFFALO RIDGE TRAIL

9500'

9000'

8500'

# BUILDING A MOUND FIRE

Many people enjoy an evening campfire for camaraderie, warmth, storytelling, and even security. From other perspectives, fires can damage the vegetation underneath them, as well as leave ugly scars on ground and rock. However, there are ways to have your fire and prevent damage too.

A mound fire is an ecological and aesthetic way to build a fire and prevent both damage to the environment and ugly scars. First, make sure no fire bans are in effect and that you are below treeline. Next, find a big level rock imbedded in the ground, make a rock base out of "flat" rocks, or find exposed soil with less than 3 inches of plant remains. Make sure not to build your fire right under tree branches. Find some "mineral soil" along a creek or by an uprooted tree. Mineral soil is dirt and/or sand that has minimal organic matter such as pine needles, leaves, or twigs in it. Put enough soil on a large plastic garbage bag to make a flat-topped mound about 6 to 8 inches thick and about 18 inches or less in diameter. Carry the garbage bag and soil to your chosen spot and shape the mound.

To gather firewood, spread out and pick up downed and dead wood that's no larger in diameter than your wrist. Gather the wood from various places on the ground so as not to remove all dead wood in an area. Birds use dead branches on trees, so please don't break any off. Build your fire on the mound within 1 inch of the edges. Enjoy!

When finished, let the fire cool to white ash. Scatter the cold ash and any unused wood over a large area. That way no one will see that you had a fire. Return the soil to where you found it. If the garbage bag has no burn holes, you passed the mound fire test!

an appropriate distance from the water. The Forest Service requests that all camps be located at least 100 feet away from lakes, other water sources, and trails, and that no new campfire rings be built. Use existing fire rings, make a mound fire, or preferably use a stove. Be aware of lightning danger in open areas.

While visiting Seven Lakes, take time to explore the open spaces up to the Continental Divide to the south, or maybe take a side trip up Davis Peak to the north.

## Miles and Directions

**0.0** Start at Seven Lakes trailhead near Big Creek Lakes Campground. Elevation: 9,020 feet. Head up Seven Lakes Trail (Trail 1125). The Red Elephant Nature Trail shares the trail. (Pick up a nature guide at the trailhead.)

**1.25** The Red Elephant Nature Trail breaks left. Stay right, continuing on Seven Lakes Trail.

**2.3** Reach the Wilderness boundary sign. Big Creek Falls is off to the left. Elevation: 9,200 feet. GPS: N40 54.55'/W106 38.17'. **(Option:** For a shorter hike, turn around and return the way you came for a moderate 4.6-mile out and back.)

**3.4** Come to a creek crossing.

**4.3** Reach the top of a steep climb with switchbacks.

**5.1** Come to a nice meadow on left, followed by an old-growth spruce forest.

**5.7** Reach a trail junction with the Buffalo Ridge Trail (Trail 1151). Stay to the left and head uphill.

**6.0** Come to a trail junction with Seven Lakes Trail and the trail to Seven Lakes. Stay to the left (more straight ahead) and hike to the lakes.

**6.1** Reach the first of the Seven Lakes. **(Side trip:** Hike an additional 0.25 mile to view the biggest of Seven Lakes. Elevation: 10,733 feet. GPS: N40 53.78'/W106 40.98') Otherwise, return the way you came.

**12.2** Arrive back at the trailhead.

# Hike Information

### General Information
**North Park Chamber of Commerce:** Walden; (970) 723-4600; www.northparkchamber.com
**North Park Visitor's Bureau:** www.northparkvisitorsbureau.com

### Local Events/Attractions
**Arapaho National Wildlife Refuge:** Walden; (970) 723-8202; www.fws.gov/arapaho/
**McCallum Field (Oil & Gas) Auto Tour:** BLM Kremmling Field Office, Kremmling; (970) 724-3400
**North Park Museum:** 365 Logan St., Walden; (970) 723-8371

### Accommodations
**National Forest campgrounds:** Parks Ranger District, Walden; (970) 723-2700; www.fs.usda .gov/mbr

### Restaurants
**Moose Creek Cafe:** 508 Main St., Walden; (866) 850-6971; www.moosecreekcafe.net
**Paradise Lanes:** 688 Main St., Walden; (970) 723-8616
**River Rock Cafe:** 460 Main St., Walden; (970) 723-4670; www.waldenriverrock.com

Springs, was the site of a wildland firefighting tragedy in 1994. Fourteen firefighters died when the fire blew up and overtook them.

After a long day hiking, have a soak in Glenwood Springs' hot springs pool. Volcanoes may no longer erupt, but the earth still heats water for hot springs across western and central Colorado. Limestone caves are common in this area, and Glenwood Caverns offers tours of one.

The Flat Tops Trail, Grand Mesa, and Dinosaur Diamond are the Colorado scenic and historic byways to explore in northwest Colorado.

# 23 Storm King Fourteen Memorial Trail

This trail, built by volunteers, is a memorial to fourteen firefighters who lost their lives on Storm King Mountain in July 1994. Interpretive signs explain wildland fire-fighting and this unfortunate disaster. You can stop at the observation point to look across to the ridge where the firefighters died, or hike farther to the memorial sites. The trail is a journey into a burned land, now recovering. The steep trails give you a brief insight into and feeling for the work of those who fight wildland fires.

**Start:** From Storm King Fourteen Memorial Trail trailhead

**Distance:** 4.4-mile out and back

**Approximate hiking time:** 3.5 to 4.5 hours

**Difficulty:** Moderate to the observation point; most difficult to the memorial sites due to steepness

**Elevation gain/loss:** 1,280-foot gain / 440-foot loss

**Seasons:** Best from Apr through Nov

**Trail surface:** Dirt trail mainly on south and southwest-facing slopes; short and fairly steep; slippery when wet; open ridge near observation point

**Land status:** BLM land

**Nearest town:** Glenwood Springs

**Other trail users:** Hunters (in season)

**Canine compatibility:** Dogs must be on leash. No water on trail.

**Schedule:** Year-round. Call first for trail conditions Dec through Mar

**Fees and permits:** None

**Maps:** USGS Storm King Mountain; Nat Geo Trails Illustrated 123 Flat Tops SE/Glenwood Canyon

**Trail contact:** Bureau of Land Management, Colorado River Valley Field Office, Silt; (970) 876-9000; www.blm.gov/co/st/en/fo/crvfo.html

**Finding the trailhead:** From Glenwood Springs, take I-70 west to exit 109 / Canyon Creek. Turn right, then immediately right again onto the frontage road. Head back east past Canyon Creek Estates for 1 mile to a dead end with a parking lot. The trail starts by several interpretive signs at the east end of the lot. There is a portable toilet but no water at the trailhead. GPS: N39 34.43' / W107 26.02'

## The Hike

On July 2, 1994, a very natural event occurred. A lightning strike started a small fire in a piñon-juniper-Gambel oak forest on Storm King Mountain (8,793 feet). Several large wildland fires were already burning across Colorado, strapping firefighting resources. The small fire received low priority. By July 5, the fire covered five acres and crews arrived to build fire lines. But Mother Nature had other plans. By mid-afternoon on July 6, a dry cold front passed through the region, causing very

*Clothes memorial on a ghost tree* ▶

strong winds that fanned the fire into a roaring inferno traveling much faster than any human could run, especially uphill. The fire soon consumed over 2,100 acres. Fourteen firefighters could not escape the 100-foot-high flames racing toward them. Thirty-five others escaped either by hunkering down in their fire shelters or by slipping down an eastern gully to the highway.

Although forest fire is a natural and important process, the fire on Storm King Mountain endangered homes and businesses in West Glenwood to the east and Canyon Creek Estates to the west. The trees on Storm King also provided essential erosion control. Storm King and surrounding mountains are a combination of red sandstone and shale, called the Maroon Formation, deposited over eons by inland seas. When shale gets wet, mudslides often result.

Volunteers built this trail in 1995 to honor wildland firefighters nationwide and to provide an insight into their experiences. The trail begins with several interpretive signs about the July 1994 fire. They invite you to imagine being a firefighter, hiking up steep slopes, and carrying thirty to sixty pounds of equipment.

The trail climbs steeply along the south side of a ridge, through rabbitbrush, wild roses, Mormon tea, and cheatgrass, with numerous log steps to hike up. Where the trail turns to follow the west side of a ridge, a small sign relates the camaraderie of firefighters and gives you a chance to take a few deep breaths. The Colorado River roars below, as does I-70. The trail continues to climb through piñon-juniper forest. The steepness of the trail is tiring even with a light pack. About 0.25 mile up, a sign announces entry into Bureau of Land Management (BLM) lands. Switchbacks take you steadily uphill. A bench provides a handy place to check out the western view and catch your breath. Down valley, I-70 twists like a serpent, following the river's contours. The Grand Hogback and Coal Ridge form the horizon to the south.

At 0.6 mile, the trail reaches a ridge at 6,280 feet. Storm King Mountain, with scorched sticks and green Gambel oak, comes into view. You can see how the fire raced up gullies to different ridges. The trees to the right of the trail are snags of their former selves. To the left, most trees are green and alive. Narrow-leaved penstemon and blue flax flowers grow among the ghostly trunks. Across the gully, Gambel oak once again covers the slopes, although junipers and piñon pines may take forty to one hundred years to reestablish themselves.

The trail follows a mostly flat ridge for 0.4 mile to the observation point. Three large interpretive signs explain the events of that fateful July day. With a pair of binoculars, you can see the slope that twelve firefighters scrambled up trying to reach safety. Look closely for the pair of crossed skis marking one memorial site. You can turn around here or continue to the memorial sites.

To reach the memorial sites on the next ridge, continue on the trail left of the interpretive signs. If you hike this trail, be aware several sections are very steep with

◀ *Memorial sites*

loose footing. Once on that ridge, a trail to the left leads to where two helitack crew-members died, across a steep little gully by a rock outcropping. The trail to the right leads to the slope where nine members of the Prineville, Oregon, Hotshots crew and three smokejumpers died. To reach the twelve sites, walk about 0.1 mile to a trail that switchbacks down the west slope. Memorial sites are noted with the firefighters' names. The BLM and families request that you stay on the trail and do not walk straight down between the crosses—however, the trail is hidden by bushes and hard to find. The area between crosses is extremely steep and prone to erosion. Look around, see and feel the steepness of the slope. Imagine what it would be like to have a fire chasing you up that hill. Read the poem at trail's end below the memorial sites and reflect for a moment on people who are willing to give their lives to protect the lives and property of others.

## Miles and Directions

**0.0**  Start at the trailhead east of Canyon Creek Estates. Elevation: 5,680 feet. Take a few minutes to read the interpretive signs. **(Note:** The first part of the trail crosses private property, which the BLM has permission to use for this trail. Please respect the owners' property rights.)

**0.25**  Reach the BLM boundary sign.

**0.3**  Reach a bench and interpretive sign on the right side of the trail. This is a good place to catch your breath and enjoy the view down the Colorado River.

**0.6**  Gain a ridge with views of Storm King Mountain and the burned area.

**1.0**  Arrive at the observation point with interpretive signs. Elevation: 6,360 feet. GPS: N39 34.68'/W107 25.35'. **(Option:** You can turn around here for a shorter, moderate hike.)

**1.2**  Reach the bottom of the first gully, contour around into the second gully, and start climbing up to the next ridge.

**1.7**  The trail comes to a T intersection. Elevation: 6,680 feet. GPS: N39 34.66'/W107 24.95'. Take the left trail to the helitack crew memorial site.

**2.0**  Arrive at the helitack crew memorial site. Look across the deep little gully near a rock outcropping to see the crosses. Head back toward the T intersection.

**2.3**  Arrive back at the T intersection. Proceed ahead to the other twelve memorial sites.

**2.4**  The trail switchbacks downhill past the memorial sites that are marked with signs along the trail. **(Note:** Please remember to stay on the trail that switchbacks [versus the trail that goes straight downhill]. When you see the Scott Blecha sign, the trail turns right into the bushes. If you walk to Blecha's stone, you'll end up walking straight down an extremely steep slope between the crosses. The area between crosses is prone to erosion.)

**2.5**  The trail ends below the twelve memorial sites. GPS: N39 34.59'/W107 25.08'. Walk to the end to read the poem. Return the way you came.

**2.7**  Arrive back at the T intersection. Turn left to head downhill and return to the observation point.

**4.4**  Arrive back at the trailhead.

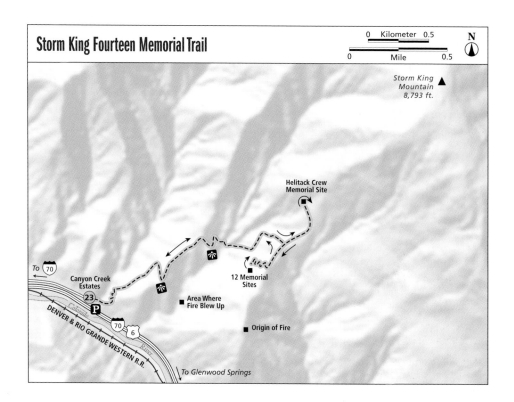

Storm King Fourteen Memorial Trail

0    Kilometer    0.5

0    Mile    0.5

N

Storm King
Mountain
8,793 ft.

Helitack Crew
Memorial Site

To 70

Canyon Creek
Estates

23

P

DENVER & RIO GRANDE WESTERN R.R.

70    6

Colorado River

12 Memorial
Sites

Area Where
Fire Blew Up

Origin of Fire

To Glenwood Springs

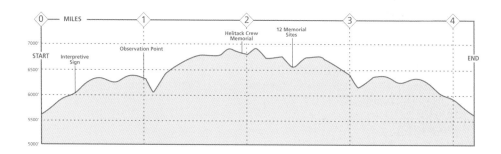

0    MILES    1    2    3    4

Helitack Crew
Memorial

12 Memorial
Sites

7000'

START

Interpretive
Sign

Observation Point

6500'

END

6000'

5500'

5000'

## Hike Information

### General Information

**Glenwood Springs Chamber of Commerce:** Glenwood Springs; (970) 945-6589 or (888) 4-GLENWOOD; www.glenscape.com

# MORE ABOUT STORM KING

Two Rivers Park in Glenwood Springs contains a memorial to the fourteen firefighters who died on Storm King Mountain. A bronze sculpture depicting three wildland firefighters is surrounded by a garden, pictures, and information about each of the lost firefighters.

To reach Two Rivers Park from the Storm King Fourteen Memorial Trail, take I-70 eastbound. Exit at West Glenwood and turn left under the highway. Then turn right onto US 6 eastbound. Go 1.8 miles to Devereux Drive and turn right. Drive 0.3 mile, crossing over I-70, and look for the park on the left. Turn left into the park. The memorial garden is straight ahead.

The story of the Storm King Mountain Fire (mistakenly reported as being in South Canyon) is captured in the book *Fire on the Mountain* by John N. McLean, published in 1999. The History Channel produced a video, *Fire on the Mountain*, in 2002; www.historychannel .com. Many interesting articles, including the report of the investigation team, can be found via the Internet.

## Local Events/Attractions
**Glenwood Caverns, Glenwood Springs:** (800) 530-1635; www.glenwoodcaverns.com
**Glenwood Hot Springs Pool:** Glenwood Springs; (970) 945-2955 or (800) 537-7946; www .hotspringspool.com
**Strawberry Days:** Glenwood Springs; (970) 945-6589; www.strawberrydaysfestival.com

## Accommodations
**Glenwood Springs Hostel:** 1021 Grand Ave., Glenwood Springs; (970) 945-8545 or (800) 946-7835; www.hostelcolorado.com
**Hot Springs Lodge:** historic site; 401 North River St., Glenwood Springs; (970) 945-6571 or (800) 537-7946; www.hotspringspool.com
**Hotel Colorado:** historic site, 526 Pine St., Glenwood Springs; (800) 544-3998 or (970) 945-6511; www.hotelcolorado.com

## Restaurants
**Glenwood Canyon Brewing Co.:** 402 Seventh St., Hotel Denver, Glenwood Springs; (970) 945-1276; www.glenwoodcanyon.com
**Italian Underground:** 715 Grand Ave., Glenwood Springs; (970) 945-6422
**Narayan's Nepal Restaurant:** 6824 Highway 82, Glenwood Springs; (970) 945-8803; www .nepalrestaurant.us.com

# 24 Coyote and Squirrel Trails

Coyote Trail winds past limestone caves, through a lush riparian and forested area, then above for a bird's-eye view of Rifle Falls. Kids of all ages will love exploring the caves. Bring a flashlight for the largest one. Squirrel Trail crosses East Rifle Creek and winds through Gambel oak forest to the base of a red sandstone cliff. The trail continues along the Grass Valley Canal, which takes water to Harvey Gap Reservoir. Hiked together, the trails make a lopsided figure eight through a naturally and historically interesting area along East Rifle Creek.

**Start:** From the Rifle Falls State Park picnic ground

**Distance:** 1.8-mile double loop

**Approximate hiking time:** 1 to 2 hours

**Difficulty:** Mostly easy with some steep sections

**Elevation gain:** 140 feet total: two at 70 feet each

**Seasons:** Year-round except after snowstorms

**Trail surface:** Paved road, dirt road, and dirt trail

**Land status:** State Park

**Nearest town:** Rifle

**Other trail users:** Wheelchair users (on first part of Coyote Trail), anglers, and mountain bikers

**Canine compatibility:** Dogs must be on leash

**Schedule:** Year-round, except after snowstorms. Day-use hours are 5 a.m. to 10 p.m. Call first for winter trail conditions.

**Fees and permits:** Daily entrance fee or annual parks pass required

**Maps:** USGS Rifle Falls; Nat Geo Trails Illustrated 125 Flat Tops SW/Rifle Gap

**Trail contact:** Rifle Falls State Park, Rifle; (970) 625-1607; parks.state.co.us/parks /riflefalls

**Finding the trailhead:** From I-70 exit 90 for Rifle, head north on CO 13 through town. In about 4 miles, turn right onto CO 325 and drive another 4 miles to Rifle Gap Reservoir. Stay on CO 325, which turns right and goes over the dam. Drive another 5.6 miles to the Rifle Falls State Park entrance. Pay the fee here or at the self-serve kiosk. Turn left and drive 0.2 mile through the campground to the picnic area. Park here. A vault toilet and water are available. GPS: N39 40.58' / W107 41.92'

## The Hike

Lined with red sandstone and limestone cliffs, Rifle Falls State Park is a showplace with a 60-foot triple waterfall, lush riparian and forested areas, wildlife habitat, and a nice picnic area and campground. Two trails, named after local inhabitants, wander through the park for a complete tour. Interpretive signs along Coyote Trail explain the natural and social history of the area.

The original configuration of Rifle Falls consisted of one wide sheet of water, with some early pictures showing multiple ribbons of water. In 1908, the Rifle Light, Heat, and Power Company was incorporated to provide electricity to the town of

Rifle. This group built the first hydroelectric plant in Colorado by diverting part of East Rifle Creek through a pipe descending the cliff at Rifle Falls. As a result, Rifle Falls became two ribbons of water plus the pipeline. Thirteen miles of transmission cable linked Rifle with the power plant. In town, 8 miles of wires, twenty-five streetlights, and wiring for most buildings were installed. Rifle received its first electricity from the power plant on December 31, 1909. The company merged with Public Service Company in 1926. Public Service sold the property to the Colorado Game and Fish Department in 1959, at which time the plant was closed. The stone power plant was torn down in 1971. With the removal of the pipe, the falls have reverted to three streams of water.

▶ **Various stories exist about how Rifle Creek was named. Most stories develop the theme of someone leaving or finding a rifle leaning against a tree along the creek. Another legend refers to a custom of cowboys firing their rifles at a roundup ground near the confluence of the three creeks.**

The cliffs that create the falls are made of calcium carbonate from creeks flowing underground in limestone deposits upstream. Thousands of years ago, the creek ran over some obstacle, which geologists believe was a giant beaver dam. The water left deposits that developed into today's cliffs. You can approach the falls from various sides, getting sprayed no matter which way you choose. To the right of the falls, Coyote Trail winds past limestone caves, created by water eroding the cliff from the inside out. Some are shallow, while one is large enough (90 feet) to need a flashlight to explore. Bats live in these caves, so be respectful if they are hanging out. The caves contain interesting formations such as flowstone, popcorn stone, and stalactites hanging from the ceiling. Watch your head as you hike from cave to cave. One place in particular has very low clearance.

Outside the caves, cottonwoods, box elders, chokecherry trees, hawthorns (emphasis on thorns), coyote willows, and a little stream line the trail. Blue Steller's jays squawk overhead. The trail curves around and up until you are on top of the cliff. The Bobcat Trail to the Rifle Fish Hatchery branches to the north just before the falls. The hatchery was completed in 1954 as the largest trout hatchery in the state. Old metal pipes and wooden water diversions still remain from the hydroelectric plant days. The quickly flowing water disappears over the cliff in a white froth as it takes the plunge. Observation decks hang beyond the cliff for a bird's-eye view and a potential adrenaline rush. The trail down is steep, but stairs make the trek a little easier. The riparian area around the falls creates wildlife-watching opportunities.

After arriving back at the picnic area, walk through the main campground past the fee kiosk to Squirrel Trail. This trail takes you to the Grass Valley Canal, built between 1891 and 1894. At the same time, a dam was being built about 5 miles away (as the crow flies), across a gap in the Grand Hogback. This tilted ridge is the western

◀ *Rifle Falls from overlook*

*Trail along Grass Valley canal*

Colorado version of the Dakota Hogback west of Denver. The canal brings water from East Rifle Creek to Harvey Gap Reservoir, which stores irrigation water for farms and ranches. The reservoir is in Harvey Gap State Park.

Squirrel Trail follows the creek through the walk-in campground, then crosses it on a swinging bridge. Gambel oaks on the other side create a thick forest, a cool treat on a hot day. The trail twists and climbs up the side of the canyon to the base of the cliff. A T intersection appears after one steep stretch. Turn left and head uphill to where the trail meets the canal before it enters the tunnel. The water is clear and deep. The dirt road along the canal takes you back to the picnic ground by going downhill at the left-hand curve.

Rifle Falls has attracted visitors since the 1880s. Many people consider this area the Hawaii or Costa Rica of Colorado. The swank Zerbe Resort housed tourists for a number of years, starting around 1903 until, unfortunately, it burned down in 1922.

## Miles and Directions

**0.0** Start at the picnic ground at the closed pipe gate on the paved road. Elevation: 6,500 feet. Head north toward Rifle Falls on the Coyote Trail.

**0.1** View the Rifle Falls area and interpretive signs. (**Note:** You might get sprayed by the falling water mist.)

**0.2** Reach the start of the limestone caves.

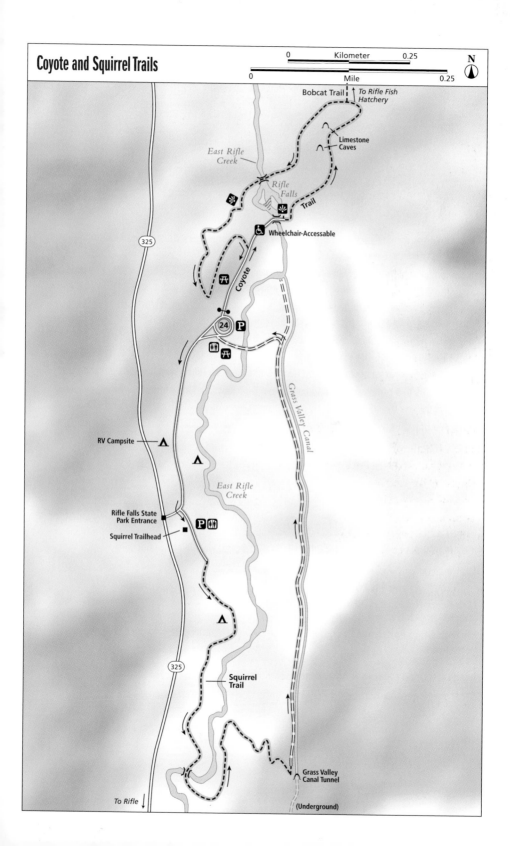

# Coyote and Squirrel Trails

Kilometer
0 — 0.25

Mile
0 — 0.25

N

Bobcat Trail — To Rifle Fish Hatchery

Limestone Caves

*East Rifle Creek*

*Rifle Falls*

Rifle Falls Trail

Wheelchair-Accessable

325

Coyote

24 P

RV Campsite

*East Rifle Creek*

Rifle Falls State Park Entrance

Squirrel Trailhead

P

*Grass Valley Canal*

325

Squirrel Trail

Grass Valley Canal Tunnel

(Underground)

To Rifle ↓

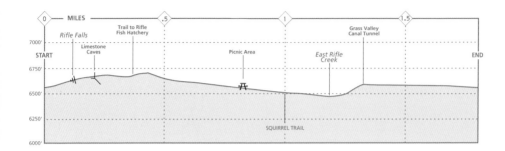

**0.3** Come to the intersection with Bobcat Trail to the fish hatchery. Go straight ahead to the falls overlook. Elevation: 6,600 feet.

**0.5** Turn left onto the observation deck for a great view of the falls. Just beyond, the trail drops downhill, sometimes steeply down concrete steps, back to the picnic area.

**0.6** Arrive back at the dirt road in the picnic area. Turn right and walk on the road back to the parking lot then through the campground toward the entrance station.

**0.8** Reach the Squirrel Trail trailhead to the left of the entrance station. GPS: N39 40.40'/W107 41.93'.

**1.1** Stay to right at campsite 20, drop down, and cross East Rifle Creek on a swinging bridge.

**1.35** Squirrel Trail climbs steeply and comes to a T intersection. Turn left and continue uphill on the trail.

**1.4** The trail joins the dirt road along the canal at the water tunnel.

**1.7** Come to a fork and go left down the road.

**1.8** Arrive back at the picnic ground.

## Hike Information

### General Information
**Rifle Area Chamber of Commerce:** Rifle; (970) 625-2085; www.riflechamber.com

### Local Events/Attractions
**Garfield County Fair:** Rifle; (970) 625-5922; www.garfieldcountyfair.com

### Accommodations
**Rifle Falls State Park campground:** Rifle; (970) 625-1607; parks.state.co.us/parks/riflefalls

### Restaurants
**Shanghai Garden Chinese & American:** 1538 Railroad Ave., Rifle; (970) 625-4430

# 25 Marvine Loop

This hike takes you to the top of the White River Plateau in the Flat Tops Wilderness via East Marvine Trail and loops back to the same trailhead via Marvine Trail for a multiday backpacking trip. The public resource and wilderness preservation history in this area is significant. Part of the hike travels through dense spruce-fir forest conveying a primeval feeling. Once on the plateau, the land rolls along through subalpine meadows and alpine tundra punctuated by clumps of trees and short peaks. Small lakes and ponds abound. Take time to climb Big Marvine Peak or explore the various lakes on your own. Camping is available below the plateau and on top.

**Start:** From the East Marvine Trail (Trail 1822) trailhead

**Distance:** 23.2-mile loop backpack.

**Approximate hiking time:** 3 days minimum to explore the Flat Tops

**Difficulty:** Most difficult due to length, elevation gain, and steep sections

**Elevation gain/loss:** 3,120-foot gain with a 290-foot loss

**Seasons:** Best from late June to mid-Oct

**Trail surface:** Dirt trail with some muddy sections and several bridgeless creek crossings

**Land status:** National forest and wilderness

**Nearest town:** Meeker

**Other trail users:** Equestrians, anglers, and hunters (in season)

**Canine compatibility:** Dogs must be under control

**Schedule:** The access road to the trailhead opens from mid- to late May and remains open through the end of the hunting seasons in Nov. Trails are neither maintained nor marked for winter use.

**Fees and permits:** No fees or permits are required. Group size limit: No more than 15 people per group with a maximum combination of 25 people and pack or saddle animals in any one group.

**Maps:** USGS Big Marvine Peak, Lost Park, Oyster Lake, and Ripple Creek Pass; Nat Geo Trails Illustrated 122 Flat Tops NE/Trappers Lake

**Trail contact:** White River National Forest, Blanco Ranger District, Meeker; (970) 878-4039; www.fs.usda.gov/whiteriver/

**Finding the trailhead:** From Meeker, drive east on CO 13 to where it curves north, and turn right onto Rio Blanco County Road (RBCR) 8. Follow the FLAT TOPS TRAIL SCENIC BYWAY sign. In about 28.5 miles (past mile marker 28), turn right onto a dirt road by the Marvine Creek sign. In 0.2 mile, turn left by Fritzlans Guest House onto RBCR 12, which later becomes FR 12. Trailhead parking is 5.1 miles down FR 12 on the left. Park away from the corrals reserved for outfitters. There is no water or toilet at the trailhead. Both are available at the two nearby campgrounds (fee areas). GPS: N40 00.55'/W107 25.47'

## The Hike

While hiking up the trail, notice the pockmarked rocks. The White River Plateau is capped with dark basalt from volcanic eruptions that started around 25 million years

*Big Marvine Peak and top of plateau*

ago. These eruptions lasted about 17 million years. After cooling off for another 7 million years, the Ice Age took hold. An ice cap formed over the plateau between 18,000 and 12,000 years ago. Melting glaciers left numerous little lakes and ponds below and on top of the plateau.

Many years later Ute Indians, also called the People of the Shining Mountains, camped in the Flat Tops on the northern end of the White River Plateau during the summer. Deer, elk, bison, and rabbits provided meat. Berries, wild onions, and the root of the yampa rounded out their diet.

As white settlers moved into the area, grazing and timber harvesting ran rampant and forest fires raged. Concerned citizens lobbied to protect western public resources. In 1891, President Benjamin Harrison set aside the White River Timber Land Reserve. White River is the second-oldest national forest in

▶ When meeting horses on the trail, step off on the downhill side until the horses pass. If a horse wants more room, it will move off the trail away from you. It is safer for both the horse and rider if the horse heads uphill. If the trail is narrow, ask the rider for instructions.

the United States. The Flat Tops area earned another special place in history in 1919. The USDA Forest Service sent landscape architect Arthur Carhart to Trappers Lake, at the base of the Flat Tops, to survey the area for summer cabins. Instead, Carhart recommended that this beautiful area be set aside and protected from development. He noted: "There are a number of places with scenic values of such great worth that they are rightfully property of all people. They should be preserved for all time for the people of the Nation and the world. Trappers Lake is unquestionably a candidate for that classification."

▶ When hiking on muddy trails, get muddy! Walking around the mud destroys the trail edge, making the bog bigger. By wearing waterproof boots and even gaiters, walking through the mud is less painful. Gaiters help keep water out of your boots when rock-hopping or wading across shallow creeks, too.

Carhart later joined Aldo Leopold and began the movement that created the Wilderness Preservation System. The Flat Tops Primitive Area was established in 1932 with special protections. After many years of negotiation President Lyndon B. Johnson signed the Wilderness Act of 1964. Congress elevated the Primitive Area to the Flat Tops Wilderness in 1975. The second-largest wilderness area in Colorado is home to the largest elk herd in the state. Keep an eye open for deer and elk while you're hiking. Other wildlife you might encounter includes black bears, bobcats, pine martens, foxes, coyotes, marmots, and pikas.

The trail follows East Marvine Creek through aspen, Gambel oak, and lodgepole pine forests. Occasional grassy meadows provide views of the Flat Tops escarpment and Little Marvine Peaks. Follow along a small stream, then past the 2-mile mark, where ponds and small lakes start to appear. The trail climbs steadily up through aspens, Engelmann spruces, and subalpine firs. Numerous creeks intersect the trail, and some can be tricky to cross depending on water level. Most creeks have muddy edges and no log bridges, so you'll have to rock hop.

After contouring around a ridge, Rainbow Lake lies to the left. A few campsites can be found on the ridge above it. Beyond Rainbow Lake, the trail levels off and loses some elevation as it runs across meadows and tiny creeks. It finally rejoins East Marvine Creek and passes an energetic cascade before climbing steeply up the side of the Flat Tops. The spruce-fir forest is thick and dark here. Bark beetles infested the forest in the 1940s and many dead snags make the forest appear ancient. Wood decays slowly in the high, dry Colorado climate. How large animals like elk can maneuver through the tangled dark forest almost defies the imagination.

Two long switchbacks lead to the base of the escarpment. When you find a flat spot, take a breather and enjoy the view. Scan the surrounding cliff bands for silver ribbon waterfalls. Six short switchbacks take you even higher, and two final switchbacks bring you close to the edge of the plateau. The climb is still not quite over, but becomes gentler now. You have gained about 1,000 feet in the last mile.

A large cairn holding up a tree trunk greets you at the top edge. A small lake is

*Rainbow Lake*

just beyond, then another and another. Little Marvine Peaks rise to the north, with Big Marvine Peak dominating the southwest view. The subalpine meadows roll along with patches of spruce-fir. After the third little lake, the trail splits. The left branch heads for Twin Lakes and Oyster Lake Trail, while the right branch (unofficial trail) leads to a good fishing lake and toward Big Marvine Peak. From here you can explore and camp many places. Take a couple of days to enjoy the open high country of the Flat Tops. Then head south on the Oyster Lake Trail to Marvine Trail to make a loop back to the trailhead parking area where you started.

Please remember to camp at least 100 feet (about thirty-five adult steps) away from streams, lakes, and trails. Using a lightweight cookstove instead of a fire will avoid leaving permanent scars on the land. By practicing Leave No Trace techniques, hikers can enjoy a pristine experience and find solitude in the Flat Tops Wilderness for many years.

# Marvine Loop

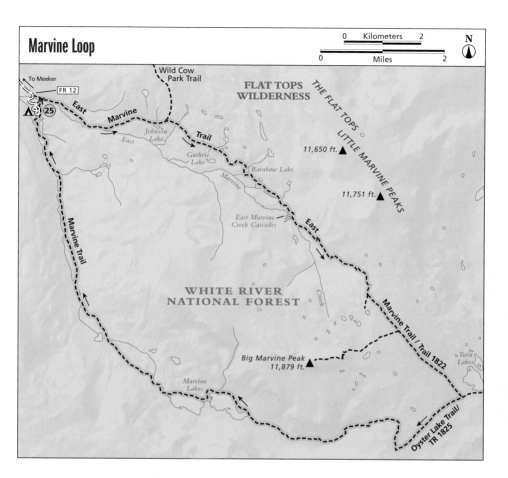

## Miles and Directions

**0.0**   Start at the East Marvine trailhead (Trail 1822). Elevation: 8,091 feet.

**0.1**   Cross the sturdy bridge over East Marvine Creek. At the T intersection, turn right onto the trail and head uphill with the creek on your right.

**1.4**   The trail leaves East Marvine Creek to follow a small stream.

**1.7**   The trail splits; stay to the right. **(Note:** The trail can get very muddy in this stretch.)

**2.7**   Johnson Lake is on the right. GPS: N40 00.27' / W107 23.30'.

**3.25**   Come to the junction with Wild Cow Park Trail (Trail 2244). Stay to the right on East Marvine Trail.

**5.0**   Reach Rainbow Lake.

**7.3**   The trail splits. The right spur (nonsystem trail) goes to Ned Wilson Lake. The high point is just past here at about 11,180 feet.

**8.5**   Reach the junction with the trail to Big Marvine Peak. Continue on the East Marvine Trail.

**10.75**   Reach the junction with the Oyster Lake Trail (Trail 1825). Elevation 10,989 feet. GPS: N39 56.52' / W107 17.75' Turn right onto Oyster Lake Trail.

| 12.2 | Turn right onto the Marvine Trail (Trail 1823) and drop down the escarpment. GPS: N39 55.83'/W107 18.90'. |
| 17.4 | Reach Marvine Lakes. |
| 19.2 | Reach Slide Lake. Ford Marvine Creek near the lake, being very careful, especially if the creek is high. |
| 23.2 | Arrive at the Marvine Trail trailhead, at the same parking area where you started. GPS: N40 00.53'/W107 25.46'. |

## Hike Information

### General Information
**Meeker Chamber of Commerce:** Meeker; (970) 878-5510; www.meekerchamber.com

### Local Events/Attractions
**Meeker Classic Sheepdog Championship Trials:** Meeker; (970) 878-5510 or (970) 878-0111; www.meekersheepdog.com

**Range Call Celebration:** Meeker; (970) 878-5510; www.meekercolorado.com/rangecall.htm

**The White River Museum:** Meeker; (970) 878-9982; www.meekercolorado.com/whiteriver museum/index.htm

### Accommodations
**Marvine campgrounds:** White River National Forest, Blanco Ranger District, Meeker; (970) 878-4039; www.fs.usda.gov/whiteriver

### Restaurants
**Clark's Big Burger:** 858 EastMarket St., Meeker; (970) 878-3240

**Ma Famiglia:** 410 Market St., Meeker: (970) 878-4141

**Meeker Cafe:** 560 Main, Meeker; (970) 878-5062; www.themeekerhotel.com

# A LITTLE UTE INDIAN HISTORY

Ute territory once covered about 150,000 square miles of mountainous Colorado, Utah, and southern Wyoming. The Utes were divided into seven bands, each with its own hunting territory. The White River band called a large area of northwest Colorado their home, including the Flat Tops. For hundreds of years they roamed the huge territory, following game with the seasons. The southern bands had early contact with the Spanish and obtained horses. Accomplished horsemen, their battle skills were feared by whites and other Native American tribes alike.

The Utes tried to live in peace with the new white settlers. Chief Ouray of the Tabeguache band realized that fighting would result in disaster. Although the Utes lived in different bands, Ouray was recognized as the spokesman for all Utes by the United States government. He crafted treaties very favorable to his people. The treaties, however, were either broken or modified as the pressure for gold and homesteading increased. The treaty of 1868 stipulated that no white man could enter Ute territory, covering the western third of Colorado, without Ute permission.

The government created agencies to provide supplies for the Utes and hopefully keep the peace. One agency was located near present-day Meeker on the White River. Nathan Meeker became agent in 1878. The next year Meeker decided that the Utes should farm a grassy pasture being used for their prized horses. Farming was not part of the Ute way of life and a disagreement ensued. Meeker requested reinforcements. Led by Major Thornburgh, troops crossed into Ute territory without permission. Who fired the first shot is unknown, but the resulting battle ended in the death of Meeker, as well as many soldiers and Utes. Angry whites banished all Utes to reservations in 1880, with the White River band going to the Uintah Reservation in Utah.

# 26 Black Mountain (West Summit) Trail

This hike climbs to the west summit of Black Mountain, a volcanic plateau in the Elkhead Mountains. The trail first winds through an aspen forest with vegetation so thick at times that you might feel the need for a machete. The trail proceeds into drier lodgepole and spruce-fir forests. Once up on the plateau, a spur trail takes you to a raptor viewing area complete with an interpretive poster and views west toward Dinosaur National Monument and Utah.

**Start:** From the Cottonwood trailhead at the east side of Freeman Reservoir

**Distance:** 7.4 miles out and back

**Approximate hiking time:** 3.5 to 5 hours

**Difficulty:** Difficult due to elevation gain and some rough trail sections

**Elevation gain:** 2,055 feet

**Seasons:** Best from mid-June to mid-Oct

**Trail surface:** Dirt trail with wet areas and some rocky sections

**Land status:** National forest

**Nearest town:** Craig

**Other trail users:** Equestrians, mountain bikers, and hunters (in season)

**Canine compatibility:** Dogs must be on leash at the trailhead, in the parking lot, and in the campground and under control elsewhere. Water is sparse on the trail.

**Schedule:** Year-round. The access road is closed by snow about 7.2 miles from the trailhead in winter. The road is used by snowmobiles. The trail is neither maintained nor marked for winter use.

**Fees and permits:** Day-use fee required for Freeman Recreation Area; America the Beautiful pass accepted

**Map:** USGS Freeman Reservoir

**Trail contact:** Medicine Bow-Routt National Forest, Hahns Peak/Bears Ears Ranger District, Steamboat Springs; (970) 870-2299; www.fs .usda.gov/mbr

**Finding the trailhead:** From the intersection of US 40 and CO 13 in Craig, head north on CO 13 to just past mile marker 103, 13.4 miles. Turn right onto Moffat CR 11 (which becomes FR 112) and drive 9.2 miles to Freeman Recreation Area. Pay the day-use fee at the self-service station. Continue another 0.4 mile to the east end of the reservoir, turn left, and go another 0.1 mile to the parking area at the trailhead near the campground. The hike description starts at the east trailhead. Water and vault toilets are at the campground (fee area). GPS: N40 45.83'/W 107 25.37'

## The Hike

In the Elkhead Mountains of northwestern Colorado, Black Mountain forms a 1.75-mile-long plateau that rises north of Craig. From a distance, it does indeed look black. The Elkheads were formed by the same volcanic eruptions that shaped the Flat Tops and White River Plateau between 25 million and 17 million years ago. At the eastern edge of a desert zone, the Elkheads capture enough moisture to feed the Elkhead, Little Snake, and Yampa Rivers. Ute Indians lived and hunted here. Although

*Black Mountain Trail through aspen*

very popular in fall with hunters because of large elk, deer, and pronghorn antelope herds, summer finds the area less used than the Wilderness areas to the east and south. Aspens flourish in the Freeman Reservoir area and on the lower part of Black Mountain, making this trail a colorful fall hike.

Aspens and willows growing along Little Cottonwood Creek border the first part of the trail. The lush aspen forest provides a home to many animals and plants. Colorado columbine, the state flower, grows in aspen forests. Pink Wood's rose, white geranium, yellow heartleaf arnica (named for its heart-shaped leaves), pinkish-purple fireweed, dandelion, blue harebells, various paintbrushes, pussytoes, white Mariposa lily, and wild strawberries cover the ground. Larkspur, pearly everlasting, and white to pinkish yarrow are common. In moister areas, tall cow parsnip, with its teeny flowers forming a lacey doily, and deep purple monkshood grow in profusion. Cow parsnip is often confused with Queen Anne's lace. Monkshood is aptly named, with its monk's cowl flowers. Listen for the *chick-a-dee-dee-dee* of the mountain chickadee, a small gray and black bird that lives here year-round. Elk and deer find ample food in aspen forests, including grasses and bushes such as serviceberry, snowberry, twinberry, and chokecherry, along with Rocky Mountain maple.

The aspen tree is an interesting plant. Started from seed, expansion of a stand occurs when lateral roots sprout new shoots, forming a clone. If you notice how various sets of aspen change color at different times or exhibit different hues, the look-alike bunch is the same plant. Aspens sprout quickly after a fire, mining, logging, or other disturbance has denuded an area. Because they shed leaves that decompose faster than evergreen needles, aspens return nutrients to the soil more rapidly than other trees. The soil is richer, fostering an environment for other plants, which in turn contribute nutrients to the soil. Aspens, however, are susceptible to about twenty different diseases, making one wonder how they survive so well.

Elk depend on aspen trees, especially during harsh winters when they cannot uncover buried grasses. Scraping bark off with their lower teeth, they feast on the cambium layer just under the bark. Watch for elk teeth marks as you hike. Black bears enjoy many fruits of the aspen forest, from aspen buds and catkins in spring to berries produced by the numerous shrubs. They sometimes climb aspens, leaving claw marks as testimony to their exploits. Avoid surprising bears that are trying to fatten up before winter.

The hike starts along the east shore of Freeman Reservoir, then heads up the Little Cottonwood Creek drainage. The trail can be very muddy after heavy rains. Farther on, one section is very rocky as it climbs to the Bears Ears Trail (Trail 1144). When you reach Black Mountain Trail (Trail 1185), head north to a big aspen stand. Thick forest undergrowth sometimes obscures the trail. Watch your footing as aspen forests are notorious for hidden roots and fallen trees waiting to twist an ankle. Some large boulders lend a rock-garden atmosphere along trail sections. A few clearings present views to the south and west, including of Freeman Reservoir about 1,000 feet below.

The trail curves up a ridge and enters spruce-fir forest. It climbs steadily to a flat spot below the plateau with views to the north. The big boulders make a nice rest spot. The trail then drops about 60 feet into an open area where a large boulder field on the right lines a thumb of the plateau. After a few tight switchbacks, the trail continues to climb to a saddle on the plateau. After hiking around a boulder field, you'll come to another open area. A spur trail heads north to the raptor viewing area, where an interpretive sign explains why golden and bald eagles enjoy soaring and playing above the edge of Black Mountain. The west summit is a little farther to the northeast. A sign denotes the summit, barely discernible on the fairly flat plateau top. The trail beyond the west summit continues another 1.5 miles to the east summit (10,801 feet), with views of the Yampa Valley.

## Miles and Directions

**0.0**  Start at the Cottonwood trailhead at the east end of Freeman Reservoir. Elevation: 8,760 feet. Follow Cottonwood Trail (Trail 1183).

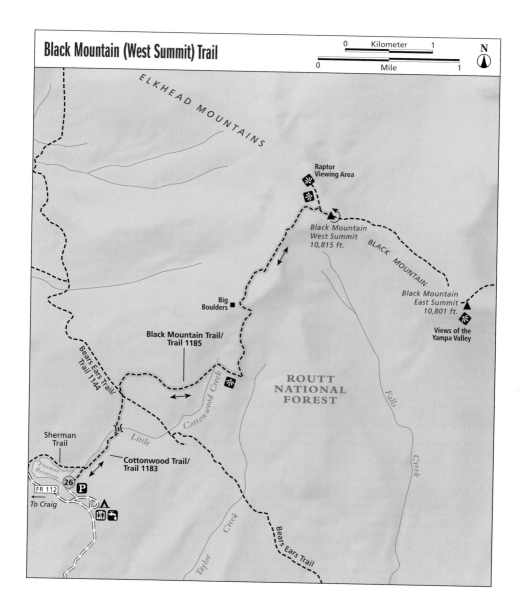

# Black Mountain (West Summit) Trail

ELKHEAD MOUNTAINS

Raptor
Viewing Area

Black Mountain
West Summit
10,815 ft.

BLACK MOUNTAIN

Black Mountain
East Summit
10,801 ft.

Big
Boulders

Views of the
Yampa Valley

Black Mountain Trail/
Trail 1185

Bears Ears Trail/
Trail 1144

Cottonwood Creek

ROUTT
NATIONAL
FOREST

Falls

Sherman
Trail

Little

Cottonwood Trail/
Trail 1183

Freeman
Reservoir

26

FR 112

P

To Craig

Creek

Creek

Taylor

Bears Ears Trail

**0.2** Pass the junction with the Sherman Trail (Trail 1010) coming in from left. Keep hiking straight on Cottonwood Trail.

**0.6** Cross Little Cottonwood Creek on a bridge.

**0.8** Reach the trail junction of Cottonwood and Bears Ears Trails. Turn left and head uphill on the Bears Ears Trail (Trail 1144).

**0.9** Reach the trail junction of Bears Ears Trail and Black Mountain Trail (Trail 1185). Turn right up Black Mountain Trail. GPS: N40 46.41'/W107 24.97'.

**1.8** Enjoy the views to the south and east as you leave the aspen forest.

*Freeman Reservoir from Black Mountain Trail*

**2.6** Come to a right switchback and a flat area near big boulders. **(FYI:** This is a good rest stop.)

**3.3** The trail reaches the edge of a plateau.

**3.6** The spur trail to the raptor viewing area. Stay right to go to the summit. **(Side trip:** Taking the out-and-back spur to the raptor viewing area will add a total of 0.5 mile to your hike. Raptors enjoy the thermals in this area. The viewpoint has an interpretive sign explaining the soaring birds of prey you might be lucky to see. GPS: N40 47.65'/W107 23.50'. On a clear day, you can see west to Dinosaur National Monument and the Uinta Mountains in Utah.)

**3.7** Reach the west summit of Black Mountain (10,815 feet). GPS: N40 47.45'/W107 23.30'. Turn around and retrace your tracks back to the start.

**7.3** Reach the junction with a trail from the left, but with no sign. Keep going straight ahead or you'll end up back at the campground.

**7.4** Arrive back at the trailhead.

# Hike Information

## General Information

**Moffat County Tourism Association:** Craig; (866) 332-8436 or (970) 824-2335; www.moffat
countytourism.com

**Moffat County Visitors Center:** Craig; (800) 864-4405 or (970) 824-5689; www.craig-chamber.com

## Local Events/Attractions

**Grande Olde West Days:** end of May; Craig; (800) 864-4405; www.grandoldewestdays.com

**Museum of Northwest Colorado:** Craig; (970) 824-6360; www.museumnwco.org

## Accommodations

**Colorado State Parks–Yampa (Elkhead Reservoir):** Hayden; (970) 276-2063; http://parks
.state.co.us/parks/yampariver/

**National Forest campgrounds:** Hahns Peak/Bears Ears Ranger District, Steamboat Springs;
(970) 879-2299; www.fs.usda.gov/mbr

## Restaurants

**Serendipity Cafe & Coffee Shop:** 576 Yampa Ave., Craig; (970) 824-5846

## Hike Tours

**Yampatika:** Steamboat Springs; (970) 871-9151; www.yampatika.org

# 27 Gates of Lodore Nature Trail

Gates of Lodore Nature Trail takes you through semidesert shrubland to a viewpoint near the Gates of Lodore. Here the Green River cuts through the Uinta Mountains, creating the Canyon of the Lodore, a spectacular gorge with towering 2,000-foot vermilion cliffs. Take time to read the nature trail guide. Then sit for a while on the sandstone, looking down the canyon. Listen to the breeze and the crickets, and watch the dragonflies. Look for raptors soaring above. Think back to the time when John Wesley Powell passed here in 1869, at the beginning of his first journey down the Colorado River through the Grand Canyon.

**Start:** From Gates of Lodore Campground
**Distance:** 1.0-mile out and back
**Approximate hiking time:** 30 to 50 minutes
**Difficulty:** Easy due to shortness
**Elevation gain:** 60 feet
**Seasons:** Year-round except after a big snowstorm
**Trail surface:** Dirt trail with some rock steps
**Land status:** National Monument
**Nearest town:** Craig
**Other trail users:** Hikers only

**Canine compatibility:** Dogs not permitted
**Schedule:** Year-round, except after a big snowstorm
**Fees and permits:** There is no entrance fee for using the Gates of Lodore area. A campground fee is charged.
**Maps:** USGS Gates of Lodore; Nat Geo Trails Illustrated 220 Dinosaur National Monument
**Trail contact:** Dinosaur National Monument, Dinosaur; (435) 781-7700; www.nps.gov/dino

**Finding the trailhead:** Drive west out of Craig on US 40 for about 31 miles to Maybell. Turn right onto CO 318 west. Drive 40.3 miles to Moffat County Road (MCR) 10 and turn sharply left onto it. This road is dirt, but well maintained. It could get muddy when wet. In 0.6 mile, turn right onto MCR 34. Stay on MCR 34 for 8.8 miles until you reach the Gates of Lodore Ranger Station in Dinosaur National Monument. (Do not turn right onto MCR 34N). Drive to the far end of the campground to the trailhead. Water and vault toilets are available at the campground. GPS: N40 43.39'/W108 53.22'

## The Hike

The Uinta Mountains of northeastern Utah and northwestern Colorado are unusual in that the spine runs east-west instead of the typical north-south. Like most of the Rockies, the Uintas are a faulted anticline, meaning that ancient Precambrian rocks have been lifted and the rock layers on top arched. The spectacular walls of Canyon of Lodore are the red sandstones and siltstones of the Uinta Mountain Group, formed in Precambrian times over 600 million years ago. Between 65 million and 45 million years ago the land started to rise, forming the present Rocky Mountains, including the Uintas. The rising mountains probably caused the Green River to slow its eastern flow. Some geologists believe that Browns Park, to the north of Gates of Lodore, filled

*Gates of Lodore from overlook*

with sediments from rivers going nowhere. As the sediments filled Browns Park to the top of the Uintas, the Green River also rose to the top, spilled over the southern edge, and started downcutting the canyon. By about 5 million years ago, the entire region had been lifted another 5,000 feet higher. The rising land and downcutting action of the river probably worked together to create the great canyon.

In the 1860s and 1870s, several surveys explored the unknown western lands belonging to the United States. John Wesley Powell, a Civil War veteran who had lost his right arm during combat, led one of these surveys. After the war, Powell became professor of geology at Illinois State Normal University. During the summers, he ventured west, exploring what is now western Colorado and eastern Utah. He believed the best way to explore the canyons in this area would be by boat. In 1868 he came to the edge of the Uintas with his wife and about twenty students and neighbors. They spent the winter in three small cabins along the White River near present-day Meeker. In the spring Powell headed east and secured four boats and supplies for a six-month trip. On May 24, 1869, Powell and nine other men left Green River City, Wyoming, and headed down the Green for the Colorado River.

> In John Wesley Powell's time, the official Colorado River started at the confluence of the Grand and Green Rivers in Utah. The Grand River started in what is now Rocky Mountain National Park. According to Powell: "The Green River is larger than the Grand, and is the upper continuation of the Colorado."

On June 6, the motley crew had floated the calm Green River through Browns Park and camped near the head of the canyon. The next day Powell and a few others climbed to the summit of the cliff. In his journal he wrote: "The cañon walls are buttressed on a grand scale, with deep alcoves intervening; columned crags crown the cliffs, and the river is rolling below . . . the sun shines in splendor on vermilion walls, shaded into green and gray, where the rocks are lichened over; the river fills the channel from wall to wall, and the cañon opens, like a beautiful portal, to a region of glory."

On June 9, one of his men suggested they call the canyon "Cañon of Lodore." During the day, one of the boats missed a pullout to examine the next set of rapids. After hitting a few huge rocks, the boat was "dashed to pieces." Luckily the crew survived. A previous party, led by a man named Ashley, had also swamped in this spot and some of his crew drowned. Powell's group decided to christen the rapids Disaster Falls. Barometers (used for determining altitude), a package of thermometers, and a keg of whiskey were rescued from the wreckage of the boat.

The group eventually arrived in the Grand Canyon. After many portages, lowering boats down the river, drying out wet food and supplies, and continually being drenched, three men decided to go no farther down the river. They traveled overland and were later killed by Native Americans, who thought the white men had killed a squaw. Powell and the rest of his crew successfully floated the last section of the Grand Canyon, finishing on August 30, 1869. Powell was later funded for a second expedition down the Grand Canyon, which he undertook from 1871 to 1872.

The hike starts at the far end of Gates of Lodore Campground. Take a nature trail guide for an introduction to semidesert shrubland, piñon-juniper forests, area history, and geology. After two steep switchbacks, the trail levels off on a bench above the Green River. Take some time to relax on the rocks overlooking the Gates of Lodore. This part of Dinosaur National Monument is less crowded than the Quarry area and has few visitors other than boaters putting in on the Green River. If you have time, take a multiday raft trip down the Green River to Split Mountain near the Dinosaur Quarry Visitor Center and Exhibit Hall (scheduled to open in fall 2011). The Browns Park area has a classic storybook western history, complete with American Indians, wildlife, ranching, and outlaws. Butch Cassidy and the Sundance Kid of the Wild Bunch used this area for a hideout, while other local characters included outlaws Matt Warner, Isom Dart, and Ann Bassett, Queen of the Rustlers. Take time to explore this remote area of Colorado.

# Gates of Lodore Nature Trail

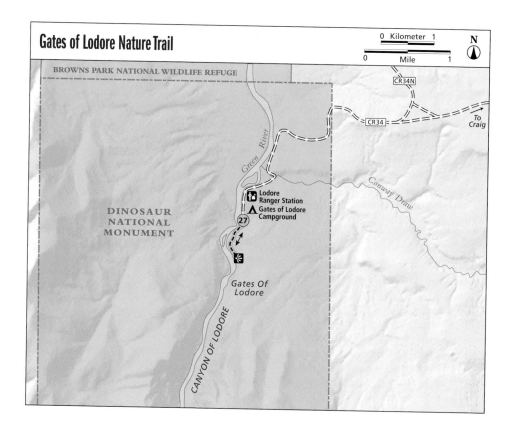

0   Kilometer   1

0      Mile      1

N

BROWNS PARK NATIONAL WILDLIFE REFUGE

CR34N

CR34

To
Craig

Green River

Conway Draw

Lodore
Ranger Station

Gates of Lodore
Campground

27

DINOSAUR
NATIONAL
MONUMENT

Gates Of
Lodore

CANYON OF LODORE

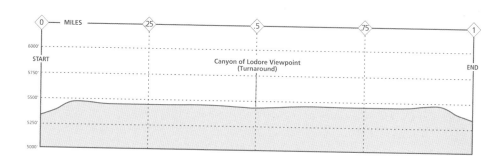

0 — MILES —    .25      .5      .75      1

6000'

START

Canyon of Lodore Viewpoint
(Turnaround)

END

5750'

5500'

5250'

5000'

## Miles and Directions

**0.0**    Start at the far end of the Gates of Lodore Campground. Elevation: 5,340 feet. In 210 feet, the trail switchbacks. After the switchbacks, stay to the left—the right trail heads to an overlook.

**0.5**    Come to a viewpoint of Gates of Lodore and Canyon of Lodore. Elevation: 5,400 feet. GPS: N40 43.08'/W105 53.36'. This is a great place for lunch and relaxation. Return the way you came.

**1.0**    Arrive back at the trailhead.

## Hike Information

### General Information
**Moffat County Tourism Association:** Craig; (866) 332-8436 or (970) 824-2335; www.moffat countytourism.com
**Moffat County Visitors Center:** Craig; (800) 864-4405 or (970) 824-5689; www.craig-cham ber.com

### Local Events/Attractions
**Browns Park National Wildlife Refuge:** Maybell; (970) 365-3613; www.fws.gov/brownspark/
**John Jarvie Historic Ranch (BLM):** Browns Park, UT; (435) 885-3307; www.blm.gov/ut/st/en /fo/vernal/recreation_/browns_park.html
**Lodore Hall National Historic Site:** Browns Park National Wildlife Refuge, Maybell; (970) 365-3613
**Swinging Bridge:** Browns Park National Wildlife Refuge, Maybell; (970) 365-3613

### Accommodations
**Browns Park NWR campgrounds:** Browns Park National Wildlife Refuge, Maybell; (970) 365-3613; www.fws.gov/brownspark/
**Gates of Lodore Campground:** Dinosaur National Monument, Dinosaur; (435) 781-7700; www .nps.gov/dino

### Restaurants
**Serendipity Cafe & Coffee Shop:** 576 Yampa Ave., Craig; (970) 824-5846

# 28 Devils Canyon

This hike takes you into an easily accessible canyon in the Black Ridge Canyons Wilderness Area. The trail first crosses open high-desert country of rabbitbrush, junipers, and other thorny plants. It then makes a loop in Devils Canyon, below huge walls of Wingate sandstone and interesting rock formations. Part of the loop follows the creek bottom and should be avoided during thunderstorms. Hiking beneath immense sandstone cliffs and past amphitheaters in a colorful canyon is a real treat! Keep an eye out for desert bighorn sheep and rattlesnakes.

**Start:** From Devils Canyon Trail trailhead

**Distance:** 6.9-mile double lollipop

**Approximate hiking time:** 3 to 5 hours

**Difficulty:** Moderate due to length and terrain

**Elevation gain:** 620 feet, plus lots of undulations over gullies and drainages

**Seasons:** Year-round; avoid hot summer days

**Trail surface:** Dirt roads (nonmotorized) and trails

**Land status:** BLM land and wilderness

**Nearest town:** Fruita

**Other trail users:** Equestrians, hunters (in season)

**Canine compatibility:** Dogs must be under control. There is little to no water on the trail.

**Schedule:** Year-round, except this area may be closed between Jan 15 and May 15 to protect bighorn sheep lambing areas

**Fees and permits:** None

**Maps:** USGS Mack and Battleship Rock; Nat Geo Trails Illustrated 502 Grand Junction/ Fruita; Latitude 40° Fruita, Grand Junction

**Trail contact:** Bureau of Land Management, Grand Junction; (970) 244-3000; www.co.blm .gov/co/st/en/fo/gjfo.html

**Special considerations:** Bring plenty of water (one gallon per person per day), especially if it's hot.

**Finding the trailhead:** From I-70 take exit 19 for Fruita. Drive south on CO 340 about 1.3 miles to Kingsview Road. Turn right and drive another 1.2 miles to the turnoff to Devils Canyon. Turn left and drive to the big parking lot 0.2 mile down this dirt road to the left. There are vault toilets at the trailhead. GPS: N39 08.39' / W108 45.36'

## The Hike

The Black Ridge Canyons Wilderness Area was designated by Congress on October 5, 2000, and signed into law by President Bill Clinton on October 24, 2000. The wilderness shares its eastern border with Colorado National Monument. The Black Ridge Canyons area includes the second-largest collection of arches in the country outside of Arches National Park. Access to the arches is via a long trail or a rough 4WD road, then a hike. The grandeur of this area can also be seen on an easier hike into Devils Canyon. If you ask how the canyon got its name, locals will simply state: "It's hotter than Hell!"

Devils Canyon lies on the northeastern edge of the Uncompahgre Plateau. Uncompahgre roughly means "rocks that make the water red" in the Ute language.

About 300 million years ago forces pushed ancient (over 1.7 billion years old) "basement" rock upward to form Uncompahgria, the forerunner of today's Uncompahgre Plateau. About 65 million years later, Uncompahgria had eroded to a plain barely above the level of an inland sea. A delta or floodplain collected red sand on the coastal plain. As the climate changed, the sea receded and windblown sand filled the area. Visualize tall buff and salmon-colored dunes, like those in Great Sand Dunes National Park and Preserve.

Then the climate changed again, becoming moister, and streams began to flow across the area. Conglomerate, comprised of mud and pebbles, formed, as did other sand deposits. Over the millennia, other seas and dunes covered these sediments and under great pressure the dunes and conglomerate became rock. The Kayenta Formation of sandstone and conglomerate forms a caprock, or hard-to-erode sandstone, that protects the old dunes, now known as Wingate sandstone. The red floodplain sand changed into the Chinle Formation. Cliffs of Wingate sandstone tower 100 to 200 feet into the sky in Devils Canyon. Look around at the cliffs and try to find the elephant's tail, the coke bottles or ovens, and the tiki head formations eroded by the elements.

This area is harsh and wild. Temperatures soar in the summer, creating an oven effect. In winter, temperatures can drop below freezing. Desert bighorn sheep and mountain lions live here. An interpretive sign near the trailhead explains ways to watch wildlife without disturbing them. Bighorn sheep are especially affected by humans and pets during lambing season, from February through May. Please watch and enjoy from a distance and keep dogs next to you! The cliffs shelter peregrine falcons—watch for these beautiful birds of prey.

Another area resident that is very fragile is the crypto, a black lumpy growth on the sand. This interesting combination of green algae, bacteria, fungi, lichens, mosses, and cyanobacteria holds the sandy soil together so other plants may grow.

The hike starts out on a road closed to public motorized vehicles. The first part is relatively flat, with sparse vegetation of rabbitbrush, sagebrush, some thorny plants, and a few hardy junipers. After traveling along several roads, the hike turns onto a singletrack trail. A few places require careful observation to find the cairns that mark the route. The cliffs of the canyon loom ahead. Drop into a creekbed and follow it for a little while among cottonwood and ash trees and some tamarisk. Do not hike here if there are thunderstorms anywhere in the area in case of flash floods.

At the start of the long loop, the trail climbs steeply to the right out of the creek bottom. As you hike along, look back down into the canyon bottom to your left to see black rock walls with shiny mica and lots of lichen. These rocks are the "basement" rocks of Uncompahgria. On the right, sandstone cliffs are a colorful parfait of yellow and pink (think ice cream). Continue climbing through black rocks, mica, and

◀ *Former sheepherder's cabin in Devils Canyon*

white quartz. The trail traverses the Chinle Formation at the base of the cliffs, undulating across many little creek gullies. Look to the right into each little amphitheater for alcoves or other interesting rock features. The buzz of cicadas and lyrical song of the canyon wren may fill the air.

Domesticated sheep once grazed in Devils Canyon. At the south end of the loop, an old sheepherder's cabin still stands. The cabin provides a little shade and a great place for lunch. To finish the loop the trail drops, crosses the creek, then climbs to the bench above. Again, the trail undulates across many little dry creek gullies. Near the close of the loop is a great view of the Grand Valley and the Book Cliffs to the north. A little farther downstream, continue along the creekbed to add variety to your hike and another mini-loop back to the trailhead.

## Miles and Directions

**0.0**   Start at the Devils Canyon Trail trailhead kiosk with bulletin boards. Elevation: 4,580 feet.

**0.15**  Come to a trail junction. Turn left and continue down the dirt road (Trail D1), which is closed to public motorized vehicles.

**0.2**   Stop and read the bulletin board, containing interesting area information.

**0.4**   Come to the trail junction with Trail D5. Turn left on Trail D1 and follow the dirt road, passing any singletrack trails.

**0.5**   Reach a junction with multiple trails. Turn right here on Trail D1 and follow the dirt road. You'll return via the left road. GPS: N39 08.14'/W108 45.54'.

**0.8**   Come to a trail junction. Turn left here onto Trail D4. When you reach a wash, look carefully for rocks and cairns and cross the wash.

**1.1**   Look carefully for cairns as trail drops about 60 feet into the canyon to the left. GPS: N39 07.77'/W108 45.84'. When you reach the creekbed, cross the creek, turn right on Trail D3, and travel upstream. **(Note:** During thunderstorms, do not enter in case of flash flood!)

**1.2**   Reach the Wilderness boundary sign, which is off to your right.

**1.4**   Reach the start of the loop. Turn right on Trail D3. Cross the creek and head steeply uphill. The trail meanders past various amphitheaters, cliffs, and up and down little gullies.

**3.7**   Reach the south end of the loop at the old sheepherder's cabin. Elevation: 5,200 feet. GPS: N39 06.21'/W108 45.93'. This is a great lunch spot. Find the trail on the north side of the cabin to finish the loop. The trail drops into Devils Creek, then follows the bank on the east side.

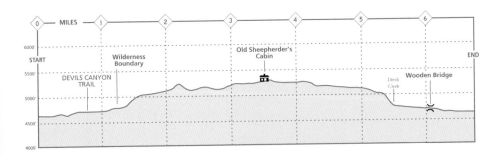

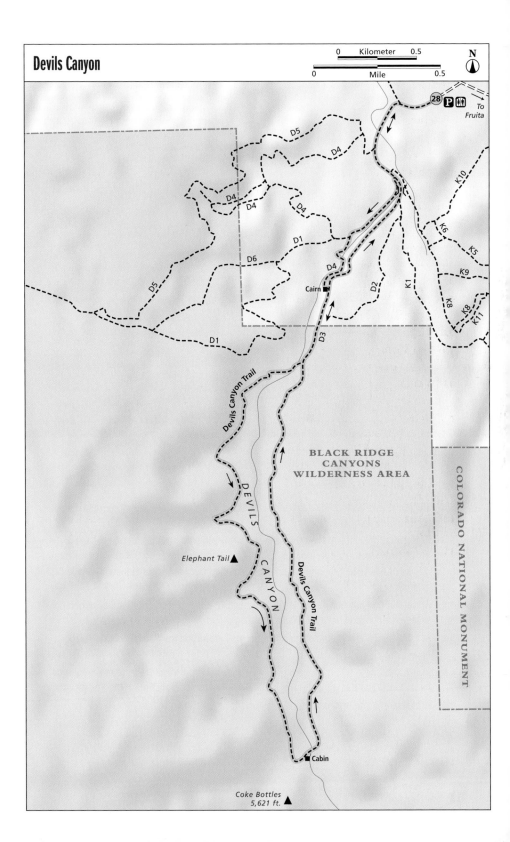

# Devils Canyon

0 Kilometer 0.5
0 Mile 0.5

N

To Fruita

D5
D4
D4
D4
D4
D1
D6
D5
D1
D4
Cairn
D3
D2
K1
K10
K6
K5
K9
K8
K8
K11

Devils Canyon Trail

BLACK RIDGE
CANYONS
WILDERNESS AREA

COLORADO NATIONAL MONUMENT

DEVILS CANYON

Elephant Tail ▲

Devils Canyon Trail

Cabin ■

Coke Bottles
5,621 ft. ▲

*View at mile 1.5 of cliffs in Devils Canyon*

**5.5** The trail drops back down into Devils Creek and starts to retrace the route on which you came (same as mile 1.4).

**5.8** Come to a trail junction (same as mile 1.1). You came into the canyon via the left trail. For more variety on the return trip, stay to the right in the creekbed on Trail D3 (unless there's danger of flash flood) and make another mini-loop back to the trail junction at mile 0.5 above.

**6.2** Arrive at a trail junction. Take the left trail, still D3, which climbs out of the creekbed on a slickrock ledge to avoid a tight spot, but then drops back down to the creek.

**6.3** At a trail junction with a road, turn left and walk down the road across a little wooden bridge.

**6.4** Come to a trail junction (same as 0.5 mile). Go straight on Trail D1 to return to the trailhead. Trail D1 to the left is the way you walked into the canyon. Return the way you came.

**6.9** Arrive back at the trailhead.

# CRYPTOBIOTIC SOIL CRUST

When hiking in Colorado's desert country, notice black lumps in between plants and sand. This cryptobiotic soil crust, sometimes called cryptogamic soil or "crypto," is actually a combination of living creatures! Green algae, bacteria, fungi, lichens, mosses, and cyanobacteria live together in the soil crust. Cyanobacteria are an ancient life-form, about 3.5 billion years old. In this area, cyanobacteria is a filament in a sheath that becomes active when moistened. It moves through the soil, leaving behind a sticky glue. Soil particles (think sand grains) stick to the gooey sheath. When wet, cyanobacteria swell to as much as ten times their dry size. Plants growing in areas with crypto soils tend to have much higher levels of nutrients than plants in noncrypto soils. In particular, cyanobacteria help the soil obtain nitrogen. This special combination of living creatures binds soil particles together, creating the topsoil of the arid West.

Human activity can easily destroy this delicate topsoil. Dry crusts are very brittle and break up easily when crunched under foot. Breakup by tires on bikes or vehicles causes even worse damage, as their continuous strips create a minigully for water to carry soil away, creating larger channels. Wind also gets in the act by blowing loosened soil around, covering other crypto and preventing it from photosynthesizing. Damaged cryptobiotic soil crusts can take fifty years or more to recover to a well-developed state.

When hiking in drier areas where crypto is common, please watch your step. Walk in gullies, on trails, and on rocks. If you must walk through crypto, walk single file stepping in the leader's footprints to minimize damage. Remember the wonder of these ancient life-forms and the important function they provide by holding sandy and silty soil together. Sand dunes are probably not the landscape of preference one hundred years from now!

## Hike Information

### General Information

**Fruita Chamber of Commerce:** Fruita; (970) 858-3894; www.fruitachamber.org

### Local Events/Attractions

**Dinosaur Journey:** 550 Jurassic Court, Fruita; (970) 858-7282; www.dinodigs.org
**Mike the Headless Chicken Statue and Festival:** Fruita; (970) 858-3894; www.mikethehead lesschicken.org
**The Museum of Western Colorado:** 462 Ute Ave., Grand Junction; (970) 242-0971; www.mu seumofwesternco.com

## Accommodations

**Colorado National Monument Campground:** Fruita; (970) 858-3617; www.nps.gov/com

**James M. Robb–Colorado River State Park:** Fruita Section, Fruita; (970) 434-3388; http://parks .state.co.us/Parks/JamesMRobbColoradoRiver

## Restaurants

**Fiesta Guadalajara of Fruita:** 103 US Highway 6 and 50, Fruita; (970) 858-1228

**Hot Tomato Cafe:** 124 North Mulberry St., Fruita; (970) 858-1117; http://hottomatocafe.com

## Clubs and Organizations

**Colorado Mountain Club–West Slope Group:** Grand Junction; www.cmc.org

**Friends of McInnis Canyons:** Fruita; (970) 270-7853; www.mcinniscanyons.org

*View west from old sheepherder's cabin*

# Honorable Mentions

## Northwest

Compiled here is an index of great hikes in the Northwest region that didn't make the A-list this time around but deserve recognition. Check them out and let us know what you think. You may decide that one or more of these hikes deserves higher status in future editions or, perhaps, you may have a hike of your own that merits some attention.

### L Hanging Lake

The trail to Hanging Lake is very popular and leads to a beautiful little lake fed by Bridal Veil Falls. The 2.8-mile out-and-back trail gains 1,100 feet in 1.2 miles and is considered most difficult to strenuous (start at 6,100 feet and end at 7,200 feet). Dogs are not allowed on the trail and swimming and fishing are prohibited in the lake to protect it. The trail is very steep in spots, with switchbacks and stone steps. Please stay on the boardwalk around the lake to protect the fragile shoreline. The hike is a trip back into geologic history, with the area around the lake composed of limestone. Take a little side trip to Spouting Rock, where water spouts from a cliff wall by a waterfall. From Glenwood Springs drive east on I-70 to Hanging Lake, exit 125. Park in the lot and walk about 0.25 mile east to start up Deadhorse Creek just before a bridge. For more information contact White River National Forest at (970) 328-6388 or visit the website at www.fs.usda.gov/whiteriver.

### M Harpers Corner Trail

Harpers Corner Trail in Dinosaur National Monument gives you an excellent view of this park's canyon country. The trail follows a promontory that was once used as a natural corral. While you hike, you'll learn about geology, seashells along the trail, trees and animals living above the canyon, and John Wesley Powell's trip down the Green River. Fremont Indians carved petroglyphs down on the canyon walls, and later the Chew family ranched along Pool Creek. Echo Canyon can be seen from above and is close to the confluence of the Green and Yampa Rivers. This enjoyable 2-mile out-and-back hike has moderate elevation gains and losses for an easy trip (start at 7,625 feet and end at 7,510 feet). Do watch out for lightning! Remember the binoculars and water. It can be hot on the trail in the summer. From the town of Dinosaur, drive east on US 40 about 1.8 miles to the Harpers Corner Road (not marked as such) and Dinosaur National Monument Visitor Center. Turn left onto Harpers Corner Road and stop at the visitor center. You can purchase a Harpers Corner Trail guide and a Harpers Corner Scenic Drive Guide at the visitor center. There is no entrance fee to drive the Harpers Corner Scenic Drive. Drive north from the visitor center about 32 miles to the Harpers Corner Trail. For more information, contact the Dinosaur National Monument Canyon Area Visitor Center at (970) 374-3000 or check out the website at www.nps.gov/dino.

## N Trail through Time

Located near the Colorado-Utah border in the Rabbit Valley Research Natural Area, this trail takes you by dinosaur bones still imbedded in rock! The 1.5-mile loop trail is moderate, with some steep, slippery sections (elevations from 4,600 to 4,700 feet). You'll first come to a quarry, still worked by paleontologists. A trail guide explains the dinosaur bones and also various geological and plant features. The trail starts at the quarry, about 0.1 mile from the parking lot. Best times to hike are spring and fall because summers can be incredibly hot (over 100°F.). Bring water. There's a restroom near the trailhead. Pets and smoking are discouraged along the trail. Because the area is fragile, please stay on the trail and remember to leave what you find. To reach this unique hike, travel west on I-70 from Grand Junction to exit 2 (about 30 miles) and turn right. The parking lot is straight ahead of you. Trail guides may be available at the trailhead. If not, contact the Museum of Western Colorado at (970) 242-0971 or visit the website at www.museumofwesternco.com, or contact the Bureau of Land Management in Grand Junction at (970) 244-3000 or www.blm.gov/co/st/en/nca /mcnca/recreation/Hiking/Trail_Through_Time.html.

## ○ Monument Canyon

Monument Canyon Trail takes you by some of the famous rock sculptures of Colorado National Monument. To Independence Monument, the crown jewel, the hike is a 6-mile out-and-back trip. As it drops about 600 feet in about 0.5 mile, the hike is rated as difficult to most difficult (elevation change from 6,200 to 5,300 feet). Remember to bring water and avoid hiking on really hot summer days. The trail takes you through millennia of time, past the Kayenta Formation (caprock) and Wingate sandstone (massive cliffs and monuments). At about 2 miles, you'll find the Kissing Couple, followed in about another mile by Independence Monument, a 450-foot-high monolith, the largest freestanding rock formation in the park. Dogs are not allowed on park trails. You can make this a 6-mile point-to-point hike by parking a second car at the east trailhead along CO 340, 2.1 miles to the southeast of the west entrance to Colorado National Monument. Turn right just beyond mile marker 5 into the trailhead. To reach the upper (west) trailhead, from the I-70 interchange (exit 19) in Fruita, drive south on CO 340 into Colorado National Monument (fee area). Drive about 10 miles to the trailhead on the left side of the road, just beyond the Coke Ovens Overlook. For further information contact Colorado National Monument at (970) 858-3617 ext. 360, or visit the website at www.nps.gov/com.

# P Crag Crest National Recreation Trail

Crag Crest Trail, high point 11,189 feet, traverses the backbone of Grand Mesa southeast of Grand Junction. Fantastic scenery to the south, east, and north keeps popping into view. Lone Cone, the San Miguels, La Platas, and San Juan Mountains line the southern skyline. The West Elks are to the east, with the Book Cliffs and the Roan Cliffs to the north, an interesting contrast of high peaks and more desertlike formations. Numerous lakes, small and large, dot the landscape below. Wildflowers bloom colorfully and profusely in July and early August along the sometimes narrow path with steep drop-offs. The trail provides three options: a 9.9-mile loop, a 6.5-mile point-to-point, or a 6.2-mile out-and-back. The point-to-point and out-and-back hikes are the most scenic. Start your hike at the East Trailhead (10,150 feet), near Crag Crest Campground, about 3.5 miles east on FR 121 from the Grand Mesa Visitor Center. Starting at the East Trailhead puts the sun to your back in the morning for better light. For the point-to-point, leave a second car at the West Trailhead (10,380 feet), about 1 mile west of the visitor center on CO 65. To reach Grand Mesa from Grand Junction, head east on I-70 to exit 49 for CO 65/Grand Mesa Scenic Byway. Head south for about 35 miles to the visitor center at the intersection of CO 65 and FR 121. Pick up a trail brochure and check the weather. Make sure to bring plenty of water and insect repellant. Grand Mesa cradles over 300 lakes and plenty of mosquitoes. For more information, contact Grand Mesa National Forest at (970) 874-6600 or (970) 856-4153, or check out the website at www.fs.usda.gov/gmug.

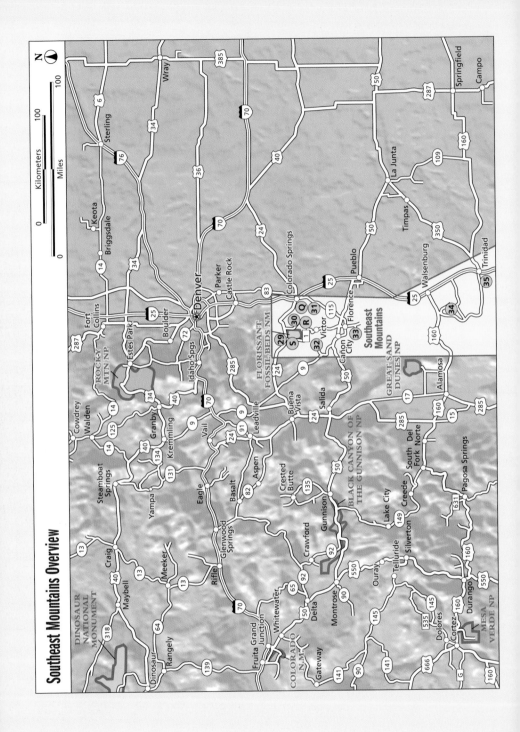

# Southeast Mountains Overview

# Southeast Mountains

The geological feature called the Front Range ends at Cheyenne Mountain near Colorado Springs. But to keep things reasonably equal north and south, Colorado Springs and the area immediately west is included in this section.

Colorado Springs, at the base of Pikes Peak (14,109 feet), contains an interesting assortment of businesses and attractions. The U.S. Air Force Academy is located to the north, and the Olympic Training Center is in town. El Paso County has developed a system of trails, and the Pike National Forest offers many hiking opportunities as well. By no means the highest of the fourteeners, Pikes Peak holds the honor of rising the farthest above its base, giving it a formidable profile. Inspired by the view from the top of Pikes Peak in 1893, Katherine Lee Bates wrote the lyrics for "America the Beautiful," which read: "Oh beautiful for spacious skies, for amber waves of grain, for purple mountains majesty, above the fruited plain . . ."

To the west of "the Springs," Florissant Fossil Beds National Monument holds a treasure trove of petrified giant redwood trees and a world-famous source of fossilized insects. Mueller State Park and Dome Rock State Wildlife Area offer both a refuge for elk and bighorn sheep, and a multitude of hiking trails through this former ranching area.

Explore Cripple Creek and Victor by following the Gold Belt Tour Scenic and Historic Byway drive. Fortunes were gained and lost in the goldfields of Cripple Creek and Victor and the tradition continues into the twenty-first century at Cripple Creek's casinos. Hikes on the Twin Rock Trail and Thompson Mountain are located off this tour route. The Vindicator Valley Trail, a 2-mile loop near Victor, explores mining remnants from the 1890s. In winter the trail is groomed for cross-country skiing.

Cañon City makes a good base of operations for exploring the northern half of this region. Goldfields and the graveyard of famous dinosaurs such as allosaurus, diplodocus, and stegosaurus lie to the north. (Check out the dinosaur museum in Cañon City.) Stop at the Museum of Colorado Prisons for a present-day piece of history. The Royal Gorge, an incredible canyon carved by the Arkansas River, lies to the west, and

Colorado's oldest oil field is to the south. A trail around Thompson Mountain, north-west of Cañon City, is featured, along with an interesting hike to an old steam boiler.

Follow the Frontier Pathways Scenic & Historic Byway into the Wet Mountain Valley, which contains several historic ranches and farmsteads. The valley provides access to trails on the eastern side of the Sangre de Cristo Range. Nine of Colorado's fifty-four fourteeners (peaks over 14,000 feet) are located in this beautiful range.

The area encircling the Spanish Peaks is steeped in various Indian and Spanish legends. Be sure to drive the Scenic Highway of Legends to learn more. Volcanic dikes radiate from the Spanish Peaks, designated as a Wilderness area in 2000. The Wahatoya Trail was extended in 1999, so you can hike among the dikes on West Spanish Peak's south flank and then continue to cross the saddle between these two majestic mountains.

At the southern end of this region, Trinidad still has streets of cobblestones and beautiful old historic buildings. Once connecting Trinidad with Santa Fe, the Mountain Branch of the Santa Fe Trail over Raton Pass was replaced by railroads. Now cars and trucks move easily on I-25 over the pass where wagons once struggled. A coal miners' strike that ended in disaster is memorialized at the Ludlow Massacre site to the north. A few miles farther west on the Highway of Legends, you can visit historic Cokedale and the relics of coke ovens near Trinidad Lake State Park.

# 29 Twin Rock Trail

The Twin Rock Trail is a gentle hike through ponderosa pine forests and open meadows so scenic you might wonder where the bison are. The trail meanders through old ranchlands and across an ancient lakebed. It then turns east and follows an unnamed stream to South Twin Rock. This part of the trail wanders along a riparian area, past open meadows, through a beautiful aspen grove, and past several other rock formations. Summer brings a profusion of wildflowers.

**Start:** From the Hornbek Homestead
**Distance:** 6.0 miles out and back
**Approximate hiking time:** 2.5 to 4 hours
**Difficulty:** Moderate due to length
**Elevation gain:** 440 feet plus small undulations
**Seasons:** Best from May through Oct
**Trail surface:** Dirt trail and nonmotorized dirt road, with one highway crossing
**Land status:** National Monument
**Nearest town:** Florissant
**Other trail users:** Hikers only
**Canine compatibility:** Dogs not permitted
**Schedule:** Day use only. Open 8 a.m. to 6 p.m. Memorial Day to Labor Day. Open 9 a.m. to 5 p.m. from Labor Day to Memorial Day. Closed Thanksgiving, Christmas, and New Year. Call first for trail conditions from Nov to Apr. You can cross-country ski or snowshoe in winter. The trail is not marked for winter use.
**Fees and permits:** Entrance fee, annual pass, or America the Beautiful pass required
**Maps:** USGS Lake George and Divide; Nat Geo Trails Illustrated 137 Pikes Peak/Cañon City
**Trail contact:** Florissant Fossil Beds National Monument, Florissant; (719) 748-3253; www.nps.gov/flfo/
**Other:** Please do not cross onto private property at the trail's end.

**Finding the trailhead:** From Florissant, head south on Teller County Road (TCR) 1 from its intersection with US 24 at the center of town. Drive 2.3 miles and turn right onto the visitor center road. The parking lot is about 0.3 mile from the highway. Pay the entrance fee, check out the displays, and if you have time hike the short and very interesting 1-mile Petrified Forest Loop trail. Then, return north to the Hornbek Homestead, which is located 0.9 mile north of the visitor center road on the west side, and park in the parking lot. A vault toilet and picnic tables are available. GPS: N38 55.60'/W105 16.92'

## The Hike

The hike starts at the old Hornbek Homestead. Take a few minutes either before or after the hike to look around at the bunkhouse, carriage shed, barn, and root cellar. Walk inside the main house (when it's open), built in 1878. A single mother with four children, Adeline Hornbek homesteaded this land in 1878 under the 1862 Homestead Act. Grasslands, nearby water and timber, and fertile soil made this an ideal area for ranching. Adeline Hornbek's was the first homestead in the Florissant Valley.

After looking at the restored house, stay to the left and head southeast on the Hornbek Wildlife Loop, crossing TCR 1. Keep an eye open for mountain bluebirds. While you hike across the grasslands, picture this area 34 million years ago, during the Eocene epoch. Beechlike and elmlike trees were overshadowed by 200-foot giant redwoods. Volcanic activity increased in the nearby Thirtynine Mile volcanic field. Mudflows caused by the volcanoes reached the giant redwoods, smothering them in 15 feet of mud. The upper portions of the trees decayed, while the lower portions, permeated with dissolved silicates and other minerals, started to petrify.

> **The fossil insect and leaf collection at Florissant Fossil Beds National Monument is a real treat. Insects are very delicate and rarely preserved. Volcanic ash the consistency of talcum powder gently covered the dainty creatures, preserving their impressions in shale. Over 1,700 different species have been found here, one of the most diverse collections in the world.**

Mudflows also blocked a small stream, creating a long and skinny lake that occupied the area where you are walking. Airborne ash clouds and poisonous gases often killed insects and butterflies, which dropped into the lake. Over the years, eruptions continued and the ash layer built up in the lake, eventually filling it. Insects, leaves, and fish lay buried under the ash layers. Mudflows continued to cover the old lake. Over many millennia, erosion took its toll in the valley, uncovering petrified tree stumps. A treasure of ancient insects, butterflies, leaves, and fish fossils were also discovered. Be sure to check out the fossil collection in the visitor center.

As homesteaders populated the valley, they collected petrified wood and fossilized insects. Scientific investigations started in the 1870s and continue today. Talk of preserving the area began back in 1911, but designation as a national monument only occurred in 1969.

Continuing on your hike, the trail meanders along the edge of ponderosa pine forest and grassland. In more recent times bison roamed here, getting fat on the nutritious grasses. Ute Indians hunted the bison for meat and hides. Today the bison and Utes are gone, but the grassland remains. Abert's squirrels, also known as tassel-eared squirrels, frolic amid the ponderosas.

The trail drops down to a little stream and crosses it on a nice wooden bridge. A riparian area lines the right side of the trail to South Twin Rock. Willow and aspen trees, along with cinquefoil (potentilla), butter-and-eggs, and sage plants inhabit the area. An old stock pond lies to the right, reflecting nearby aspen trees. In the dry climate of Colorado, ranchers built little earthen dams across creeks, creating ponds for their cattle. Mountain mahogany bushes grow along the creek, their seeds looking

*Elephant head on South Twin*

*Meadow from Hornbeck Wildlife Loop*

like feathery question marks. Grasshoppers abound and an occasional green-armored locust sits in the trail.

When the trail passes next to granitic rocks, look closely at the colorful lichen. Lichens are an interesting combination of algae and fungus that live together synergistically. Colored rusty orange, black, gray, and various greens, they brighten up the granite. Their job is to break rocks into soil. On warmer south-facing slopes, look for yucca and mountain ball cactus.

Cross an open area. Look ahead to see South Twin Rock (8,963 feet). One part looks like an elephant head with a long trunk. South Twin Rock is in Florissant Fossil Beds National Monument and North Twin Rock is on private land. The area just before the monument boundary is a good place for lunch, either sitting on some boulders or a log in a thick stand of aspen. Please do not hike out of the monument onto private property. The monument boundary is near a road, so you may hear modern vehicle sounds—quite a contrast with the memory of a volcanic-ash-filled lake!

## Miles and Directions

**0.0**   Start at the parking lot and walk to the Hornbek Homestead entrance gate. Elevation: 8,300 feet. The hike starts here. Take the left trail, signed as Hornbek Wildlife Loop with mileage to the visitor center.

**0.2**   Cross TCR 1.

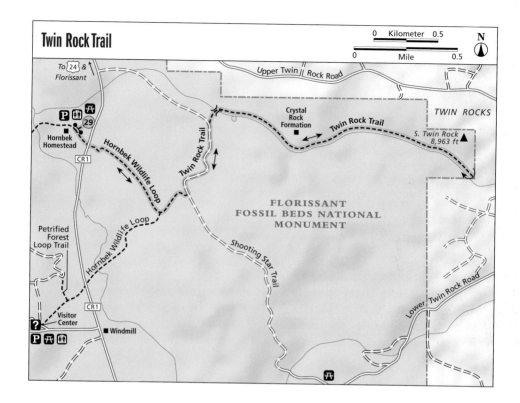

# Twin Rock Trail

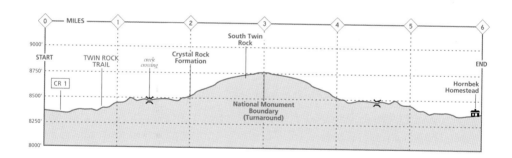

**0.6** Turn left at the junction of Twin Rock Trail, Shootin' Star Trail, and the Hornbek Wildlife Loop. GPS: N38 55.30' / W105 16.47'.

**0.8** Turn left at the junction of Twin Rock and Shootin' Star Trails onto Twin Rock Trail.

**1.3** Turn right where the old road goes left, staying on the trail. GPS: N38 55.68' / W105 16.20'.

**1.4** Cross the bridge over an unnamed creek and veer right (east) on the Twin Rock Trail, heading upstream.

**1.6** Reach an old stock pond.

**2.0** Reach a rock formation with large quartz crystals to the left of the trail. GPS: N38 55.57'/W105 15.75'. (**FYI:** Look at the band of quartz in the rock. You can see where looser grains eroded into a small fan and gully below the rock.)

**2.1** Reach an open area.

**2.7** Reach South Twin Rock.

**3.0** Arrive at the National Monument boundary and the turnaround point. Elevation: 8,740 feet. GPS: N38 55.43'/W105 14.77'. Return the way you came.

**6.0** Arrive back at the trailhead.

## Hike Information

### General Information
**Cripple Creek Heritage Center:** 9283 South Highway 67, Cripple Creek; (877) 858-4653; www.cripple-creek.co.us

### Local Events/Attractions
**Cripple Creek & Victor Mining Districts, Casinos, Mine Tours, and Narrow Gauge Railroad:** Cripple Creek and Victor; (719) 689-3315 or (877) 858-4653; www.cripple-creek.co.us
**Florissant Heritage Museum:** Florissant; (719) 748-8259
**Gold Belt Scenic Byway Tour:** Gold Belt Byway Association, Guffey; (719) 689-2485

### Accommodations
**Eleven Mile Motel:** a rustic motel; Lake George; (719) 748-3931
**Eleven Mile State Park campgrounds:** Lake George; (719) 748-3401; http://parks.state.co.us/parks/elevenmile
**Mueller State Park campgrounds:** Divide; (719) 687-2366; http://parks.state.co.us/parks/Mueller
**National Forest campgrounds:** Pike National Forest, Colorado Springs; (719) 636-1602; www.fs.usda.gov/psicc

### Restaurants
**One & Oney's Ice Cream & Pizza:** 37 Costello Ave., Florissant; (719) 748-3315

### Clubs and Organizations
**Friends of the Florissant Fossil Beds, Inc.:** Florissant; (719) 748-3253; www.fossilbeds.org

### Hike Tours
**Florissant Fossil Beds National Monument:** Florissant; (719) 748-3253; www.nps.gov/flfo

# 30 Rock Pond to Werley Ranch Loop

The Rock Pond to Werley Ranch Loop takes you into the heart of Mueller State Park and Dome Rock State Wildlife Area. Descending through forests of aspen, limber pine, and Douglas fir, the trail follows old ranch roads, closed to the motorized public. A side trip brings you to Brook Pond, reflecting big rounded rock formations of Pikes Peak granite. The trail continues through grasslands and meadows, popular with the abundant elk population. The old Werley Ranch is an excellent lunch spot, giving you a chance to reflect on ranch life. The loop continues back to the trailhead, ascending on singletrack and old ranch roads.

**Start:** From the Rock Pond Trail trailhead near the visitor center

**Distance:** 7.6-mile lollipop

**Approximate hiking time:** 3 to 5 hours

**Difficulty:** Moderate due to gentle trails and distance

**Elevation loss/gain:** 1,110-foot loss/180-foot gain

**Seasons:** Best from mid-May to Nov

**Trail surface:** Dirt trail and old dirt ranch roads

**Land status:** State Park and State Wildlife Area

**Nearest town:** Divide

**Other trail users:** Equestrians, mountain bikers (in state park only), and hunters (in season)

**Canine compatibility:** Dogs not permitted

**Schedule:** Year-round. Day-use hours: 5 a.m. to 10 p.m. daily. Call first for trail conditions in winter. The trails are used by cross-country skiers and snowshoers.

**Fees and permits:** Daily entrance fee or annual parks pass required for Mueller State Park

**Maps:** USGS Cripple Creek North (20-foot contours) and Divide (40-foot contours); Nat Geo Trails Illustrated 137 Pikes Peak/Cañon City

**Trail contact:** Mueller State Park, Divide; (719) 687-2366; http://parks.state.co.us/parks/Mueller. Dome Rock State Wildlife Area, Colorado Division of Wildlife, Colorado Springs; (719) 227-5200; http://wildlife.state.co.us/LandWater/StateWildlifeAreas/

**Finding the trailhead:** From Divide drive 3.9 miles south on CO 67 to the entrance to Mueller State Park. Turn right into Mueller State Park, and pay the fee at the entrance station. The visitor center is about 1.6 miles from CO 67. Turn left into the visitor center parking lot and park. Take a few minutes to check out the many interesting exhibits and interpretive displays. The trailhead is at the south end of the parking lot by a bulletin board. The visitor center has restrooms and water. Trailhead GPS: N38 52.73'/W105 10.77'

## The Hike

The Mueller family ranched in the meadows and valleys west of Colorado Springs, slowly buying up neighboring ranches. W. E. Mueller envisioned his ranch becoming a wildlife preserve. The Muellers sold the land in 1978, resulting in the creation of two preserves: Mueller State Park, managed by Colorado State Parks (CSP), and

*Rock Pond*

the 7,000-acre Dome Rock State Wildlife Area (SWA), managed by the Colorado Division of Wildlife (CDOW). Exhibits and interpretive displays in the visitor center convey more of the area's history.

In 1986 CDOW entered into a lease management agreement with CSP, allowing CSP to manage the wildlife area under the state park umbrella. The 12,103 acres of the two preserves became known as Mueller State Park. In June 2000, CDOW resumed management of the leased lands, changing the name back to Dome Rock SWA. Mueller State Park now contains 5,121 acres. The Rock Pond to Werley Ranch Loop starts in Mueller, loops through the Dome Rock State Wildlife Area, and wanders back into Mueller. Watch for golden eagles, red-tailed hawks, great horned owls, and turkey vultures. Elk, mule deer, coyote, black bear, and mountain lions are some of the larger mammals you may see.

From the visitor center the mountain views are excellent. Pikes Peak (14,110 feet) to the east is the most obvious, but numerous 14,000-foot peaks—Yale, Columbia, Harvard, and others—stand out to the west. The Sangre de Cristo Range and Mount Pisgah (10,343 feet), near Cripple Creek, rise in the south. Interpretive signs in a gazebo near the trailhead identify the many peaks. Walk down the trail to the right of the trailhead bulletin board, along a mowed path to the gravel road. Notice the Douglas fir trees along the way and look at a fir cone. They're easy to spot as they have distinctive three-pronged bracts between the scales. Naturalists' stories relate that once upon a time, a hungry fox chased a little mouse, hoping for a tasty meal. Not wanting to be eaten, the little mouse begged a nearby tree for help. The

# 31 Aiken Canyon

Aiken Canyon harbors a rich diversity of life where plains and foothills converge. The nature preserve is home to bear, mountain lion, elk, mule deer, bobcat, fox, squirrels, rattlesnakes, and over one hundred species of birds, including the threatened Mexican spotted owl. The canyon also provides a wildlife corridor between the plains of Fort Carson Military Reservation to the east and the higher hills and forests to the west. In an area experiencing housing development pressures, Aiken Canyon preserves a foothills ecosystem that is rapidly disappearing along the Front Range.

**Start:** From behind the bulletin board near Aiken Canyon Preserve's visitor center
**Distance:** 3.4-mile lollipop
**Approximate hiking time:** 2 to 3 hours
**Difficulty:** Easy
**Elevation gain:** 420 feet
**Seasons:** Year-round except after big snowstorms
**Trail surface:** Dirt trail with some rocks and tree roots, and a creekbed
**Land status:** Nature preserve
**Nearest town:** Colorado Springs
**Other trail users:** None
**Canine compatibility:** Dogs not permitted

**Schedule:** Year-round on Sat, Sun, and Mon from dawn to dusk. The visitor center is open those three days between Memorial Day to Labor Day; for the rest of year it is open on Sun only. Call first to check conditions after big snowstorms.
**Fees and permits:** None
**Maps:** USGS Mount Pittsburg and Mount Big Chief; Nat Geo Trails Illustrated 137 Pikes Peak/Cañon City
**Trail contact:** Aiken Canyon Preserve, The Nature Conservancy, Colorado Springs; (719) 632-0534; www.nature.org

**Finding the trailhead:** From I-25 in Colorado Springs, take exit 140, Highway 115. Drive south on Nevada Avenue (CO 115) for 15.5 miles to just beyond mile marker 32. Turn right onto Turkey Canyon Ranch Road. Drive another 0.1 mile and turn right into the parking lot for Aiken Canyon Preserve. Vault toilets are available near the visitor center (field station). Trailhead GPS: N38 37.23' / W104 53.26'

## The Hike

Back in the 1870s, ornithologist Charles Aiken first surveyed this area, which contains two globally rare plant communities: the piñon pine, one-seeded juniper / Scribner needlegrass woodland, and Gambel oak / mountain mahogany shrubland. When a quarry was proposed on state land in Aiken Canyon in the 1980s, strong local outcry prompted protection of the area. The Nature Conservancy and the Colorado State Land Board formed a partnership in 1991 allowing the conservancy to lease and manage the state land, thus saving it from the mining operation. Aiken Canyon Preserve consists of 1,080 acres of state land and another 541 acres owned by The Nature

*View from the overlook*

Conservancy. In 1993 volunteers with Volunteers for Outdoor Colorado built the current trail. Later other volunteers built the short trail to the overlook.

The loop trail passes through an amazing number of plant communities in a small area. Big bluestem grass with its trident or turkey-track heads grows over 5 feet tall. Watch for spiny yucca, a cactuslike plant that is really a member of the lily family. Pincushion and prickly pear cactus grow here, too. The trail crosses a seasonal creek numerous times. When the creek is running you can easily cross using stones. The creek is usually dry in summer, but thick vegetation grows along the banks, fed by spring runoff. In some places the creek disappears underground, and the trail and creek continuously wind together and apart, giving the impression of crossing many creeks over a long distance instead of one creek over a relatively short distance.

The red rocks of the Fountain Formation rise in interesting shapes or just lean against the area's foothills. The Fountain Formation, commonly found along the Front Range, is a combination of sandstone and conglomerate, the latter being a mixture of pebbles and sand cemented together. About 300 million years ago, the Ancestral Rockies, also known as Frontrangia, slowly rose above the surrounding land parallel to today's Front Range, but about 30 to 50 miles west. Frontrangia eroded into red-colored gravel and sand that reached depths of 7,000 to 12,000 feet. Over time, the sand became sandstone and the gravel turned into conglomerate. Fountain Formation rock formations can be seen in other places west and north of Colorado Springs, including at Garden of the Gods, Roxborough State Park, Red Rocks Park, and the Boulder Flatirons.

The trail winds in and out of meadow, creekbed, and forest. Trees and bushes intermix to form an interesting mosaic. Interpretive signs along the first 0.7 mile explain the vegetation and wildlife. It's easy to understand why so many animals and birds are attracted to life in the canyon, as the area offers deluxe habitat and a cornucopia of food. Ponderosa pines tower over an assortment of currant bushes. The great variety of grasses can be identified by the different seed heads.

As you approach the hills, the trail gets rockier. Cairns direct you, but sometimes blend in with the trail, so take care to stay on course. Green lichens cover the trunks of one particular patch of piñon pine. Most people associate lichens with rocks, but many varieties exist, some of which live on trees.

Soon you reach a meadow where a spur trail to the right heads up a side canyon. If you have time, explore this 2.0-mile out-and-back route. The spur trail takes you farther up the narrowing canyon, where Douglas firs start to appear in the cooler, moister environment. Take note that it's easy to confuse the creekbed and the trail in some places. When you come to a big pile of boulders between you and the creekbed, step on over and continue up the canyon. The old cabin remains signal the spur trail's end.

Returning to the loop trail, turn right (or continue straight if you skipped the canyon spur) and climb up a somewhat steep ridge. Near the top of the climb, to the right of the trail, is a boulder that's an excellent example of conglomerate rock. A trail to the left leads up one of the little hills to an overlook of the area to the south. On these south-facing slopes, Gambel oak, mountain mahogany, sagebrush, and cactus predominate, a noticeable change from the first half of the hike. Little lizards zip along the rocks. Ridges run down the sides of the foothills. Gambel oak, reaching 10 to 12 feet tall, form a canopy over the trail. The trail crosses several arroyos, where the deep, narrow gullies cut by flash floods remind you of the power of water. Flash floods occur infrequently here, but be mindful of lightning, which signals a storm upstream. Cross a final meadow to complete the loop part of the trail. Head back the way you came.

## Miles and Directions

- **0.0** Start behind the interpretive kiosk near the visitor center. Elevation: 6,440 feet.
- **0.1** The trail drops into the streambed for several hundred feet.
- **0.7** The loop section of the trail starts. Turn onto the right branch. GPS: N38 37.60'/W104 53.18'.

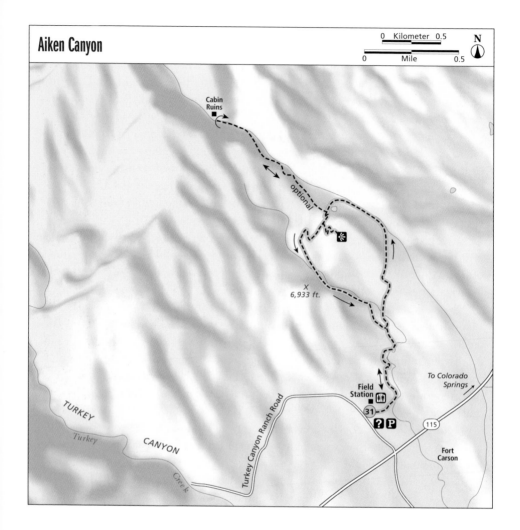

**1.7** Come to the junction with the canyon spur trail. GPS: N38 38.11'/W104 53.53'. Stay on the trail straight ahead. **(Side trip:** If you have time to explore the canyon spur, turn right and hike about 1 mile to the cabin ruins. Check out the iris garden! You gain 420 feet in elevation. Return the same way back to the loop trail and take the right branch. This side trip will add 2 miles to your overall trip.)

**1.8** Arrive at the junction with the trail to the overlook. **(Side trip:** Turn left and wind your way to the top of the small hill for a nice 360-degree view. This will add less than 0.4-mile round-trip and a 140-foot gain to your hike.)

**2.7** Return to the loop trail junction. Turn right and retrace your steps.

**3.4** Arrive back at the trailhead.

# THE NATURE CONSERVANCY

The Nature Conservancy (TNC) is a nonprofit organization. Its mission is "to preserve the plants, animals and natural communities that represent the diversity of life on Earth by protecting the lands and waters they need to survive." Several ecologists, who wanted to use their knowledge to conserve endangered areas, founded TNC in 1951. Their first accomplishment in 1955 protected a small area in New York State. Since then TNC has grown to be an international organization, preserving more than 1,500 areas just in the United States.

When evaluating a property, TNC first conducts scientific studies in areas suspected to contain imperiled species of plants, animals, and natural communities. These areas are ranked based on rarity of the species. Using money contributed by individuals and corporations around the world, TNC works with willing landowners to preserve the lands by either purchasing the land outright or forming management partnerships. Management of the preserves is accomplished using the latest ecological techniques. With some restrictions, most areas are open to the public for the purpose of nature study, wildlife watching, photography, and hiking. Ongoing projects include inventorying species and reviewing habitat health.

For more information about supporting or getting involved with The Nature Conservancy, please contact the Colorado Field Office in Boulder at (303) 444-2950 or www.nature.org.

## Hike Information

### General Information
**Experience Colorado Springs (Convention & Visitors Bureau):** Colorado Springs; (719) 635-7506 or (800) 368-4748; www.coloradosprings-travel.com

### Local Events/Attractions
**Cheyenne Mountain Zoo:** 4250 Cheyenne Mountain Zoo Rd., Colorado Springs; (719) 633-9925; www.cmzoo.org
**Garden of the Gods:** 1805 North 20th St., Colorado Springs; (719) 634-6666; www.gardenof gods.com
**Pikes Peak Cog Railway:** 515 Ruxton Ave., Manitou Springs; (719) 685-5401; www.cograilway.com
**US Air Force Academy:** 2346 Academy Dr., U.S. Air Force Academy; (719) 333-2025; www.usafa .af.mil/information/visitors/
**US Olympic Visitors Center:** Colorado Springs; (719) 866-4618 or (888) 659-8687; www .teamusa.org

### Accommodations
**Cheyenne Mountain State Park:** 410 JL Ranch Heights, Colorado Springs; (719) 576-9099; http://parks.state.co.us/Parks/CheyenneMountain

## Restaurants

**The Blue Star:** 1645 South Tejon St., Colorado Springs; (719) 632-1086; www.thebluestar.net

**La Casita Patio Cafe:** 306 South Eighth St., Colorado Springs; (719) 633-9616; www.lacasitapatiocafe.com

**Poor Richard's Restaurant:** 324 1/2 North Tejon St., Colorado Springs; (719) 632-7721; www.poorrichards.biz

## Clubs and Organizations

**Colorado Mountain Club–Pikes Peak Group:** Colorado Springs; (719) 635-5330; www.cmc.org

**Volunteers for Outdoor Colorado:** Denver; (303) 715-1010; www.voc.org

## Hike Tours

**Aiken Canyon Preserve:** tours by The Nature Conservancy; Colorado Springs; (719) 576-4336; www.nature.org

*Cabin remains*

# 32  Thompson Mountain

This interesting hike makes a rolling loop through part of the Deer Haven Ranch, managed by the Bureau of Land Management to preserve its natural values and provide recreational opportunities. The trail winds through ponderosa pines, Douglas firs, and meadows. Open areas, including a side trip to Thompson Point, provide nice views of Pikes Peak, the Wet Mountains, and the Sangre de Cristo Range.

**Start:** From Wilson Creek Trail (T5827) trailhead
**Distance:** 7.6-mile lollipop
**Approximate hiking time:** 3.5 to 5.5 hours
**Difficulty:** Difficult due to elevation gain
**Elevation gain/loss:** 1,420-foot gain / 420-foot loss
**Seasons:** Year-round except after big snowstorms
**Trail surface:** Dirt trail, singletrack, and doubletrack
**Land status:** BLM land
**Nearest town:** Cañon City
**Other trail users:** Equestrians, mountain bikers, and hunters (in season)

**Canine compatibility:** Dogs must be under control. Minimal water is found along the trail.
**Schedule:** Year-round, except after a big snowstorm. The trail is neither marked nor maintained when snow-covered.
**Fees and permits:** None
**Maps:** USGS Gribble Mountain and Rice Mountain; Nat Geo Trails Illustrated 137, Pikes Peak/Cañon City
**Trail contact:** Bureau of Land Management, Royal Gorge Field Office, Cañon City; (719) 269-8500; www.blm.gov/co/st/en/fo/rgfo .html
**Special considerations:** No facilities at trailhead. Bring water!

**Finding the trailhead:** From the intersection of CO 115 and US 50 in Cañon City, drive west on US 50 about 9.5 miles, past the Royal Gorge turnoff (restaurants and motels here), to CO 9. Turn right on CO 9 and head north approximately 8.7 miles to Fremont County Road (FCR) 11. Turn right onto FCR 11, watching for deer along this twisty paved road. (You're on the Gold Belt Scenic Byway.) Drive 5.3 miles to the Deer Haven Ranch sign, just past mile marker 5, and turn right onto FCR 69, a well-graded narrow dirt road. Drive slowly to avoid collisions with oncoming traffic or cattle because this area is open range. Drive 3.3 miles to the Wilson Creek Trail (T5827A) sign and turn right. Park immediately in the meadow. **(Note:** Drive the extra 0.2 mile to the trailhead bulletin board *only* if the road is dry and you have high clearance. The road can be extremely wet and muddy, and driving through the mud only makes the muddy area larger. Even the BLM has been known to get stuck on this road.) Meadow parking GPS: N38 36.62'/ W105 20.98'

## The Hike

Charlie and Lee Switzer first started cattle ranching in the Thompson Mountain area back in the 1870s. Their 640 acres covered open range, rolling hills, and bunchgrass. During the Cripple Creek–Victor gold rush, they supplied beef to the miners. Around 1900 Toll Witcher bought the ranch from the Switzers, then sold it to Lon

*Pikes Peak from stem part of trail*

Gribble in 1914 or 1915. During World War I the price of cattle rose. With his profit, Gribble built a new house in 1917. While digging the basement, he struck solid rock in one corner. After digging 4 feet into the rock, he struck water. Gribble built a water tank of sorts and built the kitchen right above it. The two-story house had two bedrooms downstairs and four upstairs, a big fireplace, and a full basement. Lumber for the house was hauled from Cañon City with a four-horse team. The house cost $12,000 to build, a substantial sum in those days. You passed the historic house (still a private residence) on the way to the trailhead.

Gribble also established a sawmill, with a Case tractor to run it. He hired a worker to run the mill and others to cut the timber. He sold the lumber to the coal mines south of Cañon City for mine props. By 1932, cattle prices had fallen and a hard winter took its toll on Gribble's ability to pay his loans, resulting in foreclosure on Gribble's ranch.

According to a story titled "Last Wilson Creek Roundup," in the June–July 1976 *Frontier Times,* Dud Van Buskirk, who was Lon Gribble's brother-in-law, bet Gribble that Fred Short could hold a cow by the tail for five minutes. Short walked into the herd of cattle and grabbed the tail of a two-year-old heifer. The heifer ran as fast as she could, out of the herd and up along the fence. Fred was hanging on. After about 100 feet, the heifer decided to head back to the herd, "stopped right quick and turned back down the fence. Fred, however, just kept going—about 10 feet to a step—till he fell and lit on his face."

In 1940 Floyd Murphy bought the old Switzer Ranch and actually made it profitable. He grazed a string of relay horses and was one of the best relay riders in America. He also grazed cattle. He sold the ranch about ten years later at $10 per acre.

After several other owners, The Richard King Mellon Foundation and the Conservation Fund of Arlington, Virginia, bought the land, then donated it to the Bureau of Land Management in 1992 to "provide significant wildlife habitat, riparian, and wetland habitat, recreation opportunities, protect scenic quality and to improve stewardship and access to adjoining public land." The donation amounted to 4,900 acres. On National Trails Day in 1993, a groundbreaking ceremony was held to initiate the current trail. The Rocky Mountain Back Country Horsemen and the Medicine Wheel Bicycle Club have steadily worked on the trail.

The hike starts up a drainage, then turns up another drainage at a check dam. The first part climbs steadily through the forest, then up a ridge. As you gain elevation, keep an eye open to the right for views of Pikes Peak. In a beautiful ponderosa pine forest, the trail is marked with brown carsonite signs. Mica flecks sparkle in the trail.

Pass through a gate at 2.2 miles, then descend through a flower-filled meadow to a pond where the loop part of the trail begins. Take the left fork first. The trail follows occasional trail markers. It heads down another drainage to a metal cattle trough. From the descending trail you can see the rocky knob of Thompson Point. After the cattle trough, the trail heads up a broad drainage to a saddle. A spur trail, T5827B, heads to the left to Thompson Point. Wilson Creek Trail (T5827A) turns right here and eventually climbs, descends, and climbs again to an open area with views of Cap Rock. Turn right here and follow the two-track trail that winds through forest and meadow and back to a gully. Turn right at the gully and walk back to the first pond and dam to end the loop. Head back to your vehicle the way you came.

Thompson Mountain covers a large area, its gentle ridges surrounding drainages and meadows. It's definitely not the typical Colorado pointy-topped mountain.

## Miles and Directions

- **0.0** Start in meadow near the Wilson Creek Trail (5827A) sign. Elevation: 7,620 feet. Hike up the dirt road.
- **0.2** Reach the bulletin board for the trail. Please stop and read the area information and regulations.
- **0.4** Look for an old rock fence to your right.
- **0.6** Curve left at the directional sign.
- **0.7** Reach the remains of an old one-room house with corrugated siding

# Thompson Mountain

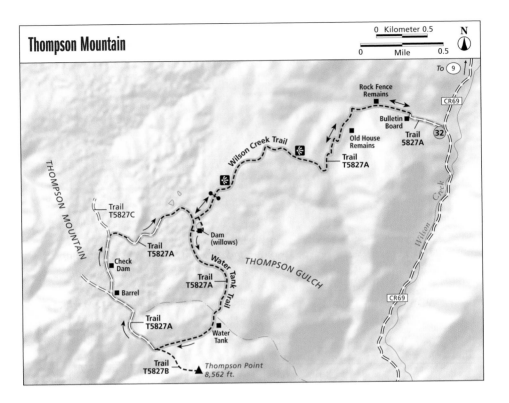

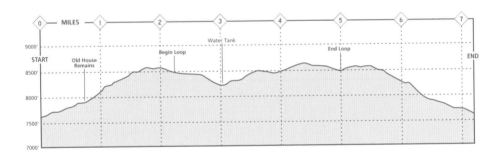

**1.2** The trail reaches a saddle and turns right up the ridge. **(FYI:** During the next 0.4 mile, look to the right for views of Pikes Peak through the trees.)

**2.2** Reach a fence and gate. Elevation: 8,250 feet. GPS: N38 36.28' / W105 22.51'. Use the metal gate to the left—remember to close the gate behind you. The trail descends the meadow to a trail junction sign. **(FYI:** Nice views to the southwest of the Wet Mountains and the Sangre de Cristo Range.)

**2.4** Reach the junction of Water Tank Trail and Thompson Mountain Trail. The loop trail is really across the gully to the west. You can turn left onto Water Tank Trail and follow the trail through the trees, turning right to cross the little dam. However, willows are overtaking the top of the dam. Instead, head toward the gully to the west on the north side of the pond and make your way to the other side. The trail comes to a T intersection. The loop in the trail starts here. Turn left and follow the trail through the forest, then descend toward a creek.

**3.0** Enter a meadow. Look downhill as you hike, and you'll see a circular water tank, a narrow water trough, and a creek. Head to the water tank.

**3.1** Drop down past the metal water tank and cross the creek. GPS: N38 35.67'/W105 22.56'. You'll find the trail on the other side that takes you up and around into a grassy open meadow and drainage. Head uphill toward a saddle.

**3.6** Reach the saddle and a trail junction. Turn right and follow the two-track T5827A uphill. **(FYI:** Look to your left for some interesting rock formations.) **(Side trip:** If you'd like to hike up to Thompson Point, turn left onto T5827B. Out-and-back distance to Thompson Point is about 1 mile, to a point beyond the rocky outcropping.)

**3.8** Follow the trail downhill to the right. As you approach a gully, the road turns left and starts heading uphill again.

**4.1** Enter an open area with a rusted barrel stuck in the ground to your right. Continue uphill on the trail to a check dam at mile 4. Continue along the trail to the left of the dam.

**4.4** Enter an open, flat area with three trail posts. Elevation: 8,580 feet. GPS: 38 36.08'/W105 23.27'. T5827A turns right while T5827C goes straight ahead and starts heading slightly downhill. Turn right here and follow T5827A as it curves toward some ponderosas. **(FYI:** There are great views of various hills ahead, with Thompson Point and the Sangre de Cristo and Wet Mountains behind you.)

**4.9** Arrive in an open meadow. A big rock outcropping is on your left. Continue across the meadow toward ponderosas. The trail curves a little to the left, then the right. You'll come to a gully, then turn right and follow the trail back to the start of the loop.

**5.2** Reach the trail junction sign for Water Tank Trail and Thompson Mountain Trail. Head uphill and return the way you came.

**7.4** Arrive back at the trailhead bulletin board.

**7.6** Arrive back at the parking area in the meadow.

## Hike Information

### General Information
**Cañon City Chamber of Commerce:** 403 Royal Gorge Blvd., Cañon City; (719) 275-2331 or (800) 876-7922; www.canoncitycolorado.com

### Local Events/Attractions
**Dinosaur Depot:** 330 Royal Gorge Blvd. A, Cañon City; (800) 987-6379 or (719) 269-7150; www.dinosaurdepot.com
**Museum of Colorado Prisons:** 201 North 1st St., Cañon City; (719) 269-3015 or (877) 269-3015; www.prisonmuseum.org
**Royal Gorge Bridge & Park:** Royal Gorge; (719) 275-7507 or (888) 333-5597; www.royalgorgebridge.com
**Royal Gorge Route (train ride):** Santa Fe Depot, 401 Water St., Cañon City; (888) 724-5748 or (719) 276-4000; www.royalgorgeroute.com

*Water trough along trail*

## Restaurants

**El Caporal:** 1028 Main St., Cañon City; (719) 276-2001
**McClellan's Grill and Brewing Company:** 413 Main St., Cañon City; (719) 276-3400; www .mcclellansbrewingco.com
**Le Petit Chablis:** 512 Royal Gorge Blvd., Cañon City; (719) 269-3333

## Clubs and Organizations

**Rocky Mountain Back Country Horsemen:** P.O. Box 41, Penrose, 81240

# 33 Newlin Creek Trail

Newlin Creek Trail wanders up a narrow canyon following the remains of an old logging road. Due to floods and deterioration, it's tough to tell that this trail was once a road. Rocky cliffs loom over the trail in spots, while little waterfalls and cascades dance down the creek. After crossing one wooden bridge, the trail crosses the creek numerous times on logs and rocks. The most interesting features of this hike lie in the destination meadow. An old steam boiler, flywheel, and chimney are all that remain of a sawmill operation.

**Start:** From the Newlin Creek Trail (Trail 1335) trailhead near Florence Mountain Park

**Distance:** 5.0 miles out and back

**Approximate hiking time:** 2.25 to 4 hours

**Difficulty:** Difficult due to elevation gain

**Elevation gain:** 1,400 feet plus lots of little undulations at creek crossings

**Seasons:** Best from mid-May to early Nov

**Trail surface:** Dirt trail with numerous creek crossings, rocky in places

**Land status:** National forest

**Nearest town:** Florence

**Other trail users:** Equestrians and hunters (in season)

**Canine compatibility:** Dogs must be under control

**Schedule:** Year-round; access road closed 0.5 mile from trailhead in winter

**Fees and permits:** None

**Map:** USGS Rockvale

**Trail contact:** San Isabel National Forest, San Carlos Ranger District, Cañon City; (719) 269-8500; www.fs.usda.gov/psicc

**Special considerations:** No facilities. Bring water in case the creek is low. Treat water obtained from Newlin Creek.

**Finding the trailhead:** From the intersection of CO 115 and CO 67 in the middle of Florence, drive south on CO 67 for 4.3 miles to Fremont County Road (FCR) 15. The intersection is marked as national forest access and for the Newlin Creek Trail trailhead. Turn right onto FCR 15. The road forks in 2.7 miles; stay on FCR 15 by driving on the right fork. The road turns to dirt in another 0.9 mile. The road forks in another 0.8 mile; stay right, following the sign to Florence Mountain Park. The entrance to the mountain park is designated by two big log posts on either side of the road in another 1.2 miles. At the junction in another 0.1 mile, marked Amphitheater, go straight. In another 0.2 mile, there's an intersection where you continue straight, then pass the caretaker's house on the left. Follow the signs to Newlin Creek Trail trailhead. In 0.5 mile, pass the national forest boundary sign and the road narrows. It's another 0.1 mile to the trailhead. The trailhead is about 10.8 miles from the middle of Florence. GPS: N38 16.00'/W105 11.30'

## The Hike

Newlin Creek is nestled in the northeastern end of the Wet Mountains. Early explorers, such as the Gunnison Expedition of 1853–1854, perceived that rain constantly fell on this mountain range and named it accordingly. Streams ran high in late winter and early spring, and summer thunderstorms flooded creekbeds. Newlin Creek was probably named after a local by the same name who lived in Locke Park to the west.

*Boiler and flywheel*

Oil was discovered near the town of Florence in 1881 and some wells are still producing oil today. Coal mining also became a big industry in the late 1800s. Coal Creek lies just north of Newlin Creek. The discovery of silver on the west side of the Wet Mountains created booming mining towns such as Silver Cliff and Westcliffe. Coal and silver mines needed much timber for shoring up mine shafts and for residential and commercial buildings. The forests of the Wet Mountains provided an opportunity for an entrepreneur to supply lumber to industries on both sides of the range.

Nathaniel F. Herrick, originally from Canada, lived in Galena near Locke Park, southwest of Cañon City and a few miles west of Newlin Creek, with his wife and children. He grabbed at the opportunity to build a lumber mill and built a road and sawmill up Newlin Creek. The hand-built road measured about 5 feet in width and in places was supported with rock walls. Herrick hauled a huge steam boiler and flywheel to a nice meadow where he also built a cabin, complete with stone chimney. The boiler used water from Newlin Creek to run the flywheel and power a saw to cut lumber.

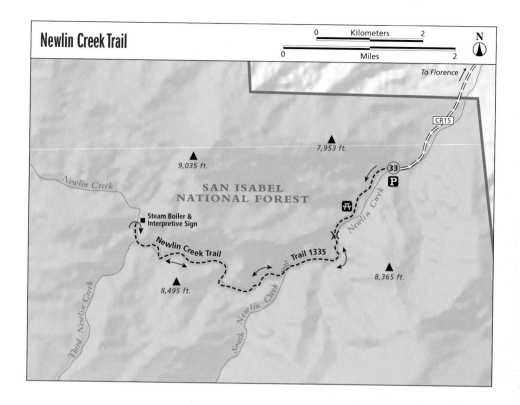

On November 28, 1887, Herrick signed a chattel mortgage with W. D. McGee and W. F. Hasidy for $900. The "chattel" involved the sawmill, including the engine, boiler fixtures, and tools; five horses and one mule with their harnesses; and two log wagons and a Studebaker wagon along with the log chains. According to the mortgage record, the sawmill was "situated on Newland Creek in said County of Fremont, 23 or 24 miles from Cañon City." Unfortunately, after Herrick had all the equipment set up and mortgaged, he died the very next month at the age of sixty-one. The lumber mill was apparently abandoned soon thereafter. Between floods and rockslides, the road was destroyed and the equipment remained in place.

Today the steam boiler lies rusting amidst aspen trees next to Newlin Creek. Some bricks lie near its base. Pipes point in different directions, and the flywheel sits forlorn and disconnected. Exactly how much time it took to haul this equipment from Cañon City or Florence is unknown, but it must have been quite an effort. Look carefully at the boiler for an interesting gargoyle-type face and other inscriptions.

The hike follows Newlin Creek up to the steam boiler meadow. Between rock-slides and floods, it's hard to tell today that any type of wagon road existed along the creek. The trail twists through forests of Douglas fir, ponderosa pine, and Gambel oak. A picnic table sits just before the trail slips between steep canyon walls. Enjoy the fancy wooden bridge that crosses Newlin Creek, since you'll be using rocks and logs to cross creeks numerous times over the duration of the hike. Watch the creek for mini-waterfalls and cascades. Look up occasionally for interesting pointy cliffs and rocks. Farther up the canyon, you'll hike along an open slope with Gambel oak above. Then head back into the trees, where the undergrowth is dotted with red columbine, heart-leafed arnica, Wood's rose, strawberries, pussytoes, and some nice aspen.

A few creek crossings later, you enter a little meadow on the left (west) side of the creek. An interpretive sign outlines the history of the equipment beyond, along with a location diagram. The old boiler and other equipment lie among the trees. Remember the equipment is protected as historical items under the Antiquities Act. Please do not climb on or disrupt the remains. The meadow is a wonderful picnic spot. Enjoy and return the way you came.

## Miles and Directions

**0.0** Start at trailhead parking area for Newlin Creek Trail (Trail 1335). Elevation: 7,000 feet. Please sign the trail register.

**0.5** Come to a picnic table.

**0.6** The trail crosses Newlin Creek on a wooden bridge with handrails.

**0.9** The trail goes through an area of big boulders with rocks in the trail.

**1.0** Come to the first of many creek crossings without a bridge.

**1.5** Reach a nice 4-foot-high waterfall off to the right of a creek crossing.

**1.7** There's a tricky creek crossing on slopey rock (like slickrock).

**2.5** Arrive in a little meadow. A nice interpretive poster explaining the history of the boiler and location of artifacts is to your right. Elevation: 8,400 feet. GPS: N38 15.71'/W105 13.00'. Return the way you came.

**5.0** Arrive back at the trailhead.

*Little waterfall near mile 1.5*

## Hike Information

### General Information
**City of Florence:** (719) 784-4848; www.florencecolorado.org

### Local Events/Attractions
**The Price Pioneer Museum:** open Memorial Day to Labor Day, 1099 County Road 95, Florence; (719) 784-3157; www.museumsusa.org/museums/info/1161444

### Restaurants
**Aspen Leaf Bakery:** 113 West Main, Florence: (719) 784-3834
**Jade Cafe:** 129 Church, Florence; (719) 784-3888; http://jadecaferestaurant.com
**Mainstreet Grille:** 132 West Main, Florence; (719) 784-3224

*Rusty machine parts of an old sawmill.*

# 34 Spanish Peaks Traverse

This hike wanders past several volcanic dikes on the south side of West Spanish Peak. The dikes are fascinating and the views into New Mexico go forever on a clear day. The trail winds through forests of bristlecone, limber, and lodgepole pine, aspen, spruce, subalpine fir, and white fir, with some Gambel oak for good measure. An unmarked overlook by a little dike provides a good view of East Spanish Peak—a good turnaround point for the out-and-back hiker. Beyond the overlook, the hike continues descending to the Trujillo cabin, then climbs to the saddle between the two peaks. It descends a final time along the north side of West Spanish Peak to the north trailhead at the upper end of FR 442 then descends to Huerfano CR 360.

**Start:** Apishapa (a-PISH-a-pa) trailhead
**Distance:** 12.9 miles point to point
**Approximate hiking time:** 6.5 to 8.5 hours
**Difficulty:** Most difficult due to length and elevation gain and loss
**Elevation gain/loss:** 2,540-foot gain / 3,860-foot loss
**Seasons:** Best from June to mid-Oct
**Trail surface:** Dirt trail with some rocky sections across talus fields, and rough dirt road
**Land status:** National forest, wilderness area
**Nearest towns:** La Veta and Cuchara
**Other trail users:** Equestrians
**Canine compatibility:** Dogs must be under control; little to no water on the trail

**Schedule:** FR 46 is closed by snow 9.3 miles from the trailhead in winter. The trail crosses several avalanche paths on south side of West Spanish Peak. The trail is neither maintained nor marked for winter use from either trailhead.
**Fees and permits:** No fees. Group size limit: No more than 15 people per group with a maximum combination of 25 people and pack or saddle animals in any one group
**Maps:** USGS Spanish Peaks and Herlick Canyon
**Trail contact:** Pike/San Isabel National Forest, San Carlos Ranger District, Cañon City; (719) 269-8500; www.fs.usda.gov/psicc
**Special considerations:** No facilities. Bring water.

**Finding the trailhead:** *For shuttle:* Drive to the south end of La Veta on CO 12 to Cuchara Street, next to La Veta Medical Clinic. Turn left on Cuchara Street. In about 0.3 mile Cuchara Street ends but the road curves right and becomes Huerfano CR 36. Continue on HCR 36. In 1 mile, turn left at the HUAJATOLLA VALLEY sign (HCR 360). In 0.5 mile, turn right where the road lazy Ts onto HCR 360. The road straight ahead is a dead end. In 4.1 miles the road Ys—go right on HCR 360. Drive another mile on this somewhat twisty but maintained dirt road to the WAHATOYA TRAIL (TRAIL 1304), FR 442 sign. GPS: N37 25.34' / W104 58.65'. There's a good place to park in about 0.1 mile down the hill. Set up your car shuttle here. With a high-clearance vehicle, you can drive 2 miles up FR 442 to the north Wahatoya Trail trailhead.

*To get to the southern trailhead,* where the hike starts, return to La Veta the way you came. Drive south on CO 12 about 17 miles to the top of Cucharas Pass. Turn left onto Cordova Pass Road (FR 46) and drive another 10.8 miles, keeping left at two intersections that are well marked. Pass through the Apishapa Arch, which was cut through a dike by the Civilian Conservation Corps. A little farther down the road, the Apishapa Trail trailhead will be on your left. Trailhead GPS: N37 20.63' / W104 59.45'

*Dike and Sangre de Cristo Mountains*

## The Hike

Seeing rain clouds gather over what are today known as the Spanish Peaks, Indians named them Wahatoya, "Breasts of the World." Rain provided drinking water and helped crops grow—both essential to life. You might also see spellings of Huajatolla or Guajatolla. Over the years, the peaks have been named Twin Peaks, the Mexican Mountains, and Dos Hermanos (Two Brothers).

The first documented sighting of these peaks came in 1706, when Juan de Ulibarri explored this area for Spain. The peaks, long a landmark for Native Americans, trappers, and explorers, became a welcomed sight for travelers on the Mountain Branch of the Santa Fe Trail, indicating an end to the dry, open plains.

The peaks are also important in the world of geology. About 100 million years ago, an inland sea covered much of North America. Sediments were deposited as the sea rose and subsided, then turned into rock over millennia. About 35 million years ago, after the present Rockies had risen, and while volcanic eruptions were creating the San Juan Mountains to the west, molten magma pushed its way up into the sedimentary rocks, which cracked and buckled from the pressure. The magma oozed into vertical cracks still below the earth's surface, then cooled and hardened. When the entire region was uplifted about 5,000 feet some 5 million years ago, these volcanic intrusions rose also. Erosion washed away the softer sedimentary rocks, leaving behind two peaks and many dikes. Geologists have identified more than 400 dikes around the Spanish Peaks. Looking like huge stone fences, they have been given colorful names like Devils Stairsteps. This hike between the Spanish Peaks and through the dikes is a trip through geologic time.

Circumnavigating the peaks is the Scenic Highway of Legends, commemorating the many legends that surround the peaks. One legend tells of a tribe of giants who once lived around Wahatoya. They quarreled among themselves and built rock walls about chest high for protection. They hurled huge boulders at each other. The gods of Wahatoya, angered by the wars, stopped the rains. The giants stopped fighting and left in search of water. One warrior remained behind to guard the valley, but the others never returned. The guard grew tired and sat to rest. The gods turned him to stone for his dedication. The rock is now known as Goemmer's Butte, a volcanic plug south of La Veta.

In pre-Spanish days, a saga told of gold being used as offerings to the Aztec deities. One of the Aztec rulers established a dazzling court and "the gods of the Mountain Huajatolla became envious of the magnificence of his court and they placed demons on the double mountain and forbade all men further approach." Years later, in the mid–1500s, when Coronado returned to Mexico after abandoning his search for the fabled cities of gold, three monks remained behind to convert the natives. Legend has it that two were killed, while the third monk, Juan de la Cruz, found the gold mines. He forced Native Americans to extract the precious metal from the mines. Ready to return to Mexico, he killed the tribesmen and left with the gold carried by pack animals. The demons became angry, and the priest and his treasure disappeared. According to some versions, a settler found gold nuggets years later. In any case, the tales of lost treasure drew people to the area in search of the lost gold and mines.

The area (not including FR 442) was designated the Spanish Peaks Wilderness area in November 2000. Volunteers for Outdoor Colorado helped the USDA Forest Service build a new 4-mile section of trail higher on the south slope of West Spanish Peak to connect the Wahatoya and Apishapa Trails and avoid private property. Many different types of trees line the trail, including ancient bristlecone pines. You can see

▶ Volunteers for Outdoor Colorado (VOC) is "a nonprofit organization formed in 1984, dedicated to promoting and fostering a sense of personal responsibility for Colorado's public lands among its citizens and visitors." VOC sponsors work projects throughout Colorado from April to October, partnering with various land management agencies. For more information contact (303) 715-1010 or check out www.voc.org.

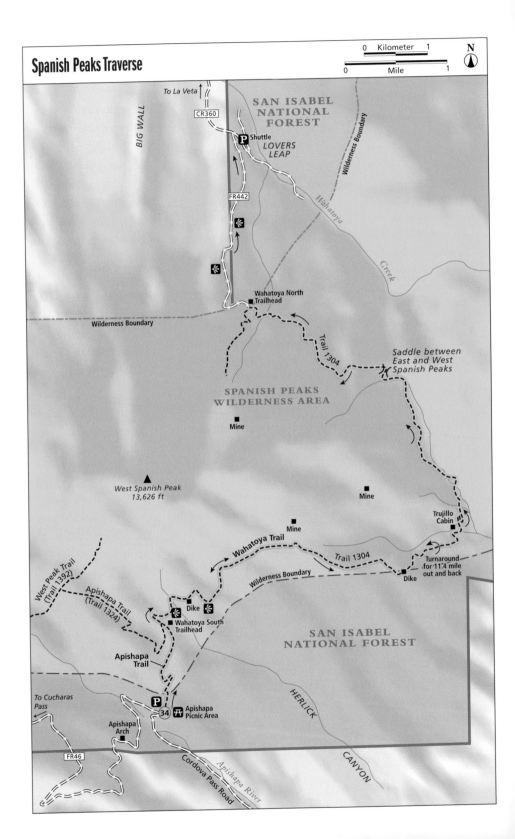

# Spanish Peaks Traverse

**0** Kilometer **1**

**0** Mile **1**

**N**

BIG WALL

To La Veta

CR360

Shuttle

SAN ISABEL
NATIONAL
FOREST

LOVERS
LEAP

FR442

Wilderness Boundary

Wahatoya

Creek

Wahatoya North
Trailhead

Wilderness Boundary

Trail 1304

Saddle between
East and West
Spanish Peaks

SPANISH PEAKS
WILDERNESS AREA

Mine

West Spanish Peak
13,626 ft

Mine

Mine

Trujillo
Cabin

Wahatoya Trail

Trail 1304

Turnaround
for 11.4 mile
out and back

West Peak Trail
(Trail 1392)

Apishapa Trail
(Trail 1324)

Wilderness Boundary

Dike

Dike

Dike

Apishapa
Trail

Wahatoya South
Trailhead

SAN ISABEL
NATIONAL FOREST

HERLICK

To Cucharas
Pass

P
34

Apishapa
Picnic Area

Apishapa
Arch

CANYON

FR46

Cordova Pass Road

Apishapa River

west to the Sangre de Cristos, south to the mesas near Trinidad, and farther yet to the volcanoes in northeastern New Mexico. The most interesting parts are the little passages through the volcanic dikes.

The featured hike is a roller-coaster ride, climbing about 1,160 feet in elevation, then losing about 1,920 feet, only to climb another 1,380 feet to the saddle between the two peaks. Finally, the trail traverses the north flank of West Spanish Peak, descending 480 feet to the north trailhead at the wilderness boundary, then descending another 1,460 feet to HCR 360. The longer hike between the two peaks gives you an intimate view of the Spanish Peaks Wilderness, but those looking to make an equally enjoyable out-and-back hike can turn around at a little dike with a viewpoint of East Spanish Peak, after dropping only 1,430 feet. The shorter hike allows you to experience the large variety of trees and the area's geology without the roller-coaster effect.

## Miles and Directions

**0.0**  Start at the Apishapa Trail trailhead, following the Apishapa Trail. Elevation: 9,720 feet.

**1.5**  Turn right onto the Wahatoya Trail (Trail 1304) GPS: N37 21.42'/W104 59.53'. **(FYI:** The Apishapa Trail continues to the left and intersects with West Peak Trail [Trail 1392], which in turn heads up West Spanish Peak.)

**2.1**  Pass through a little dike.

**5.3**  Cross through a passageway (gap) in a large dike.

**5.7**  Reach an unmarked overlook at a dike. The trail curves right here and continues downhill. Walk ahead and uphill about 90 feet to a good view of East Spanish Peak. Elevation: 9,450 feet. GPS: N37 21.88'/W104 55.67'. Continue on the trail as it heads downhill. **(Option:** This is an excellent turnaround point for an 11.4-mile out-and-back hike. Simply return the way you came. Approximate hiking time: 6 to 7.5 hours.)

**6.3**  Reach the Trujillo cabin. Continue on the trail downstream about 0.1 mile to the crossing of South Fork Trujillo Creek.

**8.9**  Reach the saddle between East Spanish and West Spanish Peaks and the Huerfano and Las Animas County line. Elevation: 10,340 feet. GPS: N37 23.40'/W104 57.05'.

**10.9**  Arrive at the Spanish Peaks Wilderness boundary, the Wahatoya Trail trailhead, and the upper end of FR 442. GPS: 37 23.91'/W104 58.45'. From here, hike down FR 442 (not in wilderness), which is open to motorized use.

**11.6**  There's a great view of a big dike to the west from an imbedded dike to the left of the trail.

**12.9**  Arrive at the trailhead at HCR 360. Elevation: 8,400 feet.

## Hike Information

### General Information

**Huerfano County Tourism:** Walsenburg; www.spanishpeakscountry.com
**La Veta Cuchara Chamber of Commerce:** La Veta; (719) 742-3676 or (866) 615-3676; www .lavetacucharachamber.com

## Local Events/Attractions

**Fort Francisco Museum:** 306 South Main, La Veta; (719) 742-5501; www.spanishpeakscountry .com/FortFrancisco.aspx

**Rio Grande Scenic Railroad:** Alamosa; (877) 726-RAIL; www.riograndescenicrailroad.com

**Scenic Highway of Legends:** Trinidad; (719) 846-9285 or (866) 480-4750; www.coloradoby ways.org

## Accommodations

**National Forest campgrounds:** Pike/San Isabel National Forest, San Carlos Ranger District, Cañon City; (719) 269-8500; www.fs.usda.gov/psicc

## Restaurants

**Dog Bar & Restaurant:** 34 Cuchara Ave. East (Main Street), Cuchara; (719) 742-6366; www .dogbarcuchara.com

**Ryus Ave Bakery:** 129 West Ryus Ave., La Veta; (719) 742-3830; www.ryusavebakery.com

**Sammie's Restaurant:** 124 North Main, La Veta; (719) 742-5435

◀ *Apishapa Arch on way to trailhead*

# 35 Reilly and Levsa Canyons

This hike first follows the Levsa Canyon Nature Trail and then about 2.6 miles of the Reilly Canyon Trail. Winding through piñon pine and juniper forest gives you an idea of the land through which early settlers traveled, especially on the Mountain Branch of the Santa Fe Trail (where I-25 now exists). The suggested turnaround point is a bench where the trail approaches Trinidad Lake and has a good view of the dam. Look for deer in some of the meadows. While hiking you can catch views of Fishers Peak, as well as the old coal mines and town sites on or below the south shore.

**Start:** From the Trinidad Lake State Park Campground
**Distance:** 6.4 miles out and back with a loop
**Approximate hiking time:** 2.5 to 4.5 hours
**Difficulty:** Moderate due to length and a few steep sections
**Elevation gain/loss:** 390-foot gain/360-foot loss
**Seasons:** Year-round except after big snowstorms
**Trail surface:** Dirt trail with a few steep sections

**Land status:** State Park
**Nearest town:** Trinidad
**Other trail users:** Mountain bikers
**Canine compatibility:** Dogs must be on leash
**Schedule:** Year-round, except after a big snowstorm; day-use hours 5 a.m. to 10 p.m.
**Fees and permits:** Daily entrance fee or annual parks pass required
**Map:** USGS Trinidad West
**Trail contact:** Trinidad Lake State Park, Trinidad; (719) 846-6951; http://parks.state.co .us/parks/trinidadlake

**Finding the trailhead:** From Trinidad drive 3.9 miles southwest on CO 12 from its intersection with I-25 to the Trinidad Lake State Park entrance. CO 12 is the Scenic Highway of Legends, so follow the scenic byway signs. Turn left onto the park road. The entrance station is about 0.5 mile on the left. Stop and pay the entrance fee. Drive less than 0.1 mile and turn right at the campground entrance. At the fork in the road, turn left and drive to the restrooms. The trailhead is across from the restrooms. Parking is available, as well as restrooms and water. Take water with you. GPS: N37 08.65' / W104 34.18'

## The Hike

The Mountain Branch of the Santa Fe Trail passed nearby what is today Trinidad Lake State Park. I-25 basically follows the old trail over Raton Pass, just south of the city of Trinidad. These lands were home to many Native American tribes: Comanche, Kiowa, Cheyenne, Arapaho, Jicarilla Apache, and Ute. They traveled over the plains, hunting bison, elk, antelope, and deer and creating trails that laid the foundation for the Santa Fe Trail.

What we now know as New Mexico belonged to Mexico and the Spanish in the early 1800s. Spain prohibited trade between the United States and Santa Fe. In 1821, the Mexican people revolted against Spanish rule and gained their independence.

*View of Trinidad Lake from interpretive post 11*

One American entrepreneur, William Becknell, left Franklin, Missouri, in August 1821 and headed to Santa Fe with trade goods on pack animals. He traveled over Raton Pass, taking two days to roll boulders out of the way so his pack animals could pass. This route later became the Mountain Branch of the Santa Fe Trail. Becknell reached Santa Fe in mid-December and quickly sold his goods. In exchange for manufactured goods and supplies, the Mexicans traded gold, silver, fur, and mules. Becknell returned to Missouri by an overland route that avoided Raton Pass, arriving home in January 1822. Later that year Becknell traveled back to Santa Fe with more trade goods, using wagons on the 780-mile overland route, which became known as the Cimarron Cutoff. The round-trip between Missouri and Santa Fe took two to three months.

For the next twenty-five years, the Cimarron Cutoff was the preferred route to Santa Fe, being 100 miles shorter than the Mountain Branch, with rolling plains and no mountain obstacles. Two disadvantages were a lack of water along one 60-mile stretch, and travel through the hunting grounds of unpredictable Comanche, Kiowa, and Apache tribes. In 1846, two events caused the Mountain Branch over Raton Pass to become the preferred route. First, a bad drought occurred in 1846, drying out the few springs and streams along the Cimarron Cutoff. The Mountain Branch followed the Arkansas River, which always had some water, even if one had to dig in the streambed to find it. Second, Bent's Fort was also located on this route. General

▶ If you stay at the campground, try your hand at horno (pronounced *OR-no*) cooking. The horno is a beehive-shaped oven made of adobe used by Spanish settlers, and still in use in the Southwest today. One is available for use at Trinidad Lake State Park near the amphitheater. Inquire at the visitor center for details.

Stephen Kearney moved his army along the Mountain Branch to run military excursions into Mexico. Kearney also drove his wagon supply trains over Raton Pass after improving the trail. The Mexican-American War started in 1846 and resulted in New Mexico becoming part of the United States in 1848.

Raton Pass provided many challenges to early trail users. Before crossing the pass, people camped along the Purgatoire River on the east side, a welcomed relief after the endless dry prairies. The town of Trinidad was founded here around 1862. From a travel account written in 1846, progress could be as little as 600 to 800 yards a day as men hauled wagons by hand over the great rocks. It took five days to cross the pass, a distance of about 30 miles. One place was so narrow that one little slip sent mules, wagons, and people to a certain death.

In 1865 the legislatures of Colorado and New Mexico granted "Uncle Dick" Wooton a charter to build a toll road over Raton Pass. Wooton blasted away the rocks and widened the road. Tolls ranged from five cents per head of cattle to $1.50 per wagon. In one fifteen-month period, the collected tolls totaled $9,193! The completion of a railroad line from Trinidad to Santa Fe in 1880 eliminated the need for the Santa Fe Trail.

As you hike the Reilly Canyon Trail, imagine driving a horse-drawn wagon through the area. Some of the trail appears fairly negotiable while other sections, dropping into the canyons and ravines, would be a bit dicey. The route starts at the trailhead near the campground. Hike up the first part of Levsa Canyon Nature Trail, then take the right fork and follow the Reilly Canyon Trail for about 2.2 more miles (the mileage noted on the bulletin board starts at this intersection). The trail drops into Levsa Canyon, then climbs out and wanders across a high stretch. Dropping down another little canyon to a flat stretch, the trail then climbs to a big slab of slickrock and descends to Trinidad Lake. A bench to rest on awaits you. From here, you can see the dam at the east end of the lake.

If you want to add some mileage, hike another 1.4 miles west to Reilly Canyon itself, for a 9-mile round-trip. Either way, on the way back, take the right fork at the Levsa Canyon Nature Trail / Reilly Canyon intersection and continue back along the nature trail. It drops, climbs, and drops, providing good views of the area across the lake where coal mines and towns resided before the dam was built, plus of Fishers Peak (9,655 feet) to the south. Watch for blue piñon jays and deer as you hike.

# Reilly and Levsa Canyons

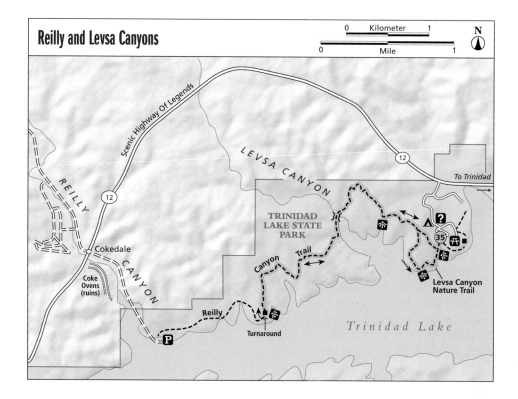

## Miles and Directions

**0.0**   Start at trailhead near restrooms in campground. Elevation: 6,340 feet.

**0.05** At the fork, go right to follow the Levsa Canyon Nature Trail.

**0.1**   At the fork, take right branch of the Levsa Canyon Nature Trail and head uphill.

**0.3**   Arrive at the intersection of the Reilly Canyon Trail and Levsa Canyon Nature Trail. Turn right onto Reilly Canyon Trail.

**1.5**   Cross the bridge in Levsa Canyon.

**2.6**   There's a mound of slickrock on the right.

**2.9**   Reach a bench and a view of the dam. This is the turnaround point. Return the way you came. Elevation: 6,370 feet. GPS: N37 08.18' / W104 35.59'.

**5.6**   Come to the trail intersection of Reilly Canyon Trail and Levsa Canyon Nature Trail. Turn right (more like straight) onto Levsa Canyon Nature Trail.

**5.9**   Reach a bench at sign #11 for the nature trail with a nice view of Trinidad Lake.

**6.3**   Reach the other end of the Levsa Canyon Nature Trail loop. Take the trail on the right. At the next intersection, turn left.

**6.4**   Arrive back at the trailhead.

# Hike Information

## General Information

**Colorado Welcome Center:** 309 Nevada Ave., Trinidad; (719) 846-9512

**Trinidad/Las Animas County Chamber of Commerce:** Trinidad; (719) 846-9285 or (866) 480-4750; www.trinidadchamber.com

## Local Events/Attractions

**El Corazón de Trinidad National Historic District:** Trinidad; (719) 846-7217

**Louden-Henritze Museum of Archaeology:** 600 Prospect, Trinidad; (719) 846-5508

**Trinidad History Museum:** 300 East Main St., Trinidad; (719) 846-7217; www.coloradohistory.org

## Accommodations

**Trinidad Lake State Park Campground:** Trinidad; (719) 846-6951; http://parks.state.co.us /parks/trinidadlake

## Restaurants

**El Capitan Restaurant & Lounge:** 321 State St., Trinidad; (719) 846-9903

**Mission at the Bell Restaurant:** 134 West Main St., Trinidad; (719) 845-1513

**Rino's Restaurant & Steak House:** 400 East Main St., Trinidad; (719) 845-0949; http://rinos trinidad.com

# Honorable Mentions

## Southeast Mountains

Compiled here is an index of great hikes in the Southeast Mountains region that didn't make the A-list this time around but deserve recognition. Check them out and let us know what you think. You may decide that one or more of these hikes deserves higher status in future editions or, perhaps, you may have a hike of your own that merits some attention.

### Q Blackmer Loop

This 4.7-mile moderate lollipop hike twists and turns up and down along the pleasant Blackmer Loop on the toe of Cheyenne Mountain in Cheyenne Mountain State Park. After passing a group of car-size boulders, you'll come upon one with a ponderosa pine growing out of it. The trail generally travels in ponderosa pine and Douglas fir forest, but occasional openings present expansive views of Fort Carson and the Eastern Plains, and of rugged Cheyenne Mountain to the west. Rustic remnants of ranching equipment lie unused in fields along the north section of the trail. Interpretive signs along Blackmer Loop and Zook Loop explain different park features. From I-25 exit 140, Highway115, in Colorado Springs, head south on CO 115 (Nevada Avenue). In 5.5 miles, just past mile marker 42, turn right at the traffic light onto JL Ranch Heights Road. At the roundabout, drive halfway around so you continue heading west. The Cheyenne Mountain State Park visitor center is 0.7 mile farther, and the entry station is 0.8 mile from CO 115. After paying the fee, drive 0.1 mile and turn left into the day-use (Limekiln Grove) trailhead parking lot. There are restrooms and water at both the visitor center and at the day-use trailhead. Dogs are not allowed. Bring water because none is available on this hike. Beware of rattlesnakes. Smoking is not allowed on the trails or in the backcountry. For more information contact Cheyenne Mountain State Park at (719) 576-2016 or check out the website at www.parks .state.co.us/Parks/cheyennemountain.

### R Vindicator Valley Trail

This 2-mile loop trail winds through historic gold mining areas near Victor. A series of interpretive signs explains the history of the area. The trail is also packed for cross-country skiing or hiking in the winter. Two trailheads access the trail, both off of Teller County Road (TCR) 81. Drive north from Victor on TCR 81 (Diamond Avenue). The first trailhead is 1.7 miles north of Goldfield, on the left side of the road. The second trailhead is 0.4 mile farther north, then left on TCR 831. For more information contact the Southern Teller County Focus Group at P.O. Box 328, Victor, 80860, or visit the website at www.web-xpres.com/stcfgtrail.htm.

## S Petrified Forest Loop

The 1-mile easy Petrified Forest Loop in Florissant Fossil Beds National Monument takes you past several petrified giant redwood stumps, once 200 to 250 feet tall. Buried by volcanic ash, it's an amazing reminder of how old the earth is and of things that lived long before humans arrived on the scene. At the end of the loop are posts that indicate time since the earth was formed to present, noting such events as the reign of the dinosaurs to how long humans have been on earth. It's very eye-opening! You can combine this loop with the easy 0.5-mile Walk Through Time Loop. Both start near the visitor center. To reach the visitor center from US 24 in Florissant, drive south on Teller County Road (TCR) 1 about 2.3 miles and turn right into the visitor center, about 0.3 mile from TCR 1. For more information, contact Florissant Fossil Beds National Monument at (719) 748-3253 or visit the website at www.nps.gov/flfo.

# South Central Mountains

The great rift valley of the Rio Grande cuts right through the heart of the South Central Mountains region. To the west, the San Juan Mountains contain some of the most rugged country in Colorado. The last grizzly in Colorado was supposedly killed here and some may still hang out undercover. Farther north, the Collegiate Peaks are 14,000-foot summits named after Ivy League universities. To the east, the jagged crest of the Sangre de Cristo Range rises above the sand dunes it helps create. Centered around an unusual geological feature, the Great Sand Dunes National Park and Preserve encompasses a 30-square-mile area in the San Luis Valley with 700-foot-high sand dunes. From Native American tribes to Spanish explorers to settlers and miners all searching for their own riches, the South Central Mountains region has a rich and diverse history.

The Spanish first journeyed into the San Luis Valley in the late 1500s. Their legacy remains in the town of San Luis, the oldest permanent settlement in the state (established in 1851), and Our Lady of Guadalupe in Conejos, the oldest parish in Colorado. The state's Spanish history is also reflected in many place names, such as Del Norte, Costilla County, and Antonito. Most streams flowing into the San Luis Valley, one of the highest alpine valleys in the world, sink into its sandy and gravelly floor. The Alamosa, Monte Vista, and Baca National Wildlife Refuges, San Luis Lakes State Park, and Blanca Wetlands provide welcome resting spots for migrating waterfowl and shorebirds. Surprisingly, potatoes are the main farm crop in the San Luis Valley. Even more surprising, an unusual farm and tourist attraction north of Alamosa called Colorado Gators harbors alligators and raises tilapia (a tropical freshwater fish) in 87°F water flowing from a 2,000-foot-deep geothermal well.

One of Colorado's historic narrow gauge railroads still carries visitors back in time to the late 1800s, when trains transported silver and gold. Leaving from Antonito, the Cumbres-Toltec Scenic Railroad heads west and south through beautiful country, a spectacular fall trip when the aspens turn gold. Crossing the Colorado–New Mexico border eleven times, the trip ends in Chama, New Mexico. The Rio Grande Scenic Railroad connects La Veta to Alamosa, Antonito, and Monte Vista, offering entertainment at an outdoor amphitheater along the way.

# South Central Mountains Overview

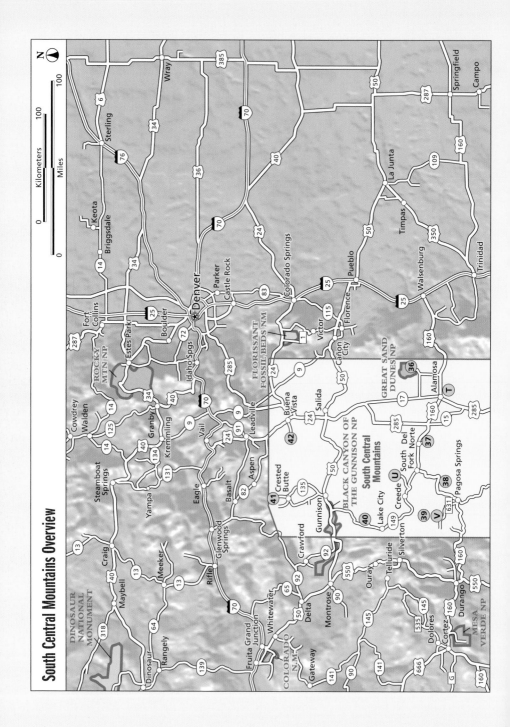

Crested Butte, north of Gunnison, hosts a wildflower festival each summer in early July, and the incredible flowers are truly worthy of the celebration. An area known for mountain biking, it's also a hiker's paradise, with the Raggeds and Maroon Bells–Snowmass Wilderness areas nearby. The former mining town of Gothic now hosts scientists and students at the Rocky Mountain Biological Institute, instead of rowdy miners.

Eleven of Colorado's fifty-four peaks over 14,000 feet are located in this region. A long section of the Colorado Trail winds through the South Central Mountains region, mostly following the Continental Divide and sometimes joining its cousin, the Continental Divide Trail. Wheeler Geologic Area, located northeast of Creede, is famous for its pinnacles and domes eroded from lava and ash.

The Buena Vista and Salida areas access the Collegiate Peaks, as well as exciting white-water rafting on the Arkansas River. The Alpine Tunnel, a marvel of railroad engineering, can be visited via Saint Elmo. Mount Princeton and Cottonwood Hot Springs soothe muscles and weary bones after a long day hiking or peak bagging.

Mining touched this region, too, with Crested Butte, Creede, Lake City, and Summitville being founded after rich strikes were discovered. Del Norte, once a major mining supply town, now supplies area farms and ranches. A few surprise trails are located here if you poke around a little. Middle Frisco Trail, near Del Norte, is featured in this book.

Scenic and historic byways exploring the riches of this area include Los Caminos Antiguos, West Elk, Collegiate Peaks, and Silver Thread.

# 36  Dunes Hiking

This is a make-your-own hike through the Great Sand Dunes National Park and Preserve. Starting and exit points are suggested for a hike across the east side of the dune mass and back along Medano Creek. A few plants and various insects live in the dunes—try to be careful as you walk. Making footprints and seeing the patterns are great fun, as is sliding down the dunes. Hiking in the sand takes a lot of energy, but it's an experience you won't soon forget! Fall is a beautiful time to visit. Watch out for thunderstorms—lightning can be extremely dangerous on the dunes!

**Start:** From the Dunes parking area

**Distance:** Suggested route is an approximately 4.3-mile loop, but you can create your own hike

**Approximate hiking time:** 3 to 6 hours for the suggested route

**Difficulty:** Difficult due to sand and steepness

**Elevation gain/loss:** Varies with route selected

**Seasons:** Year-round, but sands can be extremely hot in summer

**Trail surface:** Mostly loose sand, with some pockets of firmer sand

**Land status:** National park and wilderness area

**Nearest towns:** Mosca (small) and Alamosa (full service)

**Other trail users:** Hikers only (in dune mass) and equestrians (along Medano Creek)

**Canine compatibility:** Dogs must be on leash in the Main Dunes day-use area and along Medano Creek, but are not permitted elsewhere. Check with the visitor center for the exact location. There is no water in the dunes and summer sand temperatures can be extremely hot.

**Schedule:** Year-round

**Fees and permits:** Per person entrance fee, annual pass, or America the Beautiful pass required for park entry. Overnight backcountry camping requires a free backcountry permit. Camping at Pinyon Flats Campground requires a nightly fee. Always check for current regulations at the visitor center.

**Maps:** USGS Liberty and Zapata Ranch; Nat Geo Trails Illustrated 138 Sangre De Cristo Mountains/Great Sand Dunes National Park

**Trail contact:** Great Sand Dunes National Park and Preserve, Mosca; (719) 378-6399; www.nps.gov/grsa

**Special considerations:** In summer the sand surface temperature can reach 140°F.

**Finding the trailhead:** From Alamosa drive east on US 160 to CO 150 at mile marker 248. Turn left (north) onto CO 150 and drive about 20 miles to Great Sand Dunes National Park and Preserve. Pay your fees at the entrance station, then stop at the visitor center. Take a few minutes to browse through the displays and watch the introductory video. From the visitor center, turn left onto the main park road and drive 0.3 mile to the road to the Dunes parking area. Turn left and drive 0.6 mile to the parking lot. Restrooms and water are available. GPS: N37 44.37'/W105 31.00'

*Footprints on dune ridge*

## The Hike

These sand dunes, the tallest in North America, cover about 30 square miles on the eastern edge of the San Luis Valley. Hiking up and around them is a real treat and a lot of exercise, with fun slides down. After leaving the trees at the trailhead and wading across Medano Creek (usually dry in late summer, fall, and winter), enter the Great Sand Dunes Wilderness. By designating the dune field and western sand sheet a Wilderness area in 1976, Congress provided extra environmental protection to this unique area. Medano (Spanish for sand dune) Creek fluctuates throughout the year, depending on season and recent moisture, and may be a damp streambed or ankle deep. Even during a single day, the water levels vary slightly. As the creek flows downhill, it eventually disappears into the sand. Medano Creek rises 13 miles upstream in the Sangre de Cristo Range.

Start at the trailhead at the Dunes parking area and cross Medano Creek (8,060 feet). A nice loop hike can be made by hiking up the dune of your choice, heading north, then curving east along dune ridges or whatever path you desire until you drop

*Dunes and Mt. Herard from visitor center*

down to Medano Creek. Hike back along the creek to the Dunes parking area.

While crossing the first flat area, some green plants may surprise you. Scurfpea, blowout grass, and Indian ricegrass manage to survive here. Sunflowers and rabbitbrush bloom yellow against the dunes in fall. The wind makes interesting patterns in the sand. You can see who or what passed this way recently by the different tracks—that is until the wind wipes them out.

At the first dune start climbing and sometimes sinking in the sand. There is no formal trail; just cruise around wherever it looks interesting to you. Watch for other footprints as their patterns will tell you if the surface is firm or very soft. The hike becomes an exercise in finding the path of least resistance. Climbing up a dune ridge in the steep sand you take three steps forward only to slide back two! Once on top of

▶ If a dunes hike isn't appealing, try Sand Ramp Trail. This trail starts in Loop 2 of the Pinyon Flats Campground and wanders north past "escape dunes" (small dunes created by sand that escaped from the main dune mass). Walk as far as you'd like. The trail goes for 11 miles.

the ridge, look behind at the patterns you made, especially if you're the first to pass that way. Keep an eye open for sand avalanches. Sand grains tumble down when the surface angle reaches 34 degrees. Of course, try hiking up these slipfaces, and you'll swear they're even steeper!

The dunes are deceiving. A path that looks easy becomes a steep descent followed by an equally steep ascent to get up the next ridge. Some low spots display an amazing amount of green plant life. Sand stays moist about 5 inches below the surface. Where sand doesn't cover and snuff out life, plants hang on. Little bugs, perhaps blown by the wind, struggle to climb in the sand. A ladybug may fight mightily, its little legs moving quickly and going nowhere. Several formerly unknown insect species have been found in the dunes since 1990, some of which are found nowhere else in the world! Insects, kangaroo rats, and ravens leave telltale tracks in interesting patterns. A dust devil may swirl by, rearranging sand grains into new patterns.

The sand itself comes in different colors. The black grains that streak the dunes are magnetite from the Sangre de Cristo Mountains, just east of the dunes. Tan grains come mostly from the San Juans, the volcanic mountains to the west. Larger, coarser grains come from the Sangre de Cristos to the east. The dunes are anchored more or

▶ **Summer hiking requires closed shoes to prevent burning your feet on the hot sand. At other times of year bare feet and sandals may work. To avoid getting large quantities of sand in your shoes and boots, wear short gaiters. Protect your camera! Blowing sand gets in everything.**

# GREAT SAND DUNES BECOMES A NATIONAL PARK

The expansion of Great Sand Dunes National Monument (38,659 acres in 2000) was authorized by President Bill Clinton when he signed the Great Sand Dunes National Park & Preserve Act on November 22, 2000. This act transferred public land lying between the dunes and the crest of the Sangre de Cristo Range from the USDA Forest Service to the National Park Service, creating Great Sand Dunes National Preserve. Another provision in the act enabled procurement of the 100,000-acre Baca Ranch, which adjoined the national monument's northwest boundary. The Nature Conservancy (TNC) began securing the ranch in 2002. After procurement was completed, the monument became Great Sand Dunes National Park and Preserve in 2004, and the federal government reimbursed TNC for the purchase. The two units total about 150,000 acres. With the acquisition of the Baca Ranch, the Baca National Wildlife Refuge was created, and Kit Carson Peak (14,165 feet) and surrounding lands were added to the Rio Grande National Forest.

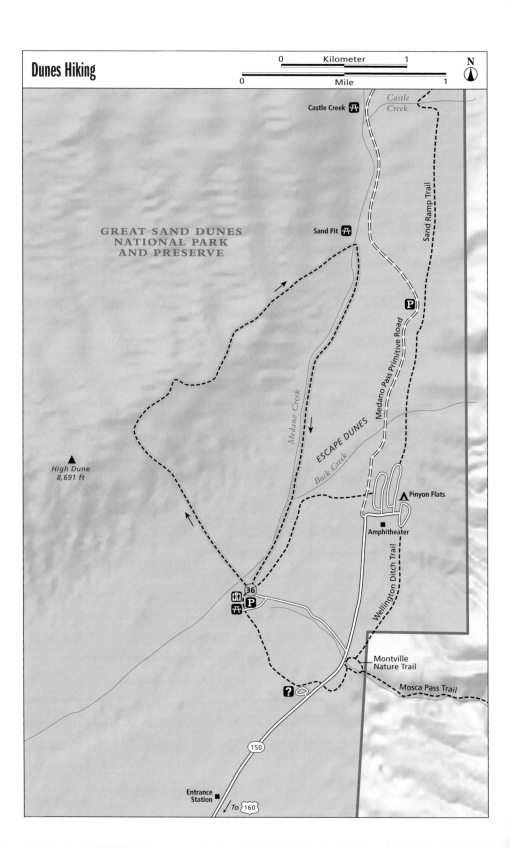

# Dunes Hiking

Kilometer
0                1

Mile
0                1

N

Castle Creek 🏕️

Castle
Creek

GREAT SAND DUNES
NATIONAL PARK
AND PRESERVE

Sand Pit 🏕️

Sand Ramp Trail

P

Medano Pass Primitive Road

Medano Creek

ESCAPE DUNES

Buck Creek

▲
High Dune
8,691 ft

▲ Pinyon Flats

■
Amphitheater

36
🚻 P
🏕️

Wellington Ditch Trail

Montville
Nature Trail

Mosca Pass Trail

❓

150

Entrance ■
Station
To 160

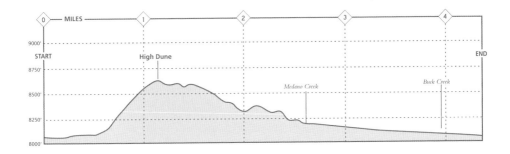

less in place by southwesterly winds that blow the sand toward the Sangre de Cristos, and by northeasterly winds blowing them back. Meanwhile, Medano Creek carries grains downstream and deposits them where the wind can blow them back into the dune mass.

Two joys of dune hiking are playing in a big sandbox and sliding down the sandy dune slopes. Listen for the jet engine roar as your feet slide with each step—the sand grains sing a song when rubbing against each other. Some disadvantages include biting, gnat-like bugs, and irritating, but nonbiting piñon flies in early summer. Nearby Mosca (fly in Spanish) Pass is aptly named.

Once you've slid down to Medano Creek, if water is flowing you can sit and watch the surges for a while. Little dunes build up beneath the water, only to break down. Waves become minibreakers, and the process begins again. A mountain bluebird or piñon jay may fly by. Dragonflies dart through the air. Parts of the wide creek bottom are filled with ankle-twisting rocks. Willows and other plants send shoots to the sky. As you proceed downstream, the creek slowly diminishes. Footsteps fill with water as you pull your foot from moist sand. Tracks of larger animals tell who visited overnight. Mule deer, coyote, and bobcat tracks may be seen.

No one knows for sure how long the dunes have been here. Recent research estimates they started forming less than 440,000 years ago. In millions of years, will they be exposed as petrified dunes in some sandstone formation? In the meantime, have fun playing in the sand!

## Hike Information

### General Information
**Alamosa Convention & Visitors Bureau:** Alamosa; (800) 258-7597; www.alamosa.org

### Local Events/Attractions
**Colorado Gators:** 9162 County Road 9 North, Mosca; (719) 378-2612; www.gatorfarm.com
**Cumbres-Toltec Railroad:** Antonito; (888) 286-2737; www.cumbrestoltec.com
**Fort Garland Museum:** 29477 Highway 159, Fort Garland; (719) 379-3512; http://museumtrail
.org/fortgarlandmuseum.asp
**Los Caminos Antiguos Scenic Byway:** Fort Garland; (719) 379-3500; www.loscaminos.com

## Accommodations

**The Great Sand Dunes Lodge:** mid-May through early October, 7900 Highway150 North, Mosca (adjacent to the park); (719) 378-2900; www.gsdlodge.com

**Pinyon Flats Campground:** Great Sand Dunes National Park and Preserve, Mosca; (719) 378-6399; www.nps.gov/grsa

**San Luis Lake State Park Campground:** Mosca; (719) 378-2020; http://parks.state.co.us/parks/sanluis

## Restaurants

**East-West Grill:** 408 4th St., Alamosa; (719) 589-4600

**The Sand Dunes Oasis Cafe:** 5400 Highway 150 North, Mosca (adjacent to the park); (719) 378-2222

**True Grits Steakhouse:** 100 Santa Fe Ave., Alamosa; (719) 589-9954

## Clubs and Organizations

**Friends of the Dunes, Inc.:** Mosca; (719) 378-6381; www.friendsofgreatsanddunes.org

## Hike Tours

**Great Sand Dunes National Park and Preserve:** Mosca; (719) 378-6399; www.nps.gov/grsa

# 37 Middle Frisco Trail

Middle Frisco Trail follows sparkling, gurgling Middle San Francisco Creek and its tributaries up to San Francisco Lakes. Starting among stands of ponderosa pine and Douglas fir, the trail slowly gains elevation, eventually switchbacking up to a nice spruce-fir forest and subalpine meadows. Wildflowers are abundant along the trail in July. Keep an eye open for elk and cattle. Near the upper lake, there is an ancient bristlecone pine forest. The lower part of the trail is fantastic when the aspen are golden yellow and orange. The lakes are snuggled in high basins between Bennett Peak and Pintada Mountain.

**Start:** From Middle Frisco Trail (Trail 801) trailhead

**Distance:** 12.9 miles out and back

**Approximate hiking time:** 6 to 8.5 hours

**Difficulty:** Most difficult due to length and elevation gain

**Elevation gain:** 2,520 feet

**Seasons:** Best from mid-June to mid-Oct

**Trail surface:** Dirt trail

**Land status:** National forest

**Nearest town:** Del Norte

**Other trail users:** Equestrians, mountain bikers, and hunters (in season)

**Canine compatibility:** Dogs must be under control

**Schedule:** Year-round; but the trail is not marked for winter use. Locals snowshoe and cross-country ski the first section.

**Fees and permits:** None

**Maps:** USGS Jasper and Horseshoe Mountain; Nat Geo Trails Illustrated 142 South San Juan Wilderness/Del Norte (Middle Frisco Creek is on this map, but the trail isn't.)

**Trail contact:** Rio Grande National Forest, Divide Ranger District, Del Norte; (719) 657-3321; www.fs.usda.gov/riogrande

**Special considerations:** Bring your own water or a water treatment system with you.

**Finding the trailhead:** In Del Norte head toward the east end of town to find French Street (Rio Grand CR 13). There's a big green-and-white sign stating NATIONAL FOREST ACCESS SAN FRANCISCO CREEK. Turn south onto French Street. In about 1.8 miles the pavement ends and RGCR 13 becomes a good gravel road. Stop and read the bulletin board on the right side of the road in another 1.9 miles. The trailhead is another 6.1 miles down the dirt road (total 9.8 miles from Del Norte). The trail starts on the left after passing the cattle guard/fence where FR 320 starts. There's a large parking area with no facilities. Cattle graze in the area. GPS: N37 33.40'/W106 23.75'

## The Hike

Locals and several signs call these trails, creeks, and lakes by the nickname "Frisco." The official name on topo maps is "San Francisco." So, you're in the correct spot at Middle Frisco trailhead. A little farther down the road is West Frisco Trail, open to all-terrain vehicles (ATVs) and dirt bikes.

San Francisco Creek is a tributary of the mighty Rio Grande del Norte (Great River of the North) named by Spanish explorers. On the western edge of the San

*Lower Frisco Lake*

Luis Valley, the town of Del Norte took its name from the river. Early native peoples of the Folsom culture lived in the valley more than 10,000 years ago. Starting around 1300, the Moache and Tabeguache bands of Utes called this area home. Juan Bautista de Anza headed north from Santa Fe in 1779 to quiet the Comanches who were causing trouble for the Spanish. He commanded an army of 700 men from Santa Fe, and 200 Ute-Apaches. They camped about 5 miles downstream from Del Norte.

The Spanish divided parts of southern Colorado into land grants. These huge tracts were normally given to individuals or small groups. The Guadalupe Land Grant on the west side of the Rio Grande was designated for one hundred families and their descendants. In 1859, Juan Bautista Silva led fourteen families 200 miles, from New Mexico to the fertile pastures along San Francisco Creek, to settle part of this land grant. It took one month to travel that distance! The newcomers named their town La Loma de San Jose, planted crops, and raised livestock.

In 1870 gold was discovered in the San Juan Mountains southwest of La Loma, and Summitville became the major gold camp. Del Norte, founded in 1871, developed into a major mining supply center for Lake City, Silverton, Summitville, and others. Del Norte was so prosperous that one rich mine owner proposed a separate state called San Juan with Del Norte as its capital!

▶ According to records in Del Norte, in 1932 during the Depression, calves sold for three cents per pound, and two dozen eggs cost fifteen cents.

In the 1880s, cattlemen and sheepherders disputed over ranges, but actually agreed to boundaries. Sheep grazed between the Rio Grande and San Francisco Creek, while cattle ruled the grasses from San Francisco Creek south to Rock Creek. Today, cattle graze near Frisco Lakes.

The trail heads off through aspen groves and meadows, and is soon surrounded by forests of limber pine, ponderosa pine, and Douglas fir. Middle Frisco Creek is tiny and lively, a pleasant hiking companion. Aspen becomes the dominant tree species, occasionally alternating with conifers. The trail breaks out of the woods into a meadow area with Pintada Mountain (12,840 feet) to the left, a large ridge delineating the drainage's east side. A few bristlecone pines have stood guardian here for centuries. A series of twelve switchbacks soon take you even higher. Colorful wildflowers like cinquefoil, death camas, Indian paintbrush, stonecrop, and columbine brighten the climb. As you hike up the ridge, the cliffs above the upper lake resemble the edge of a volcanic crater. The mountains here are part of one of the ancient volcanic calderas that formed the San Juan Mountains. Glaciers carved the upper cirques. A stand of ancient bristlecone pines grows west of the trail.

If you want to hike up the peak above the cliffs, walk back to the junction with the Middle Frisco Cut-off Trail, turn left onto it, and hike about 0.7 mile to the West Frisco Trail. Turn left and head to the summit.

To either overlook the lower lake or hike down to it, cross the creek below the upper lake, wander through a field of old-man-of-the-mountain (alpine sunflowers), then descend a little. There are some good campsites along the hike in and near the lakes. Remember to camp at least 100 feet away from streams, lakes, and trails. The area around the lakes is high subalpine, and trees take years to grow. Wildlife and birds depend on the trees and dead branches. If you camp up high, bring a stove and candles and forgo the campfire to protect the fragile ecosystem.

A little bird you may notice flying overhead near the lakes is the white-crowned sparrow. It indeed looks like a sparrow, but has white around its eyes and a black cap. Watch for a while if you catch sight of one. They pick insects off dead branches. These little sparrows winter as far south as Mexico. When spring arrives, they fly north to mate and nest in the tundra. Their nests are hidden beneath willows, which provide both shelter and the proper temperature to hatch their tiny eggs.

Middle Frisco Trail is an enjoyable hike in a pretty area. The Trail Wise Back Country Horsemen help maintain the trail. The area shows little sign of human use, so please practice Leave No Trace skills.

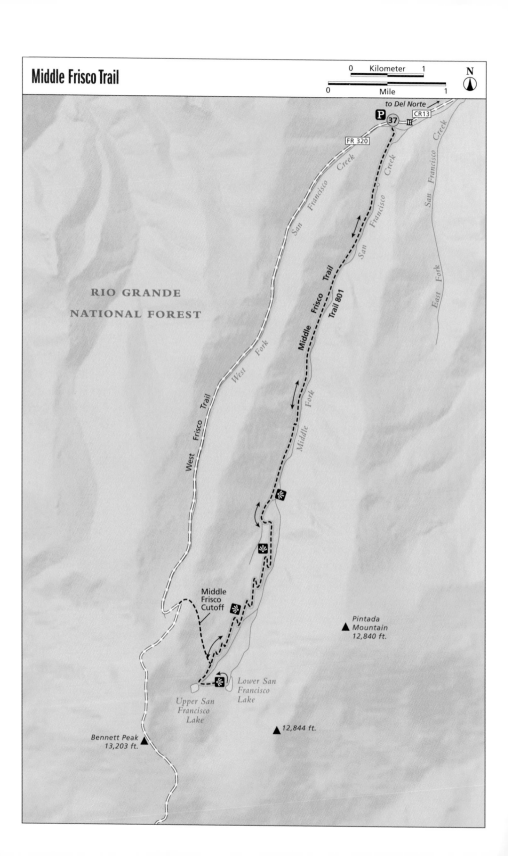

# Middle Frisco Trail

to Del Norte

P  37  CR13

FR 320

San Francisco Creek

San Francisco Creek

San Francisco Creek

East Fork

RIO GRANDE
NATIONAL FOREST

West Fork

West Frisco Trail

West Fork

Middle Frisco Trail

Trail 801

Middle Fork

Middle Fork

Middle
Frisco
Cutoff

Pintada
Mountain
12,840 ft.

Lower San
Francisco
Lake

Upper San
Francisco
Lake

12,844 ft.

Bennett Peak
13,203 ft.

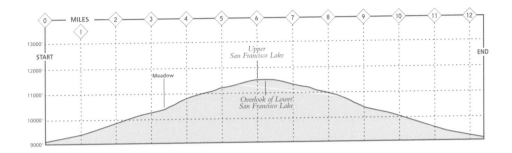

## Miles and Directions

**0.0** Start at the Middle Frisco Trail (Trail 801) trailhead. Elevation: 9,500 feet. Head toward the creek on Middle Frisco Trail. Reach a brown carsonite post shortly after the trailhead. Go past this post to the left. At the creek's edge, look right. You'll see a little bridge that looks like a flat ladder. Walk across the bridge to find the trail on the other side, which climbs up through aspen and into a meadow. The trail is easy to follow from here.

**3.4** The trail enters a large meadow area with a view of Pintada Mountain to the left. GPS: N37 30.77'/W106 24.82'. **(FYI:** Look for some bristlecone pines here.)

**3.6** The trail makes a big U-curve. Follow the curve and not a spur trail.

**4.1** The trail starts a series of switchbacks. Occasionally a spur trail leads off a switchback but stick to the main trail unless you're looking for a campsite. **(FYI:** Look north occasionally for good views of the San Luis Valley and the Sangre de Cristo Range.)

**5.1** The trail crosses a flatter area with a nice view of the cliffs above upper San Francisco Lake. More switchbacks to come!

**5.8** The switchbacks are finished, and the trail follows a little creek down to the left. There are many cattle trails in this area. Stay on the trail heading toward the cliffs.

**6.1** The Middle Frisco Cut-off Trail (nonmotorized) goes to the right and connects to the West Frisco Trail (Trail 850/motorized). **(Side trip:** You can climb Bennett Peak from the West Frisco Trail [watch out for lightning]. Turn right on the cut-off trail and hike 0.7 mile to West Frisco Trail, turn left, and follow the ridge about 1.3 miles to the peak.)

**6.3** Arrive at the outlet to upper San Francisco Lake. Elevation: 12,000 feet. GPS: N37 29.40'/W106 25.52'. Continue left across the outlet toward the lower lake.

**6.45** Enjoy a nice overlook of the lower lake. GPS: N37 29.37'/W106 25.37'. Return the way you came. **(FYI:** This area makes a good lunch spot if you don't want to hike down and back up again. Watch for white-crowned sparrows nearby and elk in the high meadows to the east and south.)

**12.9** Arrive back at the trailhead.

# COLORADO OUTDOOR RECREATION SEARCH AND RESCUE (CORSAR) CARD

In Colorado more than 1,300 search and rescue missions are conducted each year for over-due hikers, lost hunters, and other outdoor enthusiasts who run into some problem in the backcountry. Colorado has many well-trained volunteer search and rescue (SAR) groups. They devote numerous hours to training and to actual rescues. SAR groups have to raise funds for equipment such as climbing gear, radios, rescue vehicles, and snowmobiles. In 1987 the Colorado Legislature created the Colorado Search and Rescue Fund. The legislation levies a 25-cent surcharge on hunting licenses, fishing licenses, and snowmobile and off-highway vehicle registrations to help finance this fund. The fund's purpose is to help sheriffs recover costs of SAR operations and to provide money for SAR equipment and training.

As more hikers, skiers, mountain bikers, and climbers required rescue, the legislature created the Colorado Hiking Certificate for other outdoor recreationists in 1997. In July 2001 the Colorado Outdoor Recreation Search and Rescue (CORSAR) card replaced the hiking certificate. You can purchase a CORSAR card that is good for either one year or five years. Two-thirds of the few dollars charged for the card goes to the SAR fund and one-third to the vendor. Many SAR groups and outdoor organizations sell the card as a fundraiser.

If you need rescue in the backcountry, a SAR team will come (depending on where you are), CORSAR card or not. The card is *not* insurance. SAR missions can cost a lot of money, more when a helicopter is used in the search effort or if an SAR group's equipment is dam-aged during the mission. If the rescuee has a CORSAR card, certain expenses incurred by the SAR group or sheriff during the rescue can be immediately refunded from the Colorado Search and Rescue Fund. If the rescuee does not have a CORSAR card, sheriffs must wait until the end of the year, apply for a grant to replace damaged SAR equipment, and hopefully receive enough money.

The CORSAR card does not pay for medical helicopter evacuation. Sheriffs will not charge for rescue efforts except in cases of extreme negligence.

Do buy a CORSAR card and help Search and Rescue groups stay equipped and prepared! For more information call (970) 248-7308 or visit http://dola.colorado.gov/dlg/fa/sar/index.html.

# Hike Information

## General Information
**Del Norte Chamber of Commerce:** 505 Grand Ave., Del Norte; (719) 657-2845; (888) 616-4638; www.delnortechamber.org

## Local Events/Attractions
**Covered Wagon Days:** Del Norte; (719) 657-2845
**Rio Grande County Museum and Cultural Center:** 580 Oak St., Del Norte; (719) 657-2847; www.rgcm.org
**La Ventana Natural Arch:** Del Norte; (719) 657-3321; www.fs.usda.gov/riogrande

## Restaurants
**Boogie's Restaurant:** 410 Grand Ave., Del Norte; (719) 657-2907
**Organic Peddler & Peace of Art Cafe:** 14475 US Highway 160, Del Norte; (719) 657-9042; www.organicpeddler.com

## Clubs and Organizations
**Trail Wise Back Country Horsemen:** Del Norte; www.bchcolorado.org

# 38 Alberta Peak: Continental Divide National Scenic Trail

This hike follows the Continental Divide National Scenic Trail south from Wolf Creek Pass to Alberta Peak. It climbs through a pleasant spruce-fir forest and passes near a ski lift at Wolf Creek Ski Area. Beyond the ski lift the trail winds through the forest, then out onto the edge of a ridge with great views to the south and west. Passing through willows, the trail ascends above treeline with views in all directions and beautiful alpine wildflowers. A short scramble takes you to the top of Alberta Peak (11,870 feet), with its resident pikas.

**Start:** From the top of Wolf Creek Pass, on the south side by the interpretive signs

**Distance:** 6.0 miles out and back

**Approximate hiking time:** 2.5 to 4 hours

**Difficulty:** Moderate due to mostly gentle trail and distance

**Elevation gain:** 1,013 feet, plus about 80 feet in undulations

**Seasons:** Best from July to Oct

**Trail surface:** Dirt trail

**Land status:** National forest

**Nearest town:** South Fork

**Other trail users:** Equestrians, mountain bikers, and hunters (in season)

**Canine compatibility:** Dogs must be under control

**Schedule:** The trail is neither maintained nor marked for winter use. Some of the trail goes through the ski area.

**Fees and permits:** None

**Maps:** USGS Wolf Creek Pass; Nat Geo Trails Illustrated 140 Weminuche Wilderness

**Trail contact:** Rio Grande National Forest, Divide Ranger District, Del Norte; (719) 657-3321; www.fs.usda.gov/riogrande

**Special considerations:** No water on the trail; bring your own. Do not hike along the ridge if a thunderstorm and lightning are in the vicinity!

**Finding the trailhead:** From South Fork, drive west on US 160 for 19.4 miles to the top of Wolf Creek Pass. Park on the south side by the interpretive signs. There are no facilities here. The last part of this trail is above treeline. GPS: N37 28.98'/W106 48.09'

## The Hike

In 1978 Congress designated a National Scenic Trail along the Continental Divide, snaking from the Canadian border across Montana, Wyoming, Colorado, and New Mexico to the Mexican border. Because some ridges on the actual divide might be difficult or dangerous, a 50-mile-wide corridor on either side could be used for the trail. Approximately 1,900 miles of trails and seldom-used roads shaped the initial configuration of the 3,100-mile trail. Ultimately designated the Continental Divide National Scenic Trail (CDNST), most of the trail is closed to motor vehicles.

Benton Mackaye, founder of the Appalachian Trail, first proposed the idea for the CDNST in 1966. Congress authorized a study of his idea under the National Trails System Act of 1968. The study reported that trail users would access great scenery, various ecosystems and life zones, and historical areas while crossing twenty-five

*Trail and view northwest from summit*

national forests and three national parks (Glacier, Yellowstone, and Rocky Mountain). In 1971, Baltimore attorney Jim Wolf finished hiking the Appalachian Trail and looked for another such adventure. He started hiking the divide trail from the Canadian border and became a strong proponent for the CDNST.

The CDNST legislation gave the USDA Forest Service responsibility for coordinating the completion of the trail. Congress, however, did not appropriate funding to finish it. The corridor crosses National Park Service and Bureau of Land Management lands and even though existing trails would be used in places, many miles needed maintenance or improvement. Proposed routes also crossed private property in some areas, requiring negotiations with landowners for either purchase or access of the trail corridor.

Two organizations formed to aid the CDNST. First, Jim Wolf founded the Continental Divide Trail Society (CDTS) in 1978. Today the CDTS continues with its mission: "[Dedicated to] the planning, development, and maintenance of the [Continental Divide Trail] as a silent trail." CDTS's efforts focus on the selection and

*Trail along ridge with ski lift in distance*

development of the best possible route and in providing reliable information to trail users. Check out www.cdtsociety.org for more information.

The second organization, Continental Divide Trail Alliance (CDTA), was founded by Bruce and Paula Ward in 1995. CDTA assists the federal land managers to complete, manage and protect the trail. They organize volunteer efforts to build and maintain new and old sections of trail, coordinate an Adopt-a-Trail program, and work with legislators to appropriate funding. Find more information at www.cdtrail.org.

By 2010, about 71 percent of the CDNST had been completed. However, many miles of existing trail are in need of repair or need to be rerouted from motorized routes or environmentally sensitive areas.

The trail to Alberta Peak travels across a meadow to the south of Wolf Creek Pass. After you cross the bridge and enter the trees, the trail splits in several directions. Turn left to follow the official trail, which then curves right and up. The trail climbs gently

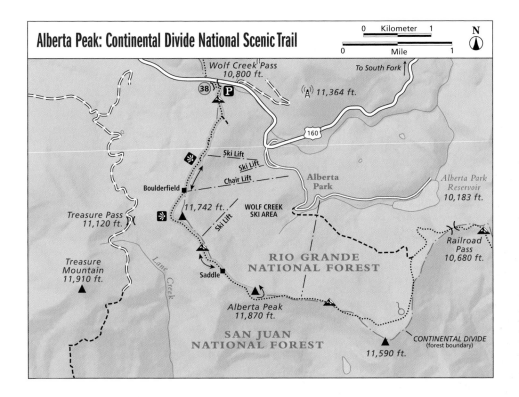

## Alberta Peak: Continental Divide National Scenic Trail

Wolf Creek Pass
10,800 ft.

To South Fork

11,364 ft.

160

Ski Lift
Ski Lift
Chair Lift

Boulderfield

Alberta
Park

Alberta Park
Reservoir
10,183 ft.

11,742 ft.

WOLF CREEK
SKI AREA

Treasure Pass
11,120 ft.

Ski Lift

Railroad
Pass
10,680 ft.

Treasure
Mountain
11,910 ft.

Lane Creek

Saddle

RIO GRANDE
NATIONAL FOREST

Alberta Peak
11,870 ft.

SAN JUAN
NATIONAL FOREST

CONTINENTAL DIVIDE
(forest boundary)

11,590 ft.

along the west side of the ridge. The Wolf Creek Ski Area's ski runs are on the east side. People from the San Luis Valley have skied on Wolf Creek Pass since the 1930s. In 1937, they formed the Wolf Creek Association and installed rope tows in 1938 on the north side of the highway. In 1956, another corporation formed and built a poma lift at the existing site. In 1976, the Pitcher family purchased Wolf Creek Ski Area and continues to own and manage it today. You can get a first-hand view of what a ski area looks like without snow at about 1.5 miles, where the top of a ski lift stands silently, waiting for snow to give it life again.

After another patch of forest, you'll arrive at an expansive view of Treasure Mountain (11,910 feet) and points to the southwest. Treasure Mountain earned its name from several legends about a chest full of gold that was buried in the area. Unfortunately, no one has ever found the gold. The trail follows the edge of the ridge, which drops steeply to the west. Curving left, it sneaks between willow bushes and emerges above treeline. The lake to the east is Alberta Park Reservoir. The snowshed to the northeast protects US 160 from frequent avalanches. Wolf Creek Pass typically receives the most snowfall in Colorado, averaging 460 inches of snow annually. Colorful alpine wildflowers bloom along the trail.

From this section, Alberta Peak, the hike's destination, rises meekly to the southeast. It's an easy scramble up the boulder field and grassy slopes to the top. The 360-degree view is worth the extra effort. Resident pikas sun themselves between hasty trips collecting grass and flowers for their winter hay piles. Continue farther along the CDNST if you wish. Watch out for lightning!

## Miles and Directions

**0.0**  Start at the trailhead at the top of Wolf Creek Pass, on the south side. The Continental Divide National Scenic Trail (CDNST) continues south from the left side of the interpretive signs. Elevation: 10,857 feet.

**0.1**  Cross a bridge and turn left at the T intersection.

**0.4**  The trail comes to a lazy T intersection. Turn right and continue uphill. (The branch straight ahead takes you to a ski run.)

**1.1**  The trail makes several switchbacks, with great views to the west and northwest.

**1.5**  The trail passes near a chairlift to the left and a boulder field to the right. Stay to the right above the boulder field and you'll see the trail. GPS: N37 28.16'/W106 48.34'.

**1.9**  The trail opens up to the right with a view of Treasure Mountain.

**2.2**  The trail travels the edge of a ridge with a steep drop-off.

**2.6**  The trail drops slightly to a saddle with good views in most directions. You can readily see Alberta Peak from here. GPS: N37 27.52'/W106 48.00'.

**2.9**  The CDNST continues along the steep south side of Alberta Peak. You can continue on from here for as long as you like. **(Note:** Just be aware of any lightning danger!) Turn left by the post and scramble up the gentle northwest side of Alberta Peak.

**3.0**  Reach the top of Alberta Peak, with wonderful panoramic views. Elevation: 11,870 feet. GPS: N37 27.35'/W106 47.65'. Return the way you came.

**6.0**  Arrive back at the trailhead.

## Hike Information

### General Information
**South Fork Visitors Center:** South Fork; (800) 571-0881 or (719) 873-5512; www.southfork.org

### Local Events/Attractions
**Logger Days Festival:** South Fork; (800) 571-0881 or (719) 873-5512
**Silver Thread Scenic Byway:** Creede; (719) 658-2374; www.coloradobyways.org
**Wildflower & Mushroom Forays:** South Fork; (800) 571-0881 or (719) 873-5512
**Wolf Creek Ski Area:** Pagosa Springs; (970) 264-5639; www.wolfcreekski.com

## Accommodations

**Chinook Lodge & Smokehouse:** cabins, 29666 West US 160, South Fork; (719) 873-1707; www .chinooklodge.net

**National Forest campgrounds:** San Juan National Forest, Pagosa Ranger District; (970) 264-2268; www.fs.usda.gov/sanjuan or Rio Grande National Forest, Divide Ranger District, Del Norte; (719)657-3321; www.fs.usda.gov/riogrande

## Restaurants

**Chalet Swiss:** 31519 West US 160, South Fork; (719) 873-1100
**Hungry Logger:** 47 State Highway 149, South Fork; (719) 873-5504
**Rockaway Cafe & Steakhouse:** 30333 West US 160, South Fork; (719) 873-5581

## Clubs and Organizations

**Continental Divide Trail Alliance:** 1200 Arapahoe St., Golden; (303) 278-3177; www.cdtrail.org
**Continental Divide Trail Society:** Baltimore, MD; (410) 235-9610; www.cdtsociety.org

*Hikers near Alberta Peak*

# 39 Williams Creek Trail

The Williams Creek Trail (Trail 587) in the Weminuche Wilderness reaches the Continental Divide in 10.1 miles. This hike description guides you to the first crossing of Williams Creek. Traveling above the creek, you'll see various volcanic rock shapes from eroded fins to fluted cliffs. The trail progresses through forests of Douglas and white fir, limber pine, Gambel oak, aspen, and some beautiful wildflowers. Watch for deer. At the creek crossing, a little area to the right makes a great lunch stop. You can continue on the trail for a long day hike or a multiday backpack. Crossing Williams Creek can be challenging or unsafe during spring runoff.

**Start:** Williams Creek Trail (Trail 587) trailhead

**Distance:** 6.0 miles out and back

**Approximate hiking time:** 2.5 to 4 hours

**Difficulty:** Moderate due to mostly gentle trail

**Elevation gain:** 720 feet plus 340 feet of undulations

**Seasons:** Best from mid-June to mid-Oct

**Trail surface:** Dirt trail, sometimes rocky

**Land status:** National forest and Wilderness area

**Nearest town:** Pagosa Springs

**Other trail users:** Equestrians and hunters (in season)

**Canine compatibility:** Dogs must be under control

**Schedule:** The access road is typically closed in the winter beyond the boat ramp at Williams Creek Reservoir, about 3 miles from the trailhead. The trail is neither maintained nor marked for winter use.

**Fees and permits:** None. Group size limit: No more than 15 people per group with a maximum combination of 25 people and pack or saddle animals in any one group. Check with the USDA Forest Service for up-to-date camping restrictions around certain lakes and hot springs, and fire restrictions in certain drainages. Also check on the latest information about bears and protecting food if you're backpacking.

**Maps:** USGS Cimarrona Peak; Nat Geo Trails Illustrated 140 Weminuche Wilderness

**Trail contact:** San Juan National Forest, Pagosa Ranger District, Pagosa Springs; (970) 264-2268; www.fs.usda.gov/sanjuan

**Special considerations:** There is a vault toilet here. The Palisades Horse Camp across the parking lot has water, if the pump by the vault toilet doesn't work.

**Finding the trailhead:** The Williams Creek trailhead is just past Cimarrona Campground, about 27 miles total from Pagosa Springs. The road intersections are well marked. Starting on the west side of Pagosa Springs, turn north onto Piedra Road (Archuleta CR 600) from US 160. In about 6.4 miles the road becomes dirt (FR 631). At about 13 miles, the road forks; stay to the left on FR 631 (the right fork is FR 633). The road crosses Piedra Bridge at about 16.1 miles; continue straight ahead on FR 631. The road forks again at about 17.8 miles; take the left fork (right fork is FR 636). At about mile 22 the road forks yet again; this time take the right fork onto FR 640 (Williams Lake Road). In a little over 1 mile, Williams Creek Reservoir is on the right. When the road forks again at about mile 25.6, take the right fork (the left fork goes to Poison Park). Drive about another 1.4 miles to the Williams Creek Trail (Trail 587) trailhead. GPS: N37 32.49' / W107 11.84'

## The Hike

The Williams Creek Trail is one of many gateways into the Weminuche Wilderness. Multiday loop trips can be designed starting at the Williams Creek trailhead and returning via Indian Creek Trail or Cimarrona Creek Trail. Hikers can also traverse the Wilderness and exit in the Rio Grande Valley to the north.

The Weminuche Wilderness is the largest designated wilderness in Colorado. The process started back in 1927, when the concept of preserving land in its natural state started to become popular. In 1932, the Forest Service established the San Juan Primitive Area, which covered the southern slopes of the San Juans. The Rio Grande Primitive Area was also created on the northern San Juan slopes. In 1964, Congress passed the Wilderness Act; however, the Weminuche was not one of the initial wilderness areas. This area was considered for wilderness status starting in 1968, causing both alarm and enthusiasm among locals. Sheep and cattle had grazed in the area for many years. Ranchers feared they might lose their grazing permits and the predator population would increase. Mining interests in the western part of the San Juans became a hot topic, too. Existing mining claims were not immediately impacted by the Wilderness Act, nor were grazing permits.

According to *Walking in Wildness: A Guide to the Weminuche Wilderness* by B. J. Boucher, during the early efforts for wilderness designation in the 1960s, Ian M. Thompson, then editor of *The Durango Herald,* was an avid wilderness advocate. Thompson wrote in a special wilderness supplement to the newspaper: "The 'Wilderness' effort we are engaged in at this time is, in one respect, a pitifully futile struggle. Earth's total atmosphere is man-changed beyond redemption. Earth's waters would not be recognizable to the Pilgrims. Earth's creatures will never again know what it is to be truly 'wild.' The sonic thunder of man's aircraft will increasingly descend in destructive shock waves upon any 'wilderness area' no matter how remote or how large. We are attempting to save the battered remnants of the original work of a Creator. To engage in this effort is the last hope of religious men."

A proposal to create the Weminuche Wilderness by combining the San Juan and Rio Grande Primitive Areas and adding some additional land was submitted to Congress in 1971. Recreational opportunities were emphasized, as were water quality and quantity. Water is the liquid gold of Colorado, and disputes over water rights and control are a never-ending battle in the state. For three years the proposal suffered through political haggling and boundary adjustments. Finally, in 1975, Colorado senators Peter H. Dominick and Floyd K. Haskell sponsored the bill that created the 405,031-acre Weminuche Wilderness. The name came from the Weeminuche band of Utes, who once thrived here.

Congress expanded the Weminuche in 1980 and again in 1993. Today the total area stands at approximately 488,210 acres in both the San Juan National Forest (Pacific drainage) and the Rio Grande National Forest (Atlantic drainage). A wilderness team comprising land managers from both forests provides consistent management for the Weminuche Wilderness.

The hike starts along a doubletrack that quickly becomes a trail. After crossing a boulder-filled waterway, which is often dry, you'll enter the Weminuche Wilderness. The trail gradually ascends. The large pinecones on the ground belong to the limber pine. Limber pines have five needles to a packet on very flexible branches that give the species its moniker. As the trail becomes steeper, it narrows considerably, so watch for oncoming horse traffic and ask what to do if you meet equestrians. Usually the hiker steps off the trail on the downhill side, but this could prove difficult in one stretch. Along with the first view of Williams Creek, you'll notice an interesting area with eroded volcanic rock to your right.

The trail winds up and down around little creek drainages while slowly gaining elevation. The undergrowth thickens in several places with ferns, geraniums, subalpine larkspur, Woods' rose, and aspen trees. In some areas, subalpine larkspur and cow parsnip stand about 5 feet tall. The Spanish called Williams Creek *huerto,* meaning "gardenlike" or "orchard." About 2.5 miles in, you cross a nice meadow with cliffs to the left that appear fluted. Cross over a ridge and drop to the Williams Creek crossing for lunch.

If you are backpacking, please remember to camp at least 100 feet away from streams, lakes, and trails per Forest Service regulations for this area. By practicing Leave No Trace techniques, the Weminuche will remain pristine for your next visit and for future generations.

## Miles and Directions

**0.0**   Start at the Williams Creek Trail (Trail 587) trailhead. Elevation: 8,360 feet. Please remember to sign the trail register.

**0.2**   Enter the Weminuche Wilderness Area.

**1.2**   The trail switchbacks above eroded features in the cliff along Williams Creek.

**2.1**   Reach the junction with Indian Creek Trail. GPS: N37 33.84' / W107 10.98'. Stay left on Williams Creek Trail.

**2.6**   Enter a large meadow with fluted cliffs to the left.

**2.8**   Cross a ridge and drop down to Williams Creek.

**3.0**   Arrive at the creek crossing. Elevation: 8,960 feet. GPS: N37 34.34' / W107 10.51'. **(FYI:** There's a nice lunch spot to the right along the creek.) Return the way you came.

**6.0**   Arrive back at the trailhead.

## Hike Information

### General Information
**Pagosa Springs Area Chamber of Commerce:** Pagosa Springs; (800) 252-2204 or (970) 264-2360; www.pagosaspringschamber.com

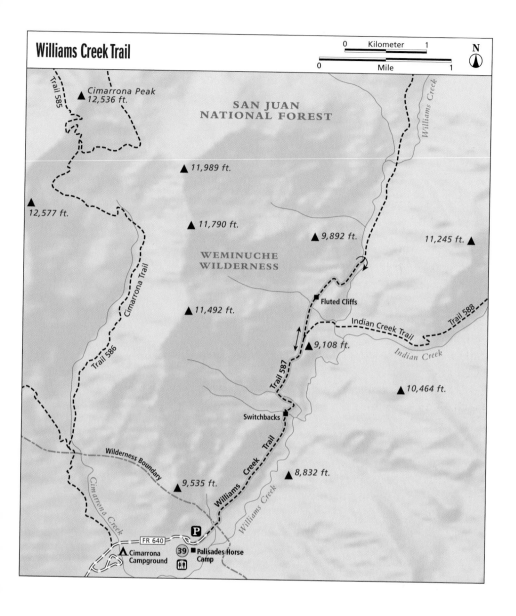

# Williams Creek Trail

| | Kilometer | | |
|---|---|---|---|
| 0 | | | 1 |
| 0 | Mile | | 1 |

**N**

Trail 585

▲ Cimarrona Peak
12,536 ft.

SAN JUAN
NATIONAL FOREST

Williams Creek

▲ 11,989 ft.

▲
12,577 ft.

▲ 11,790 ft.

▲ 9,892 ft.

11,245 ft. ▲

WEMINUCHE
WILDERNESS

Cimarrona Trail

■ Fluted Cliffs

Indian Creek Trail

Trail 588

▲ 11,492 ft.

Trail 587

▲ 9,108 ft.

Indian Creek

Trail 586

▲ 10,464 ft.

■ Switchbacks

Williams Creek Trail

Wilderness Boundary

▲ 9,535 ft.

▲ 8,832 ft.

Williams Creek

Cimarrona Creek

FR 640

🅿

🅲 Cimarrona
Campground

39 ■ Palisades Horse
Camp

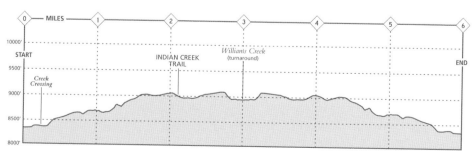

| MILES | 1 | 2 | 3 | 4 | 5 | 6 |
|---|---|---|---|---|---|---|

10000'

START

INDIAN CREEK
TRAIL

*Williams Creek*
*(turnaround)*

END

9500'

*Creek*
*Crossing*

9000'

8500'

8000'

## Local Events/Attractions

**Chimney Rock Archaeological Area:** Pagosa Springs; (970) 883-5359 (between May 15 and Sept 30) or (970) 264-2287 (between Oct 1 and May 14); www.chimneyrockco.org

**Four Corners Folk Festival:** Pagosa Springs; (877) 472-4672 or (970) 731-5582; www.folk west.com

**Pagosa Hot Springs pools:** Pagosa Springs; (800) 225-0934 or (970) 264-4168; www.pagosa hotsprings.com

**Southern Ute Cultural Center and Museum:** Ignacio; (970) 563-9583; www.southern-ute.nsn.us

## Accommodations

**National Forest campgrounds:** San Juan National Forest, Pagosa Ranger District; (970) 264-2268; www.fs.usda.gov/sanjuan

## Restaurants

**Boss Hogg's Restaurant & Saloon:** 157 Navajo Trail Dr., Pagosa Springs; (970) 731-2626

**JJ's Upstream Restaurant & Pub:** 356 East Highway 160, Pagosa Springs; (970) 264-9100; www.jjsriverwalk.com

**Pagosa Brewing Company:** 118 North Pagosa Blvd., Pagosa Springs; (970) 731-2739; www .pagosabrewing.com

## Clubs and Organizations

**San Juan Mountain Association:** Durango; (970) 385-1210; www.sjma.org

*Fluted cliffs*

# In Addition

## Leave No Trace

Leaving no trace in the backcountry is a true backcountry skill. How good are your skills?

As the number of people visiting our public lands increases, impacts are also on the rise. Conflicts between visitors, dogs harassing wildlife and other visitors, trash, messy campsites, degraded trails, undesignated (user-created) trails, and improper waste dis-

# leave no trace
CENTER FOR OUTDOOR ETHICS

posal are a few obvious problems. You may be only one hiker, but there are hundreds of thousands of us now. Think of 200,000 feet (or more) instead of just two!

If each of us takes a little time to learn about the environments that we love to explore, we can minimize many impacts. The concept of Leave No Trace was developed to help us make informed decisions about our behavior and habits in the backcountry and also on public lands closer to home (frontcountry).

The Leave No Trace program establishes a widely accepted code of outdoor ethics to shape a sustainable future for wildlands. Originating in the 1960s with the USDA Forest Service, Leave No Trace was developed to help recreationists minimize their impacts while enjoying the outdoors. In 1993, the Forest Service teamed with the National Outdoor Leadership School (NOLS), other federal land management agencies, and various private and nonprofit organizations in the Leave No Trace program. NOLS, a recognized leader in developing and promoting minimum-impact practices, began developing and distributing LNT educational materials and training.

Today, the Leave No Trace Center for Outdoor Ethics (a nonprofit organization established in 1994 as Leave No Trace, Inc.) manages the national program as well as international programs. The center partners with federal and state land management agencies, manufacturers, outdoor retailers, user groups, educators, and individuals to maintain and protect "recreational resources on natural lands for all people."

1.  Plan Ahead and Prepare. Prior Planning Prevents Poor Performance.* The basic tenet is to know where you're going, what the environment is like, and come prepared for current conditions. Things to check on include the weather forecast, area regulations, fire restrictions, difficulty of the trail versus your group's abilities, availability of water, etc. Knowing items such as these will help you decide what

---

\* The Leave No Trace Seven Principles have been reprinted with the permission of the Leave No Trace Center for Outdoor Ethics: www.LNT.org.

to pack, how far you can travel per day, etc. Wet trails imply waterproof boots, not running shoes. Good backcountry skills include map and compass reading and perhaps Global Positioning System (GPS) use. Repackaging the needed amount of food into unbreakable containers minimizes trash. A good mountain-oriented first aid course helps prepare you for various emergencies. Remember, cell phones don't always work in mountains, canyons, or away from main highways and towns. Your brain is your most important resource. By planning ahead, you can avoid most problems that typically result in leaving a trace.

> **The principles of Leave No Trace are:**
> 1. **Plan ahead and prepare.**
> 2. **Travel and camp on durable surfaces.**
> 3. **Dispose of waste properly.**
> 4. **Leave what you find.**
> 5. **Minimize campfire impacts.**
> 6. **Respect wildlife.**
> 7. **Be considerate of other visitors.**

2. Travel and Camp on Durable Surfaces. Durable surfaces do not easily sustain damage. Dry grass is less susceptible to damage than wet areas and woody plants. Special care is needed in fragile environments such as alpine tundra and desert cryptogamic soil. What is appropriate for one is not appropriate for the other. Until trails dry out, either avoid muddy ones or get muddy! Walking around mud holes kills the veggie and widens the bog. To protect riparian areas on which much wildlife depends, and to minimize being seen by others, camp 200 feet (70 adult paces) away from streams, lakes, and trails. Use an existing campsite that's an appropriate distance whenever possible.

3. Dispose of Waste Properly. Who wants to see trash when they're hiking? Pack out everything you bring in. Food scraps, apple cores, orange peels, etc. harm animals. They become used to human food or get sick. Animals dig up buried food and tampons. For human feces, walk at least 200 feet away from water sources and trails, dig a cathole 6 to 8 inches deep, then cover it; or pack it out. Pack out or bury dog feces, too. If you're above treeline, pack out feces because holes damage the tundra. Likewise, to wash yourself or dishes, carry water 200 feet (70 adult paces) away and use and dispose of it there. Use only biodegradable soap away from water sources. Contaminated water affects all of us!

4. Leave What You Find. Indian artifacts, petroglyphs and pictographs, and old cabins and equipment are protected by law. Even antlers or cool rocks belong where they are. Enjoy them where you find them and leave them for others to enjoy. Wildflowers die quickly after being picked. If you find berries, pick only one out of ten. Animals depend on the rest. Leave the area cleaner than you found it, taking some time to restore pine needles, twigs, etc. to hide your traces. Besides leaving no trace, leave no weeds! Noxious weeds are becoming a major problem

in our wild places. Clean your boots and other equipment between trips to avoid transporting nonnative weed seed.

5.  Minimize Campfire Impacts. Campfires are really an indulgence and not a necessity. Lightweight stoves are easier to cook on and don't leave scars. Candles propped in aluminum foil create a nice cozy atmosphere. Enjoy the stars! Fires can leave scars for years. Many areas are picked clean of dead and downed wood. If you do build a fire, learn to build a mound fire or use an existing fire ring. Gather no bigger than wrist-size dead and downed wood from dispersed places. Make sure your fire has burned completely, and when the ashes are thoroughly cooled, scatter them.

6.  Respect Wildlife. With development encroaching farther into the backcountry and more people recreating, wildlife is under more stress than ever. Never let your dog chase wildlife, even squirrels. It's illegal under Colorado state law to harass wildlife anyway. Make sure to hang your food and trash or use bear-proof containers. Mice, chipmunks, and pine martens rip into packs, too! Feeding wildlife can be very harmful to them and possibly to you. Watch wildlife from a distance—they need personal space like we do.

7.  Be Considerate of Other Visitors. Remember you are not alone in the back-country very often. Others come to enjoy peace and quiet. Avoid talking loudly or using boom boxes. Barking dogs can ruin a peaceful setting. Camp and take breaks off the trail to allow others a sense of solitude. "Natural quiet" is becoming a precious resource these days. Please help preserve it. Horses have the right of way. Backcountry users are typically friendly and thoughtful. Let's keep the tradition going!

Leaving no trace in the backcountry is a true backcountry skill. Accept the challenge to Leave No Trace!

For further information contact the Leave No Trace Center for Outdoor Ethics at (800) 332-4100 or (303) 442-8222; www.LNT.org.

# 40 Devils Creek and Lake

The hike to Devils Lake is a great warm-up or trial hike for anyone wanting to climb the 14,000-foot peaks near Lake City. The elevation gain is similar, but at lower altitude. For those wishing a shorter hike, the old cow camp at mile 2.6 is a good turnaround point. The Devils Creek Trail into the Powderhorn Wilderness was constructed in 1994. The relatively undisturbed Cannibal and Calf Creek Plateaus contain one of the largest, relatively flat alpine tundra areas in the lower United States. The Cannibal Plateau is named after the area's famous cannibal, Alferd Packer.

**Start:** From the Devils Creek Trail trailhead

**Distance:** 13.6 miles out and back

**Approximate hiking time:** 7 to 12 hours (recommended 2- to 3-day backpack)

**Difficulty:** Strenuous due to elevation gain and altitude

**Elevation gain:** 3,600 feet

**Seasons:** Best from mid-June to mid-Oct; closed Apr to mid-June to protect elk calving areas

**Trail surface:** Dirt trail and old nonmotorized ranch road, steep in places, through alpine tundra

**Land status:** BLM land and wilderness area

**Nearest town:** Lake City

**Other trail users:** Equestrians and hunters (in season)

**Canine compatibility:** Dogs must be under control

**Schedule:** The area is closed Apr to mid-June. The access road may be closed by snow in winter. The trail is neither maintained nor marked for winter use.

**Fees and permits:** None, except for commercial guides or outfitters

**Maps:** USGS Alpine Plateau, Cannibal Plateau, and Powderhorn Lakes; Nat Geo Trails Illustrated 141 Telluride/Silverton/Ouray/Lake City and 139 La Garita Wilderness/Cochetopa Hills; Latitude 40° Southwest Colorado (shows part of the trail)

**Trail contact:** Bureau of Land Management, Gunnison Field Office, Gunnison; (970) 641-0471; www.blm.gov/co/st/en/fo/gfo.html

Gunnison National Forest, Gunnison Ranger District, Lake City; (970) 641-0471 or (970) 944-2500; www.fs.usda.gov/gmug

**Other:** The road along the creek is mostly one vehicle wide, so be very careful. The bridge over the Lake Fork Gunnison River is closed until June 15 each year to protect elk calving areas.

**Special considerations:** Bring your own water!

**Finding the trailhead:** From Lake City, drive north on CO 149 for about 7 miles, from the post office to a dirt road heading northeast. The turn is about 0.5 mile north of mile marker 79. Turn right onto the next road, which drops steeply to the river, and follow it 0.5 mile across the Lake Fork Gunnison River and up a hill to a dirt road signed TRAILHEADS. Turn left onto this road and continue about 0.4 mile to the Devils Creek Trail trailhead. With slow, careful driving, most 2WD cars should be able to reach the trailhead. There are no facilities at the trailhead, and camping is not allowed. Trailhead GPS: N38 08.04'/W107 17.07'

*Cow camp*

## The Hike

High peaks and high plateaus surround Lake City. The plateaus were formed by both lava and ash flows, estimated to be as thick as 5,000 feet. More recently, Ice Age glaciers scraped and molded the land, leaving U-shaped valleys, moraines, lakes, and tarns (ponds).

Volcanic activity also deposited gold, silver, and other precious metals in cracks and crevices. In 1871 J. K. Mullen and Henry Henson found the Ute-Ulay veins west of Lake City. This treasure, however, lay in Ute Territory guaranteed by the Treaty of 1868.

In fall 1873 Alferd Packer was serving a jail sentence in Salt Lake City, Utah Territory, for counterfeiting. Hearing of gold discoveries in Colorado Territory, Packer bragged of his knowledge of the area. A group from Provo heard his boasts, paid his fine, and hired him to guide them to the Breckenridge area. The group of twenty-one men left Provo in November 1873. By mid-January, they arrived at the winter camp of Chief Ouray, the Ute's spokesman. Chief Ouray warned them against proceeding, especially with the unusually severe winter. But gold blinds wisdom, and five men plus Packer left Ouray's camp in early February. They headed toward Los Pinos Indian Agency southeast of Gunnison via a shortcut across the mountains.

Alferd Packer arrived alone at the agency on April 16, 1874. Apparently healthy, his first request was for a drink of whiskey. He also started spending money on drinks and games in nearby Saguache, although he was known to have little money when he left Utah. Packer's various stories conflicted, and local Utes reported finding strips of human flesh along his trail. At one point Packer agreed to lead a party to the bodies, but then became disoriented and refused to go farther. Artist J. A. Randolph found five skeletons near Lake City during the summer and sketched the gruesome site. Another story credits Captain C. H. Graham, a prospector, with the discovery. All five men had been shot, and one body was headless. Packer was jailed in August 1874, but soon escaped. He was recaptured in 1883.

▶ From Devils Lake, hike northeast on the North Calf Creek Trail (Trail 460) then north to the top of Calf Creek Plateau for an overlook into beautiful Powderhorn Lakes.

Packer was found guilty of premeditated murder and sentenced to execution on May 19, 1883, in Lake City. The execution was overturned because the murders occurred in Ute territory. Packer was tried again in Gunnison in 1886, found guilty of five counts of murder, and sentenced to forty years in the state penitentiary at Cañon City. In 1900, the owners of the *Denver Post* requested parole for Packer as part of a publicity maneuver for the paper. After several interesting incidents, Governor Charles S. Thomas paroled Packer in 1901. Packer died in 1907 and is buried in a Littleton cemetery. Just south of Lake City, local citizens established a memorial to Packer's victims.

The Devils Creek Trail was completed in 1994 as a western access to the Powderhorn Wilderness. The area sees relatively little use (more during hunting season), so take care to keep it pristine. The trail climbs steadily and fairly steeply through forests of ponderosa pine, Douglas fir, juniper, aspen, and sage to an old cow camp. The trail also crosses a large meadow. Be careful during thunderstorms—this section is very exposed to lightning. The historic cow camp is protected as an antiquity, so please be respectful and leave it untouched. No camping is allowed inside or within 50 feet of the cabins. For a shorter 5.2-mile out-and-back hike, return the way you came from here. To reach Devils Lake in another 4.2 miles, continue hiking up the trail.

The trail winds more gently up along Devils Creek, through aspen groves and into thick spruce-fir forest, finally traveling along the creek at times. Switchbacking away from the creek, the trail enters another open meadow where a forest fire raged more than thirty years ago. Several steep switchbacks through thick forest bring you to a beautiful subalpine meadow, full of colorful wildflowers in July. Cairns mark the trail. Enter a final patch of forest where you need to look closely to find the path. After another flower meadow, the trail reaches treeline at about 12,000 feet. Follow the cairns while climbing through open alpine tundra and rocks. The trail then flattens, crossing more alpine tundra and rocks that reflect the area's volcanic history. Head south across the tundra to Devils Lake.

If you are backpacking, please camp below treeline during thunderstorm season for your own safety. Water is usually available in Devils Creek—be sure to treat it—to

*Uncompaghre Peak from Devils Creek Trail*

about the meadow created when a forest fire killed the trees. If you camp near the lake, please follow BLM's regulations and camp at least 150 feet away, out of sight of other visitors, and use only camp stoves to protect the fragile tundra. Several grassy bluffs above the lake provide excellent camping spots and are more resistant to damage than the alpine tundra near the lake.

As you hike, think of the volcanic flows and seas of ice that have been replaced with fragile alpine tundra plants. Imagine Alferd Packer's party, trudging through snow and meeting its gruesome death.

## Miles and Directions

- **0.0** Start at the Devils Creek Trail trailhead. Elevation: 8,480 feet. Remember to sign the trail register.
- **0.6** The trail makes a left "L" by a big rock thumb.
- **0.8** The trail comes to a T intersection with an old road. GPS: N38 07.90'/W107 16.65'. Turn left and continue uphill on the road.
- **1.0** The road enters a long sagebrush meadow and continues in the open for 0.5 mile. **(Note:** Be careful of lightning.)
- **1.5** The road curves left above the aspen grove.
- **1.8** Reach the Wilderness boundary sign. GPS: N38 08.22'/W107 15.95'.

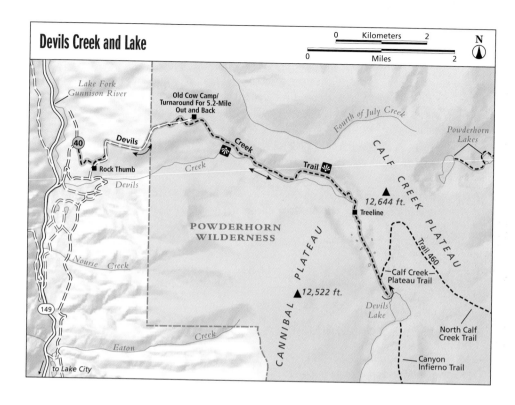

# Devils Creek and Lake

Lake Fork
Gunnison River

Old Cow Camp/
Turnaround For 5.2-Mile
Out and Back

Fourth of July Creek

Powderhorn
Lakes

40

Devils

Creek

CALF

Rock Thumb

Creek

Trail

CREEK

Devils

12,644 ft.

PLATEAU

POWDERHORN
WILDERNESS

Treeline

Trail 460

PLATEAU

CANNIBAL

Nourse   Creek

12,522 ft.

Calf Creek—
Plateau Trail

149

Devils
Lake

North Calf
Creek Trail

Creek

Eaton

to Lake City

Canyon
Infierno Trail

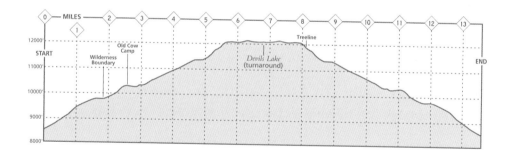

**2.0** The trail turns right and leaves the road. Please follow the trail and do not return to the road as the trail crosses it a few more times. **(Note:** The BLM requests visitors stay on the trail when it departs from the old road to avoid creating areas where erosion will occur.)

**2.6** The old cow camp appears on the left side of the trail. GPS: N38 08.39' / W107 15.27'. **(FYI:** There's a big flat rock that's ideal for a break.) **(Option:** For a day hike [three to five hours], return the way you came, arriving back at the trailhead at 5.2 miles.)

**3.1** Pass some huge Douglas firs. **(FYI:** In an open spot, look back to the west for a view of Uncompahgre Peak, which at 14,309 feet is Colorado's sixth highest peak. The Cannibal Plateau is above on your right.)

**3.4** The trail is finally next to the creek, and you can see it!

**4.4** The trees thin as you enter an old burned area. The trail follows a little ridge. **(Note:** Be careful of lightning.)

**5.3** The trail leaves the forest and enters a colorful meadow. Follow the cairns along the right side of the meadow until you see some crossing the meadow. Cross and enter another patch of trees (the trail is faint here), across another meadow, and then follow more cairns.

**5.5** The trail is now above treeline. GPS: N38 07.20' / W107 12.78'. Follow the cairns across the alpine tundra and rocks. When cairns no longer exist, keep heading south and downhill to Devils Lake.

**6.8** Reach Devils Lake. Elevation: 11,980 feet. GPS: N38 06.33' / W107 12.28' Return the way you came. **(Option:** You can make a longer trip by connecting with other trails in the area.)

**13.6** Arrive back at the trailhead.

## Hike Information

### General Information
**Lake City Chamber of Commerce:** Lake City; (800) 569-1874; www.lakecity.com

### Local Events/Attractions
**Alferd Packer Massacre Site:** Lake City; (970) 944-2050
**Hinsdale County Museum:** Lake City; (970) 944-2050
**Silver Thread Scenic Byway:** Creede; (719) 658-2374; www.coloradobyways.org
**Slumgullion Slide:** Lake City; (800) 569-1874 or (970) 641-0471

### Accommodations
**National Forest and BLM Campgrounds:** Gunnison Ranger District/Gunnison Field Office, Lake City; (970) 641-0471 or (970) 944-2527; www.fs.usda.gov/gmug or www.blm.gov/co/st/en/fo/gfo.html

### Restaurants
**Alpine Moose Lodge:** 1221 North Highway 149, Lake City; (970) 944-2415; www.alpinemoose lodge.com
**Poker Alice:** 188 South Gunnison Ave., Lake City; (970) 944-4100; www.pokeralice.org
**Sweet Peas Natural Foods:** 219 Silver St., Lake City; (970) 944-8020

### Hike Tours
**The Sportsman Outdoors & Fly Shop:** 238 South Gunnison Ave., Lake City; (970) 944-2526; www.lakecitysportsman.com

# 41 Washington Gulch Trail

Washington Gulch Trail offers several options. The main goal is the ridge at about 11,400 feet, with spectacular views of the Maroon Bells–Snowmass Wilderness and the Raggeds Wilderness. The flowers are sensational during July. The hike starts at the Gothic-side trailhead, climbing through fields of wildflowers and spruce–fir forest to the ridge. The out-and-back option returns from here. The point-to-point option descends to the Washington Gulch side, passing an old mine with relics. A high-clearance vehicle is required to reach the west-side trailhead. Be mindful of mountain bikers the entire way.

**Start:** From the Washington Gulch Trail (Trail 403) trailhead near Gothic Campground on Gothic Road

**Distance:** 3.9 miles point to point

**Approximate hiking time:** 1.5 to 2.5 hours

**Difficulty:** Difficult due to elevation gain

**Elevation gain/loss:** 1,940-foot gain / 410-foot loss

**Seasons:** Best from mid-June through Sept

**Trail surface:** Dirt trail with some steep sections

**Land status:** National forest

**Nearest towns:** Crested Butte and Mount Crested Butte

**Other trail users:** Equestrians, mountain bikers, and hunters (in season)

**Canine compatibility:** Dogs must be on leash.

This is a popular mountain bike trail so keep dogs leashed for their safety as well as bikers' safety.

**Schedule:** Call first for winter trail conditions. Access roads are closed by snow in winter.

**Fees and permits:** None

**Maps:** USGS Oh-Be-Joyful; Nat Geo Trails Illustrated 133 Kebler Pass / Paonia Reservoir; Latitude 40° Crested Butte, Taylor Park

**Trail contact:** Gunnison National Forest, Gunnison; (970) 641-0471; www.fs.usda.gov /gmug

**Other:** Gothic Campground is about 0.1 mile south of the Gothic-side trailhead.

**Special considerations:** No facilities at either trailhead.

**Finding the trailhead:** *With shuttle* (requires high-clearance vehicles): Drive north and east on Gothic Road from the Crested Butte Chamber of Commerce (located in the old train station at the corner of Elk Avenue and Gothic Road in Crested Butte) toward the town of Mount Crested Butte. Turn left at Washington Gulch Road (GCR 811/FR 811) in about 1.7 miles. From this intersection drive about 8 miles up Washington Gulch. The trailhead is on the right side of the road, just up the hill beyond a very sharp and steep left switchback, and above the cabins at Elkton by the Painter Boy Mine. Drop one vehicle off here and return to Gothic Road. GPS: N38 58.05' / W107 02.53'

*To reach the Gothic-side trailhead for the start of the hike,* turn right at the intersection of Gothic Road and Washington Gulch Road, continuing north on Gothic Road (GCR 317). The pavement ends at mile 3.7. Drive down the dirt road, which becomes FR 317 just past Gothic and the Rocky Mountain Biological Laboratory. The Washington Gulch Trail trailhead is located on the left side of the road about 10 miles from Crested Butte, or 6.4 miles from where the pavement ends. GPS: N38 58.93' / W107 00.40'

*Ruby Range and Raggeds*

## The Hike

Gothic Mountain (12,625 feet), south of the Washington Gulch Trail, received its name from the interesting rock formations on its east side that resemble Gothic cathedral spires. In May 1879, John and David Jennings discovered silver at the head of Copper Creek east of Gothic Mountain and named their discovery the Sylvanite. The deposit of silver in wire form was so rich that it often brought in over $15,000 per ton. From 1880 to 1910, the Sylvanite Mine produced over $1 million worth of silver.

Hopeful miners arrived in droves, searching the surrounding hills and valleys for ore, praying to strike it rich. A few months after the deposit was discovered the town of Gothic was laid out at the confluence of East River and Copper Creek. In one week's time, one hundred tents and cabins reportedly sprang up. Two sawmills were set up and had a hard time keeping up with the demand for lumber. By the end of 1879, more than 200 buildings had been constructed and over 500 people lived in the area. The next summer the town boasted five law firms, four grocery stores, three restaurants, two general mercantile stores, a bank, three doctors, two hotels, and the usual assortment of saloons, gambling halls, and dance halls. A nightly bonfire on Main Street allowed the locals to tell stories and smoke their tobacco. Gothic became the supply center for the area's various small camps and mines.

Transporting ore out of, and goods into, town was a challenge. The East River Toll Road was the main route in 1879. Eventually another road was built around the west side of Crested Butte (12,162 feet), saving several miles. Gothic even supplied Aspen via a road up Copper Creek, over East Maroon Pass, and down Maroon Creek. Gothic eventually boasted a population of 8,000 people, until the Silver Panic of 1893 signaled the end of the "City of Silver Wires."

In 1928, the Rocky Mountain Biological Laboratory (RMBL) moved into the remaining buildings at Gothic, tearing down some and remodeling others. RMBL was the dream of Dr. John C. Johnson, a biology professor at Western State College at Gunnison. Johnson purchased land and old buildings to create a research and training facility for field biologists. Scientists use the surrounding national forest, wilderness, and Gothic Research Natural Area to hone their investigative and research skills.

> An amazing toll road was built over Schofield Pass, connecting the towns of Marble and Aspen with Gothic and Crested Butte. The road was only 7 to 8 feet wide in places, instead of the usual 10 feet. Freight traffic normally negotiated an 8 percent grade, with 12 percent being the maximum. Schofield Pass, near the Devil's Punchbowl, however, is a steep 27 percent grade!

The hike starts at the Gothic side of Washington Gulch Trail, as it is more accessible and easier to find. The trail starts by climbing up switchbacks through a field of cornhusk lilies and tall larkspurs. As the trail winds higher, the Elk Mountains expand into view to the east. Columbine, Indian paintbrush, and varieties of sunflowers add color along the trail. Rock Creek rumbles downhill to the left. At times the vegetation is so tall and hanging over the trail that you might feel a machete would be useful. In about 1 mile, a cirque on Gothic Mountain comes into view. The mountain will dominate the southern view for most of the hike. Keep an eye out for deer. The trail enters a relatively flat meadow with a red mountain looming just beyond. This is Mount Baldy (12,805 feet).

After crossing Rock Creek, the trail meanders a long way through spruce-fir forest and meadows before making a final steep zigzag climb to a fantastic scenic overlook. There's even a "scenic pullout" to the right of the main trail, a great place for lunch. Looking east, you can see into the Maroon Bells–Snowmass Wilderness, including the top of one of the Bells. Notice how the rock is folded on one ridge of Avery Peak, across Gothic Road. Tremendous uplifting forces created these mountains. Walk west across the trail to a field of beautiful flowers. Looking west to the Raggeds Wilderness and Ruby Range, you can see Daisy Pass (11,600 feet) snaking upward to the ridge. Washington Gulch lies below.

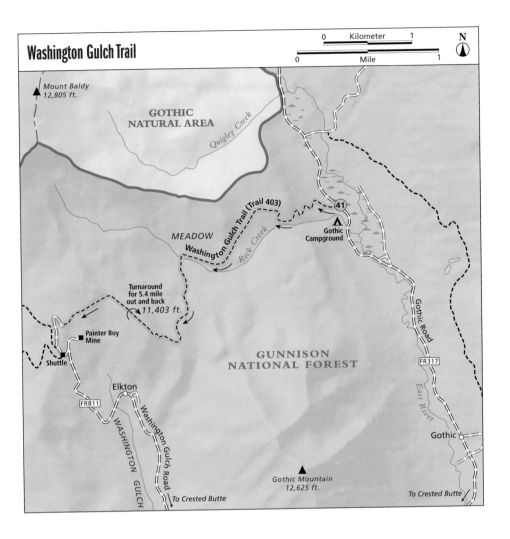

# Washington Gulch Trail

▲ Mount Baldy
12,805 ft.

GOTHIC
NATURAL AREA

Quigley Creek

MEADOW

Washington Gulch Trail (Trail 403)

Rock Creek

41

⛺ Gothic
Campground

Turnaround
for 5.4 mile
out and back
▶ 11,403 ft.

■ Painter Boy
Mine

Shuttle

Elkton

FR811

Washington Gulch Road

WASHINGTON GULCH

GUNNISON
NATIONAL FOREST

Gothic Road

FR317

East River

Gothic

▲ Gothic Mountain
12,625 ft.

To Crested Butte

To Crested Butte

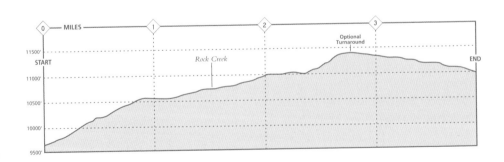

0 — MILES —          1          2          3

Optional
Turnaround

11500'

START

Rock Creek

END

11000'

10500'

10000'

9500'

The overlook area is the turnaround point for the optional out-and-back hike. To continue into Washington Gulch, the trail gently descends about 1 mile to Washington Gulch Road near the Painter Boy Mine, another great ore producer in its day. Remember, old mines can be extremely dangerous—stay out!

As you hike along, enjoying the fabulous views and fantastic wildflower show, visualize miners streaming through the area, searching for the strike that would make them rich.

## Miles and Directions

**0.0**  Start at Washington Gulch Trail (Trail 403) trailhead north of Gothic. Elevation: 9,460 feet.

**1.3**  Reach a meadow with a view of Mount Baldy.

**1.5**  Cross Rock Creek.

**1.7**  Encounter steep switchbacks.

**2.1**  Reach a marshy meadow with a view of Gothic Mountain.

**2.5**  Encounter more steep switchbacks. Views of Ruby Range are to the left and Elk Mountains are to the right.

**2.7**  Reach a scenic overlook. Elevation: 11,380 feet. GPS: N38 58.22' / W107 01.87'. Great place for lunch! Make sure to check out the spectacular views both east and west, then continue down the trail toward Washington Gulch. **(Option:** For a 5.4-mile out-and-back without a shuttle, turn around here and return the way you came. Approximate hiking time: 2.5 to 3.5 hours)

**3.7**  Reach an old mine and relics. GPS: N38 58.18' / W107 02.57'.

**3.9**  Arrive at the Washington Gulch-side trailhead. Elevation: 10,990 feet. **(FYI:** This trailhead is an optional starting point. It can also be the turnaround point for a 7.8-mile out-and-back hike.)

## Hike Information

### General Information

**Gunnison-Crested Butte Tourism Association:** Gunnison; (970) 349-1168 or (800) 814-7988; www.gunnisoncrestedbutte.com

### Local Events/Attractions

**Mountain Bike Hall of Fame & Museum and Crested Butte Mountain Heritage Museum:** 200 Sopris Ave., Crested Butte; (800) 454-4505 or (970) 349-1880

**Wildflower Festival:** Crested Butte; (970) 349-2571; www.visitcrestedbutte.com

### Accommodations

**Crested Butte International Hostel:** 615 Teocalli Ave., Crested Butte; (970) 349-0588 or (888) 389-0588; www.crestedbuttehostel.com

**The Forest Queen Hotel & Restaurant:** Crested Butte; (970) 349-5299 or (888) 830-1882; www.forestqueenhotel.com

**National Forest campgrounds:** Gunnison National Forest, Gunnison; (970) 641-0471; www.fs.usda.gov/gmug

## Restaurants

**Brick Oven Pizzeria:** 229 Elk Ave., Crested Butte; (970) 349-5044
**Donita's Cantina:** 330 Elk Ave., Crested Butte; (970) 349-6674
**Pitas in Paradise:** 212 Elk Ave., Crested Butte; (970) 349-0897

## Clubs and Organizations

**High Country Citizens Alliance:** Crested Butte; (970) 349-7104; www.hccaonline.org
**Rocky Mountain Biological Laboratory:** Crested Butte; (970) 349-7231; www.rmbl.org

## Hike Tours

**Crested Butte Mountain Guides:** Crested Butte; (970) 349-5430; www.crestedbutteguides.com

*View near the east trailhead*

# 42 Ptarmigan Lake

The hike to Ptarmigan Lake winds through spruce-fir forest, gently climbing into an area of beautiful subalpine meadows dotted with tarns and little lakes. For flower aficionados, the meadows show off beautiful wildflowers in July. After a little climb up the side of a cirque, you arrive at crystal-clear Ptarmigan Lake. Another 0.3 mile leads to a saddle with a view down into South Cottonwood Creek. This hike travels above treeline, so if the weather is threatening a thunderstorm, stay at the lower lakes.

**Start:** From Ptarmigan Lake Trail trailhead off Cottonwood Pass Road
**Distance:** 6.6 miles out and back
**Approximate hiking time:** 3 to 4 hours
**Difficulty:** Difficult due to elevation gain and altitude
**Elevation gain:** 1,490 feet to the lake
**Season:** Best from July through Sept
**Trail surface:** Dirt trail with some boulders and rocks
**Land status:** National forest
**Nearest town:** Buena Vista
**Other trail users:** Equestrians, anglers, mountain bikers, and hunters (in season)

**Canine compatibility:** Dogs must be under control
**Schedule:** The Cottonwood Pass road is closed by snow from late November to May about 4 miles before the trailhead. The trail is neither maintained nor marked for winter use.
**Fees and permits:** None
**Maps:** USGS Mount Yale and Tincup; Nat Geo Trails Illustrated 129 Buena Vista/Collegiate Peaks
**Trail contact:** San Isabel National Forest, Salida Ranger District, Salida; (719) 539-3591; www.fs.usda.gov/psicc
**Special considerations:** Vault toilet; no water!

**Finding the trailhead:** From Buena Vista, drive about 14.5 miles west on Chaffee CR 306, which later becomes FR 306, heading to Cottonwood Pass. The trailhead is on the south (left) side of the road about 0.1 mile in. GPS: N38 48.22'/W106 22.45'

## The Hike

Cottonwood Pass was originally a toll road from Buena Vista, connecting with other roads leading to Crested Butte, Gothic, and eventually Aspen in the 1870s. Harvard City, which you pass on the way from Buena Vista to the trailhead, boomed for a couple of years as placer claims were located along Cottonwood Creek. Lode mines were discovered and developed in 1874. Freighters also stopped at Harvard City to repack their loads for the long and difficult climb over the Continental Divide. Times changed, and the road connecting Aspen and Leadville over Independence Pass, opened in 1881, drew traffic away from Cottonwood Pass. The mines in the area couldn't match new mines farther west, and the miners moved on.

Cottonwood Pass, named after the many trees lining the creek alongside the road, fell into disrepair. The USDA Forest Service repaired and improved the road for automobile travel in the late 1950s. Several trailheads and good fishing are all accessible

*Ptarmigan Lake from saddle*

via the road today. The pass is closed during the winter, but is open to various winter sports.

Several lakes in Colorado bear the name Ptarmigan. The white-tailed ptarmigan, *Lagopus leucurus*, is a member of the grouse family that lives year-round above treeline and in the krummholz just below. Krummholz refers to the stunted, twisted tree hedges growing at the edge of treeline. It's usually made up of subalpine fir, Engelmann spruce, or limber pine. Ptarmigans are masters of disguise: During winter they wear snow-white feathers, which turn mottled brown and white in the summer. It's easy to almost step on one because they blend in so well with the rocks. As you hike, look for these birds. Little chicks follow after mom in the summer. If approached, the mother pretends to have a broken wing to draw predators away from her chicks. Please do not harass ptarmigans to see if they'll pretend an injury, and do not let your dogs chase them.

Winter finds the male ptarmigan still above treeline, sometimes in the shelter of the krummholz and sometimes in willow thickets hidden below the snow. Females winter in willows below treeline. The ptarmigan is one animal that may gain or maintain weight during harsh Colorado mountain winters by eating the energy-rich buds of the willow bushes. To save energy in the spring, willows set their leaf buds during the prior autumn.

White-tailed ptarmigan appear to be monogamous, although after the chicks hatch, the female raises them alone. Mating time in the spring, like molting, is triggered by lengthening daylight and other changes in climate.

If you head around the lake on the trail to the little saddle, look up to the left and notice the streams

▶ The raspberries found along the trail are edible. Because animals, including bears, depend on the berries for food, please take no more than one berry in ten from a raspberry patch for your group.

of rocks heading down toward the lake. Freezing and thawing, which occurs most of the year, can force rocks buried underground up to the surface. On steep slopes the unearthed rocks roll into depressions. If one rock stops, others may roll into it or along a small water depression causing a streamlike appearance. In more level places, the rocks may form polygons or garlands. This "patterned ground" is common in Colorado's alpine tundra.

The hike starts in thick spruce-fir forest, opening occasionally as two boulder fields flow over the trail. Watch for raspberry bushes among the boulders. Although you can hear Ptarmigan Creek in the distance, the trail keeps a good distance until you are almost to the lake. The hike continues through spruce-fir forest without much of a view. At about mile 1.2, cross a dirt road (FR 346—4WD access to the trail). Go straight and don't turn onto the road. The trail continues to wind and switchback gently through the forest.

About 2.4 miles in, the trees are less dense and more flowers appear. Some possible campsites come into view away from the trail. (Camp at least 200 feet from the trail, lakes, and streams.) Then the world opens, with Jones Mountain on the right and Gladstone Ridge on the left. You can see the edge of the cirque that contains Ptarmigan Lake. Flower-filled meadows dotted with little ponds and a lake line the trail.

Continue hiking through the meadows, jump across Ptarmigan Creek, and two switchbacks later arrive at the lake. Mount Yale (14,196 feet) looms large to the northeast. Two other high peaks rise above other ridges. Those high points are Mount Harvard (14,420 feet) and Mount Columbia (14,073 feet). The pointy peak between you and the fourteeners is Turner Peak (13,233 feet).

If the weather is good, continue another 0.3 mile to the saddle for views down Grassy Gulch and South Cottonwood Creek. The views to the east and northeast of the Collegiate Peaks are worth the short climb.

## Miles and Directions

**0.0** Start at the Ptarmigan Lake Trail (Trail 1444) trailhead. Elevation: 10,650 feet. In 350 feet cross a bridge over Middle Cottonwood Creek. The trail register is on the other side—please sign in.

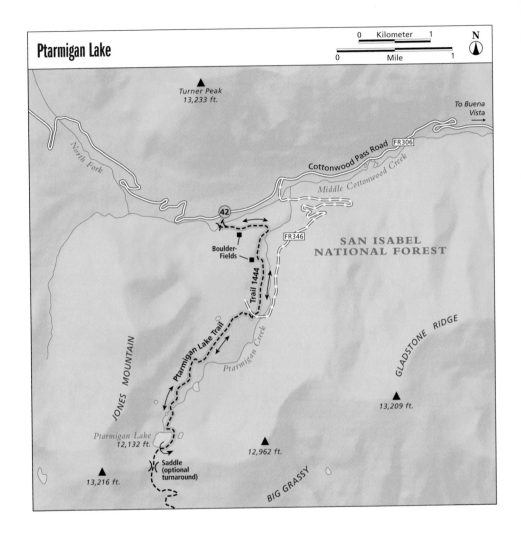

# Ptarmigan Lake

| 0 | Kilometer | 1 |
| 0 | Mile | 1 |

**N**

Turner Peak
13,233 ft.

*To Buena Vista →*

*North Fork*

Cottonwood Pass Road  FR306

*Middle Cottonwood Creek*

42

Boulder-Fields

FR346

**SAN ISABEL NATIONAL FOREST**

Trail 1444

*Ptarmigan Lake Trail*

JONES MOUNTAIN

*Ptarmigan Creek*

GLADSTONE RIDGE

13,209 ft.

12,962 ft.

*Ptarmigan Lake*
12,132 ft.

Saddle
(optional turnaround)

13,216 ft.

BIG GRASSY

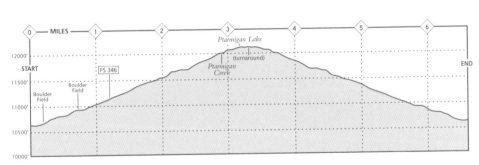

| 0 | MILES | 1 | 2 | 3 | 4 | 5 | 6 |

*Ptarmigan Lake*

12000'

(turnaround)

*Ptarmigan Creek*

**START**

FS 346

11500'

END

Boulder
Field

Boulder
Field

Boulder
Field

11000'

10500'

10000'

**0.2**  Reach the first boulder field.

**0.7**  Reach the second boulder field.

**1.2**  Cross a dirt forest road. GPS: N38 47.53' / W106 22.15'. The trail is clearly marked. (FR 346 provides access to the trail, but only by 4WD vehicle.)

**2.5**  Reach the first little kettle pond on right, and a lake down to left.

**2.9**  Cross Ptarmigan Creek.

**3.2**  Arrive at Ptarmigan Lake. Elevation: 12,132 feet. GPS: N38 46.68' / W106 02.93'. Hike another 0.1 mile to the other side of lake.

**3.3**  Reach the south side of the lake. Return the way you came. (**Side trip:** Continue another 0.3 mile to the saddle between the Middle Cottonwood and South Cottonwood drainages. This side trip will add 0.6 mile and about 20 minutes to the hike.)

**6.6**  Arrive back at the trailhead.

## Hike Information

### General Information

**Buena Vista Chamber of Commerce:** Buena Vista; (719) 395-6612; www.buenavistacolor ado.org

**Buena Vista Heritage:** Buena Vista; (719) 395-8458; www.buenavistaheritage.org

### Local Events/Attractions

**Annual King Boletus Mushroom Festival:** Buena Vista; (719) 395-8458; www.buenavistaher itage.org

**Gold Rush Days:** Buena Vista; (719) 395-6612; www.fourteenernet.com/goldrush/

### Restaurants

**Buffalo Bar & Grill:** 710 North US Highway 24, Buena Vista; (719) 395-6472

**Evergreen Cafe:** 418 US Highway 24, Buena Vista; (719) 395-8984

### Hike Tours

**Noah's Ark Whitewater Rafting Co. and Adventure Program, Ltd.:** Buena Vista; (719) 395-2158; www.noahsark.com

# Honorable Mentions

## South Central Mountains

Compiled here is an index of great hikes in the South Central Mountains region that didn't make the A-list this time around but deserve recognition. Check them out and let us know what you think. You may decide that one or more of these hikes deserves higher status in future editions or, perhaps, you may have a hike of your own that merits some attention.

### T Alamosa National Wildlife Refuge

A 4.0-mile out-and-back doubletrack trail follows the Rio Grande and various canals/ditches in the wildlife refuge. The Rio Grande lazily meanders along here. Various ponds, as well as the river, host numerous waterfowl. The Sangre de Cristo Mountains, especially the 14,000-foot summits of Little Bear, Ellingwood, and Blanca peaks, rise to the northeast. Located in the San Luis Valley southeast of Alamosa, the wildlife refuge seems out of place in this high-desert basin. The trail starts at the headquarters/visitor center, which has interesting displays. From Alamosa, drive about 3 miles east on US 160 to El Rancho Lane, just past mile marker 236. A sign for Alamosa National Wildlife Refuge marks the intersection. Turn right and drive about 2.4 miles to the headquarters/visitor center and park. The trail is called the River Road Walk and is open from sunrise to sunset. Dogs must be on leash. The trail provides an interesting look at a riparian area along a major river. For more information contact Alamosa National Wildlife Refuge at (719) 589-4021 or visit the website at www.fws.gov/alamosa.

Another interesting area to visit (and camp) is San Luis Lakes State Park, a fantastic wildlife viewing area. Contact the park at (719) 378-2020 or visit the website at http://parks.state.co.us/parks/sanluis.

### U Wheeler Geologic Area (East Bellows Trail)

Wheeler Geologic Area is well known for its unusual, colorful, and picturesque formations, eroded from volcanic ash. The East Bellows Trail provides a difficult 16.8-mile out-and-back hike. Camping spots can be found along the trail. From Creede, drive south on CO 149 for 7.3 miles to FR 600/Pool Table Road. Turn left and drive about 9.9 miles to the Hanson's Mill Trailhead. Park here. Crossing East Bellows Creek can be difficult during spring runoff because there is no bridge, so be very careful. The trail eventually joins the 4WD road. Turn left and walk up the road to the foot trail, then another 0.5 mile into the area. Follow the signs. The pinnacles and domes are very fragile, so please stay on the trail and don't climb on the formations. The formations lie within the La Garita Wilderness. For more information contact

Rio Grande National Forest, Divide Ranger District, in Creede at (719) 658-2556 or check the website at www.fs.usda.gov/riogrande. Additional information at www.sangres.com/features/wheelergeologic.htm.

## ∨ Piedra River

The Piedra Special Area is one of those pristine places that earned wilderness protection except for water rights. It's a beautiful little canyon that you can explore from either the north or south end, or traverse the entire length of about 12 miles. Being lower in elevation, this area is a good place to hike when the high country is still covered with snow. Old-growth forests surround the river, where you might catch a glimpse of river otters at play. The Piedra forms an important wildlife corridor between the Weminuche Wilderness and winter range to the south. To reach the north trailhead, drive about 16 miles north of Pagosa Springs on Piedra Road/Archuleta CR 600, which becomes FR 631. After you cross the Piedra River bridge, the parking lot is up on your left (elevation 7,700 feet). The south trailhead is called First Fork trailhead. Drive about 22 miles west of Pagosa Springs on US 160 to First Fork Road (FR 622). Turn right onto FR 622 and drive about 12 miles to the trailhead at 7,200 feet. For more information contact the Rio Grande National Forest, Pagosa Ranger District, at (970) 264-2268 or visit the website at www.fs.usda.gov/riogrande.

# Southwest Overview

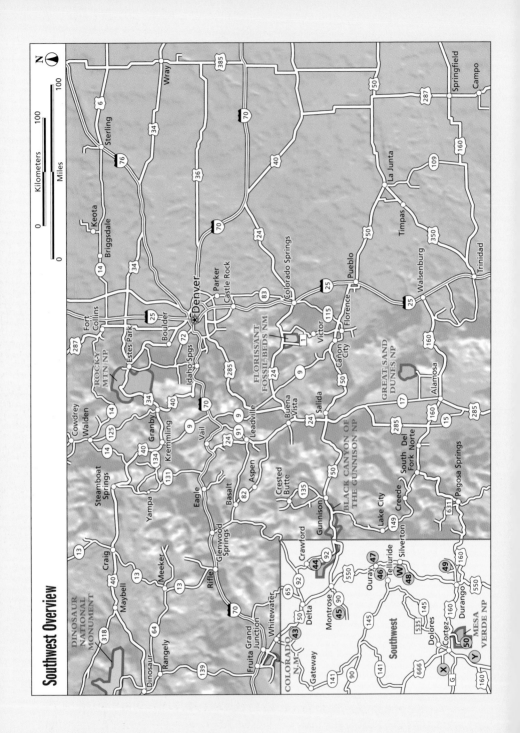

N

Kilometers
0       100       100

Miles
0       100

DINOSAUR NATIONAL MONUMENT

ROCKY MTN NP

FLORISSANT FOSSIL-BEDS NM

GREAT SAND DUNES NP

BLACK CANYON OF THE GUNNISON NP

COLORADO N.M.

Southwest

MESA VERDE NP

Denver

Fort Collins
Boulder
Estes Park
Idaho Spgs
Castle Rock
Parker
Colorado Springs
Victor
Florence
Cañon City
Buena Vista
Salida
Leadville
Vail
Granby
Kremmling
Walden
Cowdrey
Steamboat Springs
Yampa
Eagle
Basalt
Aspen
Crested Butte
Gunnison
Crawford
Lake City
Creede
South Fork
Del Norte
Pagosa Springs
Alamosa
Walsenburg
Trinidad
Pueblo
La Junta
Timpas
Springfield
Campo
Sterling
Wray
Keota
Briggsdale
Maybell
Craig
Meeker
Rifle
Glenwood Springs
Whitewater
Fruita
Grand Junction
Gateway
Delta
Montrose
Ouray
Telluride
Silverton
Durango
Cortez
Dolores
Rangely
Dinosaur

43 44 45 46 47 48 49 50
W X Y G

# Southwest

L and of the Ute and the Ancestral Puebloans (formerly called Anasazi), the Four Corners area and San Juan Mountains are rich in culture, history, and beauty. Hiking opportunities abound in both canyons and on rugged mountain trails. Thirteen of Colorado's fifty-four peaks over 14,000 feet are located in this region. Ouray has long been known as the Little Switzerland of America and also boasts about its hot springs for those weary bones and muscles. Telluride is just 10 miles away from Ouray as the crow flies, about 18 miles on 4WD roads, or 49 miles by twisty highway. The feats of miners and road builders from Ouray to Durango and Telluride to Lake City take on a new meaning after touring and hiking the steep, rough terrain of this region. The San Juan Mountains, born of explosive volcanoes and later carved into sharp pinnacles and cirques by several glacial periods, provide years of exploring for any hiker. The Million Dollar Highway, connecting Ouray and Silverton, is another accomplishment of stubborn humans who had to get from Point A to Point B through horrendously rugged country. Avalanches still claim lives today on this highway.

To the west lies the Uncompahgre Plateau, an interesting geological uplift between mountains and canyons. To its east and west, rivers have carved canyons through its back and along its edges. Dominguez Canyon Wilderness and National Conservation Area, on the east edge of the Uncompahgre Plateau, contains petroglyphs, an old mine, and a seasonal waterfall, plus desert bighorn sheep. Farther east, the Gunnison River has carved its skinny canyon through ancient Precambrian bedrock, now preserved by the Black Canyon of the Gunnison National Park and the Gunnison Gorge National Conservation Area.

Mesa Verde National Park, world-renowned for its superb cliff dwellings, lies in the southwest corner. Here you can visit mesa-top pueblo sites or take a guided tour of the cliff dwellings. The lesser-known Ute Mountain Tribal Park, just south of Mesa Verde, also contains ancient treasures. The Utes offer tours of their reservation for a less-developed view of the ancient world. The Canyons of the Ancients National Monument adds to the cultural, natural, and historical offerings. Ancient sites are hidden in and around the many little canyons west and northwest of Cortez.

Telluride, an old mining town turned ritzy ski resort, offers strong hikers interesting loops over steep ridges, with a few easier hikes to get acclimated. The Bluegrass Festival in mid-June draws people from all over, while other music, outdoor activities, and arts events keep the town hopping all summer.

The Durango-Silverton Narrow Gauge Railroad is a ride not to be missed. Connecting Durango and Silverton, the railroad has been operating since 1882. You can even depart and board at two points (Elk Park and Needleton) for a spectacular 35-mile loop hike in the Weminuche Wilderness northeast of Durango. Colorado's largest wilderness, the Weminuche contains jagged peaks, high alpine lakes, and many miles of trails. Durango is also the western terminus of the 485-mile-long Colorado Trail.

The scenic and historic byways in this area are the San Juan Skyway, Unaweep-Tabeguache, Trail of the Ancients, Grand Mesa, and Alpine Loop (4WD required).

# 43 Big Dominguez Canyon

The Big Dominguez Canyon Trail wanders up a beautiful canyon cut in the side of the Uncompahgre Plateau. Desert bighorn sheep were reintroduced here in 1983 and 1985—watch rocky areas and cliff tops for them. Ancient people have traveled through the canyon for at least 1,500 years. Keep your eyes open for (but hands off) petroglyphs pecked in boulders along the trail. Remains of an old mine straddle the trail 6 miles from the parking lot. This red sandstone canyon is part of the Dominguez Canyon Wilderness, designated by Congress in March 2009.

**Start:** From the Bridgeport trailhead
**Distance:** 13 miles out and back (you can turnaround sooner for shorter hikes)
**Approximate hiking time:** 5.5 to 8.5 hours
**Difficulty:** Difficult due to distance, but shorter, moderate hikes can be done
**Elevation gain:** 680 feet plus some small undulations
**Seasons:** Best in spring and fall. Summer can be very hot.
**Trail surface:** Dirt trail, rocky in a few areas
**Land status:** BLM Wilderness and National Conservation Area
**Nearest towns:** Delta and Grand Junction
**Other trail users:** Equestrians
**Canine compatibility:** Dogs must be under control
**Schedule:** Year-round
**Fees and permits:** None
**Maps:** USGS Triangle Mesa
**Trail contact:** Bureau of Land Management, Dominguez-Escalante National Conservation

Area, 2465 South Townsend Ave., Montrose; (970) 240-5367; www.blm.gov/co/st/en/nca/denca.html
**Other:** Plans have been in the works to reroute the trail from its current location along the railroad tracks to a safer alternative. Check the website or call the BLM office to check current status.
**Note for backpackers:** If you camp along the Gunnison River, please camp in designated campsites. The first part of Big Dominguez Canyon (to about 4 miles from the parking lot) and Little Dominguez Canyon (to the south end of the Rambo property) are day use only and closed to camping. Please use Leave No Trace techniques and camp at least 100 feet away from small streams.
**Special considerations:** Big Dominguez Creek is dry part of the year, the creek is not always near the trail, and the water, when available, must be treated. Bring your own water—one gallon per person per day is recommended.

**Finding the trailhead:** *From the junction of CO 92 and US 50 in Delta,* drive 19.2 miles north on US 50 to Bridgeport Road. Turn left onto Bridgeport Road and drive 3.3 miles to the dead end, where there's a parking lot but no facilities.

*From Grand Junction,* drive south on US 50 to Bridgeport Road, near mile marker 52. Turn right onto Bridgeport Road; drive 3.3 miles to the parking lot at the dead end. No facilities.

Be sure to read the visitor information at the trailhead on the left (south) side of the parking lot. Please follow all safety recommendations regarding hiking near the railroad tracks. Trailhead GPS: N38 50.95' / W108 22.30'.

## The Hike

On March 30, 2009, President Barack Obama signed legislation designating the Dominguez-Escalante National Conservation Area (NCA) and the Dominguez Canyon Wilderness Area. Encompassing 209,610 acres of beautiful canyon country carved out of the eastern edge of the Uncompahgre Plateau, the NCA designation will conserve and protect these lands for wildlife, flora, and future human generations. Public meetings and discussions held over three years set the stage for the legislation. The lands are managed by the Bureau of Land Management, and the agency is tasked with creating a resource management plan to provide for the long-term protection and management of the NCA and Wilderness. A citizen's advisory committee has been established to aid in the process. The lands are withdrawn from mining and mineral leasing, but grazing, access to inholdings, control of invasive species, fire prevention, and existing water rights protection are still allowed. The Dominguez Canyon Wilderness consists of 66,280 acres within the NCA.

Long before the Spanish and white settlers arrived, Native Americans wandered these western canyons hunting game and collecting plants, successfully living in the arid climate. These Archaic peoples arrived perhaps as far back as 6500 BC. Over time, people living around the Uncompahgre Plateau in western Colorado borrowed ideas from their neighbors, the Fremont and the Ancestral Pueblo (Anasazi), and incorporated them into their culture, while maintaining a unique way of living. Archaeologists describe their lifestyle as the Uncompahgre Complex or Gateway Tradition. The petroglyph panel by the BLM's Archaeological Site sign, located along the trail, is categorized as Uncompahgre Style, which existed for about 2,000 years between 1000 BC and AD 1000. The figures on the rock were pecked or carved into it, typically with a bone or an antler. The Uncompahgre Style differs from the Fremont style found farther north in Colorado and Utah. Fremont rock art typically uses huge-bodied figures to depict heroes or supernatural beings. The figures in Big Dominguez Canyon tend to be smaller and more humanlike. Bears are common in the Uncompahgre Style, and one is apparent on the panel you'll see. Bighorn sheep figures are plentiful. Unfortunately, a few modern folks have defaced parts of the rock art panels in the area—notably with words and a spaceship. Please respect this ancient art and do not touch. Oils from our hands promote deterioration. Human-like figures riding horses and other shapes were pecked into another rock by the Utes, who later roamed these canyons.

Petroglyph panels throughout western Colorado indicate that bighorn sheep were hunted by these early peoples. Over time, with westward expansion in the 1800s and early 1900s, bighorn were extirpated from this area. The Colorado Division of

*Bridge across Gunnison River*

*Rock art panel*

Wildlife reintroduced the desert bighorn (*Ovis canadensis nelsoni*) to the Big Dominguez area in 1983 and 1985. Slightly smaller and lighter in color than their cousins, the Rocky Mountain bighorn, they live in small groups in arid canyons, using the rocks and cliffs for protection from predators. Ewes (females) and lambs stay together while the rams create their own herds. They eat sparse desert vegetation, from which they gather water, and drink at water holes or creeks every few days. They even eat cacti, using hooves and horns to remove the spines. During summer's hot days, they find shady shelter. At other times, they eat during the day and rest at night. Rams grow spiral horns with a new ring emerging each year. Horns can reach thirty inches long with a base circumference of fifteen inches. Ewes' horns are 12- to 17-inch spikes. Weighing up to 200 pounds, the rams win mating privileges through head-butting contests with each other. Mating season typically occurs in late fall, with lambs born in April and May.

Watch for bighorn sheep on the canyon rims. If they are down in the canyon, be sure to keep your dog under control. Bighorn sheep have been adversely affected by human activities, from loss of habitat to overhunting to contracting diseases from domestic sheep and cattle.

The trail up Big Dominguez Canyon sometimes looks like a road—it was. Miners built the road to access the uranium mine at mile 6.1. Not much else is known about this mine, although it was probably active during the region's uranium boom between 1940 and the 1960s.

This hike takes you to the junction with the Cactus Park Trail, but turn around sooner if you'd like. The canyon contains many beautiful features, from red rock cliffs with interesting formations to various desert plants to old mining remains. Enjoy your visit to this wonderful canyon.

## Miles and Directions

**0.0**  Start at the trailhead to the left (south) of the parking lot. The first 0.3 mile travels along the railroad tracks. If a train is present, wait until it passes. If the train is stopped, wait until the train moves before crossing at the one designated crossing. Delays can be up to one hour. Elevation: 4,720 feet.

**0.3**  Cross the tracks at the designated railroad crossing.

**1.0**  Walk past the trail to the first bridge on the right. This bridge is private. Continue straight ahead, then turn right on the trail to the interpretive signs and the second bridge. N38 50.19'/W108 22.81'. Cross the Gunnison River and turn left.

**1.7**  Arrive at the trailhead bulletin board near the Wilderness boundary.

**2.3**  Arrive at a trail junction. Turn right to hike up Big Dominguez Canyon. The two-track trail to the left goes up Little Dominguez Canyon. GPS: N38 49.34'/W108 22.75'.

**3.1**  A side trail marked by cairns heads to the left to a big waterfall (when Big Dominguez Creek has water in it).

**3.25**  Reach an archaeological site. Please take only pictures—touching, defacing, or tracing any rock art is prohibited. Please leave the petroglyphs intact for others to enjoy. These sites are sacred to Native Americans. **(Option:** For a shorter, moderate hike, turn around here and return the way you came.)

**3.7**  The trail curves left over rocks—follow the cairns. In another 0.1 mile, the trail passes through a tunnel created by two huge rocks leaning against each other.

**4.0**  Reach the approximate end of the day-use area.

**4.6**  The trail climbs up black lava rock.

**6.1**  The trail passes by the remains of a mine. Please remember to leave all artifacts for others to enjoy.

**6.5**  Arrive at the Cactus Park Trail junction. Elevation: 5,400 feet. GPS: N38 48.13'/W108 26.12'. Turn around and return the way you came. Just before this junction is a flat area to the south that is a great lunch spot.

**13.0**  Arrive back at the parking lot.

## Hike Information

### General Information
**Delta Country Tourism:** Delta; (800) 436-3041; www.deltacolorado.org/tourism
**Grand Junction Visitor and Convention Bureau:** 740 Horizon Dr., Grand Junction; (800) 962-2547; www.visitgrandjunction.com

# Big Dominguez Canyon

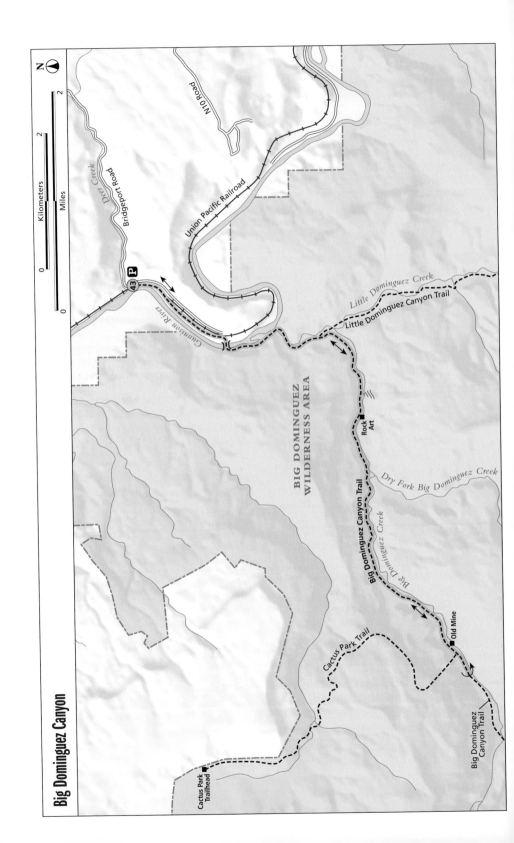

BIG DOMINGUEZ
WILDERNESS AREA

# THE DOMINGUEZ-ESCALANTE EXPEDITION

In 1776 Fray Francisco Atanasio Dominguez and Fray Francisco Silvestre Vélez de Escalante, Spanish Franciscans, embarked on an expedition to find a route from Santa Fe to the California missions near Monterey. Dominguez provided leadership, while Vélez de Escalante kept a detailed journal. While the main purpose of the expedition was route finding, details about native peoples, plants, animals, potential farming areas, terrain, and rivers were recorded.

The expedition left Santa Fe on July 19, and followed a route north and west through Durango, Mancos, and north to Montrose. They followed today's Uncompahgre River, which they named El Rio de San Francisco. On August 28, they turned north near Delta, and followed today's North Fork of the Gunnison River, called Tomichi by the Ute Indians. By early September the expedition crossed Grand Mesa. From mid-October to early November, the expedition spent much time trying to cross the Colorado River, El Rio Grande, in what is now northern Arizona. But the Grand Canyon and its tributary canyons proved too difficult. They returned to Santa Fe on January 2, 1777. Although Dominguez and Escalante did not find a route to Monterey, the party explored and documented a large area of the West.

## Local Events/Attractions

**Colorado Mountain Winefest:** Palisade; (970) 464-0111; www.coloradowinefest.com
**Colorado National Monument:** Fruita; (970) 858-3617; www.nps.gov/colm
**Dinosaur Journey Museum:** 550 Jurassic Court, Fruita; (970) 858-7282; www.museumofwesternco.com/visit/dinosaur-journey
**Fort Uncompahgre History Museum:** open Apr to Oct; Confluence Park, Delta; (970) 874-8349

## Restaurants

**The Garden Center Bistro:** 1970 South Main St., Delta; (970) 874-3073; www.deltagardencenter.com
**Main Street Bagels Artisan Bakery and Cafe:** 559 Main St., Grand Junction; (970) 241-2740; www.mainstreetbagels.net
**Rockslide Restaurant & Brewery:** 401 Main St., Grand Junction; (970) 245-2111; www.rockslidebrewpub.com
**Wilson Bar-B-Que & Bean Company:** 1410 Valley View Drive, Delta; (970) 874-6867

## Clubs and Organizations

**Colorado Mountain Club-Western Slope Group:** www.cmc.org

# 44 North Vista Trail

The North Vista Trail follows the north rim of the Black Canyon of the Gunnison, traveling through Gambel oak and piñon-juniper forest. Dramatic canyon views appear along the trail and at two unprotected overlooks accessed by short spur trails. A third and longer spur loops out to the accurately named Exclamation Point, with an incredible view into the canyon. From here, the trail continues along the north rim, then switchbacks up to the top of Green Mountain (8,563 feet). The spectacular, aerial view of the Black Canyon is almost surrealistic. A short loop takes you around the top of Green Mountain, offering a 360-degree view of western Colorado.

**Start:** From the North Vista Trail trailhead near the North Rim Ranger Station
**Distance:** 6.8 miles out and back
**Approximate hiking time:** 3 to 5 hours
**Difficulty:** Moderate due to length and terrain
**Elevation gain/loss:** 1,095-foot gain / 255-foot loss
**Seasons:** Best from May through Oct
**Trail surface:** Dirt trail
**Land status:** National park
**Nearest town:** Crawford
**Other trail users:** None
**Canine compatibility:** Dogs not permitted
**Schedule:** The access road is closed by snow in winter 6.7 miles from the trailhead. The trails are neither maintained nor marked for winter use.
**Fees and permits:** Entrance fee, annual pass, or America the Beautiful pass required (pay at the North Rim Ranger Station). A camping fee is charged for developed campgrounds. Free backcountry permits are required for back-country camping or inner-canyon travel.
**Maps:** USGS Grizzly Ridge; Nat Geo Trails Illustrated 245 Black Canyon of the Gunnison National Park/Curecanti National Recreation Area
**Trail contact:** Black Canyon of the Gunnison National Park (visitor center), Montrose; (970) 249-1914, ext. 423; www.nps.gov/blca/

**Finding the trailhead:** From Crawford head south on CO 92 about 3.2 miles to Black Canyon (BC) Road. Turn right onto BC Road and follow it to the North Rim. The way is well marked, but here are some details. From the junction with CO 92, drive 4 miles, then BC Road turns right. In 0.8 mile, BC Road turns left. In another 0.7 mile the paved road becomes a good dirt road. In 1.2 miles, turn right to stay on BC Road. The park boundary is in another 1.7 miles. Cattle may be grazing here, so watch for them on the road. At the fork 3.3 miles into the park, turn right to the North Rim Ranger Station, which is another 0.5 mile. Total distance from Crawford to the ranger station is about 15.4 miles. There is a vault toilet by the ranger station. Water is available at the North Rim Ranger Station between mid-May and mid-Sept. Be sure to bring your own water at other times. The North Rim access road is typically closed by snow from Nov to May. GPS: N38 35.21'/W107 42.28'

## The Hike

Gazing into the shadowy depths of the Black Canyon of the Gunnison, the name makes sense. The shadows alone would earn the moniker, but the canyon walls

*Black Canyon of the Gunnison from Exclamation Point*

really are black. They are comprised of metamorphic "basement" rock, over 1.7 billion years old, pressed and heated into schist and gneiss (pronounced "nice"). White and pink stripes of granite and pegmatite snake across the black cliffs. They formed when hot magma worked its way into cracks in the metamorphic rocks and slowly cooled. After the present Rocky Mountains rose and volcanoes in the San Juan and West Elk Mountains erupted, the Gunnison River slowly carved the Black Canyon over the last 2 million years. Without major tributaries eroding away its sides, the canyon has remained narrow, only 40 feet wide at the bottom of "The Narrows."

The Gunnison River used to surge 12,000 cubic feet per second (cfs) during spring runoff. Imagine what force that amount of water created raging through this narrow spot. Today, with three dams upstream slowing the flow, the mighty Gunnison rarely rushes above 4,000 cfs.

▶ The juniper is a member of the cypress family. For years it has been misnamed as a cedar in many parts of Colorado and Utah.

Due to the efforts of local citizens, particularly Reverend Mark Warner, President Herbert Hoover created Black Canyon of the Gunnison National Monument on March 2, 1933, preserving the most spectacular 12 miles of the 48-mile-long canyon. In October 1976, 11,180 acres in the national monument were designated as wilderness under the Wilderness Act of 1964, further protecting the impressive canyon. The northern side of the monument was expanded in 1984. In October 1999, Congress upgraded the Black Canyon to national park status, while adding approximately 10,000 new acres to protect a valuable view corridor along the southern boundary and expanding the wilderness to include 2 additional river miles (for a total of 14 miles). An additional 14 miles of the Gunnison River is protected in the Gunnison Gorge National Conservation Area, just downstream. The visitor center on the South Rim offers interesting interpretive displays and an excellent movie about the history of Black Canyon.

▶ You can hike (slide and scramble) into the canyon to the river via six different gullies or draws. These difficult routes are not really trails, and usually drop at least 1,800 feet in 1 mile. You must obtain a backcountry permit to travel these routes. Contact the South Rim Visitor Center for information.

The North Rim attracts fewer visitors than the South Rim, and thus offers quieter hiking opportunities. The North Vista Trail, built in 1991 and 1992 by the Volunteers for Outdoor Colorado, provides impressive views not only down into the canyon from various angles, but also 360 degrees of the surrounding area.

Starting near the North Rim Ranger Station, the trail winds its way through Gambel oak, piñon pine, and juniper forest. You'll first encounter dense oak thickets and sagebrush as the trail drops slightly to cross S.O.B. Draw. Gambel oaks produce nutritious acorns that bears, chipmunks, and squirrels love, and deer browse on the lobed leaves. The thickets also provide shelter for smaller animals and their young. Gambel oak can be extremely flammable during a wildfire, but nature provided it with underground rhizomes (roots), which house dormant buds that sprout readily. Another bush along the trail is serviceberry, an important food source for the local critters.

Two little side trails lead down to overlooks between 0.6 and 0.7 miles. These overlooks don't have any type of protective barriers, so watch where you walk and make sure your children don't wander. At 1.25 miles, be sure to take the 0.2-mile spur trail to Exclamation Point, which rightly earns its name by providing a fantastic view down into the canyon. When you reach the viewpoint, walk down to the next little level spot among the rocks. The view is best here because you can see the river 1,900 feet below. Violet-green swallows and white-throated swifts enjoy soaring on the thermals along the cliff edge.

From here, the North Vista Trail continues along the canyon's edge for a little way. Some huge piñon pines grow here. Piñon pine is well known for the large tasty nuts it produces. Keep an eye open for piñon jays, a blue bird without a black crest. The

# North Vista Trail

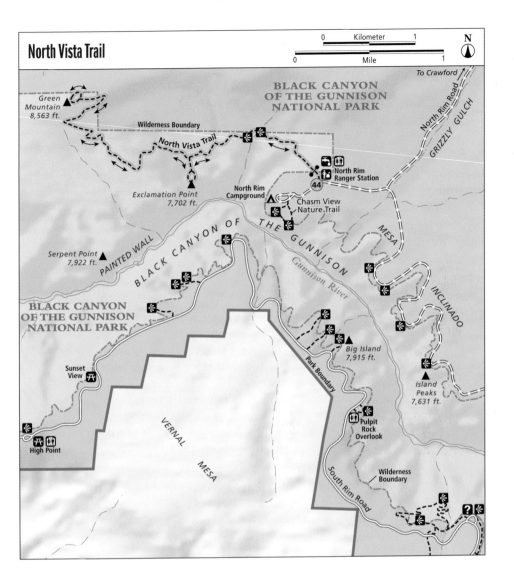

0 Kilometer 1
0 Mile 1

**N**

BLACK CANYON
OF THE GUNNISON
NATIONAL PARK

To Crawford

*Green
Mountain
8,563 ft.*

Wilderness Boundary

North Vista Trail

North Rim Road

GRIZZLY GULCH

North Rim
Ranger Station

*Exclamation Point
7,702 ft.*

North Rim
Campground

Chasm View
Nature Trail

44

MESA

INCLINADO

*Serpent Point
7,922 ft.*

PAINTED WALL

BLACK CANYON OF THE GUNNISON

Gunnison River

BLACK CANYON
OF THE GUNNISON
NATIONAL PARK

Park Boundary

*Big Island
7,915 ft.*

*Island
Peaks
7,631 ft.*

Sunset
View

VERNAL

MESA

Pulpit
Rock
Overlook

High Point

Wilderness
Boundary

South Rim Road

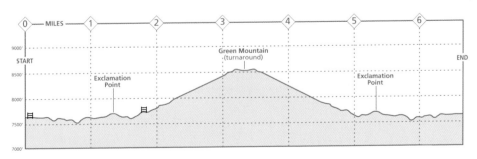

| 0 | MILES | 1 | | 2 | | 3 | | 4 | | 5 | | 6 | |

9000'

START

Green Mountain
(turnaround)

END

8500'

Exclamation
Point

Exclamation
Point

8000'

7500'

7000'

jays love piñon nuts and can store up to twenty seeds in their throats. Considering the appetite of the jays, you'd be lucky to find a pinecone with a nut still inside. Porcupines enjoy the bark and leave large wounds on the pines. Utah juniper is the other common tree along the trail. Its stringy bark has been used by Native Americans for everything from sandals to baby diapers. The berries are an important food source for the local animal and bird populations. Watch for an interesting step the trail crew created using an imbedded juniper log.

Both the trail and the top of Green Mountain provide great views. Mount Sneffels (14,150 feet) and the Dallas Divide, along with several 14,000-foot peaks in the San Juans to the east, tower above the rest of the landscape. Miniature-looking cars drive along the South Rim road across the canyon. Needle Rock near Crawford points to the West Elk Mountains to the north and east. The Grand Mesa rises in the north like a ship's prow. On a clear day, Utah's La Sal Mountains may be visible to the west. The Black Canyon lies below, trenched into the landscape.

## Miles and Directions

**0.0**  Start at the North Vista Trail trailhead by the North Rim Ranger Station (near the vault toilet). Elevation: 7,700 feet.

**0.1**  Open the gate in the fence and be sure to close it behind you. The fence keeps cattle out of visitor-use areas, such as the ranger station and the campground. Just beyond here there are some good views of the canyon walls.

**0.6**  Reach a scenic overlook on a spur trail to the left. **(Side trip:** A 0.1-mile out-and-back walk will lead you to the actual overlook.)

**0.7**  Come to a second scenic overlook on a spur trail to the left.

**1.25**  Reach the turnoff for the Exclamation Point loop. Turn left here for a spectacular view. GPS: N38 35.34'/W107 43.25'.

**1.4**  Arrive at Exclamation Point via the west branch of loop. **(Option:** For a shorter trip of 2.8 miles, return from here to the trailhead.)

**1.6**  Arrive back at North Vista Trail via east branch of loop. Turn left to continue toward Green Mountain.

**1.8**  Cross an interesting step cut in a downed juniper tree.

**2.6**  Enjoy good views to the south. The trail begins to switchback.

**3.5**  Reach the top loop on Green Mountain. Elevation: 8,563 feet. Go either right or left for a loop with panoramic views.

**3.7**  Arrive back at the start of the top loop. As you start to descend, look toward the canyon for a fantastic view. Return the way you came. **(Side trip:** Consider going back out to Exclamation Point for another view with a different sun angle. Remember to add 0.4 mile to your overall hike.)

**6.8**  Arrive back at the trailhead.

*North Rim Trail at about mile 1.5*  ▶

# The Hike

The Uncompahgre Plateau extends about 100 miles, running north-south from the San Miguel River to the Colorado River. Rising like a submarine west of Montrose, the plateau is quite rugged. It's a land of multiple uses: hiking trails, 4WD roads, and a long mountain bike route—the Tabeguache Trail. Ute Indians hunted this area, as local names attest. Tabeguache means "place where the snow melts first." As noted in a journal kept by the 1776 Dominquez-Escalante expedition, the Utes called the river to the east the "Ancapagari (which, according to our interpreter, means Red Lake), because they say that near its source there is a spring of red-colored water, hot and ill-tasting."

The Roubideau *(roo-bi-doe)* Area was created by the 1993 Colorado Wilderness Bill. Because the headwaters of its creeks start outside its designated boundaries, Congress denied it full Wilderness protection. Water rights in Colorado create many hotly contested arguments and lawsuits. To avoid potential conflicts, the "Roubideau Area" is managed as wilderness, except its water. Some people call it a baby Wilderness. The area is closed to motorized and mechanized use, logging, and mining.

Antoine Robidoux headed to Santa Fe from St. Louis in 1824. His family, long involved in the fur trade, wanted to take advantage of trading with newly independent Mexico. Robidoux and an old family friend explored regions northwest of Santa Fe in what became western Colorado and eastern Utah. Beaver were plentiful, and Ute Indians were eager to trade pelts for European tools. Antoine became a Mexican citizen, and by 1828 had obtained from the Mexican government an exclusive hunting and trading license to the area he had explored a few years earlier.

Rough terrain made for difficult travel on trading routes in those days. Instead of using the established Old Spanish (California) Trail through southwestern Colorado, then traveling north into his territory, Robidoux headed north to the San Luis Valley. Turning west he followed an old American Indian trail over Cochetopa Pass into the Gunnison Valley, then into the Uncompahgre Valley. Just below the confluence of the Gunnison and Uncompahgre Rivers, he built his first trading post, Fort Uncompahgre. For years the Utes had wintered nearby at the Ute Council Tree, a huge old cottonwood that still stands. They brought pelts from their lands in exchange for modern conveniences.

Historical documents indicate some of the inventory sold at Fort Uncompahgre included: silk and cotton bandanas, scarves, trousers, shirts, jackets, combs, mirrors, linen thread, needles, blanketing material, scissors, cotton material, steel knives, fire steels, copper cooking pots, tea, coffee, sugar, and leaf tobacco. Food staples also filled the shelves. Modern implements made life easier for the Utes. But as life improved

◀ *Old Roubideau Trail through aspen forest*

*Near Old Roubideau and Pool Creek trail junction*

in this tough country, the winds of change started blowing. The Oregon Trail farther north became the preferred trading route and more white people settled in Ute territory, creating unrest. The United States won the area during the Mexican-American War. By 1844, Robidoux's trade kingdom crumbled. Angered by a Mexican attack on a Ute village with no reparation from the Mexican government, the Utes went on a rampage in 1844, even attacking Fort Uncompahgre and killing most of the Mexican workers. Two years later, Fort Uncompahgre was in ruins.

Over the years, Fort Uncompahgre's exact location was lost. Perhaps the flooding Gunnison wiped out its traces. Local citizens built a replica of the fort closer to Delta, and opened it to visitors on June 30, 1990.

This hike lets you wander in the cool highlands of the Uncompahgre Plateau, away from the bustle of Delta and Montrose. The Old Roubideau Trail switchbacks down to Goddard Creek drainage, crosses the creek, then climbs up to wander through gently sloping aspen forest. Elk bed and graze in the lush grasses. Some aspens bear scars of carved names and dates—this practice exposes aspen to various diseases. Approaching the Pool Creek drainage, the trail drops with views down into

Roubideau Creek. Cattle enjoy the plentiful grasses in this section and their trails go every which way. Upon reaching Pool Creek, a 0.4-mile jaunt downhill (left) on the Pool Creek Trail brings you to Roubideau Creek, a pleasant place for lunch.

The hike up Pool Creek Trail gains 1,271 feet in 2.7 miles. The trail is overgrown in some areas, but it stays on the north side of the creek. Notice the difference in vegetation. The south side of the creek is sunny and grassy, while the north-facing side is steep, cool, and moist with dark spruce-fir forest dominating. At Pool Creek Trail trailhead, return to Old Roubideau trailhead via the Parallel Trail (Trail 139), which you intersect at the Pool Creek Trail trailhead. Or meet your shuttle vehicle, if you've chosen the point-to-point option; see below.

## Miles and Directions

**0.0**  Start at the cow camp where the dirt road Ys. Elevation: 9,440 feet. Walk straight ahead on the road to the right of the old buildings. (The right fork dead ends.) About 260 feet down the road, look to your right for the brown carsonite post that indicates the trail is open to hikers and equestrians. The Old Roubideau Trail (Trail 105) starts at this post, which is easy to miss so be observant.

**0.5**  Reach the Roubideau Special Area boundary. The trail switchbacks down into Goddard Creek.

**1.25**  Cross Goddard Creek.

**1.9**  Cross another drainage. The trail contours along a hill through pleasant aspen forest.

**2.3**  The trail curves left but isn't obvious. Look for blazes on trees to the right to find the faint trail. GPS: N38 21.91' / W108 12.76'.

**2.8**  The trail splits. Turn left and drop to the southeast. It then curves to the south, then turns east. Arrive at a tall clump of Gambel oak (GPS: N38 21.88' / W108 12.35'). The trail heads uphill slightly to the left, then disappears. Head east cross-country until you intersect a trail. Turn right. Cross the flatter bench area, with some luck find a trail, and continue downhill to the right. If you lose this trail, find the easiest way to walk down to Pool Creek.

**3.3**  Reach a T intersection with the Pool Creek Trail (Trail 113). GPS: N38 21.78' / W108 12.30'. **(Option:** Turn left here for an 0.8-mile out-and-back spur to Roubideau Creek.) Turn right here to head uphill toward the Pool Creek Trail trailhead.

**3.9**  The trail crosses a gooey gully, which can be a little tricky. You might need to walk down the dry creek a few feet to find an easy place to walk across.

**5.3**  Cross a little water seep coming from under a boulder to the right side of the trail.

**5.6**  Arrive at the Pool Creek Trail trailhead. GPS: N38 20.57' / W108 14.07'. Turn right and walk a few steps to the access road, where you go straight ahead onto Parallal Trail (Trail 139), also called the Tabeguache Trail on the sign. This trail is multiple use.

**6.0**  Cross a road and head straight ahead.

**7.75**  Arrive at FR 546 (East Bull). Turn right and walk down this road. Turn right when the road forks at FR 547.

**8.6**  Arrive back at your vehicle and the trailhead near the cow camp.

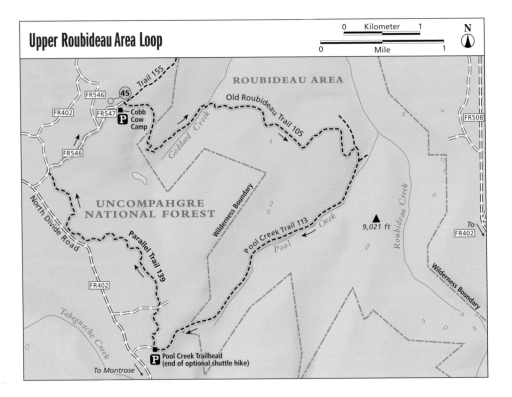

Kilometer
Mile
N

ROUBIDEAU AREA

Trail 155

FR546
45
FR402
FR547
Cobb
Cow
Camp

Old Roubideau Trail 105

FR546

Goddard Creek

FR508

UNCOMPAHGRE
NATIONAL FOREST

North Divide Road

Parallel Trail 139

Wilderness Boundary

Pool Creek Trail 113

Creek

Pool

9,021 ft

Roubideau Creek

To
FR402

FR402

Wilderness Boundary

Tabeguache Creek

Pool Creek Trailhead
(end of optional shuttle hike)

To Montrose

## Option

For a shorter point-to-point hike—5.6 miles, leave a shuttle vehicle at the Pool Creek Trailhead. Turn right off FR 402 at the 5.4-mile mark, where the sign reads POOL CREEK TRAILHEAD. Do not turn right at 3.6 miles at Pool Creek FR 548. The trailhead and shuttle drop-off is 0.2 mile in. GPS: N38 20.58'/W108 14.07'. Park one car here and drive the second back to FR 402 and turn right, resuming with the directions to the Cow Camp trailhead above. Approximate hiking time: 2.5 to 4 hours.

## Hike Information

### General Information
**Montrose Visitors & Convention Bureau:** 1519 East Main St., Montrose; (800) 873-0244 or (970) 252-0505; www.visitmontrose.com

### Local Events/Attractions
**Fort Uncompahgre:** Delta; (970) 874-8721
**Rocky Hill Winery:** Montrose; (970) 249-3765
**Unaweep/Tabeguache Scenic & Historic Byway:** Bureau of Land Management, Montrose; (970) 249-6047
**Ute Indian Museum and Ouray Memorial Park:** Montrose; (970) 249-3098

## Accommodations

**National Forest campgrounds:** Ouray Ranger District, Montrose; (970) 240-5400; www.fs.usda .gov/gmug

## Restaurants

**Camp Robber:** 1515 Ogden Rd., Montrose; (970) 240-1590; www.camprobber.com
**Red Barn Restaurant and Lounge:** 1413 East Main St., Montrose; (970) 249-9202
**Smugglers Brew Pub and Grille:** 1571 Ogden Rd., Montrose; (970) 249-0919; www.smugglers brew.com

## Clubs and Organizations

**Colorado Mountain Club-West Slope Group:** Grand Junction; www.cmc.org

*View to east from Old Roubideau Trail*

# 46 Jud Wiebe Memorial Trail

The Jud Wiebe Trail climbs up and across the hill north of Telluride between Butcher and Cornet Creeks. Although short, it has its steep moments as very precipitous mountains surround Telluride. This trail is a good early season south-facing hike and a great warm-up for longer, more difficult trails in the area. From various points, Bridal Veil and Ingram Falls, the ski area, spectacular craggy peaks, and the town below come into view. The trail was completed in 1987 in memory of Jud Wiebe, a Forest Service employee who designed the trail.

**Start:** From the trailhead at the top of Aspen Street

**Distance:** 2.7-mile loop

**Approximate hiking time:** 1.5 to 2.5 hours

**Difficulty:** Difficult due to some steeper sections

**Elevation gain:** 1,150 feet

**Seasons:** Best from June to mid-Oct

**Trail surface:** Dirt road and dirt trail

**Land status:** National forest

**Nearest town:** Telluride

**Other trail users:** Equestrians (some trail sections), mountain bikers, and hunters (in season)

**Canine compatibility:** Dogs must be on leash

**Schedule:** Year-round. The trail is sometimes hikable in winter. Call first for conditions.

**Fees and permits:** None

**Maps:** USGS Telluride; Nat Geo Trails Illustrated 141 Telluride/Silverton/ Ouray/Lake City; Latitude 40˚ Telluride, Silverton, Ouray

**Trail contact:** Uncompahgre National Forest, Norwood Ranger District, Norwood; (970) 327-4261; www.fs.usda.gov/gmug

**Finding the trailhead:** Find a parking place in Telluride or park in the free parking area across from the visitor center and take the Galloping Goose shuttle into downtown. Walk to Aspen Street (0.4 mile east of the visitor center) and walk uphill to the top of the street. The west end of the trail starts here. GPS: N37 56.45'/W107 48.71'

The other option is to walk to Oak Street and head uphill to the top of the street to the east end of the trail. GPS: N37 56.42'/W107 48.66'. Walk along Tomboy Road to the pipe gate and bulletin board, and turn left. The hike description starts at the Aspen Street trailhead.

## The Hike

Telluride, an old mining town snuggled at the mouth of a box canyon, is experiencing a second wave of success. The first came with the mining frenzy in the 1870s, as miners swarmed over the rugged San Juan Mountains looking for gold, silver, and other precious metals. Today the spectacular mountain scenery has attracted writers and artisans, and the ski area (opened in 1972) has created a new building frenzy.

The San Juan Mountains were born of volcanic fire and ash and sculpted by the scraping of glaciers. Eruptions started about 35 million years ago and lasted more than 13 million years. During one phase, the volcanoes were so explosive that they often collapsed into themselves, forming calderas. Hot mineralized water oozed up

*Ballard and Wasatch Mountains*

through cracks and faults underground and around the calderas, leaving behind gold, silver, zinc, copper, and lead. Within the last 2 million years, various glaciers covered the area. The San Miguel glacier carved the U-shaped valley floor in which Telluride sits. Spectacular Bridal Veil Falls, at the head of the box canyon, drops 365 feet from a hanging valley.

In 1875, John Fallon discovered ore rich in zinc, lead, copper, iron, silver, and gold. Nearby, the Union Mine also started recovering rich ore. J. B. Ingram discovered that Fallon's claim and the Union were bigger than the legal limit by about 500 feet. He laid claim to the area in between, calling it the Smuggler. The Smuggler's ore contained 800 ounces of silver and eighteen ounces of gold per ton. The Union and Smuggler merged and became one of the major producers in Telluride. The Tomboy Mine, about 5 miles up Tomboy Road, started operations in 1880 and continued until 1928. In 1897 it sold for $2 million!

▶ **The book *Tomboy Bride*, by Harriet Fish Backus, offers an interesting account of life in the mining camp near the Tomboy Mine from 1908 to 1910.**

*Telluride and Ballard Mountains*

The mountains around Telluride contain over 350 miles of tunnels (think San Francisco to Los Angeles), some going all the way through the mountains to the Million Dollar Highway between Ouray and Silverton. The town itself was established as Columbia in 1878, when 80 acres were laid out and incorporated. It became the county seat of newly established San Miguel County in 1883. The post office, however, had a problem getting mail to Columbia, Colorado, often sending it to Columbia, California, instead. A name change was inevitable. Telluride, the name of a gold-bearing tellurium compound, was chosen for the new moniker in the 1880s.

The rich ore-bearing peaks surrounding Telluride hold a lurking danger—the white death. Three hundred inches of annual snowfall combined with steep terrain result in fairly regular avalanches. In 1902, an avalanche demolished part of the Liberty Bell Mine (farther up the road you'll hike down), killing seven men and injuring several others. While the rescue party was recovering the bodies, a second avalanche swept through. The rescuers escaped without additional injuries or deaths. However, as they made their way back to Telluride a third avalanche roared down, killing three and injuring five. In one winter (1905–1906) with unusually heavy snows, one

# Jud Wiebe Memorial Trail

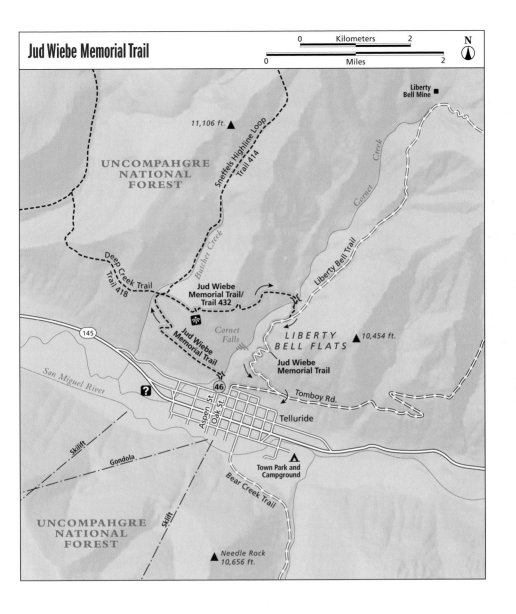

Kilometers 0 — 2

Miles 0 — 2

N

Liberty Bell Mine ■

11,106 ft. ▲

UNCOMPAHGRE NATIONAL FOREST

*Cornet Creek*

Sneffels Highline Loop Trail 414

*Butcher Creek*

Liberty Bell Trail

Deep Creek Trail Trail 418

Jud Wiebe Memorial Trail/ Trail 432

*Cornet Falls*

LIBERTY BELL FLATS ▲ 10,454 ft.

Jud Wiebe Memorial Trail

Jud Wiebe Memorial Trail

145

46

Tomboy Rd.

San Miguel River

❓

Aspen St.   Oak St.

Telluride

Skilift

Gondola

Town Park and Campground ⛺

Bear Creek Trail

UNCOMPAHGRE NATIONAL FOREST

Skilift

Needle Rock ▲ 10,656 ft.

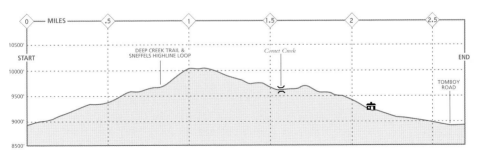

0 — MILES — .5 — 1 — 1.5 — 2 — 2.5

10500'

START

DEEP CREEK TRAIL & SNEFFELS HIGHLINE LOOP

*Cornet Creek*

END

10000'

TOMBOY ROAD

9500'

9000'

8500'

hundred people died in avalanches in the area. Snow isn't the only thing to go sliding around Telluride. In 1914, Cornet Creek overflowed, sending 8 feet of mud down Colorado Avenue, Telluride's main street.

The Jud Wiebe Trail (Trail 432) starts at the bulletin board at the top of Aspen Street. Continue uphill to the bridge over Cornet Creek and turn left. The trail climbs steadily and after a couple of switchbacks comes to a junction with the Deep Creek Trail (Trail 418). The Jud Wiebe Trail takes off to the right and continues climbing.

You soon arrive at a viewpoint, locally called Breakfast Rock, with views of Telluride and the surrounding lofty peaks. A few more switchbacks lead to an open area with more fantastic views. To the west is the San Miguel River, heading downstream along a glacial moraine. You might even catch a glimpse of the La Sal Mountains near Moab, Utah. The San Miguel Mountains, home to three 14,000-foot peaks, line up along the horizon. To the south and east, peaks rise dramatically and the gondola climbs the hill from town along ski runs. Ingram and Bridal Veil Falls tumble from cliffs to the east.

The trail meanders down through a lush aspen forest and crosses a bridge over Cornet Creek. Climbing further, the trail then intersects the nonmotorized road to Liberty Bell Mine. This flat area once served as the local playing field for baseball games between miners and town residents. Turn right and follow the steep road down past the town water tank to Tomboy Road. Turn right and walk down the road to the top of Oak Street and back to town.

## Miles and Directions

**0.0** Start at the trailhead bulletin board at the top of Aspen Street. Elevation: 8,880 feet. In a few feet, turn left and walk across the bridge that crosses Cornet Creek.

**0.7** Reach a junction with Deep Creek Trail (Trail 418) and Sneffels Highline Loop (Trail 414). Turn right to continue on the Jud Wiebe Trail (Trail 432).

**1.1** Come to an open meadow and slope with fantastic views.

**1.6** Cross the bridge over Cornet Creek.

**1.7** Reach the junction of Jud Wiebe Trail and a nonmotorized road, which leads to Liberty Bell Mine. GPS: N37 56.70' / W107 48.36'. Turn right and walk down the road.

**2.2** The town water tank is on the right.

**2.6** Reach the junction of Jud Wiebe Trail and Tomboy Road, which leads to Tomboy Mine. At a pipe gate and bulletin board, turn right and walk down Tomboy Road.

**2.7** Arrive at the Oak Street trailhead. Elevation: 8,920 feet. Return to wherever you parked your vehicle.

# Hike Information

## General Information
**Telluride Tourism Board:** Telluride; (970) 728-3041 or (888) 605-2578; www.visittelluride.com

## Local Events/Attractions
**Jazz Celebration:** Telluride; (970) 728-7009; www.telluridejazz.org
**Telluride Bluegrass Festival:** Telluride; (800) 624-2422; www.bluegrass.com/telluride
**Telluride Blues & Brews Festival:** Telluride; (866) 515-6166; www.tellurideblues.com

## Accommodations
**National Forest campgrounds:** Norwood Ranger District, Norwood; (970) 327-4261; www.fs
.usda.gov/gmug
**Town Park Campground:** Telluride; (970) 728-2173

## Restaurants
**Emilio's Grill and Bar:** 226 West Colorado, Telluride; (970) 369-1101
**Maggie's Bakery & Cafe:** 217 East Colorado Ave., Telluride; (970) 728-3334
**Tommy's:** 300 West Colorado, Telluride; (970) 728-1801

## Hike Tours
**Herb Walker Tours:** Telluride; (970) 728-0639
**San Juan Outdoor School:** Telluride; (970) 728-4101 or (866) FUN-TRIDE; www.tellurideadven
tures.com

# 47 Cascade and Portland Loop

This pleasant hike loops along Cascade Falls Trail and Portland Trail in Ouray's Amphitheater area. The trail offers nice views of surrounding mountains, jagged cliffs, and mining operations. The hike includes the trail to Upper Cascade Falls. This spur trail switchbacks its way past cliffs for great views of surrounding mountains. After enjoying the falls, you can walk to the Chief Ouray Mine's bunkhouse.

**Start:** From the trailhead at the top of the Amphitheater Campground
**Distance:** 6.8-mile lollipop (with a moderate 3.6-mile loop option)
**Approximate hiking time:** 2.5 to 6 hours
**Difficulty:** Most difficult due to the steep trail to the upper falls and bunkhouse
**Elevation gain:** 1,920-foot gain (including ups and downs)
**Seasons:** Best from May through Oct
**Trail surface:** Dirt trail, steep and narrow to Upper Cascade Falls
**Land status:** National forest
**Nearest town:** Ouray
**Other trail users:** Equestrians, mountain bikers, and hunters (in season) on lower parts of the loop

**Canine compatibility:** Dogs must be under control on the trail and must be on leash in the parking lot and in the campground. Dogs are not recommended on the upper section of the Cascade Falls Trail due to narrowness.
**Schedule:** Year-round. Call for winter access road and trail conditions.
**Fees and permits:** None
**Maps:** USGS Ouray; Nat Geo Trails Illustrated 141 Telluride/Silverton/Ouray/Lake City; Latitude 40° Telluride, Silverton, Ouray
**Trail contact:** Uncompahgre National Forest, Ouray Ranger District, Montrose; (970) 240-5300; www.fs.usda.gov/gmug
**Other:** Outhouse in campground
**Special considerations:** Bring your own water.

**Finding the trailhead:** From Ouray drive south out of town on US 550 to the entrance road to the Amphitheater Campground. Turn left onto the campground road and drive 1.1 miles on the paved road to the trailhead at the top of the campground. Trailhead GPS: N38 01.31'/W107 39.59'

## The Hike

The Ouray area is a jumble of geologic history, from ancient bedrock to glacially carved features. Leadville limestone formed in a sea over 325 million years ago. Reddish rock remains from the erosion of Uncompahgria, part of the Ancestral Rockies. Another sea helped form Dakota sandstone. Then the explosions of the San Juan volcanoes started, leaving deep deposits of ash and breccia (broken rocks) called San Juan tuff, of which the Amphitheater seen from the Portland Trail is a good example. Hot mineralized water deposited gold, silver, and other metals in the Leadville limestone during the volcanic era. Ice Age glaciers carved craggy peaks and scoured the valley north from Ouray, leaving its moraine by Ridgway.

*Amphitheater*

This combination of geologic events produced a gold and silver bonanza for prospectors. On a hunting and fishing expedition in summer 1875, A. J. Staley and Logan Whitlock meandered up the Uncompahgre River to the headwall by the current site of Ouray and discovered veins of ore, which were subsequently named the Trout and the Fisherman lodes. In August of that same year, A. W. Begole and Jack Eckles found the Cedar and Clipper lodes where the hot springs pool is today. As hopeful miners arrived in town, Captain Cline and Judge Long laid out a townsite that they called Uncompahgre City.

The next spring Chief Ouray and his wife, Chipeta, arrived in town to talk with the townspeople. Ouray was chief of the Tabeguache band of Utes, who lived in the Ouray-Montrose area. Half-Ute and half-Apache, Ouray rose to power as a skilled negotiator. He was friendly to the white man, realizing that fighting could decimate his people. He hoped that through negotiations, his people would survive and perhaps keep some of the land they had called home for hundreds of years. The latter did not happen. The Utes were organized into seven different bands, each with its

own leader. Because of his oratorical skill, the U.S. government regarded Ouray as spokesman for all Utes, a status not always acknowledged by other Ute chiefs. Over time, Chief Ouray gained much respect among white people. Uncompahgre City was renamed to Ouray in his honor.

Ouray continued to grow, its mines producing mainly silver. The transportation of ore and supplies was a struggle for many years. In 1887, the Denver and Rio Grande Railroad finally reached Ouray, adding to its prosperity. The Silver Crash of 1893, which killed many other mining towns, proved a mere burp to Ouray. A gold discovery on Gold Hill northeast of town saved the day.

Being surrounded by steep mountains poses occasional problems for Ouray. In July 1909, a downpour filled creek channels with tons of water and debris. Portland Creek, above which part of the hiking loop travels, roared into town, covering the first floor of the Elks Building with mud. It continued into J. J. Mayer's furniture store, carrying carpet rolls and furniture down Main Street.

In wintertime the drive south via Red Mountain Pass is very prone to avalanches, as is witnessed by a marker at one switchback. It commemorates a minister, his two daughters, and three snowplow drivers who met their untimely demise in the "white death."

On the way to the trailhead, stop at the first switchback just south of town. Look to the northeast, and you can see the Chief Ouray Mine buildings perched on a shelf in the cliffs. Believe it or not, the trail to Upper Cascade Falls takes you there without the need for ropes.

The hike starts by contouring around a ridge, then above a drainage. The intersection of Upper Cascade Falls Trail (Trail 213) and Portland Trail (Trail 238) is reached in about 0.8 mile. The spur trail to Upper Cascade Falls and the Chief Ouray Mine climbs steeply from the junction, zigzagging its way up a precipitous mountainside. The trail is good, although narrow in a few spots. When you reach a ledge, the walking becomes easier, but can be dangerous in bad weather. Take time to enjoy the fantastic views. The trail rounds a ridge near some interesting rock outcroppings and drops slightly to Upper Cascade Falls. You can cross Cascade Creek (**Note:** This crossing can be tricky in high water with the falls just downstream.) and continue 0.1 mile to explore the old mine bunkhouse and see Ouray far below. The trail past the bunkhouse is not maintained and can be treacherous.

Return to the junction of Upper Cascade Falls and the Portland Trail and turn left to continue the loop. When crossing the big gully, you can imagine the force of water that races down the steep cliffs. The hike continues through spruce-fir forest and climbs a little ridge to intersect with the Portland Cutoff Trail (Trail 238.1A) to

◀ *Chief Ouray Mine bunkhouse*

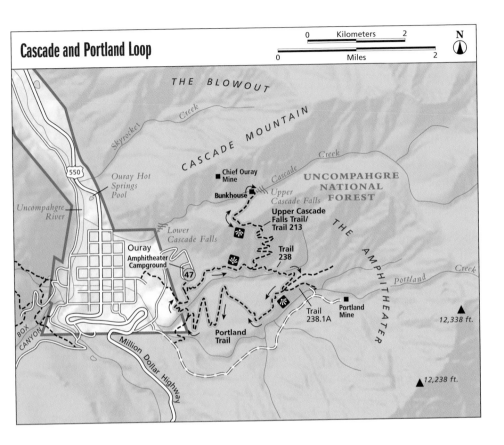

## Cascade and Portland Loop

the Portland Mine. Stay to the right on Portland Trail, enjoy the views into Portland Creek, and continue switchbacking down through a nice forest with aspens. At the next intersection, turn right onto Upper Cascade Falls Trail. After crossing the big gully again, the trail climbs back up to complete the loop and return to the trailhead.

## Miles and Directions

**0.0** Start at the trailhead at the top of Amphitheater Campground. Elevation: 8,520 feet.

**0.2** Reach a trail junction and trail register. Turn left and head uphill. (You'll return to this junction later.)

**0.5** The Lower Cascade Falls Trail (Trail 255) comes in from the left. Continue straight ahead and uphill.

**0.8** Reach the junction of the Upper Cascade Falls Trail (Trail 213) and the Portland Trail (Trail 238). GPS: N38 01.35' / W107 39.26'. Turn left on the Upper Cascade Falls Trail, heading for Upper Cascade Falls and the Chief Ouray Mine bunkhouse. **(Option:** For a shorter, easier hike turn right and follow the Portland Trail. This option will make for a 3.6-mile loop.)

**2.0**   Round a ridge by some interesting rock formations.

**2.2**   Reach Upper Cascade Falls. Elevation: 10,000 feet. GPS: N38 01.76'/W107 39.15'.

**2.4**   Arrive at the bunkhouse for the Chief Ouray Mine. Take a look inside, then return the way you came. **(FYI:** The trail beyond is not maintained and can be treacherous.)

**2.6**   Return to Upper Cascade Falls.

**4.0**   Arrive back at the junction of the Upper Cascade Falls Trail and the Portland Trail. Turn left onto the Portland Trail to complete the loop.

**4.3**   Cross a large gully that shows the power of water.

**4.6**   Reach the junction of the Portland Trail and the Portland Cutoff Trail (Trail 238.1A). GPS: N38 01.24'/W107 38.94'. Turn right to stay on the Portland Trail.

**4.7**   Enjoy the scenic view.

**6.2**   Reach a trail junction. The Portland Trail curves right here. The trail to the left goes to the Portland Trailhead. Recross the large gully that you crossed higher up.

**6.5**   Reach a trail junction. Turn right onto the Upper Cascade Falls Trail to return to the trail-head. The trail climbs up here.

**6.6**   Reach the trail junction with the trail register. This junction completes the loop. Turn left; the trailhead is just around the ridge.

**6.8**   Arrive back at the trailhead.

## Hike Information

### General Information

**Ouray Chamber Resort Association:** Ouray; (800) 228-1876 or (970) 325-4746; www.ouray colorado.com

### Local Events/Attractions

**Bachelor-Syracuse Mine Tour:** Ouray; (970) 325-0220 or (888) 227-8545; www.bachelorsyra cusemine.com

**Box Cañon Falls Park:** Ouray; (970) 325-7080

**Hot Springs Pool & Fitness Center:** Ouray; (970) 325-7073; www.cityofouray.com

### Accommodations

**Matterhorn Motel:** Ouray; (970) 325-4938; www.matterhornouray.com

**National Forest campgrounds:** Ouray Ranger District, Montrose; (970) 240-5300; www.fs.usda .gov/gmug

**Wiesbaden Hot Springs Spa & Lodgings:** has underground natural hot springs cave; Ouray; (970) 325-4347 or (888) 846-5191; www.wiesbadenhotsprings.com

## Restaurants

**Bon Ton Restaurant:** 426 Main St., Ouray; (970) 325-4951 or (866) 243-1502; www.stelmo hotel.com

**Buen Tiempo Mexican Restaurant & Cantina:** 515 Main St., Ouray; (970) 325-4544

**Outlaw Restaurant & Cookout:** 610 Main St., Ouray; (970) 325-4366; www.outlawrestaurant.com

## Clubs and Organizations

**Ouray Trails Group:** Ouray; www.ouraytrails.org

## Hike Tours

**San Juan Mountain Guides:** offers peak hikes and wildflowers along with technical climbing; Ouray; (970) 325-4925; www.ourayclimbing.com

*Creek crossing below Upper Cascade Falls*

# 48 Pass and Coal Creek Loop

This hike makes a loop above Coal Bank Pass via Pass Creek Trail (Trail 500) to the foot of impressive Engineer Mountain, then north on the Engineer Mountain Trail (Trail 508) to return on Coal Creek Trail (Trail 677). The wildflowers are spectacular on many sections of this hike during July and early August. Several places offer great views of the West Needle Mountains in the Weminuche Wilderness to the east and north to the mountains between Silverton and Telluride. The final 1.3 miles of the hike are along US 550 and can be avoided with a car shuttle.

**Start:** From the Pass Creek Trail (Trail 500) trailhead near the top of Coal Bank Pass
**Distance:** 7.8-mile loop
**Approximate hiking time:** 3 to 5 hours
**Difficulty:** Difficult due to elevation gain
**Elevation gain:** 1,700 feet including ups and downs
**Seasons:** Best from mid-June through Oct
**Trail surface:** Dirt trail with some grassy areas, steep in spots
**Land status:** National forest
**Nearest town:** Silverton
**Other trail users:** Equestrians, mountain bikers, and hunters (in season)

**Canine compatibility:** Dogs must be under control
**Schedule:** Year-round; but trail is neither maintained nor marked for winter use
**Fees and permits:** None
**Maps:** USGS Engineer Mountain; Nat Geo Trails Illustrated 141 Telluride/Silverton/Ouray/Lake City; Latitude 40˚ Durango and Southwest Colorado
**Trail contact:** San Juan National Forest, Columbine Ranger District, Bayfield; (970) 884-2512; www.fs.usda.gov/sanjuan
**Special considerations:** Bring your own water as not much is easily accessible.

**Finding the trailhead:** From Silverton, drive south about 13.6 miles on US 550. Turn right just before the top of Coal Bank Pass to enter a gravel parking area where you can access the Pass Creek Trail trailhead. There is a vault toilet on the east side of the highway at Coal Bank Pass. GPS: N37 41.95' / W107 46.71'

## The Hike

While driving from Silverton to the trailhead, compare the numerous craggy peaks to the south and east with the more rolling terrain and scattered peaks to the west. Engineer Mountain (12,968 feet) and the area of the hike are readily visible from just south of Molas Pass. Engineer Mountain itself is comprised of sandstone and shale that eroded from part of the Ancestral Rockies called Uncompahgria. These sediments add red color to the peak. The lower slopes are limestone formed from marine sediments in an ancient sea. The rolling hills were lava and ash flows, signs of the volcanic origins of the San Juan Mountains. Glaciers placed the final touches on this area. Engineer Mountain rose above an immense ice cap during more recent ice ages, the last of which only ended about 11,000 years ago.

*Engineer Mountain and trail sign*

Across the highway, craggy Twilight Peak is often seen while hiking down the Coal Creek Trail. Although some geologists say coal doesn't exist near Coal Bank Pass, records in Silverton indicate that people found some type of inefficient coal near here and used it for fuel until the coal mines near Durango were discovered.

Engineer Mountain looms large above the surrounding rolling hills. How the mountain was named is not certain, but historians believe the Hayden Survey (1870–1879) coined the name. "Engineer" most likely commemorates a survey engineer versus a railroad engineer. The San Juan region contains two Engineer Mountains, the other located on the Alpine Loop Scenic Byway (4WD) between Ouray and Lake City.

The Pass Creek Trail starts in a field of cornhusk lily, cow parsnip, subalpine larkspur, Indian paintbrush, death camas, geraniums, and columbines. Cornhusk lily (false hellebore) is the large, white-flowered plant with big green leaves resembling cornhusks. Another common name for this member of the lily family is skunk cabbage. The other large plant with clusters of white flowers is cow parsnip, which some people mistakenly call Queen Anne's lace. Both grow in moist areas such as this meadow, and are often found with another moisture-loving plant, subalpine larkspur. These three can grow taller than most hikers,

▶ **Lodging in Silverton can fill quickly in summer. Make reservations far in advance if planning a visit in July or August.**

forming green walls along the trail. The larkspur is a member of the buttercup family, sporting purple petals with a long spur. Without a close look, it can be mistaken for monkshood, which also loves moist areas. Death camas has six joined petals with a yellow band and red stamens. Both death camas and cornhusk lily are poisonous to humans.

> ▶ Picked wildflowers will only stay fresh for about two hours before fading into oblivion. So, please do not pick the wildflowers, but leave them for others to enjoy. The local animals depend on them for food too.

The amount and type of flowers change with forest and meadow as you hike along. The trail enters a spruce-fir forest and wanders around little ridges. A little pond surrounded by elephant heads lies in an open meadow at about 1.2 miles. Elephant head, also called little red elephant, is an appropriate name for these pink-to-purple flowers that love boggy areas. The elephant trunk sticks out from the ears as if trumpeting sunny days. Other boggy area plants can be seen along various sections of trail. Globeflowers with their overlapping cream-colored petals, marsh marigolds with their more separated white petals, king's crowns (ruby flowers), occasional queen's crowns (pink flowers), and Parry's primroses with magenta-to-purple flowers line the trail in wetter areas. After about 2 miles, the hills are covered with yellow, rosy, or magenta paintbrush flowers in a profusion of color. As the trees thin, Colorado blue columbine, the state flower, makes a showy appearance. Engineer Mountain towers above the seas of tiny wildflowers like a castle surrounded by its moat.

When you reach the intersection with Engineer Mountain Trail (Trail 508), turn right and follow Engineer Mountain Trail across the open alpine fields. Willows grow here, along with varieties of paintbrush, king's crown, American bistort, Parry's primrose, columbine, elephant head, and alpine avens—all commingled as if a higher power had emptied packages of mixed wildflower seeds.

The trail proceeds north, crossing the head of Coal Creek. Turn right at the marked junction and follow the trail across a little ridge. Just beyond is a trail junction. Turn right, follow the trail through willows, then head down to a saddle. At the saddle, the trail disappears in the grasses but is marked by cairns. Turn right and drop down into the Coal Creek drainage, where the trail reappears near a wooden post in the meadow. The flowers aren't as spectacular along Coal Creek, but the occasional views of Twilight Peak are. The trail drops, sometimes steeply, above Coal Creek, then makes several switchbacks down to US 550. If you haven't set up a car shuttle, follow US 550 back to the trailhead.

## Miles and Directions

**0.0** Start at the Pass Creek Trail (Trail 500) trailhead. Elevation: 10,680 feet.

**1.2** A little pond is on the left.

**1.5** The trail makes a big right switchback.

**2.3** Engineer Mountain comes into view, followed by fantastic fields of wildflowers.

**2.5** Reach the trail junction with Engineer Mountain Trail (Trail 508). Elevation: 11,660 feet. GPS: N37 42.22'/W107 47.87'. Turn right and follow Engineer Mountain Trail, heading north. **(FYI:** A left turn will take you to US 550, south of Coal Bank Pass, in about 4 miles.)

**3.3** Reach the top of the Coal Creek drainage. **(FYI:** There's a little saddle to the left for a view to the west. Good lunch spot.)

**3.5** The trail forks. Turn right onto Coal Creek Trail (Trail 677) **(FYI:** You can also go farther north on Engineer Mountain Trail to intersect with the Colorado Trail.)

**4.0** The trail rounds a ridge. Just past the top there's a sign on a tree that points to Coal Creek Trail. Just past there is a big cairn. Turn right at the cairn, then go a little downhill and look carefully to the left for the trail through a willow patch. GPS: N37 43.16'/W107 47.53'.

**4.3** The trail disappears at a saddle in the ridge, but is marked by cairns. Turn right and head downhill in the meadow. Stay to the left along a little gully. Look for a log post in the meadow below. GPS: N37 43.01'/W107 47.29'. If you don't see the trail, stay close to the little gully and you'll come upon the path in about 0.1 mile. Turn left onto the trail, which soon curves to the left.

**5.1** Enjoy the view of craggy peaks to the east, including Twilight Peak, the closest.

**6.5** Reach Coal Creek Trail trailhead along US 550. Elevation: 10,280 feet. GPS: N37 42.51'/W107 46.06'. To complete the entire loop hike, continue walking along the road, being mindful of oncoming traffic.

**7.7** Cross the highway and turn right onto the dirt road to the Pass Creek Trail trailhead.

**7.8** Arrive back at the trailhead.

## Option

If you have two vehicles, you can make this a point-to-point hike of 6.5 miles. From Silverton, drive south about 12.4 miles on US 550. At mile marker 58, leave one car at the dirt parking area on the left side of the road just before a large left switchback. GPS: N37 42.51'/W107 46.06'. Then proceed to the Pass Creek Trail trailhead for the start of the hike. There is a vault toilet on the east side of the highway at Coal Bank Pass. Turn right just before the top of Coal Bank Pass to enter a gravel parking area where you can access this trailhead. Follow the Miles and Directions to mile 6.5. Turn right, cross the road, and walk about 0.1 mile along the left side up to the parking area, and your shuttle vehicle, back at mile marker 58.

# Hike Information

## General Information

**Durango Area Tourism Office and Visitor Center:** Durango; (800) 525-8855 or (970) 247-3500; www.durango.org

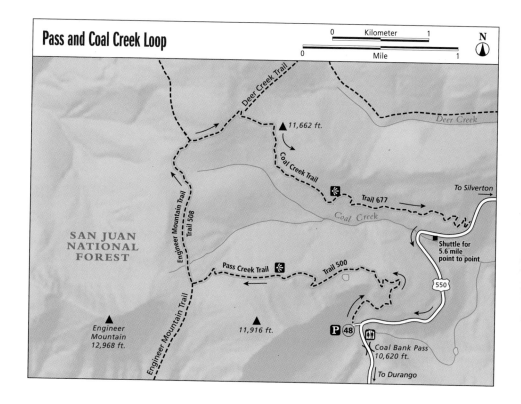

## Pass and Coal Creek Loop

Kilometer

Mile

N

11,662 ft.

Deer Creek Trail

Deer Creek

Coal Creek Trail

Trail 677

To Silverton

Coal Creek

Shuttle for
5.6 mile
point to point

Engineer Mountain Trail 508

SAN JUAN
NATIONAL
FOREST

Pass Creek Trail

Trail 500

550

Engineer Mountain Trail

Engineer
Mountain
12,968 ft.

11,916 ft.

P 48

Coal Bank Pass
10,620 ft.

To Durango

---

**Silverton Area Chamber of Commerce:** Silverton; (800) 752-4494 or (970) 387-5654; http://silvertoncolorado.com

## Local Events/Attractions

**Christ of the Miners Shrine:** Silverton; (800) 752-4494 or (970) 387-5654

**Durango & Silverton Narrow Gauge Railroad:** Durango; (877) TRAIN-07 or (970) 247-2733; www.durangotrain.com

**Mayflower Gold Mill Tour:** Silverton; (970) 387-5838 (summer); www.silvertonhistoricsociety.org

**Old Hundred Gold Mine Tour:** Silverton; (800) 872-3009 or (970) 387-5444; www.minetour.com

## Accommodations

**National Forest campgrounds:** San Juan National Forest, Columbine Ranger District, Bayfield; (970) 884-2512; www.fs.usda.gov/sanjuan

## Restaurants

**Brown Bear Cafe:** 1129 Greene St., Silverton; (970) 387-5630

**Pickle Barrel:** 1304 Greene St., Silverton; (970) 387-5713; www.thepicklebarrel.com

**Handlebars Food & Saloon:** 117 West 13th St., Silverton; (970) 387-5395

*Flowers and Engineer Mountain*

## Clubs and Organizations

**San Juan Mountains Association:** Durango; (970) 385-1210; www.sjma.org

**San Juan County Historical Society:** Silverton; (970) 387-5838; www.silvertonhistoricsociety.org

## Hike Tours

**San Juan Backcountry:** Silverton; (800) 494-8687 or (903) 477-2555; www.sanjuanbackcoun try.com

# 49 First Fork and Red Creek Loop

The First Fork Trail follows a sparkling little creek up to Missionary Ridge northeast of Durango. Although parts of this forest burned in 2002, the vegetation is lush and trees are growing again. The trail travels through a forest of Douglas fir, ponderosa pine, Gambel oak, and aspen. After joining the Missionary Ridge Trail, head northeast through mixed conifer and aspen forests and several beautiful meadows, with occasional views north to the craggy San Juan Mountains. Return via Red Creek Trail, which drops down several steep switchbacks, then past huge aspens. The trail intersects the road about 0.3 miles above First Fork Trail trailhead. A beautiful hike when aspens are golden!

**Start:** From the First Fork Trail trailhead
**Distance:** 10-mile loop
**Approximate hiking time:** 4.5 to 7 hours
**Difficulty:** Difficult due to distance and some steep spots
**Elevation gain:** 2,150 feet (including ups and downs)
**Seasons:** Best from May through Oct
**Trail surface:** Dirt trail, sometimes steep
**Land status:** National forest
**Nearest town:** Durango
**Other trail users:** Equestrians, mountain bikers, hunters (in season)
**Canine compatibility:** Dogs must be under control
**Schedule:** Year-round; access road closed by snow 0.9 mile from trailhead; trail is neither maintained nor marked for winter use
**Fees and permits:** None
**Maps:** USGS Durango East, Hermosa, Lemon Reservoir, and Rules Hill (these maps are ancient and the trail is not shown on them); Nat Geo Trails Illustrated 145 Pagosa Springs & Bayfield; Latitude 40° Southwest Colorado
**Trail contact:** San Juan National Forest, Columbine Ranger District, Bayfield; (970) 884-2512; www.fs.usda.gov/sanjuan
**Special considerations:** Although water may be available in First Fork and Red Creek, cattle graze in this area, so be sure to purify any creek water before drinking.

**Finding the trailhead:** From the intersection of US 550 and College Drive in Durango (near the train station), drive 0.2 miles into downtown on College Drive to East 3rd Avenue, turn left on East 3rd and drive 0.7 mile to intersection of East 3rd and 15th Street and Florida Road. Turn sort of right onto Florida Road / La Plata County Road (LPCR) 240, and drive 9.4 miles northeast to the sign COLVIG SILVER CAMPS. Turn left here onto dirt LPCR 246 and drive 1 mile past the camps. The road gets rougher and bumpier. In another 0.3 mile there is a gate, which you may have to open and close. You can park here, off the road. The road beyond is best negotiated with a high clearance vehicle (4WD not necessary). A parking area is available about 0.25 mile beyond the gate. Park here if the road is getting too rough for your vehicle. The trailhead and a small parking area are another 0.35 mile from this point. The trailhead is marked by a TRAIL sign on the left side of the road. Vehicles are not allowed beyond this point.

There are no facilities. Bring your own water. Because of the Missionary Ridge fire of 2002, some portions of the access road may be subject to mudslides. GPS: N37 21.31' / W107 44.50'

## The Hike

Many early settlers to the Animas Valley were Civil War veterans. Legend has it that one morning, fog cloaked a ridge northeast of Durango. The veterans noticed a similarity with Missionary Ridge, site of a famous Civil War battle near Chattanooga, Tennessee. The ridge has since been known as Missionary Ridge.

On June 9, 2002, a small fire started along the Missionary Ridge Road, allegedly by a discarded cigarette. Little moisture had fallen during winter, and spring and summer continued to be very dry and hot. Reservoirs were lower than usual and the land became parched. The very dry trees quickly became torches, as the fire burned 6,500 acres the first day. Helicopters dropped buckets of water on the fire, slurry bombers covered trees with fire retardant, and ground crews created fire breaks and put out spot fires. The fire continued to spread in the dry forest, fanned by typical afternoon winds. Because of dry vegetation, the fire even burned downhill, an unusual event. By July 17, officials declared the fire was contained after burning eighty-three buildings, 73,391 acres of forest, and causing some 2,100 people to flee at times. The fire actually continued to burn in small patches until winter snows finally extinguished the stubborn flames.

One firefighter died, his life snuffed out by a falling tree. A tour of tree carvings depicting firefighters and other emergency responders in action can be seen around Vallecito Lake, just east of this hike. The carvings were created in dead ponderosa pine trees. One tree and nearby plaque commemorates the fallen firefighter.

From the smoke and media reports, people envisioned the entire area from Missionary Ridge to Lemon Reservoir to Vallecito Lake as being burned to a crisp. Forest fires typically jump around, and this one was no exception. Burned homes were surrounded by unburned forest, while blackened forest encircled unburned homes. This hop-skip-jump phenomenon is readily observed throughout this hike.

In early August, a few rainstorms passed over the burned area. In places where trees and ground cover had been destroyed, roots no longer held the soil together. As rain moistened the charred earth, mudslides flowed downhill across roads, into homes and businesses, making a mess of everything in their way. One slide closed the access road to First Fork Trail. Geologists studied one newly created arroyo, and discovered that fires and resulting debris flows have occurred in the Vallecito Valley about every 350 years for the last 3,500 years!

By early October 2002, little Gambel oak shoots started to poke through the burned ground. Crop dusters dropped pounds of plant and grass seeds, which sprouted the next spring, along with seeds already in the ground. Within two years, grasses, aspen sprouts, and flowers grew knee-high. While you can still see the effects of the fire, nature continues to heal the burned scars.

◄  *Carving of firefighter near Vallecito Reservoir*

Starting up First Fork Trail, you'll first cross Red Creek then come upon a gate. Please close the gate behind you as cattle graze in this area. The trail follows little First Fork, where flowers sometimes grow waist high. You'll hike in and out of areas that were burned in the fire. In one place, the general area has been burned except for one tree. In a large open area, the trail climbs steeply, drops, and climbs again.

When you come to a Y intersection, know that you are not at Missionary Ridge. Turn left and continue up to a T intersection with the Missionary Ridge Trail, passing through a burned area. The fire scorched many parts of the ridge, but aspen are once again growing and the vegetation is quite thick among the ghost trees. One advantage of the fire: The view to the north of the craggy San Juan Mountains and the Hermosa Cliffs has improved.

Continue hiking along the ridge, over one saddle to a second saddle. Here the Red Creek Trail drops off the ridge to the right. After switchbacking steeply off Missionary Ridge, Red Creek Trail then wanders through a huge, beautiful aspen forest (making an excellent fall hike) and shoulder-high cow parsnip that sometimes hides the trail. Watch for elk and deer. When you come to a road, turn right to return to your vehicle.

## Miles and Directions

**0.0**  Start at the First Fork Trail trailhead. Elevation: 7,880 feet. Immediately cross Red Creek and soon arrive at a gate. Remember to close the gate behind you.

**2.7**  Arrive at an open area filled with bushes. A cliff looms ahead of you. The trail climbs steeply, then drops down and climbs up again.

**3.3**  The trail arrives at a Y intersection. Turn left here to continue climbing to Missionary Ridge Trail.

**3.4**  Reach the junction with Missionary Ridge Trail. GPS: N37 22.62' / W107 46.83'. Turn right and proceed north, then east along the ridge.

**4.8**  Arrive at a large meadow ringed with little aspen and some conifers.

**5.2**  The trail starts descending, sometimes steeply.

**5.5**  Pass by an old stile. Before the fire, the trail used to cross a fence on the stile.

**6.0**  After dropping and switchbacking down, arrive at a saddle. The trail appears to fork. Take the trail to the left that goes around the hill in front of you. Lots of bushes and flowers grow along the contouring trail.

**6.5**  Reach the junction with the Red Creek Trail. Elevation: 9,840 feet. GPS: N37 23.74' / W107 44.68'. Turn right, drop down, and follow the steep switchbacks. The trail sign faces east so look carefully for it.

**6.8**  The trail mellows out and meanders through a thick aspen forest with lush vegetation.

**8.5**  Come to a gate. Make sure to close it behind you. Cross the creek to the left. The trail crosses the creek a number of times as you continue down. There are some nice red cliffs along the trail also.

*Scorched ponderosa pine and aspen* ▷

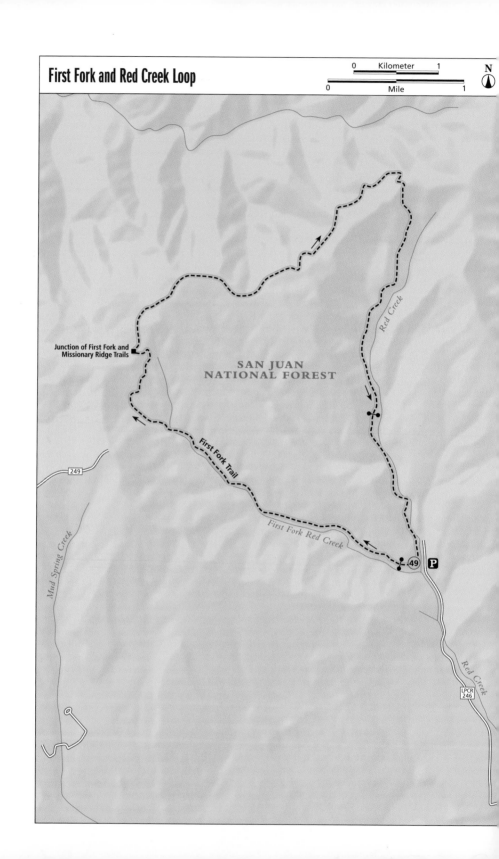

# First Fork and Red Creek Loop

0　　　Kilometer　　　1

0　　　Mile　　　1

N

**SAN JUAN
NATIONAL FOREST**

Junction of First Fork and
Missionary Ridge Trails

First Fork Trail

First Fork Red Creek

Red Creek

Mud Spring Creek

Red Creek

249

49

P

LPCR
246

**9.7** Arrive at a dirt road (closed to motorized traffic). GPS: N37 21.51'/W107 44.50'. Turn right and walk down the road back to your vehicle.

**10.0** Arrive back at the First Fork Trail trailhead.

## Hike Information

### General Information

**Durango Area Tourism Office and Visitor Center:** Durango; (800) 525-8855 or (970) 247-3500; www.durango.org

**Durango Visitor Information:** www.godurango.com

### Local Events/Attractions

**Durango & Silverton Narrow Gauge Railroad:** Durango; (877) TRAIN-07 or (970) 247-2733; www.durangotrain.com

**Trimble Hot Springs:** Durango; (970) 247-0111; www.trimblehotsprings.com

### Accommodations

**National Forest campgrounds:** San Juan National Forest, Columbine Ranger District, Bayfield; (970) 884-2512; www.fs.usda.gov/sanjuan

### Restaurants

**Ken and Sue's:** 636 Main Ave., Durango; (970) 259-2616; www.kenandsues.com

**The Red Snapper:** 144 East 9th St., Durango; (970) 259-3417; www.redsnapperdurango.com

**Steamworks Brewpub:** 801 East Second Ave., Durango; (970) 259-9200; www.steamworks brewing.com

### Clubs and Organizations

**San Juan Mountains Association:** Durango; (970) 385-1210; www.sjma.org

**Colorado Mountain Club–San Juan Group:**, Durango; www.cmc.org

### Hike Tours

**San Juan Mountains Association:** Durango; (970) 385-1210; www.sjma.org

# 50  Petroglyph Point Trail

This hike takes you below the rim of Spruce Tree Canyon along a self-guided trail, up and down various steps, between huge rocks, through skinny cracks, to a wonderful petroglyph panel. Petroglyph Point, unfortunately misnamed Pictograph Point on topo maps, is the largest and best-known group of petroglyphs in Mesa Verde National Park. The hike gives you a glimpse of what it was like to live in this area, including climbing up a little cliff using big toeholds and handholds, much larger than the Ancestral Puebloans used.

**Start:** From the Spruce Tree House Trail trailhead between Chapin Mesa Museum and the chief ranger's office
**Distance:** 2.8-mile loop
**Approximate hiking time:** 1.5 to 3 hours
**Difficulty:** Moderate due to uneven dirt trail and toeholds in one spot
**Elevation gain/loss:** 360-foot loss, then many undulations before regaining the 360 feet
**Seasons:** Best from Mar through Nov
**Trail surface:** Paved trail turning to dirt with rock steps, narrow passages, and rock footholds
**Land status:** National Park
**Nearest towns:** Cortez and Mancos
**Other trail users:** Hikers only
**Canine compatibility:** Dogs not permitted
**Schedule:** Open Mar to Nov, depending on snow. The trail is open from 8:30 a.m. to 6:30 p.m. in summer, and from 9 a.m. to 5 p.m.
in spring and fall. No visitors can enter ruins without a ranger present.
**Fees and permits:** Entrance fee, annual pass, or America the Beautiful pass required for park entry
**Maps:** USGS Moccasin Mesa; Nat Geo Trails Illustrated 144 Durango/Cortez; Latitude 40° Southwest Colorado
**Trail contact:** Mesa Verde National Park, Mesa Verde; (970) 529-4465; www.nps.gov/meve
**Other:** You must register at the trailhead (about 0.1 mile down the Spruce Tree House Trail) before hiking this trail. If you start on this trail late, you must complete the loop. A gate across the trail is locked at 6:30 p.m. (earlier in spring and fall), which prevents you from returning the way you came.
**Special considerations:** No water is available along the trail.

**Finding the trailhead:** From Cortez drive about 10 miles east on US 160. Turn right at the Mesa Verde National Park interchange. Drive about 21 miles on the park road to the parking lot for Spruce Tree House and Chapin Mesa Museum. You will have to pay the entrance fee at the entrance station near the interchange. The visitor center, about 15 miles along the park road, offers information and is the only place to purchase tickets for tours of Cliff Palace, Balcony House, and Long House. Water, food, and restrooms are available near the trailhead. Trailhead GPS: N37 11.05' / W108 29.25'

## The Hike

About AD 1200, the sounds of building, farming, grinding corn, and playing children rang through the canyons and mesa tops of Mesa Verde. Spruce Tree House, built

*Petroglyph panel*

between 1200 and 1276, is thought to have housed about one hundred people. It is the third-largest dwelling at Mesa Verde. The Ancestral Puebloan people lived in this area from about AD 550 to 1300. At first they built pit houses, partially underground, with log, branch, and mud roofs. They farmed the surrounding land and cleared piñons and junipers for their fields, using the materials for their structures, clothes, food, and firewood. Water was mainly obtained from winter snows and often meager summer rains. Dryland farming methods were used to grow corn, beans, and squash. Hunting first with atlatls (a spear-throwing device), and then bows and arrows, men brought meat home. Woven baskets were used for storage and cooking. Between AD 900 and 1100, pottery and multilevel surface structures called pueblos evolved. Circular ceremonial structures, called kivas, were built completely underground with an entrance from above.

These people progressed and prospered. Pueblos evolved into larger villages, often with several kivas. The Ancestral Puebloan culture covered many square miles of the Four Corners region (where Colorado, Utah, Arizona, and New Mexico meet). Trade

routes developed between many villages. Evidence of trade with people in Mexico and California has been found at various sites.

By 1100 the Ancestral Puebloans were entering their "golden age." Pottery was decorated with black-on-white designs. Masonry techniques had improved, and structures were built with more regularly shaped stones, resulting in nicer-looking buildings. Toward the end of the 1100s, they started building their multi-storied dwellings in alcoves in the cliffs.

No one knows for sure why the Ancestral Puebloans moved into the alcoves. Access was difficult, requiring handholds and toeholds to be carved into the solid sandstone, and sometimes ladders had to be constructed. Theories range from protection from enemies to shelter from weather—many populated alcoves face south to benefit from winter sun.

▶ **The Ancestral Puebloan people were formerly called Anasazi. The descendants of these people are the present-day Pueblo and Hopi people.** *Anasazi* **is a Navajo word meaning "different ancestors" and is not preferred by today's descendants.** *Mesa Verde* **is Spanish for "green table," an appropriate name for the mesa when viewed from a distance.**

By 1300, the people had moved away from these villages and cliff dwellings. Possibilities for the exodus range from environmental problems, severe draught, or religious reasons. According to Hopi culture, the various clans were to migrate in four directions, then eventually join together again at a common and permanent home. As they lived in, then left, their villages, they carved information about their clan, the history of their village, and their migration on rock walls. Archaeologists believe the citizens of Mesa Verde moved to pueblos along the Rio Grande to the south and the Hopi mesas to the southwest.

These ancient peoples had no written language. Traditions and knowledge about how to live were passed orally from generation to generation. They did, however, leave stories chipped and scratched on the stone cliffs. Petroglyph Point is one of their storyboards. A petroglyph is a drawing pecked into the rock, whereas pictographs are painted. The *Petroglyph Trail Guide* describes a possible interpretation of the panel.

The hike starts on the paved trail to Spruce Tree House. Switchbacks take you down into Spruce Tree Canyon. Before or after your hike, take some time to walk around Spruce Tree House. A ranger is on duty to answer any questions. A self-guided brochure explains life at the site and some information about preservation.

When you come to the intersection with Petroglyph Point Trail, make sure to sign the trail register. After the intersection with the Spruce Canyon Trail, Petroglyph Point Trail climbs up Spruce Tree Canyon, following various ledges. The trail guide explains many plants and geologic features of the area. One section of narrow trail can be a challenge if you are carrying a wide pack or dangling camera. At marker 19, stop and look at the grooves in the rock where ax heads were sharpened. The petroglyph

◀ *Skinny passage*

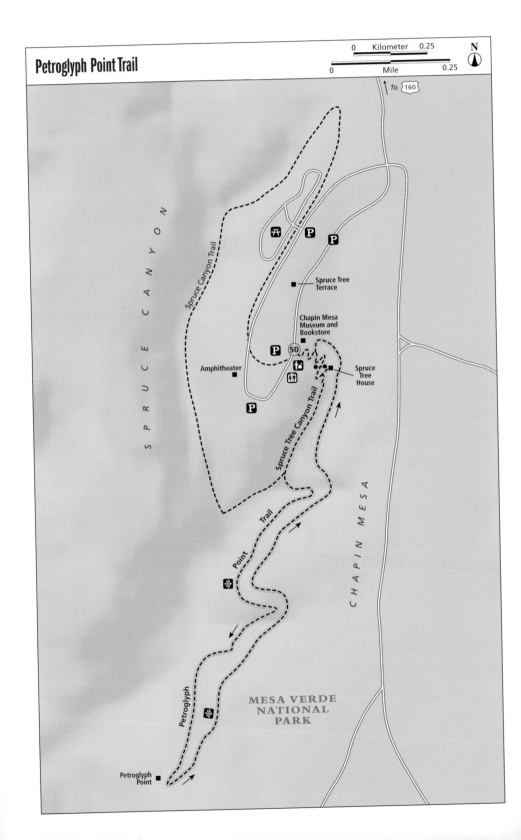

# Petroglyph Point Trail

0    Kilometer    0.25

0    Mile    0.25

N

To 160

SPRUCE CANYON

Spruce Canyon Trail

Spruce Tree Terrace

Chapin Mesa Museum and Bookstore

50

Spruce Tree House

Amphitheater

Spruce Tree Canyon Trail

Point Trail

CHAPIN MESA

Petroglyph

MESA VERDE NATIONAL PARK

Petroglyph Point

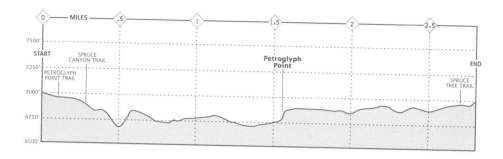

panel is at marker 24. From there, look carefully for the museum signs with arrows. The trail climbs up a very short rock face, with good steps carved into the rock and handholds that can be easily reached. Just beyond, the trail travels a few feet along a rock ledge. Once on the mesa top, the trail is easy to follow.

Please do not deface or remove any artifacts, or pick any plants. Others will follow you—leave the area clean and unspoiled for the next visitors.

As you hike the trail, envision living here 900 or 1,000 years ago. A people in tune with their environment and skilled in the ways of the land successfully lived here for more than 700 years.

## Miles and Directions

**0.0**  Start at the Spruce Tree House Trail trailhead, between the museum/bookstore and the chief ranger's office. Elevation: 6,960 feet. The trail splits at a left curve. Take the left branch downhill around the left switchback. (The right branch goes behind the chief ranger's office.)

**0.1**  Pass by a metal chain-link gate. This gate is closed and locked at night, so if you start hiking late, you'll have to complete the loop. The trail forks. Turn right onto Petroglyph Point Trail (a National Historic Trail) and sign the trail register. The trail becomes dirt here. (**FYI:** The left trail goes to Spruce Tree House.)

**0.3**  The trail forks. Turn left and go uphill on Petroglyph Point Trail. The right branch is Spruce Canyon Trail.

**0.9**  There's a good view of Navajo and Spruce Tree Canyons.

**1.6**  Reach Petroglyph Point.

**1.7**  Reach the mesa above Spruce Tree Canyon.

**1.9**  Come to a slickrock area with views.

**2.5**  A short section of forest on your right was burned in a fire in 2002.

**2.7**  Come to the trail junction with paved Spruce Tree House Trail. Turn right and head uphill to trailhead.

**2.8**  Arrive back at the trailhead.

## General Information

**Cortez Chamber of Commerce & Colorado Welcome Center:** Cortez; (970) 565-3414; www.cortezchamber.org

**Mancos Valley Visitor Center & Pioneer Museum:** Mancos; (970) 533-7434; www.mancosvalley.com

**Mesa Verde Country:** Cortez; www.swcolo.org

## Local Events/Attractions

**Anasazi Heritage Center:** Dolores; (970) 882-5600; www.blm.gov/co/st/en/fo/ahc.html

**Chapin Mesa Museum:** regular visits and scheduled special events like Indian dances; Mesa Verde National Park; (970) 529-4461; www.nps.gov/meve

**Crow Canyon Archaeological Center:** Cortez; (970) 565-8975 or (800) 422-8975; www.crowcanyon.org

**Ute Mountain Tribal Park:** Towaoc; (800) 847-5485 or (970) 565-3751 ext. 330; www.utemountainute.com

## Accommodations

**Far View Lodge:** Mesa Verde National Park; (800) 449-2288; www.visitmesaverde.com

**Morefield Campground:** Mesa Verde National Park; (800) 449-2288; www.visitmesaverde.com

# LEAVE NO TRACE AT ARCHAEOLOGICAL SITES

To preserve the legacy of the Ancestral Puebloan culture for future generations, please . . .

- **Keep Your Feet Off the Furniture.** Archaeological sites are very old and fragile. Walk carefully and avoid stepping on walls and trash middens.
- **Don't Touch the Paintings.** Oils from skin damage pictographs (rock paintings) and petroglyphs (rock carvings). Never deface artwork in archaeological sites.
- **Don't Eat in the Living Room.** Avoid picnicking in archaeological sites. Crumbs attract rodents who may tunnel and nest in the site. Make sure that you pick up and carry out all of your trash.
- **Don't Take the Knickknacks.** Leave artifacts right where you find them, so others can enjoy them, too. Out of context, artifacts lose their meaning. It is illegal to remove them.
- **No Slumber Parties.** Avoid camping in the ruins. It's easy to destroy walls and artifacts in the dark. Smoke from campfires stains walls and cliffs, and charcoal leaves a mess. Never use wood from archaeological sites in campfires.
- **Tell the Owner if You See Something Wrong.** Contact a law enforcement official if you find archaeological sites defaced or if you witness someone removing artifacts.

## Restaurants

**Main Street Brewery & Restaurant:** 21 East Main St., Cortez; (970) 564-9112

**Nero's Italian Restaurant:** 303 West Main St., Cortez; (970) 565-7366; www.subee.com/neros /home.html

**Tequila's Mexican Restaurant:** 1740 East Main St., Cortez; (970) 565-6868

## Hike Tours

**Aramark Parks and Destinations:** Mesa Verde National Park; (800) 449-2288; www.visitmesa verde.com

**Mesa Verde Tours:** Durango; (970) 247-8533; www.mesaverdetours.net

# Honorable Mentions

## Southwest

Compiled here is an index of great hikes in the Southwest region that didn't make the A-list this time around but deserve recognition. Check them out and let us know what you think. You may decide that one or more of these hikes deserves higher status in future editions or, perhaps, you may have a hike of your own that merits some attention.

### W Ice Lake Trail

This popular trail leads to high alpine lakes, passing through aspen and spruce-fir forests to fields of wildflowers in July and August. Spectacular waterfalls roar along the way. To reach upper Ice Lake requires a difficult 9-mile out-and-back hike, climbing from 9,840 to 12,260 feet. Lower Ice Lake is just below treeline. The trail then climbs up a cliff, passing three waterfalls, one close to the trail. Upper Ice Lake is tucked in a spectacular basin. Once above treeline, be careful of lightning. Thunderstorms can come in swiftly. If you explore the area, please remember the tundra is fragile and stay on any trails or rock hop. From Silverton, drive north on US 550 about 2 miles to South Mineral Creek Road (FR 585). Turn left and drive about 4.4 miles. The trailhead is on the right, across the road from the entrance to South Mineral Creek Campground. For further information contact San Juan National Forest at (970) 884-2512 or check the website at www.fs.usda.gov/sanjuan.

### X Sand Canyon

The Sand Canyon Trail is west of Cortez in the Canyons of the Ancients National Monument. Winding first over slickrock, the trail becomes dirt as it wanders through piñon-juniper forest. Several spur trails lead to archaeological sites and small cliff dwellings tucked in Entrada sandstone alcoves. Two spur trails open to views deep into Sand Canyon to the right. Sleeping Ute Mountain towers to the south. At 3.7 miles, a trail sign warns that the next mile is steep and rocky. GPS: N37 22.38'/W108 47.42'. For a moderate hike, return the way you came. You can continue on for another 2.8 miles (rated most difficult) as the trail climbs thirty switchbacks out of the canyon to end at Sand Canyon Pueblo site, which is marked with interpretive signs. From Cortez, drive south on US 491 to Montezuma CR G (McElmo Canyon Road; also the road to the airport). Turn right and drive about 12.6 miles west to the Sand Canyon Trail trailhead (5,471 feet). GPS: N37 20.50'/W108 49.03'. The trailhead is marked but easy to miss. Park on the north side of the road on the slickrock to the east of the LEAVING PUBLIC LANDS sign. To the west is private property—do not trespass. There are no facilities at the trailhead. Dogs must be under control. Bring water for you and your dog. For more information, contact the BLM Anasazi Heritage Center, 27501 Highway 184, Dolores; (970) 882-5600; www.blm.gov/co/st/en/fo/ahc.html

## Y Ute Mountain Tribal Park

Hikes in the Ute Mountain Tribal Park are by reservation only with a Ute guide. These hikes are wonderful, as you visit cliff dwellings, rock art, and historical sites in small groups. The tribal park is just south of Mesa Verde National Park and was also home to many Ancestral Puebloan people. You'll hear about Ute history, as well as information about the Wetherill brothers (who explored much of this area) and the Ancestral Puebloan residents. Some hikes require climbing on ladders to ledges to get to the cliff dwellings (Eagles Nest in particular). Dogs are not allowed on hikes. To reach the hikes, you must provide your own vehicle for an up to 80-mile round-trip on gravel roads. One full-day tour includes about 3 miles and five ladders. To reach the Tribal Park Visitor Center, drive south from Cortez on US 160/US 491, past Towaoc, to the intersection of US 160 and US 491. The visitor center is on the northwest corner in what looks like an old gas station. For further information, contact Ute Mountain Tribal Park at (970) 565-3751 ext. 330 or (970) 749-1452 or (800) 847-5485, or visit the website at www.utemountainute.com.

# In Addition

## Colorado's Long Trails: The Colorado and Continental Divide Trails

No Colorado hiking guide would be complete without mentioning two trails that traverse all or most of the state:

The Colorado Trail starts in the east at Waterton Canyon, in the foothills southwest of Denver, and traverses mountain ranges and valleys to its western end near Durango in the southwest corner of the state. Covering almost 500 miles, it crosses eight mountain ranges, seven national forests, and six wilderness areas. Some people choose to backpack this trail in one summer, while others hike sections of it over many years. Most of the trail is above 10,000 feet, with a high point of 13,334 feet. One short section, the Wheeler Trail from Copper Mountain to the top of the Tenmile Range, is a featured hike in this book. For more information on the trail, contact The Colorado Trail Foundation at (303) 384-3729, or visit the website at www.coloradotrail.org. You can buy various hiking guides describing the trail, and the website contains updates to the descriptions.

The Continental Divide Trail in Colorado starts at the Colorado–Wyoming border and travels south across the state to the Colorado–New Mexico border. Work still continues on this trail, but it is hikable. The trail is difficult as much of it is above treeline, and weather is a major factor in hiking this spectacular route. Some people hike the trail from one end of Colorado to the other in one summer. Unless you have a lot of time, hiking sections is the more practical way to go. The trail covers an estimated 800 miles through some of Colorado's most breathtaking high country. Alberta Peak and Parkview Mountain, described in this guide, are along the Continental Divide Trail. *Colorado's Continental Divide Trail: The Official Guide,* by Tom Lorang Jones, breaks the trail into sections, giving excellent descriptions, tips, and other interesting facts and figures. For more information, contact the Continental Divide Trail Alliance at (303) 278-3177 or visit www.cdtrail.org, or contact the Continental Divide Trail Society at (410) 235-9610 or visit www.cdsociety.org.

# Appendix A: Local Clubs and Organizations

## Colorado Hiking Clubs

Colorado's main hiking/climbing club is the Colorado Mountain Club. The state offices are located in Golden, but groups exist in many parts of the state. Most other clubs seem connected with places of employment, senior centers, or recreation centers. These clubs may or may not be available to drop-ins and are not listed here. However, if you're wandering through an area, it never hurts to check to see if you can hop on a hike with one of these groups. Check with the local chamber of commerce, visitor center, or land management agency.

**Colorado Mountain Club,** State Office, 710 10th St. Suite 200, Golden, 80401; (303) 279-3080; www.cmc.org

### Trail Groups (Education, Maintenance, Advocacy)

What appears below is not a complete listing of trail groups, as there are many throughout the state.

**Colorado Fourteeners Initiative,** 710 Tenth St., Suite 220, Golden, CO 80401; (303) 278-7650; www.coloradofourteeners.org

**Colorado Trail Foundation,** 710 10th St., Suite 210, Golden, CO 80401; (303) 384-3729; www.coloradotrail.org

**Friends of Dillon Ranger District,** P.O. Box 1648, Silverthorne, CO 80498; (970) 262-3449; www.fdrd.org

**Continental Divide Trail Alliance,** 1200 Arapahoe St., Golden, CO 80401; (303) 278-3177; www.cdtrail.org

**Continental Divide Trail Society,** 3704 N. Charles St. 601, Baltimore, MD 21218; (410) 235-9610; www.cdtsociety.org

**Friends of Cheyenne Mountain State Park,** P.O. Box 51453, Colorado Springs, CO 80949; www.friendsofcmsp.org

**Friends of Dinosaur Ridge,** 16831 West Alameda Parkway, Morrison, CO 80465; (303) 697-3466; www.dinoridge.org

**Friends of the Dunes, Inc.,** 11500 Highway 150, Mosca, CO 81146; (719) 378-6381; www.friendsofgreatsanddunes.org

**Friends of the Eagles Nest Wilderness,** P.O. Box 4504, Frisco, CO 80443; (970) 468-5400; www.fenw.org

**Friends of the Florissant Fossil Beds, Inc.,** P.O. Box 851, Florissant, CO 80816; (719) 748-3253; www.fossilbeds.org

**Friends of the Front Range Wildlife Refuges,** Rocky Mountain Arsenal National Wildlife Refuge, Commerce City, CO; (303) 287-8734 or (303) 287-0210; www.ffrwr.org

**Friends of Larimer County Parks and Open Lands,** 1800 South County Road 31, Loveland, CO 80537; (970) 679-4570; www.larimer.org/friends

**Friends of McInnis Canyons,** P.O. Box 245, Fruita, CO 81521; (970) 270-7853; www.mcinniscanyons.org

**Friends of Roxborough,** 4751 North Roxborough Dr., Littleton, CO 80125; (303) 973-3959; http://parks.state.co.us/parks/roxborough

**Friends of Wilderness,** Steamboat Springs, CO; www.friendsofwilderness.com

**Indian Peaks Wilderness Alliance,** P.O. Box 2214, Boulder, CO 80306; www.indianpeakswilderness.org

**Ouray Trail Group,** Ouray, CO 81427; www.ouraytrails.org

**Poudre Wilderness Volunteers,** P.O. Box 271921, Fort Collins, CO 80527; (970) 295-6730; www.poudrewildernessvolunteers.com

**Roaring Fork Outdoor Volunteers,** P.O. Box 1341, Basalt, CO 81621; (970) 927-8241 or (877) 662-5220; www.rfov.org

**Rocky Mountain Nature Association,** P.O. Box 3100, Estes Park, CO 80517; (970) 586-0108; www.rmna.org

**San Juan Mountains Association,** San Juan Public Lands Center, 15 Burnett Court, Durango, CO 81301; (970) 385-1210; www.sjma.org

**Trails and Open Space Coalition,** 1040 South 8th St., Suite 101, Colorado Springs, CO 80905; (719) 633-6884; www.trailsandopenspaces.org

**Volunteers for Outdoor Colorado,** 600 South Marion Parkway, Denver, CO 80209; (303) 715-1010; www.voc.org

**Wilderness Workshop,** P.O. Box 1442, Carbondale, CO 81623; (970) 963-3977; www.wildernessworkshop.org

**Yampatika,** 925 Weiss Dr., Steamboat Springs, CO 80487; (970) 871-9151; www.yampatika.org

## Conservation Groups

**Colorado Environmental Coalition** (also offices in Grand Junction and Craig), 1536 Wynkoop St. 5C, Denver, CO 80202; (303) 534-7066; www.ourcolorado.org

**Colorado Wild,** P.O. Box 2434, Durango, CO 81302; (970) 385-9833; www.coloradowild.org

**Colorado Wildlife Federation,** 1410 Grant St. Suite C-313, Denver, CO 80203; (303) 987-0400 ext. 1; www.coloradowildlife.org

**High Country Citizens' Alliance,** P.O. Box 1066, Crested Butte, CO 81224; (970) 349-7104; www.hccaonline.org

**Leave No Trace Center for Outdoor Ethics,** 1830 17th St., Suite 100, P.O. Box 997, Boulder, CO 80306; (303) 442-8222 or (800) 332-4100; www.LNT.org

**The Nature Conservancy,** 2424 Spruce St., Boulder, CO 80302; (303) 444-2950; www.nature.org

**Sierra Club, Rocky Mountain Chapter,** 1536 Wynkoop St., 4th Floor, Denver, CO 80202; (303) 861-8819; www.rmc.sierraclub.org

# Appendix B: Further Reading

## History

Arps, Louisa Ward, and Elinor Eppich Kingery. *High Country Names: Rocky Mountain National Park and the Indian Peaks.* Boulder, CO: Johnson Books, 1994.

Brown, Robert L. *Holy Cross—The Mountain and the City.* Caldwell, ID: Caxton Printers, Ltd., 1970.

Buchholtz, C. W. *Rocky Mountain National Park: A History.* Niwot: University Press of Colorado, 1983.

Clawson, Janet Marie. *Echoes of the Past: Copper Mountain, Colorado.* Denver, CO: Waldo Litho, 1986.

Cole, Sally J. *Legacy on Stone.* Boulder, CO: Johnson Books, 1990.

Fiester, Mark. *Blasted Beloved Breckenridge.* Boulder, CO: Pruett Publishing Co., 1973.

Gilliland, Mary Ellen. *Summit: A Gold Rush History of Summit County, Colorado.* Silverthorne, CO: Alpenrose Press, 2006.

Johnson, Kirk R., and Robert G Raynolds. *Ancient Denvers.* Denver Museum of Nature and Science. Golden, CO: Fulcrum Publishing, 2006.

Kaye, Glen. *Lulu City Colorado River Trail.* Estes Park, CO: Rocky Mountain Nature Association, 1983.

King, Larry L. *The History of Calhan and Vicinity 1888–1988.* Simla, CO: Gaddy Printing Company, 1987.

Lister, Robert H. and Florence C. *Those Who Came Before.* Southwest Parks and Monuments Association, 1993.

Lockley, Martin G., Barbara J. Fillmore, and Lori Marquardt. *Dinosaur Lake: The Story of the Purgatoire Valley Dinosaur Tracksite Area.* Denver, CO: Colorado Geological Survey, 1997.

Marsh, Charles S. *People of the Shining Mountains: The Utes of Colorado.* Boulder, CO: Pruett Publishing Co., 1982.

McGlone, Bill, Ted Barker, and Phil Leonard. *Petroglyphs of Southeast Colorado and the Oklahoma Panhandle.* Kamas, UT: Mithras, 1994.

McLean, John N. *Fire on the Mountain.* New York, NY: Harper Perennial (reprint edition), 2009.

McTighe, James. *Roadside History of Colorado.* Boulder, CO: Johnson Publishing Co., 1989.

Pedersen Jr., Henry F. *Those Castles of Wood: The Story of Early Lodges of Rocky Mountain National Park and Pioneer Days of Estes Park, Colorado.* Estes Park, CO: Pedersen, 1993.

Reyher, Ken. *Antoine Robidoux and Fort Uncompahgre.* Lake City, CO: Western Reflections, Inc., 1998.

Smith, P. David. *Ouray: Chief of the Utes.* Ridgway, CO: Wayfinder Press, 1986.

Warner, Ted J. Editor, translated by Fray Angelico Chavez. *The Dominguez-Escalante Journal*. University of Utah Press, 1995.

Wolle, Muriel Sibell. *Stampede to Timberline*. Athens, OH: The Swallow Press, Inc., Revised English Ed., 1991.

## Natural History

Armstrong, David M. *Mammals of the Canyon Country*. Canyonlands Natural History Association, 1982.

Benedict, Audrey DeLella. *A Sierra Club Naturalist's Guide to the Southern Rockies*. San Francisco, CA: Sierra Club, 1991.

Chronic, Halka and Felicie Williams. *Roadside Geology of Colorado,* 2. Missoula, MT: Mountain Press Publishing Co., 2002.

Elmore, Francis H. *Shrubs and Trees of the Southwest Uplands*, Southwest Parks and Monuments Association, 1981.

Emerick, John C. *Rocky Mountain National Park Natural History Handbook*, Lanham, MD: Roberts Rinehart Publishers, 1995.

Guennel, G. K. *Guide to Colorado Wildflowers*, Volumes 1 and 2 Mountains. Englewood, CO: Westcliffe Publishers Inc., 2004.

Kavanagh, James. *Rocky Mountain National Park Wildlife*. Guilford, CT: Globe Pequot Press, 2007.

Kavanagh, James, and Raymond Leung. *Rocky Mountain Butterflies & Moths*. Guilford, CT: Globe Pequot Press, 2008.

Matthews, Ph.D., Vincent, Katie Keller Lynn, Betty Fox, Eds. *Messages in Stone: Colorado's Colorful Geology*. Denver, CO: Colorado Department of Natural Resources: Colorado Geological Society, 2003. Printed in Canada.

Mutel, Cornelia Fleischer and John C. Emerick. *From Grassland to Glacier: The Natural History of Colorado and the Surrounding Region*. Boulder, CO: Johnson Books, 1992.

Nelson, Mike. *The Colorado Weather Almanac*. Boulder, CO: Johnson Books, 2007.

Shattil, Wendy, Bob Rozinski, and Chris Madson. *When Nature Heals: The Greening of Rocky Mountain Arsenal*. Boulder, CO and Lanham, MD: Roberts Rinehart Publishers in cooperation with the U.S. Fish & Wildlife Foundation, 1990.

Zwinger, Ann H. and Beatrice E. Willard. *Land Above the Trees: A Guide to American Alpine Tundra*. Boulder, CO: Johnson Books, 1996.

## Hiking Guides

Boucher, B. J. *Walking in Wildness: A Guide to the Weminuche Wilderness*. Durango, CO: Durango Herald Small Press, 1999.

◄ *Old Man of the Mountain* (Rydbergia grandiflora)

The Colorado Trail Foundation. *The Official Guidebook of The Colorado Trail Foundation.* 7th Ed. Revised. Colorado Mountain Club Press, 2008.

Gaug, Maryann. *Best Hikes Near Denver and Boulder.* Guilford, CT: Globe Pequot Press, 2010.

———. *Hiking Colorado's Summit County Area.* Guilford, CT: Globe Pequot Press, 2006.

Green, Stewart M. *Best Easy Day Hikes Colorado Springs,* 2nd edition. Guilford, CT: Globe Pequot Press, 2011.

Hopkins, Ralph Lee and Lindy Birkel. *Hiking Colorado's Geology.* Seattle, WA: The Mountaineers, 2000.

Ikenberry, Donna Lynn, *Hiking Colorado's Weminuche and South San Juan Wilderness Area.* Guilford, CT: Globe Pequot Press, 2005

Jones, Tom Lorang. *Colorado's Continental Divide Trail: The Official Guide.* Englewood, CO: Westcliffe Publishers, 2004.

*Alpine Forget-me-nots*

# About the Author

A native of Colorado, Maryann Gaug was born in Denver and spent much of her youth dreaming about living in the mountains. While working on a B.S. degree in Mathematics at Gonzaga University in Spokane, Washington, she started backpacking and downhill skiing. Missing the mountains of Colorado, Maryann returned and earned an M.S. in Computer Science at the University of Colorado Boulder. The Boulder Group of the Colorado Mountain Club and their Mountaineering School provided new friends and a great education in enjoying the Colorado mountains. Between the Colorado Mountain Club and the Rocky Flats Mountaineering Group, Maryann continued to hike, backpack, backcountry ski, and otherwise love doing mountain-oriented activities.

*Maryann on top of Mt. Elbert*

After twenty years at Rocky Flats, Maryann took a voluntary separation plan and moved to Silverthorne, Colorado. Her initial mountain life included working as a cross-country instructor at Copper Mountain Resort, completing a Wilderness Studies Certificate at Colorado Mountain College, and becoming a Master of Leave No Trace. She volunteered and worked for Friends of the Eagles Nest Wilderness for more than eleven years, writing grant proposals, helping create a Wilderness volunteer program, and overseeing noxious weed treatment efforts.

Maryann also started following another dream: to write about the mountains and canyons that she loves. Her articles—ranging from her outdoor adventures to natural history—have been published in several Summit County newspapers and *Cyberwest* e-zine. Her second FalconGuide is *Hiking Colorado's Summit County Area*, seventeen hikes in Summit County and eight in surrounding counties. She also wrote *Best Hikes Near Denver and Boulder*, her third FalconGuide, containing forty hikes within an hour's drive of Denver or Boulder.